Praise for

"Woman, Watching is an irresistibl[e] ... de Kiriline Lawrence was a woman [...] ...on, intellectual curiosity, and independence of mind; she paid attention during her time on the planet and left the world a richer, more storied place as a result. Merilyn Simonds returns the favour by honouring her subject in crystalline prose, applying an unfailing instinct for those details that allow meaningful ingress into another's experience. This book is a gift. Get one for yourself and another for somebody you love." — ALISSA YORK, author of *The Naturalist*

"No ordinary biography, but an observational study as compassionate and clear-eyed as those undertaken by its subject — famed amateur ornithologist Louise de Kiriline Lawrence. Beautiful and powerful. Merilyn Simonds has written a remarkable book about a remarkable woman." — HELEN HUMPHREYS, author of *Field Study* and *The Evening Chorus*

"Woman, Watching is an entrancing blend of biography, memoir, history, research, and homage that is unlike anything I've ever read. It's radical, it's ravishing. This portrait of a world rich with diversity, and the subsequent thinning of that fullness, moved me deeply." — KYO MACLEAR, author of *Birds Art Life*

"Louise de Kiriline lived several lives, and this stirring biography brings all of them vividly to the page. In sharing de Kiriline's passion for birds and concern for their survival, Simonds has created a life history that is a lens upon an entire network of women ornithologists." — TREVOR HERRIOT, naturalist, activist, and author of *Grass, Sky, Song*

"What a life! Louise deKiriline Lawrence escaped the Russian Revolution, was nurse to the Dionne Quints, moved to a log cabin and became an iconic birder, and friend of Merilyn Simonds who's written this lyrical, passionate, and deeply researched portrait." — MARGARET ATWOOD/TWITTER

"The accounts of Louise de Kiriline Lawrence's unfathomable journey across war-torn Russia and hardships faced in pursuit of someone she loved is a story unto itself, but combined with her migration to a sparsely settled area north of Algonquin Park, and the challenges she encountered on the road to becoming one of Canada's most respected ornithologists, make this an epic story. In Simonds's hands, the passion, the struggle, the celebration, and the sheer beauty of Louise's story leaps off the page." — IAN DAVIDSON, Director (Americas), BirdLife International

WOMAN, WATCHING

*Louise de Kiriline Lawrence
and the Songbirds of Pimisi Bay*

MERILYN SIMONDS

LIBRARY AND ARCHIVES CANADA CATALOGUING
IN PUBLICATION

Title: Woman, watching : Louise de Kiriline
Lawrence and the songbirds of Pimisi Bay /
Merilyn Simonds.

Names: Simonds, Merilyn, 1949- author.

Description: Includes bibliographical references
and index.

Identifiers: Canadiana (print) 20210387696 |
Canadiana (ebook) 2021038770X

ISBN 978-1-77041-659-8 (softcover)
ISBN 978-1-77305-961-7 (ePub)
ISBN 978-1-77305-962-4 (PDF)
ISBN 978-1-77305-963-1 (Kindle)

Subjects: LCSH: Lawrence, Louise de Kiriline,
1894-1992. | LCSH: Ornithologists—Ontario,
Northern—Biography. | LCSH: Women
naturalists—Ontario, Northern—Biography. |
LCSH: Naturalists—Ontario, Northern—
Biography. | LCSH: Songbirds—Ontario,
Northern.

Classification: LCC QH31.L39 S56 2022 | DDC
508.713/11092—dc23

Published by ECW Press
665 Gerrard Street East
Toronto, Ontario, Canada M4M 1Y2
416-694-3348 / info@ecwpress.com

Editor for the press: Susan Renouf
Cover design: Michel Vrana

We acknowledge the support of the Canada Council for the Arts. *Nous remercions le Conseil des arts du Canada de son soutien.* This book is funded in part by the Government of Canada. *Ce livre est financé en partie par le gouvernement du Canada.* We acknowledge the support of the Ontario Arts Council (OAC), an agency of the Government of Ontario, which last year funded 1,965 individual artists and 1,152 organizations in 197 communities across Ontario for a total of $51.9 million. We also acknowledge the support of the Government of Ontario through the Ontario Book Publishing Tax Credit, and through Ontario Creates.

PRINTED AND BOUND IN CANADA   PRINTING: FRIESENS   5 4 3 2 1

For those who watch

"Looking," said the ant, "is a very important business. He who looks long enough sees much."

—LOUISE DE KIRILINE LAWRENCE,
Jimmy Joe and the Jay

Because you see a bird, you do not know it.

—LOUISE DE KIRILINE LAWRENCE,
personal correspondence

Contents

1

The Golden Bird

The March sun wasn't yet warm enough to slump the snow when the evening grosbeaks descended on Louise's feeding station. She was watching out her kitchen window, as she always did, a cup of strong coffee in hand, her reward after a vigorous bird walk at dawn, a habit of forty years that she had not yet given up, even on the cusp of ninety.

The flock of black-and-yellow birds mobbing her tray of sunflower seeds was the largest she'd seen in years. For decades, she'd been collecting data on evening grosbeaks for her ornithologist friend Doris—how many came to her feeder, male or female, when and where they nested, how long it took the eggs took to hatch and the young to fledge. She made a mental note to check her records to see if the numbers this spring were truly record-breaking.

Suddenly, amidst the throng, a flash of pure gold. Louise lifted her binoculars. Obviously a grosbeak—those thick seed-cracking bills— but solidly yellow, like an oversize canary.

The other birds settled back to their feeding, edging the uncanny bird off the tray whenever it tried to snatch a seed, until finally, the gilded bird rose like a wisp of pure sunshine and disappeared among the trees.

My feeder was half an hour southwest of Louise's, flying as a hungry bird might, along the canopy-highway of boreal forest between her log house nestled in the pines on the edge of Pimisi Bay and my R2000 prefab, tucked into hundreds of acres of forest just south of Callander in Ontario's Near North.

Evening grosbeaks shifted across my wooden feeding tray as if by some prearranged schedule, clearly not women and children first as it was the males that were snuffling up the sunflower seeds, cracking them open and scooping out the meat with their thick, curling tongues, blackening the snow with shells.

The motorcycle gang, I called these birds, gold slashes above the eyes like cool yellow sunglasses, wings glossy as black leather jackets with a startling white blaze. My sons were at school; my husband at work. I stood alone at the sliding glass doors, counting. A hundred birds, at least.

Silvery females were jostling for seed now. Suddenly they fluttered up, a small explosion, leaving a strange golden bird alone on the tray.

"The Golden Bird" is one of the tales collected by the Grimm brothers. In the fable, when a king discovers golden apples missing from his orchard, he asks his three sons to watch for the thief. Only the youngest son stays awake to identify the culprit—a golden bird. The three sons are sent to catch the bird and bring it to the king. The two older boys ignore the advice of a fox and are distracted from their quest, but the youngest follows the animal's wise counsel, endures the trials that beset him, and returns with the golden bird, thus winning the heart of the most beautiful woman in the kingdom and releasing her brother from the spell that had turned him into the fox.

The story is found in other collections, too, although the bird often changes species—a golden blackbird in one, and in the French-Canadian version collected by Marius Barbeau, a golden phoenix. In that story, the fox is a hare, an equally mythical helper, who counsels diligence over comfort and dedication to a quest.

Nowhere is the golden bird a grosbeak, except in Louise's yard and mine.

If Louise had been younger, she might have set her drop traps to catch the golden bird, banding it and releasing it in the hope that someone, somewhere, might report its fate. If she could have figured out a way to feed it apart from the bullying flock, the pure yellow grosbeak might have built a nest in her patch of woods and she would have watched the eggs hatch, the young fledge and migrate south, to the Appalachians perhaps, returning to mate again, a unique gilded strain that scientists might have named for where she lived. *Coccothraustes vespertinus Pimisiana*. Or for her—*Coccothraustes vespertinus deKirilina*.

Very few women have a bird named for them. There is Mrs. Bailey's chickadee, *Parus gambeli baileyae*, dedicated to the nineteenth-century ornithologist Florence Merriam Bailey. And a Mexican race of song sparrow, *Melospiza melodia niceae*, named for Margaret Morse Nice, a woman who devoted herself to writing the life history of this sweetly singing bird.

Like both these women, Louise was a watcher. Florence Bailey in the American Southwest. Margaret Morse Nice in Ohio. Louise de Kiriline Lawrence in northern Ontario, where for fifty years she kept meticulous daily records of the birds she saw, the nests she watched, and the individuals she banded at what was then Ontario's most northerly banding station.

Louise was an amateur. In the late-nineteenth-century world she was born into, an amateur observed birds not for personal gain, but for the altruistic purpose of increasing human knowledge about the natural world. Until the middle of the twentieth century, it was mainly amateurs who pushed science forward, especially the natural sciences, collecting data and specimens for museums and the people who ran them. Today, despite the professionalization of scientific study, amateurs continue to make significant contributions, especially in the realm of birds. Who else would sit for days on end in forests, swamps, and meadows, observing, wondering, and recording every twitch and flight of bird behaviour?

As a self-trained amateur ornithologist, Louise de Kiriline Lawrence set a record for counting birdsong that has never been broken. She wrote life histories of wilderness birds whose daily existence were a mystery at the time. She parsed the meaning of bird behaviours that scientists are only now proving to be true. She wrote six books about birds, including a comparative life history of four species of woodpeckers that explored the age and stage patterns—birth, growth, reproduction, death—and the interactions with their environment that make up the life of every living creature. She was interested not only in songbirds—passerines—but also in the tree-dwelling near-passerines such as woodpeckers and merlins that shared her forest. She published almost a hundred articles in scientific journals and popular magazines, pounding away at her typewriter in a log house isolated in the middle of the boreal forest, remote from the privileged world of the Swedish gentry she had been born into and far from other scientists and scientific libraries. Far from anyone at all, yet for fifty years the top ornithologists on the continent beat a path to her door.

I met Louise de Kiriline Lawrence in 1980, just a few years before the golden bird landed on both our feeding trays. She was an imposing woman—tall, square-jawed, and high-cheeked with plain Scandinavian features, her hair clipped sensibly short though still elegant, her clothes finely made and artfully chosen. A handsome, no-nonsense woman with penetrating eyes. I was barely thirty, living in the bush with my artist husband and two young boys scarcely in school. I had just written my first book; Louise had just published her last, although neither of us knew that then. I had brought my copy of *To Whom the Wilderness Speaks* to her signing at the library in North Bay. I arrived late, hoping the crowd would have thinned, but the room was still jammed with people pressing to be close to Louise. I held out the book and she briskly asked my name, as she'd asked almost a hundred others before me, then she signed her own name with a flourish, and flashing me a smile, said, "*Tack så mycket!*" as I melted silently into the crowd.

We met occasionally after that. The few times we were together, we talked birds and writing and how the Northwoods inspired us and at the same time threw up its obstacles. In 1989, when she was ninety-five and I was forty, I wrote a profile of Louise for *Harrowsmith* magazine. I moved and she died, but the idea of this woman, alone in the woods, watching, stayed with me. What drove her particular brand of curiosity? What fuelled her passion for birds, a devotion that never faltered for half a century? What in her background or her character or her situation conspired to shape this immigrant woman, isolated in a log cabin in the northern Ontario bush, into one of Canada's first and finest amateur ornithologists and nature writers?

I ponder this today as I watch a gang of violet-crowned and broad-billed hummingbirds frantically licking up the nectar from the feeders outside my window in the mountains of central Mexico. Idly, I wonder what feeding schedule these birds are on. How much do they drink at each visit to the feeder? How often do they pause to check for interlopers and threats? If I were Louise, I would get out my stopwatch and my notebook to record the timing and length of each visit, each sideways glance. I'd set up a live trap and band the flitting birds to determine if one particular violet-crowned visited many times or if a shimmer of hummingbirds was feeding outside my window.

But I am not Louise. I lack the patience for scientific study. Besides, it is Louise, not hummingbirds, I have in my sights. She is gone, but still I watch her—through her vast correspondence, her speeches, her books and articles, her drawings and photographs, the birds and nests she salvaged for museums, the neatly typed records sequestered in archives across the continent.

A life history is what I'm after—not of a species, but of a watcher named Louise.

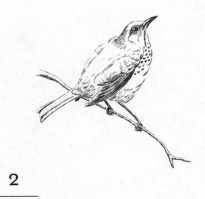

2

The View from the Terrace

Your wills grow in the forest, Louise's mother said to her two little girls, both of them headstrong, intent on having their way. Especially Louise. Red-headed and stubborn, her tantrums flared like sheet lightning, then vanished. Ebba, two years younger than Louise, was her opposite: dark-haired and dark-eyed, physically frail but with a defiance that could smoulder for days.

What do you mean? they both clamoured. Show us!

So their mother took the girls into the forest until they could no longer see their family's big wooden house with its many chimneys. She stopped where two saplings grew side by side near the path.

This one, she said, pointing to the smaller of the two, is you, Ebba. And this taller one is your sister, Louise. Every time you pass this way, you'll see how much bigger and stronger your wills have grown.

Young Louise Flach was delighted that her will was alive in the forest like her imaginary friends, the Bebborna—tiny invisible dark-skinned creatures dressed in pale blue and pink frocks. The Bebborna accompanied her everywhere, into the house and into the shops of the

Louise ("Lolo"), age two and a half, with her mother, Hillevid Neergaard, 1896

nearby town. She communicated with them by pantomime. "They were a good influence on me," Louise writes. "It was clearly up to me, for instance, to show them how one yields the way to grownups, how one opens the door, how one curtsies."

Until she was eight, Louise lived in a house on the brow of an escarpment that overlooked an elongated fjord of the Baltic Sea, three hundred kilometres south of Stockholm. Along the fjord's western shore, the Flach family homeland of Svensksund stretched far back into the forest. In 1772, during one of the ongoing wars between Sweden and Russia, the manor house had been pillaged and burned, leaving only a wide marble staircase at the end of an avenue of ancient chestnut trees. The indomitable Flachs had taken up residence in one of the outbuildings, adding on rooms until it became the Big House, where Louise's father was born in 1859.

Sixten Flach was landed Swedish gentry: he carried the courtesy title of Chamberlain of the Court and appeared at ceremonial occasions such as state visits, royal audiences, and official dinners. When Sixten married Hillevid Neergaard, a daughter of Danish nobility, he built Villan on a ridge a half mile above the Big House. The new house was set among the trees, the walls and roof clad in wooden shingles stained a deep earthy brown that made the house seem one with the forest. From the lawns of Villan, Louise could look down on the fjord glittering far below and watch the hooded crows circling overhead. Her first word was not *mama* or *papa*, but *kraa-kraa*, the raucous call of the birds.

One of the earliest photographs of Louise—or Lolo, the name she signed at the bottom of her letters until her mother died—shows her tiny two-year-old fist gripping her father's gently curving finger as they emerge from the woods. He is a tall, thin man with reddish

Lolo, two, with her father, Sixten Flach

blond hair that matches hers perfectly, and a handlebar mustache that he trained by fitting it into a transparent harness to keep the tips turned smartly up. She is wearing a white dress, and they both stride forward with determination in their stout leather boots.

It is easy to pick Louise out of photographs from Svensksund. Her features are even and strong, her hair inevitably springing out of its braid or escaping from under her hat. Her smile is wide, her teeth prominent, her gaze direct. A photo from when she was about ten is particularly telling: four little girls and a boy stand sideways, their hands resting on the shoulders of the next youngest in line—cousins, I imagine. A little boy in a miniature Cossack coat stands at one end; Lolo, the eldest, holds the beginning. The other girls squint or glare or withhold themselves from the camera, but not Louise. Even at that young age, she stands tall, smiling straight at the lens as if to say, This is me, take me as I am.

In my favourite picture, the cousins are much older, adolescent girls in gauzy white ankle-length dresses. The older ones wear their hair rolled to frame their faces, Swedish-style; the hair of the younger ones falls loose, held back with large white bows. The girls have

Louise (far right), her sister Ebba, and children visiting Villan

clasped hands and are dancing in a circle in front of the Big House, a garland of muses. Louise is not the prettiest, but she is the liveliest, even fixed in this image, leading the way, her form perfect, heart and body devoted to the dance.

As much as Louise's mother fed her imagination, it was her father who shaped her character. He had inherited self-reliance from his own mother and passed it on to Louise, along with his flaring temper. His daughters were born into the outdoor movement of the 1890s, and he insisted they be brought up hardy and fearless. They tobogganed and skied and skated through the winter, pulling on a sail or hanging onto the sharp-shod horses to slide across the frozen fjord. In summer they rode ponies their small legs could barely span. "Be never afraid!" he'd say, and Louise understood that he meant every kind of fear—of the body, of the heart, of the mind.

When Louise was nine, her grandfather died, and Svensksund passed into her father's hands. The family moved from the splendid seclusion of Villan down to the Big House, close by the farms that earned the family income. Louise left the magical forest on the ridge, but as if in exchange, she found herself in a world where peacocks strolled the terraces and swans swam mutely in the reflecting pool, and where she had her own pony. The house was within trotting distance of the bay, where crested grebes and ducks paddled among the swaying reeds and ruffs, snipes, and sandpipers filled the air during breeding season with their shrill calls. She'd run barefoot over the tussocks, lapwings rising up around her, crying, *vee-weep, vee-weep, vee-weep.*

Her father, who adored nature, was her teacher and guide. "His whole being was enwrapped in it. He could not have lived in a place he was not in the closest contact with it. He taught me to watch for the skylark's first ecstatic flight song into the blue in late February. He enjoined me to check the arrival of the pied wagtail under the great maple tree precisely on the eighth day of April, and it was never late. From his suggestion that it sounded like the pronunciation of the name of a famous regiment, I learned the phonetics of the song of a chaffinch. And with his help I discovered one day the elusive corn crake by its raspy utterance out in the hayfield, in the days when this bird was still plentiful."

In winter, her father set up a feeding place for the birds outside the drawing room windows. Sheaves of corn, plump with cobs, were tied to posts and cords strung between them to hold "bells" of seeds and fat moulded in earthen flowerpots. Her father taught her to distinguish between the great tit, the blue tit, and the scarlet-chested bullfinches, and to celebrate when the European crested tit, unremarkable in plumage but rare, came to feed.

Typical of his time, Sixten Flach took a moralist's view of nature: some animals and birds were good, others not. When Louise grew big enough to handle a gun, she was enlisted to rid Svensksund of creatures her father determined should be annihilated—domestic cats, house sparrows, crows, rats, and squirrels, paying her fifteen cents for every pair of sparrow's legs she brought him.

Yet, in one of the ironies of the nineteenth century, when killing was assumed to be an essential part of understanding nature, Louise's father was also a conservationist. He was part of a society of Swedish men who had become friends while students at Uppsala University, where Carl Linnaeus had been professor of medicine and botany in the mid-eighteenth century. Linnaeus formalized a way of naming and classifying plants, animals, and birds. Called the Pliny of the North, his influence in the field of biology is comparable to that of Shakespeare in literature. As a professor, Linnaeus attracted apostles who collected and organized newly discovered plants and animals into the Linnaean system. One of these was Peter Kalm, a Swedish naturalist who studied under Linnaeus and who travelled into what is now Ontario and Quebec in 1750, publishing an early account of North American natural history that was one of the most important of that century. The English botanist Joseph Banks, an admirer of Linnaeus, was inspired to begin the tradition that all British research ships carry a naturalist on board, which in turn led to Darwin's revolutionary studies on evolution.

Sixten Flach was born the year *On the Origin of Species* was published. His time at Uppsala in the late 1870s and early 1880s was surely steeped in the ideas of both Linnaeus and Darwin. A decade before Louise was born, her father joined with other wealthy naturalists to form a private company that gradually purchased the entire island of Stora Karlsö in the Baltic Sea, due east of Svensksund. Stora Karlsö was famous for its vast colonies of guillemots and razorbill auks that bred on the island's sheer cliffs, species whose populations were threatened by recreational hunting and the collecting of eggs for food. Once the group owned the island, they banned these practices, creating the world's second nature reserve. (The first was Yellowstone National Park in the United States, established in 1872.)

One of her father's friends who made an impression on young Louise was Bruno Liljefors, the Swedish wildlife painter. Visitors usually arrived at Villan by carriage, the horses dashing up the long drive and coming to a neighing halt in front of the main door. But Louise clearly remembered the thickset, powerfully built man walking up the avenue with a slow, slouching gait. "His mouth was half-hidden by a limp moustache but his cheeks were bright, as if, like my father, he'd spent his life out of doors. I watched as he came closer. His eyes were steel blue and sharp, used to looking into the distance. I felt he could see me where I hid by the curtain, looking out."

Her father rushed to embrace his friend, pulling him into the drawing room where they talked for hours. "What impressed my childish mind was not what they said—for I remember nothing of this—but the intensity of expression upon their faces and the seriousness of their voices as they discussed important things."

Later, when the men went into the fields, Louise tagged along, eavesdropping as Liljefors described the enclosures he'd built on his property outside Uppsala, a private wildlife park where he kept the animals and birds he used as live models—an eagle, an eagle-owl, hawks, black grouse. Sometimes he had to kill his birds and animals and dissect them to see their structure. But more important, he said, was watching the living birds, observing how they moved, how they behaved when they were alone in the wild.

"It was winter, and there was snow on the ground, more than a dusting but not so much as to make walking a bore. We were at the edge of the spruce forest, where it gave way to the open field that in spring was the breeding ground of Father's pheasants. The men looked up at the same instant, their eye caught on a sound, the rush of wings through the cold air, but I saw the white hare first, galloping through the stubble. The eagle dove, talons aching for the touch of fur and flesh. The men saw it now, too, and we watched, the three of us breathless, uncertain whether to cheer for the hare or the bird, when the hare dropped suddenly into a hole only it could see, and the eagle keened back up into the sky, settling into a lazy upward spiral almost before its screech faded from our ears."

The next morning, Louise heard her father and his guest moving down the hall and out into the yard, but the featherbed was too warm, and she was too sleepy to follow. The men returned for breakfast, muddy chin to toe.

What on earth have you been doing? Louise's mother cried.

Her father laughed like a boy caught climbing the orchard wall to steal an apple. We've been lying in the reeds of the bay, he said, watching the eiders.

In the afternoon, her father took Bruno Liljefors to the pheasant yard where the painter picked out a pair of birds that he carried in a sack over his shoulder as he slouched back down the avenue between the ancient trees.

Some months later, the postman brought a package for Louise's father. He unwrapped the painting on the kitchen table: a crouching hen pheasant, her brown-speckled feathers all but invisible among the winter grasses; a little ahead of her, under the low branch of a young conifer, stood her resplendent mate, his long barred tail half-hidden in the underbrush, his posture alert, watchful. Two birds in their world.

Another regular visitor to the Flach estate was Einar Lönnberg, head of the vertebrate department of the Swedish Museum of Natural History in Stockholm, a noted conservationist concerned about wild-fowl habitat along Sweden's Baltic coast, especially in the bay of Bråviken that bordered Svensksund.

To young Louise, Lönnberg and Liljefors were almost indistinguishable: both portly older men with drooping blond mustaches. Lönnberg would often stay several days, settling with her father in the easy chairs by the windows of the second-floor smoking room that overlooked the swans in their pond. Louise would sit cross-legged and silent on the moose hide at their feet, not missing a word. "For the first time in my life I became dimly aware of nature as something very real and very important, something of an encompassing world within which our lives are not only shaped and moulded but wherein responsibilities exist for us to fulfill. . . . If our role is to manage—I can almost imagine them using the very words—then our management should be one based on devotion and respect, on knowledge and wisdom."

Louise's naturalist values—what is worth knowing, what is worth preserving, a loving kinship with the land—came from her father, but her formal education was delivered primarily by nannies and governesses, most memorably for Louise a certain Miss Palmquist, who taught her the tenets of liberty, equality, and brotherhood. Miss Palmquist's influence on Louise was lifelong, although her teacher's stay in the Flach household was brief. Louise's mother quickly sent "the socialist vampire" packing and enrolled Louise and her sister in the Brummerska finishing school for girls in Stockholm, where she rented a small apartment to supervise her daughters while they completed their education. For a short, perfect time, while her younger sister was being "finished," Louise stayed alone at the Big House with her father, sitting at the dining table in her mother's place, touring the fields as his companion and assistant.

"He tried haltingly, for he did not easily reveal his inner thoughts and feelings, to explain to me the bond that tied him so closely to this land . . . he tacitly imparted to me his hopes that I would be his successor."

But Louise was seventeen and Svensksund was a backwater. She couldn't wait to return to the city and have some fun before taking her place in Svensksund, and so she left. A month later, when her father came to visit the family in Stockholm, he suffered a massive stomach hemorrhage from a bleeding ulcer and was rushed into surgery. He did not survive the operation.

The Flach family fortune had been declining for decades. Now, without the patriarch's guiding vision, the farm faltered. His last plea, written in a strong, clear hand and attached to his will, urged his wife not to sell. But Louise's mother saw no other choice. Louise's last memory of the Big House was of her father's room off the front hall, the office where he would sit at his sprawling desk, working on the farm accounts. The scent of his Eau de Quinine hair tonic still hung in the air, mixed with a lingering whiff of tobacco. From the sale, her mother rescued a few family heirlooms and favourite pieces of furniture; after paying off the debts, she realized enough to start a new life for herself and her daughters in a small flat on a back street in a residential area of Stockholm.

"To my dying day I shall never forget the view from the villa terrace with light and shadow playing upon the Nordic landscape. The loss of Svensksund left me with a dream, nothing else, a dream of a piece of land where once again I could live and take root."

3

_____

Hungry for Something

W hen Louise was a girl, she'd often tag along with Tante Jana, visiting the houses of the workers on the estate, caring for the sick. "At the time, I thought it was marvellous to roll up dressings." Instead, she trained as a teacher. Then suddenly she was twenty, Archduke Ferdinand had been shot, and the Great War was raging. All she wanted now was to be a nurse, however unseemly that vocation might be for a debutante who had just been presented at the court of King Gustaf V. Her mother was not pleased, but her godmother, Queen Alexandrine of Denmark, took Louise's side.

Louise had no intention of rolling bandages as a war volunteer or sweeping floors as a nursing assistant. "I was going to be the real thing. I left the opulence . . . hungry for something I could not identify or name, an opportunity to feel passion, a chance to spend energy and heart recklessly."

She was accepted immediately by the Swedish Red Cross Training School for Nurses in Stockholm. The work was hard. She never dreamed anyone would be expected to work such long hours, sometimes back-to-back twelve-hour shifts, earning nothing but experience.

By the time she finished training, the war was all but over. Most of her classmates went into private nursing, taking care of the ill and injured in their homes. Louise did, too, but not for long. She yearned to be in the thick of it. Sweden was politically neutral and so was Denmark, but the governments of both countries allowed the Red Cross to provide medical and humanitarian care to victims of war. Among its projects was the repatriation of wounded prisoners-of-war. The Danish Red Cross had set up prisoner-of-war camps on the Eastern Front, one for Russians and one for Germans waiting to be exchanged. A friend of Louise worked at the camps. Yes, she said, there was room for Louise with the Russians.

Louise was horrified. Russia was the arch-enemy of Sweden. The two countries had been at war on and off for centuries. During one invasion, the Russians had burned the Flach family estate at Svensksund to the ground. But it was wartime: she set aside her prejudice and took the job.

Louise met Gleb Nikolayevich Kirilin just before Christmas, 1917, on her third day in Barracks 42 of the Russian POW repatriation camp. She was twenty-three years old.

When the soldier-prisoners invited the nurses to their Christmas concert, Louise at first declined, exhausted from caring for the "sixty human wrecks" who were her patients. But another nurse convinced her: "You must not refuse; they like us to join in their fun." And it *was* fun—singing, poetry, a short play, and Russian folk songs sung to the balalaika. During the singing, she felt eyes upon her back and when she could stand it no longer, she turned to meet the steady stare of a lanky young man, his officer's cap pulled at a rakish angle above startling grey eyes.

Not long before, discouraged by her private nursing assignments in Stockholm, Louise had visited a fortune teller, an unkempt

woman with ratty cards who had irritated her as much as the Swedish
employers who wanted a nanny more than a nurse. She hardly paid
attention as the old woman went on about a tall, fair man with grey
eyes. Yet here he was.

A week later, on the eve of the Russian New Year, Gleb and Louise
danced, chatting in French, their common language. When the music
stopped, the other prisoners urged Gleb to recite. He began with
French poems of love, then slipped into Russian, words incompre-
hensible to Louise although the sound was thrilling, "like the wind in
the pines, like a roaring torrent, like the reverberating harmonies of
an organ, the crash of a storm." As the applause died down, Louise
leaned into Gleb, imploring, "Will you teach me Russian?"

Gleb had grown up in a military family, educated at the elite Corps
des Pages military academy before being accepted into the Imperial
Guard. These sons of noblemen and high-ranking soldiers were
among the first called up as officers in Russia's White Army when the
Great War broke out. Gleb was sent to the Polish front and within
weeks, he was wounded and taken prisoner. By the time he met Louise,
he had languished in POW camps for three years, desperately ill with
a blasted, septic hip that left him with a noticeable limp.

Louise and Gleb spent hours together, inside the camp and out.
(As an officer, he was allowed beyond the camp on the strength of his
word.) On their walks, they shared their upbringings in grand houses,
his admission into the Imperial Guard of the Tsar, her debut at the
court of King Gustaf V. Both were eager to throw off the oppression
and injustices of that privileged background, to embrace values other
than class, position, and wealth. One day they rented bicycles and rode
to Helsingør castle, and beside Hamlet's empty sarcophagus, Gleb
confessed his literary aspirations—and his love.

Romance was not easy in the throes of war. The Bolsheviks had
signed a cease fire with Germany, which meant the prisoners would
soon be exchanged. Gleb worried about the welcome Tsarist POWs
would receive in the new Bolshevik Russia, yet he couldn't stay away.

Wedding portrait, Louise Flach, age twenty-four

His two brothers had died in the trenches, and his mother had thrown herself out a window when she heard the news. She had died of her injuries, but his father, a retired general, and his sister were still alive. He had to see them.

Gleb decided to make his own way to Petrograd rather than travel with his fellow prisoners. The day before he left, he entered Louise's little room in the Danish nursing quarters. "I brought you this," he said, handing her his faded peaked cap with his officer's badge. "It is the only thing of value I have."

For the next few weeks, Louise received postcards written in purple pencil, half-English, half-French, from northern Sweden, from the top of Norway, then silence as Gleb was swallowed into the great unknown of revolutionary Russia.

She was desolate through that spring of 1918. When the POW camp was emptied, she left to spend the summer at the estate of her Danish aunt. She passed the time with her sister, Ebba, spitting into the moat to make the carp rise, willing the postman to cycle up the grand *allée*.

When Gleb's letter finally arrived, his words "changed my whole world. And I knew that life was glorious, that he and I were young and in love, that no distance existed wide enough to separate us. That there were no difficulties we could not overcome. No circumstances, no considerations could come between us, no wars, no revolutions, for at long last he had expressed the words I had longed to hear."

Louise was engaged. Her mother was horrified. Propelled by love, Louise left for Stockholm. Through her cousin Elsa Brändström, who was the daughter of the Swedish ambassador in Petrograd, Louise arranged for her letters and Gleb's to be smuggled across the closed Russian border in a Swedish diplomatic courier's bag. When Gleb asked if she could get him a Swedish visa, she appealed to a man in the Swedish foreign office with whom she'd once danced. Russian refugees are not among the most desirable immigrants, he reminded her sternly, but gave her the visa anyway. Every day Louise waited on the quay in Stockholm, watching Russian refugees walk down the gangplank into Swedish exile. Then one day, late in the fall, it was Gleb waving from a ship's railing.

Gleb had swum the Torne River that divides Finland from Sweden in order to come to her. He had nothing but the clothes he wore. And he couldn't stay: the Swedish visa allowed him to remain in the country for three months, no more. For weeks, they walked the leaf-strewn parks of Stockholm, trying to discern a path into the future. Gleb hoped eventually to find nonpartisan work in Russia, where he could help create a true democracy, a system fair and beneficial to all Russians. But first, the civil war between the Reds and the Whites, the Bolsheviks and the Tsarists, had to be resolved. Russia was his mother; he could not abandon her. And Louise could not abandon Gleb.

Three days after Christmas 1918, they were married in the Swedish Church without bridesmaids, flowers, or guests other than immediate family. Louise wore a purple tweed suit and the pink blouse she was wearing the night she'd met Gleb. Two weeks later, on January 11, 1919, they were married again, this time in the Russian Orthodox Church. The space between was their honeymoon. "The minutes fled desperately fast and became days, and each day ended was a day less. We clung with greedy determination to our small measure of bliss."

Gleb left immediately to take up a commission in the White Army that was pushing south from a front on the polar barrens of northern Russia, alongside their French, British, American, and Canadian allies. At first Gleb refused to allow Louise to join him, so she waited, "waited as if in the whole world there was nothing else to do." Then Gleb's telegram arrived, pleading with her to come to Archangel, an ancient city on the northwestern edge of Russia, just below the Arctic Circle, where the Allied Expeditionary Force and the White Army had their headquarters. In a flurry, Louise packed seven trunks with clothes, bedding, a complete Royal Danish tea service—everything she imagined she would need to start married life in Russia. According to Russian law at the time, Louise had not only taken Gleb's surname in marriage—Kirilin—but also his nationality: she would travel with a Russian passport.

On April Fool's Day 1919, she left Stockholm by train and headed for her new life, as happy as any new bride. She followed Gleb's route north through Sweden into Norway, where she caught a steamer that travelled five days along the northern fjords of the Scandinavian Peninsula to Vardø, the northernmost city in Norway. There, she just missed the boat to Murmansk, Russia's only ice-free port and the country's sole link to the Atlantic. The town was full of travellers, most of them fleeing Russia; no one but Louise was heading east into a war zone with seven trunks filled with fine clothes and family heirlooms.

Louise waited a week in Vardø. When the boat to Murmansk finally arrived, the British commandeered it to transport soldiers to the Russian front. "Women are not allowed on board troopships," the British officer told her crisply. Then, a brief smile. "If anybody asks any questions, just say you didn't see me." Louise ducked below decks to find a hiding spot. In a smoking room in the aft of the ship, she found the Russian officer and the French diplomat with whom she'd pleasantly waited in Vardø. Count Montrichard offered her the red plush settee as a bed, and behind her wall of trunks she made safe, secret passage.

A week later, the troopship steamed into Murmansk. As they entered the port, a ship heading out to sea dipped its flag. Louise read the name on the bow: *Canada*. She had just missed the last icebreaker to Archangel.

Louise refused to be discouraged. She wangled an interview with the colonel in charge of the Royal Army Medical Corps. One telephone call and she was assigned to a hospital ship in Murmansk harbour, hired as interpreter for a doctor studying scurvy. As a result of Gleb's coaching, her Russian was fluent.

She was hardly settled in her new job when the Russian officer and the French count who had hidden her informed her that two icebreakers bound for Archangel were at that very moment loading supplies. Would she object to becoming a stowaway again? Anything, she said, to get to Gleb. Under cover of darkness, her trunks were transferred to a French icebreaker, where she was given the cabin of the second mate. For four days and nights the ship crashed through the ice of the White Sea, thick floes thundering against the hull until finally, after twenty-two days of travel, Louise stood at the bow as the ship steamed down the Northern Dvina river, past the fortress of Arkhangelsk into the calm harbour.

Gleb's room was hardly as big as Louise's closet at Svensksund but it didn't matter, they were together. Within days they were assigned a room big enough for two, with large windows that held fig trees and potted palms. Light spilled through the air. In the mornings they left together, Gleb to his work as a machine-gun instructor and Louise to her two jobs: one as interpreter to the liaison officer of the White Army automobile division, the other at the American military mission. For more than a year, British, American, Canadian, and French troops had been in Archangel as part of an Allied intervention they hoped would tip the balance in the Russian civil war in favour of the Tsarists. Both of Louise's interpreting jobs paid well. As Gleb wrote to her mother, "Knowledge of this strange language is worth a small fortune."

Louise was blissfully happy. "Every day we loved each other more and more. Nobody could fit together better than us." Archangel was cosmopolitan, with a small Swedish community that included her

Louise and Gleb in Archangel, Russia, 1919

cousin Elsa Brändström, also a Red Cross nurse, revered as the "Angel of Siberia" for her work in the German and Austrian POW camps in northern Russia.

Louise and Gleb had been together only a month when he volunteered to return to the front at Pinega, about two hundred kilometres farther east. His English was so good he was assigned as liaison officer to a British colonel.

Louise applied to the Russian Red Cross to work in Pinega and was put in charge of the British soldiers' ward in what both Louise and Gleb refer to in their letters as *laʒaret* instead of *hôpital*. This unusual French word more commonly denoted a quarantine facility for infectious disease, which makes me wonder whether the Spanish flu was rampant in the Arctic, too, although neither Louise nor Gleb ever mentioned influenza.

All Louise's patients were war-wounded. One day, an English airman was admitted to her care. He'd been badly burned when the bomb he was unhooking from the undercarriage of his plane exploded. Louise sat with him for hours. As his pain subsided, he told her stories of homesteading in the Cypress Hills of Saskatchewan, his log cabin tucked amid the lodgepole pines, snow sifting in through the chinks, the woodstove billowing heat to keep him cozy. She listened, rapt, the bleak hospital ward fading in the light of that distant forest paradise.

Louise and Gleb were enjoying two weeks' leave in Archangel when they awoke one morning to a town emptied of foreigners. "Nowhere was the uniform of an Allied soldier to be seen, nowhere did a foreign flag float upon the breeze over buildings that had been flying them for months. In one short night the Allies had evaporated. The White Russians were on their own."

Communication with the outside world stopped. Louise received no word from her mother, and she sent her own letters into a void, not knowing if they would ever arrive at their destination. Gleb fell ill with bronchitis and just as he was recovering, he contracted typhus. Louise had found work in the new Red Cross hospital across the street from their room. Several times a day, she'd slip home to check on Gleb, pulling on his big leather boots and a fur-lined cloak that fell to her ankles. "Little bear," he called her when she came through the door.

Their lives became increasingly consumed with food: finding it, hoarding it, eating it—mostly porridge and tea or apples and rice and whatever else Louise could scrounge at the hospital to rebuild her husband's strength. Christmas came and went. As the Arctic winter settled in, the fighting at the front stopped. Gleb and Louise welcomed the lull. They spent their evenings by the fire, Louise teaching herself how to type, Gleb writing his novel about Russia before the revolution, pausing often to read passages aloud. Now and then gunfire would erupt or muffled drums sound in the distance, but in the absence of news, like everyone else in Archangel, they stayed focused on the spring, when the White Russians would march in victory into Petrograd.

Then suddenly, at the end of January, Louise's hospital filled with wounded, nearly all of them officers, one with a bullet in the back of his neck. The White Russian troops had taken up the Bolshevik revolution and turned on their officers.

"The beginning of the end," Gleb said quietly.

A month later, the icebreakers that regularly shuttled between Archangel and Murmansk vanished. The only vessels in the harbour were a destroyer escort and a yacht being loaded with wounded. Louise rushed to the Red Cross hospital. The nurses were being evacuated, the wards shuttered.

The Bolsheviks were closing in. The order came from the White Army generals: get to the Murman Railway and hold the front there. Escape by sea was impossible: the soldiers and their families would have to travel almost a thousand kilometres by sleigh and on foot.

Louise pulled out her seven trunks and carefully packed away their things, knowing she would never see them again. Into one light suitcase and a duffel bag she stuffed warm shirts, socks, blankets, a few toiletries, and as much food as she could lay her hands on. When she spied her father's leather portfolio filled with her love letters and Gleb's, she pressed it into the duffel, along with Gleb's manuscript. Her few valuables—two rings, a gold chain studded with pearls, and a hundred-pound note they were saving for an emergency—she sewed into a first-aid dressing that she pinned inside the knot of her hair.

On February 15, she sent a cryptic telegram to her mother. "All right. Kirilins."

They left Archangel separately: Gleb with the gunners on a machine-gun sleigh and Louise with another officer's wife in a sleigh filled with straw and heaped with wolfskin robes, pulled by a black horse that picked its way down the embankment onto the icebound river, heading west into the teeth of a blizzard. "Cold snow whirled into every crease and fold of our covering. The horse floundered knee-deep in snow, its tail and mane tossed sideways by the wind. Ahead of us the trail lay trackless."

The driver tramped through the snow beside the sleigh. Every so often, Louise would jump off, too, pushing through the snow until blood flow returned to her extremities, then she'd stumble exhausted back into the sleigh. Her skirts clung to her in icy sheets. "We went on like this for hours, endless hours . . . Ghostlike figures were moving up alongside us, blurred silhouettes bent forward against the driving gale . . . Behind them came sleighs like ours, drawn by lathered horses."

At a peasant's house where they stopped to rest, Louise changed into men's breeches. For a few hours, she and Gleb were reunited. He showed her how to unharness her horse and rub it down and reminded her to fill her sleigh with fresh hay for the animal before starting out. Louise begged to travel with him; she couldn't bear the thought of being separated as they sped into the unknown. But Gleb refused. "We're all under orders," he said.

The next morning, Louise joined the long sleigh-train that followed the column of marching soldiers winding through the bleak white landscape: more than a thousand sleigh-loads of refugees heading west along the coast of the White Sea.

In Onega, they were just sitting down to a meagre supper when they heard a shout, "To the sleighs!" Louise grabbed their half-unpacked things and rushed to the sleigh as it pulled out of the yard, Gleb's sleigh only two behind. She crouched deep in the hay as gun-shots cracked around her, then silence, broken only "by the creaking of the runners and the soft sound of reins slapping loosely against the horses' flanks."

Ahead of her, a horse fell in its tracks. She passed another, dead in the snow. Then a soldier's booted foot sticking awkwardly up out of the snow. Behind, the horizon glowed red. Onega was burning. The Reds were mere hours behind. "Hard on our heels they poured like spilled water from one village to the other. On the narrow trampled road our column pressed forward, allowing men and horses only a few hours to eat and to rest at long intervals . . . Nobody marched on foot any longer. What was left of the rank and file rode in the sleighs with the officers. Hardship erased all differences."

For three days and nights they raced across the snow, sleeping and eating on the run, in barns, deserted farmhouses, in their sleighs. Soldiers tore wires from the telegraph posts to foil enemy communication; dropped their rifles through holes chopped in the ice to keep the weapons out of enemy hands. Now and then, Louise passed a deserter huddled by the road, choosing death by cold and starvation over a firing squad.

The number of sleighs and passengers steadily diminished. On the fourth day they met a small band of soldiers who told them the Reds were already at the railway. Still, they pushed on through the night, through the next day, and the next night, too, never stopping to rest or sleep.

At one point, Louise realized Gleb was no longer behind her. "I tumbled out of the moving sleigh and began to walk against the flow of men and horses. The passing sleighs crowded me into the snow, but

I was past caring, past exhaustion. Only one sensation motivated me, a frantic fear that he was lost somewhere far back." She called his name, searching the passing sleighs frantically for a glimpse of him. The last sleigh slipped past, and he was not in that one either. The road behind was empty. "Then in the distance I saw a stumbling figure. I ran. It was Gleb, dragging himself toward me . . . Supporting each other, we walked slowly, stopping and resting often. Finally we arrived at a house. There they told us that the Red Army was in the next village."

Bolshevik soldiers had been there for two days. The race to safety had been futile.

Still, Louise and Gleb refused to give up. Maybe the sleighs could reach the Finnish border. Maybe the two of them could find skis and a compass and go it alone. Maybe, maybe, maybe. But it was no use. The White Army generals had already decided: the soldiers would surrender.

Louise filled the sleigh with fresh hay one last time. Gleb pitched his pistol into the snow. Together they covered the final distance.

The surrender was orderly. The Reds marched the captives in a long column to the railway. Each soldier was given five pounds of flour as his food ration for the trip; the women got nothing. Then they were packed into boxcars and the doors chained shut.

Every time the train stopped and they were let out to stretch their legs, Louise gathered snow in a small can and melted it for drinking and for washing their hands and faces. Gleb continued to shave as best he could. The prisoners stripped to the waist to pick lice from the seams of their clothes. The raw flour, eaten in pinches, made their stomachs ache, so Louise fashioned a frying pan from a tin can with a stick for a handle, mixed the flour with melted snow, and fried what she called bannock. At every stop, local people lined the tracks, holding out food in exchange for goods. Gleb bartered a blanket for a small bag of sugar, and Louise's green silk scarf for a round of black bread, which he shared with Louise and another officer. Sometimes the train stopped and the starving prisoners were sent into the cold to shovel snowdrifts or cut trees to stoke the engine.

Louise never gave up hope they would be rescued by the Allies that had abandoned them.

By day six, all the flour was eaten. On day seven, at midnight, the train rolled into Petrozavodsk. The prisoners were prodded out of the boxcars and marched to a prison at the edge of the town, where twenty White Russian soldiers, including Gleb and Louise, were housed in a former library the size of a bedroom.

"Imagine my Lisa in a Bolshevik prison!" Gleb joked. "What will the aunts and cousins say?"

As they stood looking out through the barred windows at the melting April snow, Gleb remembered the downed airman and his Saskatchewan cabin. If we live through this, he said, somehow we'll get to Canada and begin again.

Two days later, the men were separated from the women. When the warden checked Louise's duffel for contraband, he paused at the leather portfolio containing her love letters. With your permission, citizeness, I'll keep these, he said with a smirk.

Each prisoner received one pound of heavy black bread a day and a small tureen of soup. Louise was so hungry that once, after chopping wood all morning, when she spied a pile of potato peelings on a kitchen counter, she shoved them into her mouth before anyone could see. But the matron was kind: she smuggled messages between Gleb and Louise, hidden under the lid of a little pail of soup that Louise sent to Gleb as often as she could.

Four weeks passed. The spring equinox approached.

The women were released. They heard that the men were being moved by train to Moscow, no one knew exactly when. Louise hastily gathered her things, scrounged what food she could, and waited by the tracks with the other women. When the prison train slowed, the men pulled the women into the boxcars.

For a week, the train chugged across Russia toward Moscow. The prospect of being separated when they arrived at their destination no longer frightened Louise. Being on the outside had its advantages: she could bring Gleb food, work for his release. In a railway yard outside Moscow, Louise and the other women slipped from the slowing train.

Gleb and the other officers were held in a monastery refitted as a prison. He set himself to studying political science and philosophy in the monks' library while Louise roamed the streets of Moscow, scrounging for food, trading her best clothes on the black market for eggs and cheese—one shirt for thirty eggs. The walls she walked past were riddled with bullet holes, stores abandoned, their windows pasted over with posters. *Down with the bourgeosie! Workers of the world unite! Long live the Revolution of Workers and Peasants!*

In the prison, the White Russians were being called alphabetically for interrogation. Some had been released, which gave Gleb and Louise hope. Others had been moved to a conventional prison, but not Gleb. They took this, too, as a good sign.

On May 15, 1920, feeling feverish, Louise visited Gleb. She had diagnosed herself: typhus, from the ubiquitous lice on the prison trains. Or perhaps it was malaria. She begged the commissar for an extra visit with Gleb before she succumbed to the illness, and so they sat together in the monastery garden. Under the chestnut tree, they made love. "Alone I walked slowly down toward the gate. I turned and saw him standing there, tall in his khaki outfit, a figure framed within the fine old arches of the monastery. His hair lay sleek upon his head. A thoughtful man of quality and courage, he seemed at this moment supreme master of himself and his life."

When Louise became delirious with fever, a friend took over the task of preparing Gleb's food parcels, standing in line for hours to deliver them. One day, she was turned away. The prisoners had been moved to a high-security prison camp. The word was that the men were being transported to a work camp in the Urals. Louise sent a letter with

Elsa Brändström, telling her mother, "All is well, we have lots to eat . . . it will probably be a while before I can write to you again."

And then the men were gone.

Word trickled out. Some of the White Russians had tried to escape, and the next day, all the prisoners were loaded into boxcars and transported north. The train had arrived in a town not far from Archangel; the prisoners would be tried in a court there. One of the women received a postcard from her husband. "We are all safe at Kholmogory. Do not worry."

The passport that brought Louise Kiriline to Canada, 1926

Louise was alone in a strange country. Her husband had disappeared, and she hadn't heard from her mother for five months, not since she left Archangel in February. She wrote every week, sending letters north to people she knew in Archangel, west to Stockholm with Swedes leaving the country. To foil the censors, she wrote in English or French, saying little of substance except that she was well and urging her mother to speak to the person delivering the letter, they would tell the truth about how things were. A citizen by marriage, she couldn't leave Russia even if she wanted to, which she didn't. She stayed in Moscow, pestering the government for news of Gleb and the other officers. When the social reformer Kata Dahlström came to Moscow as the Swedish delegate to the Second Congress of the Communist International, she took up Louise's cause and arranged for her to meet top Russian officials. She also carried a letter back to Sweden and delivered it personally into Louise's mother's hands.

At the end of August, after eight months of silence, Louise finally received news from her mother. She wrote back, begging for oats, chocolate, condensed milk, soap, boots, shirts, whatever her mother could send. Her mother was working in the Swedish passport office and easily found people to carry packages to Louise. Meanwhile, Louise had been given work at the People's Commissariat for Food, where she received extra rations as well as a meagre salary of two thousand rubles a week, which didn't stretch far. The Allied blockade was starving the Russians and inflating black market prices. Two spools of thread cost her entire week's salary. She had to save three weeks to buy a bar of soap.

By September she'd exhausted every avenue she could think of to find out where her husband might be. "I feel I must go and find Gleb," she wrote to her mother. "Every hour is taken for the preparation of this rather difficult journey. I am thinking of everything in the smallest detail." She was travelling light, just one small suitcase of her own clothes and a blanket, shirt, and boots for Gleb, who had sold his warm clothes and good boots for food on the way south. She baked stacks of rusks from eggs, butter, and hearty flour and stockpiled concentrated foods and canned meats, balancing nutrition against what she'd have the strength to carry if she were forced to walk. She packed the food into a basket along with insect powder against lice and small things she could trade for information—matches, tobacco, thread. She left all her photographs behind except for a small picture of her mother and one of Gleb, which she cut to fit into a locket. "I am the only one who can get him through this and that is why I must go and I am happy that I am able to go morally, physically, and materially. He knows how strong I am and how able I am to help and live in primitive circumstances."

Her friends begged her to stay and work for Gleb's release in Moscow, the centre of power. Louise herself felt an embarrassing reluctance, "a paralyzing presentiment, a cowardly conviction of the futility of my mission." Even so, on September 27, 1920, she bought a train ticket and told her mother not to send more parcels. "It is better not to have more than just enough here, and only what is absolutely necessary."

It was all she could do to push away the feeling of doom as she took her seat on the train. The departure bell rang. Louise heard jostling in the hall outside her compartment, a familiar voice calling, then her friend was standing in the open doorway.

"Quick, Luisa, come on! They are all dead!"

Five hundred prisoners had been marched out of Kholmogory prison camp, onto the barrens, never to return.

Louise refused to believe Gleb was dead. She had heard stories of men who dropped before the firing squad pulled the triggers; they'd survived buried under corpses. Others had slipped away in the chaos to hide in the woods. Stories flew among the prisoners' wives, each more fantastic than the next.

All she knew for sure was that she loved him. "He is a magnificent character, the most honest, warmest and light-hearted and morally strongest person in the world. I can't believe how happy we were in Archangel. It is through all the difficulties and trials that you get to know and value and love each other . . . a love that has been tried like ours can never be doubted."

Louise kept Gleb's fate from her mother, just as she never told her about their breathless escape from Archangel or the real privations of her life in Moscow. She simply wrote another telegram: "Circumstances have completely been changed due to certain news, so that my journey to A was cancelled at the last minute. I shall soon write about details."

She took a train to Petrograd to wait with his sister, Marie, as she and Gleb had arranged should they become separated. From there, she kept in touch with the wives of the other officers, trading rumours of a secret concentration camp on an island in the White Sea where the most dangerous counterrevolutionaries were held; trains filled with prisoners going who-knows-where; dark columns of men marching by night across the vacant landscape. When Louise heard that White Russian officers had been seen in England, she asked her mother to pull whatever strings she could to discover their whereabouts "as there is most certainly truth to these rumours." Early in 1921, when the Russian people revolted against the Reds, her hopes rose, thinking the Bolshevik experiment might yet fail. But the uprising, like her hopes, quickly died.

Sometimes, Louise thought of leaving. "Yet how could I, in all sincerity, wish myself away from all that Gleb had lived for and loved with the most intense feelings of belonging and passion? Strange how Russia had gradually become part of my own life and being, this land, this people, this culture that were his very essence. Give me a week of soft living outside, and it would break my heart to come back to this air, these sights, the wide perspectives, the smells, the insecurity, the hunger, the despair—to Russia!"

For three more years, Louise waited and searched. She took a nursing job in the surgical department of the Petrograd children's hospital, a position that provided a private room "with heat and light and the Red Army's food rations, sounds grand but is minimal: 1 pound bread each day, a little sugar, and once or twice a month, meat."

In the hospital wards, children suffered from scurvy and epidemics of dysentery so extreme that "at times the whole corridor was full of these little patients, who wasted away in blue clamminess." She saw a day-old baby admitted to the hospital, its tiny face lacerated with rat bites; a little girl with neck burns so deep her chin had stuck to her chest in the healing. "I hope I will never again encounter that sickening stench of peccant [sic] death in a place where there are still living children. Medical science could do little but wait for the fittest to survive—perhaps—and for the weakest child-skeleton to die."

From 1921 to 1924, famine spread across Russia, a hunger so pervasive it triggered the first international humanitarian mission, led by Norwegian Arctic explorer, Fridtjof Nansen. The Swedish Red Cross joined the Nansen Mission, and Louise signed up to help, happy to stay in the country she had learned to love. But conditions in the famine district were worse than anything she imagined. "Those who would rather die than leave their humble homes worked until the hunger weakened them so much that they lay puffed up with hunger edema upon their beds, unable to move. Some, when they saw their children starve to death, killed them to relieve them from suffering—then they cut up the small bodies and cooked soup with them. Others went mad with hunger, sneaked away to the cemeteries at night where unburied corpses lay in rotting heaps, and cut pieces off the dead to take home for food. . . . Such things were still happening when I arrived to take over one of the most outlying districts of the Mission."

On the Volga steppes, among the Moldovians, she was given a house and a bodyguard and left alone to set up community kitchens to feed twenty thousand people in seventeen surrounding villages. Grave diggers received double rations so they would be strong enough to bury the dead. Within a month, under her hand, the death rate returned to normal. Once the population was being properly fed, she embarked on a private project. "I went around into the poorest houses of my district and picked out the worst children I could find, some thin little skeletons with enormous eyes in a death-skull face, some with abdomens distended like drums from the cakes made of cow manure and ground-up wood they had eaten, some with eyes hidden under puffed pouches of edema. All these I took into my home." She fed the children and examined them weekly, and when they were healthy, she sent them back to their families, replacing them with others on the brink of starvation. Disease raged through the district: a malignant form of malaria and spotted fever, a kind of bronchial plague. No one was exempt.

When her work there was done, she joined the European Student Relief, also part of the Nansen Mission, and nursed among the Cossacks in coastal towns on the Black Sea, and later, in the middle of the Siberian taiga. The work was exhausting and humbling. After the worst of the famine passed, the Mission delegates were invited to a thanksgiving service. "When we arrived, the open place outside the church was packed with peasants from near and far. Of one accord they fell upon their knees and intoned blessings over us. Through this humbly kneeling crowd, weak from hunger and ragged from poverty, we were conducted by the priests into the church up to the altar . . . I don't think there has ever been an occasion of my life in which I have felt as utterly unworthy."

Louise bought herself a motorcycle and saved up her gasoline rations to tour the countryside in her off-duty hours. In her photo album, there is a picture of her astride the big Douglas, dressed in leathers; another of her in a lacy white dress, lounging on the porch of a dacha. Turning from one image to the other is like seeing history unfold: pre-war wealth and lassitudinous elegance giving way to a powerful new determination, a thrumming energy.

Technically, she was Russian: she couldn't leave the country without permission. Then the Soviets decreed that a woman's national status did not change with marriage, a ruling intended to stop women from marrying foreigners in order to emigrate. The new law worked in Louise's favour. She was no longer Russian by marriage; she was Swedish by birth. She could go home.

She had arrived in Russia with seven trunks of family treasure. Six years later, she returned to Sweden with nothing of value but a sealskin coat and the pair of sapphire earrings that Gleb had given her as a wedding gift, his scant legacy from his mother.

4

Untrammelled Landscapes

Bone-tired after her years in Russia and heartbroken at the loss of Gleb, Louise returned to her mother and sister in Stockholm. She was only thirty years old, but already she had lived what seemed like several lifetimes. After being among people struggling so fiercely to survive, she found it difficult to adjust to her family's privileged existence in Sweden "with its shallow aims and very different set of values. I wanted to breathe freely again in a vast room and experience some more of what it really is to live."

For two years she tried in vain to find her footing, to quell her restlessness. She and Gleb had often talked about where they might settle if they made it through the war. The Russia Gleb knew and loved, the Russia of the Tsars, was gone. And his country had too long been an enemy of Sweden for him to feel comfortable there. The Canada of the downed airman seemed the perfect compromise: untrammelled landscapes, winters of deep snows, a "vision of unlimited space and open fresh air, of freedom of movement and freedom of mind . . . the same kind of breadth and width" as Russia. So when the decision fell to Louise alone, she chose Canada too—"the land of milk and honey, for those who wish to milk the cows and tend the bees," an emigration pamphlet promised.

She had never been afraid of hard work.

Louise travelled with her mother to Paris, then in the spring of 1927 she kissed her goodbye and walked up the gangplank of a ship bound for Montreal. She spent her first night in Canada at the Mount Royal Hotel, reportedly the largest in the British Empire, with a thousand beautifully appointed rooms. She intended to head west—she still dreamed of the airman's Saskatchewan—but first she stopped to visit Swedish friends in Toronto. There, she happened upon a newspaper story about the new one-nurse Red Cross outpost hospitals, and thought, This is what I am going to do.

Nursing outposts were a uniquely Canadian solution to a sparse population sprinkled over a vast, rugged geography. A community would provide room and board for the nurse, a clinic, and a housekeeper; the Red Cross would pay the nurse's salary. She would treat patients in their homes or at the outpost clinic, admitting them to the small inpatient ward if necessary. For the most severe cases, the nearest doctor would be called in. For the patient, the health care was free.

The remoteness, the independence, the need, and the challenge all appealed to Louise. Within a week, she joined the Canadian Red Cross Outpost Service. They suggested she take an extra course in obstetrics at Toronto General Hospital, which she passed easily. At the end of her course, she was invited to become nurse-in-charge of operations at another Toronto hospital, but the head of nursing at Toronto General advised against it. "She just put her foot down and said, No that doesn't suit you. You go out with the Red Cross."

And that's what Louise did. She was posted first to Haileybury, a small town in the boreal forest five hundred kilometres north of Toronto, then a few months later, to the mining town of Kirkland Lake, another hundred kilometres farther north. After that brief orientation, she was offered her own outpost hospital in Bonfield, a tiny village on the eastern tip of a lake south of North Bay, where the Red Cross was launching an experiment in serving Francophone communities.

Louise went down by train to take a look. "I saw this little place sitting on the shore of Lake Nosbonsing . . . There was a big church and a spire and behind it was bush. I thought, That's a pretty place, I'll stay."

The first time I drove with my husband and two young sons through Astorville, on the opposite end of Lake Nosbonsing from Bonfield, I felt the same. Both hamlets were founded in the late nineteenth century as train stops: Astorville on the Canadian National Railway line and Bonfield on the Canadian Pacific. By the time we arrived at our piece of forest ten minutes west of Astorville, forestry had faded as the main employment, but when Louise moved into Bonfield, almost every family would have worked for J.R. Booth, the lumber baron who owned the logging rights to thousands of acres of wilderness from Lake Nipissing to Ottawa. He had even built a five-mile-long railway—the Nosbonsing and Nipissing Railway—to carry sawlogs to the headwaters of the Mattawa. The two villages at either end of Lake Nosbonsing were predominantly French parishes: Bonfield's name derives from *bonne ville*, good settlement, and Astorville was originally called La Tête du Lac, then Astorville after its first priest, Father Antonin Astor. Both communities were dominated by a Catholic church on a hill, with a spire that rose above the trees. Small houses spilled over the slopes around the church, the roads rising, dipping, and twisting around the lake, a postcard view at every turn.

In 1928, Louise took over the storey-and-a-half wood-frame house donated by the people of Bonfield. In a few weeks, she'd transformed its eight rooms into an office, a clinic, a small ward of four hospital beds, and upstairs, a nursery as well as a bedroom and a little den-nook for herself where she could read and listen to her shortwave radio. On her first night, however, she slept in a barren room without blankets. The next day she walked three kilometres to her first case.

Louise was impressive: a statuesque Swede with a shock of short dark hair, she towered over her wiry French-Canadian patients. But she had been raised speaking French, and the community loved her. They called her Madame de Kiriline, the noble "de" creeping unannounced into her name.

Louise thrived on the independence and initiative required by the job. She was responsible for the primary health care of the people in two townships north of North Bay and two to the south, an area of approximately 2,500 square kilometres. She had twenty schools to visit and two thousand children whose health she monitored. At the time, Louise's district held the Dominion championship for large families, with an average of ten children in each of 150 families. She saw the children in their schools, checking inside their mouths and ears for infection and examining their hair for lice. She sewed a monkey puppet she named Coco, and with it, taught them to brush their teeth and wash their hands.

Through the children, Louise got into the families. Even in those Depression years, Canada was a country of relative plenty, yet the babies in her district were undernourished. "I saw children born a picture of rounded pink healthiness—that in a few weeks' times became thin and whiny and pasty of colour. I saw children with legs and arms and bellies distorted by rickets because they had missed the sunshine outside the cabin door and a bottle of cod liver oil during the winter."

Louise went house to house to plead for sunlight and fresh air for the babies and for more generous use of soap and water. She taught parents, mostly mothers, basic hygiene and sterile techniques for curbing the spread of epidemics. By the early 1930s, tuberculosis, whooping cough, diphtheria, measles, and polio were sweeping through North America, killing and maiming children by the hundreds of thousands. During a smallpox epidemic in 1930, when there were more than a hundred active cases in her district, Louise and the local doctor worked without rest to vaccinate every child over six. "With Dr. Dafoe I was treated as I was in Sweden, where nurses and doctors are equal.

We worked together hand in glove. It was extraordinary . . . I just had to phone him and he knew he could trust me and that I knew exactly what to do."

She spoke at community gatherings and set up clinics. She arranged for dentists to come up from Toronto for an all-day tonsil clinic where dozens of tonsils were removed in the parish hall, set up as a kind of field hospital. "It was the most satisfying kind of work . . . There again was primitiveness, the direct and the frugal and the genuine, people that could be helped, and effort that paid off in the greater values. I fell in love with the land, its broad contours, its stark beauty, its harshness and its wonderful benevolence."

When Louise discovered that she had to rely on local volunteers to transport her to the bedsides of her patients, she bought Henrietta, an open Ford coupe that was so cold in spring and fall that she had to

Louise on the bumper of Henrietta, her summer transport to patients, 1928

blink furiously to keep her eyelashes from freezing together. There were no snowplows; once winter arrived, the car was useless.

The community provided a sleigh and a horse, which often as not she'd unharness and ride bareback to her patients. One night, she hitched the horse to the cutter to answer a call deep in the woods, driving through canyons of snow to an ailing mother, injecting her with morphine, then bedding her down in a pile of hay in the sleigh. When they got to the railway siding, she flagged down a train and loaded her passenger into a baggage car that sped through the night to North Bay, where the woman was transferred to hospital for emergency surgery—and survived.

In the depths of winter, even the horse and cutter couldn't get through the deepest drifts. With a self-reliance and resourcefulness learned at her father's side and honed in the Russian subarctic, Louise trained three dogs to pull a sled over the winter snows, making trips night or day through the roughest weather.

"I could never get along without my three dogs—Buck, Zippy, and Brook," she told a *Star Weekly* reporter in "Swedish Girl Ministering Angel to Ontario French-Canadians," published in March 1931. "Buck was given to me by an old-timer who said the dog was part Labrador Malamute and part huskie from around the south of Hudson Bay. The dog was so savage that no one could go near him safely when first he came into my hands. But just look at him now. He is the gentlest and most faithful leader I know of." She bought Zippy, a greyhound-husky cross, as a mate for Buck and raised their offspring Brook to complete the team. Fifteen, twenty, thirty miles a day, she ran after the sled, hopping on and off the back, Buck howling like a timber wolf as he raced along the bush trails, families rushing to the windows, Louise waving and shouting as she flew past on her way to the bedsides of birthing mothers, the sick, and the dying.

Even the priests trusted her. Though they knew she wasn't a Roman Catholic, they taught her how to baptize the dying. "I can remember that I had a case of a miscarriage. The child was born, I don't know if it was alive or not, you could see that there was an embryo, and I remember baptizing this thing before they put it in a box to bury it. That made a great impression on the people."

The Red Cross paid its nurses a modest salary, but beyond having enough to get by, money never meant much to Louise, perhaps because she had grown up with plenty. "It's the work, the performance, knowing that you can do these things and that your handling of it gets better and better. You strive for excellence. Excellence, of course, is a very illusive thing and it isn't something that stops at a certain point. It goes on and on and on . . . The striving for excellence, I have always found, has been the most exciting thing."

Her first days in Bonfield were lonely, only a radio to break the silence until she made friends with her housekeeper, Lawrence, and with Allan Dafoe, the doctor on call in Louise's district. He was a shy man who kept mostly to himself, but he was open with Louise, and she with him. Both were educated and curious about the world: they talked history and medicine and music. When he learned of an especially good performance coming on the radio, he'd invite Louise to listen with him. And he kept an eye on her, making sure she didn't go where there would be drinking and trouble might erupt. At one point, he whispered a proposal of marriage through a closed door, something she laughed off.

One evening as she browsed the doctor's bookshelf before a radio concert, she came upon a book that stopped her hand. *The Red Terror in Russia* by Sergey Petrovich Melgunov.

Louise had avoided reading books about revolutionary Russia: most struck her as propaganda for one side or the other. But Melgunov was different: he delivered documented facts. In Kholmogory, the "Camp of Death" outside Archangel, thousands of prisoners, "the flower of Russian youth," had died. All through the summer of 1920, he wrote, the town had fairly groaned under the terrorizing scourge. He could not verify the total number of people slaughtered, but of one thing he was certain—eight hundred officers of the White Army had been shot.

At last she knew for certain. Gleb was dead.

Louise was living in Bonfield, nursing at the Red Cross Outpost Hospital, when she found the wedge of forest along the shore of Pimisi Bay, half an hour east of North Bay. Some call Pimisi a lake, but really, it's a widening of the Mattawa River where the water slows after foaming through the chute at the outlet of Lake Talon. At the north end of the bay, the Mattawa continues eastward through a series of rapids to empty into the Ottawa River. At the chute, where the river begins, it flows through an ancient rift valley, between sheer rock walls rising as high as a ten-storey building. When the virgin forests of the north were felled, logs tumbled down the falls of the chute, swirling frantically into the open water, carving out Pimisi Bay. Louise always said that *pimisi* meant "I rest here." But in the Algonquian language of the First Peoples in that area, it means eel, a sacred carrier of prayers.

The land around Pimisi Bay is rough and rocky, heaved through with glacial ridges and ravines. Since the days of J.R. Booth, the trees have been cut and burned over many times, the forest floor littered with slash and windfalls. At the time Louise arrived, however, the second-growth forest was still relatively young, the rock furred with bright moss and powdery lichen, and in the ravines, secluded thickets, inland ponds, and tinkling brooks that ran to the shore.

There are blanks in any effort to recreate a life. Most of what I know about Louise's early years in Canada comes from her letters to her mother, chatty weekly chronicles that rarely lapsed except during wartime. The first letters were in Swedish, but Louise soon switched to English. "If I wrote in Swedish, it would take me twice as long." She wrote often about the log cabin she was having built on Pimisi Bay, but nowhere does she tell the story of how she happened upon this three-and-a-half-acre parcel of rock and trees bounded by a river and wild tracts of forest.

What I do know is this: along the south side of the property, a road from Mattawa to North Bay was being surveyed through the bush. Since the First World War, there had been great enthusiasm in Canada for an east-west transcontinental highway; construction had already started in several places when the stock market crash of 1929 moved the project to the back burner. By the mid-1930s, however, the federal government was funding provincial programs that hired thousands of unemployed men to construct roads in remote areas. Temporary work camps, called Bennett camps after Prime Minister R.B. Bennett, each housed a hundred men or more as they built roads through the wilderness across northern Ontario.

Three Bennett camps were in the district under Louise's nursing care. When flu broke out or a man slashed himself with an axe, or when a fight left a trail of broken jaws and bruised ribs, Louise was called in to get the men back on their feet. Perhaps it was on one of these visits

Louise mushing her sled dogs through Bonfield, 1928 to 1934

that she found both the land and the builders to help her realize her dream of recreating the wooded paradise of her childhood. I imagine her mushing her dogsled, shouting out to Buck, Zippy, and Brook as they raced along the snow path that would become the Trans-Canada Highway, stopping where a frozen bay opened to the western flank of the Laurentian hills, blueing in the distance, a filigree of spruce tips etched against the sky.

In October 1933, she applied to purchase that wedge of wilderness, receiving assurances from the assistant deputy minister of the Department of Crown Lands and Forests that the land was hers for the asking. (At the time of settlement, the land was occupied by the peoples of Nipissing and Dokis First Nations, signatories to the Robinson-Huron Treaty of 1850.)

Louise immediately requested a leave of absence from the Red Cross Outpost Service and hired two Finns from the Bennett camp to build her a log cabin from stout pines they felled on the property. Her house would be a simple rectangle with a front door on the short side that opened into a main room with a fireplace and behind that, a small bedroom on the right and a kitchen on the left. No bathroom. No plumbing. No electricity.

She looked forward to the primitive conditions. "I have acquired the ability to make myself very comfortable with small means. It is amazing how one can think out all sorts of labour-saving devices even in the midst of the woods if one uses one's head a bit. I think I will be able to live very cheaply and comfortably when once I get there."

The Finns erected a small prospector's tent for themselves and a larger one as a workshop. Louise sent her mother snapshots of the tents nestled in bluffs of snow, dwarfed by the spruce and pines, and of the road, little more than a gap in the trees, narrow dogsled tracks pointing the way. In another, she is full-cheeked and grinning broadly, a tuft of hair curling out from under her woolly aviator's cap; behind her, the wilderness of Pimisi Bay. She looks like a kid who finally found the cookie jar. She was thirty-nine years old.

In January, the land office informed her that the parcel she'd applied for had too much water frontage for the depth of the property. She revised her application to include a piece of land on the other side of the road, bringing the total to five acres.

By spring, the Cabane, as she called it, was ready. Just as she was preparing to move in, she received another letter from the Crown lands agent, saying that her application could not be approved until the road that bounded the property was finished, which wouldn't happen until June at the earliest. In the meantime, any building on the property would have to be dismantled and removed.

Louise was devastated. But not daunted. She hired a lawyer and drove to Toronto where well-placed friends arranged a meeting with the minister of Lands and Forests. He was unmoved. Instead of granting her the property, he sent her a letter charging her with taking possession of Crown land without authority, felling timber that didn't belong to her, and erecting a building. "The Department does not condone an illegal act such as you have performed."

The Crown Timber Authority placed a seizure on the land and warned her "not to interfere with it in any way, shape or form."

Louise was in Toronto, defending her title to the land on Pimisi Bay, when the doctor on call at the Bonfield Red Cross Outpost Hospital tracked her down. "Get in your car and come up here at once," Dr. Dafoe demanded.

Louise was on a year's leave of absence. Nevertheless, she hopped into her Ford coupe and drove north through the night; in the morning, she dug out her nurse's uniform and headed down the back roads to the Dionne farmhouse. Louise was no stranger to the family. Just four years before, she had helped Elzire carry her youngest through a bad case of rickets and malnutrition. Louise visited every pregnant woman in her district in the months leading up to delivery, and through the winter of 1934, Elzire Dionne had been one of her mothers.

On May 28, 1934, Elzire had gone into labour. She delivered a pair of twins easily, but as soon as it was clear she was giving birth to more than two, the midwives called Dr. Dafoe and the new Red Cross nurse, Yvonne Leroux, a fresh young graduate hired to take Louise's place during her leave. The next day, Dr. Dafoe went in search of Louise. After six years of working together, he knew he could rely on his indomitable Swede.

"Go out and get order into that business out there!" he shouted into the telephone.

At the time, quintuplets occurred naturally once in every fifty-five million births. Medical history had recorded thirty-five quintuple births, but only the Dionne girls lived more than one day. Now, with in vitro fertilization, multiple births are quite common, and even an instant family of nine babies has survived. But in 1934, the successful delivery of five infants seemed like a miracle.

Louise found Elzire weak but smiling, half-buried in the bedcovers. In the corner by the woodstove, two tiny newborns lay swaddled in a butcher's basket, hot water bottles hanging off the sides. Another three babies lay crosswise in an incubator meant for one. Taken together, the five babies weighed under fourteen pounds—just 6.2 kilograms.

The farmhouse was crowded with relatives: grandparents, aunts, and cousins propped on every table, counter, and chair. Louise quickly commandeered a small room beside the parents' bedroom as the nursery, directing the men to cut a window in the adjoining wall so Elzire could see her tiny daughters. Louise and Yvonne scrubbed the walls, ceiling, and floor of the nursery and moved in the kitchen table, padding it to make a changing table. Within hours, shelves were built, equipment arranged, and netting tacked across the open windows to let in fresh air while keeping out the black flies, mosquitoes, and house flies, all mortal threats to the fragile babies. As soon as the nursery was ready, the new donated incubators were moved in, one for each of the girls.

A long room that ran the length of the house became the nursing station with an office area, reception, storeroom, and rest area for the nurses. No one—not the parents, the five other Dionne children, the relatives, the doctors, or nurses—was allowed to enter the nursery without first passing through the reception area, sterilizing their hands and donning cloth masks and white coats.

"We never knew a moment really free from anxiety in those first days," Louise said. As nurse-in-charge, she established a strict routine. The tiny babies got their first feeding at 5 a.m., then they were put into the "rat's nest," a five-foot-square padded box she devised to hold all the children at once while their bed linens were changed. Every other day, they had a four-minute sunbath in the rat's nest, under a sunray lamp. Then each baby was bathed and oiled, fed again, and as long as the outdoor temperature was above -9°C, they were put into sleeping bags and wheeled in their prams to the veranda where they would sleep until noon. Even in stormy weather, Louise made sure they got their daily dose of fresh air, their faces shielded from snow and rain.

Louise, nurse-in-charge of the Dionne Quintuplets, 1934

The babies were fed every two hours, drop by drop at first, as Louise struggled to get the infants to take sufficient liquid. Every bottle and nipple was sterilized: the slightest slip-up could mean infection and death. For the first six months, the babies survived on mothers' milk, more than Elzire could supply; the women of the Junior League in Montreal and Toronto canvassed hospitals for more and shipped it north to the Quints. "Their present [situation] is as safe as science and humanity can make it," Louise told the press.

Even in the darkest moments Louise never allowed herself to think of her task as hopeless. She had seen compromised infants before: one of her first patients in her second-year placement in Stockholm had been a tiny months-early baby boy who "lay in cotton wool in an incubator and had to be handled very delicately. I called him 'the Spider,' for his body was so small and his legs and arms so long in comparison and so thin." Yet this baby grew round and healthy. "Babies came to be something strangely wonderful to me—something that one could hardly talk about."

In August, while Louise was sterilizing baby bottles over an alcohol lamp, a jar of fuel tipped over and caught fire. The flames spread toward the incubators where the infants lay sleeping. Without thinking, Louise threw herself to the floor and rolled in the flames to extinguish the fire, burning her face, arms, hands, and legs. For the next eleven days she was confined to the little cabin near the farmhouse that had been converted into sleeping quarters for the nurses.

The fire made headlines around the world. News services from every continent stalked the perimeter of the Dionne property and dogged Louise whenever she left for a bit of down-time at a North Bay hotel. She didn't mind; she was used to being interviewed. Her scrapbook was already pasted with profiles from Russia during the famine, Sweden after she returned, Bonfield when she arrived to set up the Red Cross Outpost Hospital. She was unfazed by the attention and a good storyteller, neither embellishing nor downplaying her reports on the quintuplets, which had enough drama on their own. The media loved her. She was interviewed endlessly in her "charming accent." Although she wasn't as young and pretty as Yvonne Leroux, she was a model of Scandinavian efficiency, a dark-haired ministering angel. She described helping the Quints through their first year as a "great adventure," adding coyly, "I had not lived tamely up to then." Her backstory in the Russian Revolution and Swedish nobility, her race back from her leave of absence to take charge—it all became part of the Dionne mythology.

By summer, hordes of tourists were heading north to see the quintuplets. Every cabin and rented room was filled to bursting. Diners stayed open twenty-four hours so travellers could doze at their tables. The yard outside the Dionne house looked like opening day of a country fair, with tents and stalls selling food, mementoes, and "fertility stones." The crowds worried Louise. Only twelve hours before the fire, someone had tried to raise a window in the nursery. The 1932 kidnapping and murder of the Lindbergh baby was not far from anyone's mind. Police were brought in to keep the peace, but perfect security was impossible. Louise often felt that all that stood between the grasping hordes and the fragile babies were the round-the-clock nurses.

It was a strange, distorted time. Everyone wanted a piece of the Quints, and many were willing to pay for the privilege. Within days of his daughters' birth, Oliva Dionne, supported by Dr. Dafoe, signed a contract allowing the infants to be displayed at the 1934 Century of Progress World's Fair in Chicago. In the uproar that followed the announcement, the Dionnes signed custody of the little girls over to the Red Cross for two years, as a way of negating the World's Fair contract. In return, the Red Cross agreed to cover all the Quints' medical costs, including Louise's salary.

The pressure of nursing in that peep-show atmosphere is hard to imagine, especially as tension tightened between the parents and the medical team trying to keep the children alive. In September, the girls—three and a half months old, their health still unstable—were moved into the new Dafoe Hospital and Nursery, speedily constructed across the road from the Dionne farmstead. The structure could have passed for the charming cottage of a reclusive, neurotic lumber magnate. The building and its compound were enclosed by a seven-foot barbed wire fence and included a staff house for the nurses and another for the three policemen who provided nonstop security. There was an outdoor playground surrounded by a covered arcade that allowed tourists to observe the sisters from behind one-way screens. By the time they were two, the Quints had been visited by half a million people: at the peak of Quintmania, three thousand gawkers a day.

At first, Louise was pleased to be at the hospital, where a sterile environment was much easier to maintain. The babies flourished. Within a month of the move, Dr. Dafoe announced that Yvonne, Annette, Cécile, Émilie, and Marie Dionne now had the same life expectancy as any Canadian child. But the hospital further isolated the parents from their daughters and intensified their grievances. In February 1935, when Elzire and Oliva Dionne travelled to Chicago to go on stage as "Parents of the World Famous Babies," the premier of Ontario used what he called "the Dionne vaudeville trip" as an excuse to extend the province's guardianship. Bolstered by what the government saw as its responsibility to save the babies from exploitation, the Dionne Quintuplets Guardianship Act was passed, making the girls wards of the Crown until they turned eighteen.

For the Dionnes, Louise was part of the enemy cabal, even though Louise, in her heart, sided with the family and believed fervently in a mother's right to raise her own children. "I was thrown into a very difficult situation without experience and I don't think I was up to it properly," she said later, admitting she regretted not taking more time with the parents, not being more understanding of their predicament. "But I was too taken up just keeping the babies alive, to the detriment of my relations with the family. I really was quite brusque."

When Elzire and Oliva brought friends across the road to visit, Louise stood on the porch in front of the hospital's bright red door and refused to allow them to enter without first going through the usual sterilization procedures. The Dionnes were enraged.

By the spring of 1935, the small hospital was surrounded by tents and makeshift souvenir shops put up by anyone with even a tenuous link to the one-year-old Quints. The atmosphere around the babies was such an such an "undignified muddle," such a circus of self-interest fighting for control of the goldmine these babies had become, such a mean-spirited contest of wills that Louise resigned.

"I think this is a wise step to take, although I very much hate to do so," she confided to her mother. She had become attached to the five little girls, but "as they unhappily are not mine," she knew her separation from them was inevitable and would only get harder with time. The Dionne babies were as close as she would ever come to watching children grow—"the first waving tiny hand, the first opening of blinking eyes. Then the marvel of their first cooing sound, until they imperceptibly crept into my heart with all of a baby's endearing love-making." If the babies had needed her, she would have stayed, but they didn't. She had carried them successfully through the first and most dangerous year of their lives.

Louise was forty when the quintuplets were born, forty-one when she left the girls in the care of others. The year had been an emotional strain as she tried to hold fast to her values in the face of media attention and the countless corporations and individuals who wanted to use the Quints for their own purposes. She was appalled when Dafoe endorsed Palmolive soap, which in her view "is about the worst soap one could ever use for babies and we are, as public health nurses, always taught to warn mothers from using it." She refused to write articles recommending Libby's baby foods. When she found out Carnation Milk planned to run an ad with a quotation from her, she vetoed it. She had to hire a lawyer to ensure that Lysol would refrain from using photographs of her in their advertisements.

Louise introducing her lead sled dog, Buck, to one of the Quints

She was horrified by Dafoe's insistent self-interest, his lack of compassion, his refusal to work toward reconciliation with the parents. Could this be the same man who had said to her, in the thick of things, "You know, it is only just good luck that the babies are alive. I mean—don't let's kid ourselves." Now in letters to her mother she called him "a mean impossible little man . . . a made-up straw-figure who lives on the meanness of his soul. A Hitler en miniature."

She knew the temptations were all but irresistible. In her archives I come across a fragment of an essay called "Advertising Five Small Faces." I don't know if it was ever published, but it illuminates the ethical pressure Louise was under. "Had the inducement been alluring enough . . . I hesitate to state the possible consequences. Discretion is all too often like a bird on the wing." And even though she did not personally benefit financially from her time with the Quints, still she felt compromised. "It is of small account whether I refuse to touch any profit thereof with my own hands or merely constitute the means by which it is passed on to the pockets of others. The result is the same— that of a smutty hand touching a clean sheet."

Resigning as the Quints' nurse did not save Louise. On the girls' first birthday, she had taken part in a radio program that was broadcast around the world. Her voice was so good and she was so articulate that she received wires of congratulations from across the United States and an invitation to come to New York City as a guest of the Newspaper Enterprise Association (NEA), the world's largest syndicated news-feature distributor, supplying some seven hundred newspapers.

In New York, she was feted in the press. "She doesn't look or act like a nurse, more like an efficient private secretary. Strong and infinitely competent. Taciturn herself, but vibrating the kind of human-ness that makes her the recipient of everyone else's confidences," one columnist wrote. "In twenty minutes' conversation she is likely to talk about anything from Nijinsky to the rhumba, evening gowns, moose-hunting, Fascism, and canoes."

She stayed with the NEA president at his summer place outside the city, where she rode his horses every morning and spent the afternoons touring hospitals, being interviewed, going to nightclubs that paraded "the most naked women in the world as well as the most beautiful girls. On the whole I was treated as a queen of lesser quality, yet queen." The NEA signed her up for a five-part series on the Dionne quintuplets and promised her a book contract for the Quints story and for her Russian saga.

Her decision to quit nursing—made before the Quints were born—now made perfect sense. She would make her living with her typewriter, spending half her time alone in the woods and half in the swirling culture of the biggest, most exciting city in the world.

Before she could write a book about the quintuplets, Louise first had to overcome the feeling that such a book was not hers to write. Who was she to give advice to women on how to raise a child when she herself had never been a mother? "I, who have not been granted the sorrows and happiness of having a living child of my own, cannot speak with the subtle experience of a mother."

A living child.

In all the thousands of pages of Louise's letters and talks and published writings, there is only one hint of a pregnancy—this single offhand, unexplained comment during a speech to a local audience in small-town North Bay. Before she and Gleb were married, he had gone to a Swedish doctor and told him frankly that they did not want to have children in the middle of a civil war. "The doctor advised me not to use anything artificial, but just to be careful," Gleb wrote to Louise's mother, an intimate reassurance that suggests the concern originated with her. But how careful could a couple be who thought they might never see each other again? If Louise became pregnant on May 15, the last time she saw Gleb, the last time they made love, then she would have been four months along when she heard Gleb had been shot. Would a pregnancy survive the fevers of malaria, the starvation of post-revolutionary Moscow, the stress of not knowing where Gleb was, the terror of his death? With her next sentence, Louise intimates that the pregnancy ended not in miscarriage but in stillbirth, her in utero child at least five months old.

"More than ever I regretted that my child had not been born alive."

In her years in Russia and again in the northern Ontario woodlands, she had "tried my utmost to put myself into the place of every mother with whom I discussed the care of children and to look upon her difficulties through her eyes." But as she coached the Bonfield mothers in baby care, she always worried that they were saying to themselves, But you, who have no child of your own, how can we believe that what you say is true?

"Then came the Dionne quintuplets. And I could gloriously prove, to myself at least, that what I had taught and in which I deeply believed in the care of babies, was not only true but essentially simple and applicable to every case of a child."

Louise hunkered down to write the book she called *Mothercraft*—a story not about her, but about babies and how to bring them safely through their first year. How to give them the best possible start to a healthy life. The Dionne girls would be her examples, an extreme testing ground for her theory that what babies need most is sunshine, fresh air, cleanliness, close attention, and affection—"No more extravagant care . . . than is the birthright of every baby born."

In telling the story of the Quints' fight for life, the little girls would be the heroines. She would record every move and every action of their first year, staying faithful to the facts but telling it as a story, the sort of story one woman might tell another over coffee. Feeding. Clothing. Sleeping. Playing. Good and bad behaviour. She would talk about these children as individuals, noting the fine shadings that made each girl unique rather than writing about the five as an indistinguishable lump, as most reports did. She would show how scientific diagnoses and treatments were arrived at; how doctors and nurses worked best as a team of equal partners, each providing their own special care. "I wish every Canadian nurse to feel that this record of the nursing of the Dionne quintuplets is her own record," Louise wrote in her preface. "It would be most presumptuous of any of us not to admit that any other nurses, being entrusted with the care of these five premature small babies, could, as successfully, have replaced us."

One year later, she mailed the 137-page manuscript to Macmillan of Canada, which immediately accepted it for publication based on an enthusiastic reader report: "The style of the writing is simple, vigorous, and dramatic. Its charm is due to the enthusiasm, affection, scientific understanding, keen intelligence, and accurate observation, and to the character of the writer. It would be a loss if the Canadian public and the many thousands of others interested in the Quints were deprived of this book."

Production was swift. On September 15, 1936, *The Quintuplets' First Year: The Survival of the Famous Five Dionne Babies and Its Significance for All Mothers* was released into the same literary season as Grey Owl's *Tales of an Empty Cabin* and Margaret Mitchell's *Gone with the Wind*.

When Louise heard the first review of her book on the radio, she danced and danced. In the mass of literature that had come out of Quintmania, the announcer said, Louise's book would "stand out head and shoulders as one of the serious works. Its author deserves congratulations for its effectiveness and gratitude for having spared us from the slushy nonsense which this might easily have been." The reviewer for *The Canadian Nurse* admitted she opened the book with misgiving, due to the "nauseating commercialized publicity which has and still does beat down on these five little girls." But Louise in her disarming preface had "created quite another atmosphere and we read the book with genuine enjoyment. While it is quite apparent that the author was fond of her little patients there is a refreshing lack of sentimentality. The weaving-in of the narrative with sound and sensible advice on infant care is most skillful."

Only one reviewer, a satirist at the *Winnipeg Free Press*, saw the deeply political underpinnings of Louise's book "written with the subversive and unhallowed idea that the child is an important citizen, entitled to consideration, respect, and a reasonable amount of liberty . . . She would give children in city slums, children in backwoods shacks, as good care as that now provided for Annette, Cécile, Émilie, Yvonne, and Marie . . . You gather that she would have the resources of the state as much at the disposal of infants as it is now at the disposal of war commanders. If no one puts a stop to this sort of thing, it is hard to say where it will end. People may get the idea that infants are as important as guns."

The book was serialized in *Chatelaine* with photographs of Louise and the Dionne babies. The *New York World-Telegram* bought serialization rights in the United States. It was excerpted in *Woman's Digest* and translated for serialization in a popular Swedish magazine. Toronto General Hospital gave the book to every birthing mother to read before they left the hospital.

Yet sales were dismal. Despite the half million tourists who visited the hospital every summer to ogle the five little girls, Louise's royalties for all of 1937 were only $49.32 ($862 in 2020), including the sale of Danish rights. Just forty-five copies sold in Canada that year. The gift shop the Dionne family had set up across the road from the hospital—one of several booths selling Quintmania trinkets—flatly refused to touch it. The bookseller in North Bay was reluctant. A British deal collapsed, although rights were sold in Sweden and Denmark. Today the book has disappeared, even from the shelves of used and rare book dealers.

Louise's hope that *The Quintuplets' First Year* would be published in the United States was fading fast. The head of Macmillan of Canada was mystified: "The most talked-about children in the world, and the only really good book about them to date, and yet we have to be shopping around from publisher to publisher in the United States. I simply don't understand it." When Louise offered to do a lecture tour in the United States to pique interest, he replied, "This is a pretty heavy matter, and particularly for a girl: do you feel that you can undertake it?"

Clearly, he didn't know who he was talking to.

Louise blamed Dr. Dafoe for her book's poor reception. His own ghost written book, *Dr. Dafoe's Guide Book for Mothers*, had been released three months before hers and was lionized in both Canada and the United States.

Dafoe had grown rich on the babies, through his guardianship, product endorsements, and as consultant on the Quints movies. So, too, had Yvonne Leroux, who had become a radio darling and was living in New York City. Louise's head wasn't turned by the money; she knew from her own childhood how quickly money could be lost, how little it mattered in the long run. But she wasn't immune to jealousy and resentment, and she had a hard time containing her bitterness that Dafoe had robbed her book of its readers.

Her plan had been for the Quints book to finance her next writing project. Instead, she was penniless. Dafoe chastised her for not taking the sponsorship deals she was offered or the radio gig that went to Yvonne. But Louise held to the high road. She wouldn't even accept expense money from the Red Cross when she travelled to open their fundraising campaigns; she would not, "perhaps foolishly, allow myself to commercialize my connection with the quintuplets for the sake chiefly of my good name as a Red Cross nurse."

The year after her book came out, Louise was entertaining friends when up her path walked Oliva Dionne. She had sent him a copy of her book along with a letter of sympathy for his troubles around custody of his five world-famous daughters.

"He sat here for over two hours," she wrote to her mother, "and talked with me straight-forwardly and sincerely of the whole situation and of all that had been. He was bitter but not unjust. And I think it did him good to talk it all out to someone whom he found sincere and sympathetic. To me of course, I think his coming a great proof of confidence. He ended up saying that we are friends and that he always had valued my services and all I did for the babies."

Two weeks later, Louise delivered her speech in North Bay. She spoke on the topic of children: her experiences with them in Sweden, in Russia, in Canada at the Bonfield Red Cross Outpost Hospital, and finally, with the Dionne babies. Then she dropped her bombshell: "The separation of the Quints from their parents, brothers, and sisters was only justified in the first two or three years of their lives . . . A reunion of the Dionne family . . . I am emphatically sure, is now not only possible but might save the babies from what tends to be a most abnormal kind of childhood. For isolated as they are, they are denied that irreplaceable bond in life that exists between brothers and sisters, that family relationship upon which their background is inevitably founded."

Louise expected a furor. No one other than the Dionne parents had dared to express such an opinion publicly. But she held to her view. "What I said I said, and I had thought it well over and I stand by what I said to the last drop of my blood."

Louise always saw her time with the Dionne quintuplets as an intermezzo: a separate and unrelated episode that propelled her back to the life she had started out to live—a life in nature. But looking at it now, from a further remove, I see a single, repeating refrain: Louise watching the birds of Svensksund through the window of her father's house; Louise watching those tiny babies, keeping them alive. Louise, wherever she was, watching.

The Quints constituted her first scientific experiment, the testing of her theory that sunlight, fresh air, and cleanliness were key to cultivating health in even the most compromised newborns. Already in the mid-1930s, as she extrapolated from her year with the Quints to the appalling child mortality rate in Canada and how it might be reduced, I can see her mind moving naturally from the particular to the general, from science through scene and exposition to the universally significant, following an irresistible narrative thread.

The Quintuplets' First Year proved to Louise that she wasn't only a nurse, she was an observer and a writer—one who had just written her first life history.

Just as Louise was taking charge of the newborn Dionnes, she received a bill for the 1,121 feet of timber she had "stolen" to build her Cabane—$2.80 ($53.04 in 2020).

As soon as she paid for the felled trees, she received permission to move into her log house. On her first night in the Cabane, fire raged up a nearby hill, fanned by a strong south wind that made torches of the pines and sent live sparks drifting down over her cedar-shingled roof. She watched in horror as the conflagration reached the top of the hill and tilted toward her cabin. Then, miraculously, the fire lost its momentum and died.

Amid the chaos of Quintmania, the silence of the woods was a balm. Louise made paths through the property, naming each feature in the terrain. The slopes where the fire had raged became Brulé Hill.

The rise behind the Cabane became Peak Hill. Little Creek, where she fetched her water in summer, ran from Peak Hill down to the bay. The lofty hall of aspens and birches between the road and the creek she dubbed the Green Woods. Along the shore a wild toss of glacial boulders marked East Point, which looked across the bay; North Point faced the river. From East Point, a climax stand of evergreens climbed the Southeast Slope, sheltering the Fern Dell. Back toward the Cabane, aspens, willows, and alders grew all the way to the small cove she christened Lily-Pad Bay, where water flowed under the bridge in the road into small, round Beaver Lake.

She had just finished the Quints book when she discovered that although she had bought the timber rights, she did not, in fact, own the land. She had only leased it from the Crown. By this time, according to her own estimate, she had spent close to $2,000 (almost $38,000 in 2020) on her little piece of paradise, including the purchase of timber, clearing the bush, and the construction of the Cabane. When her lawyer told her that the three-year fight wasn't over yet, she broke down.

"I must apologize for becoming so upset yesterday over the bad news," she told him the next day, "but this little home of mine—the first I have ever been able to call really my own—has become very dear to me."

Finally, four years after she applied for the land, the minister authorized the sale of the original three and a half acres to Louise. According to the final patent, her property was 342 feet in depth at the road and 595 feet at the northern river edge, with a width of 330 feet. In other words, 3.45 acres of what she called "stony, sterile land," not the five she had petitioned for. The patent came with an invoice for $1.75—the remainder of what she owed.

Three days before Christmas 1937, Louise finally held the deed and the certificate of ownership in her hands. Ever since Svensksund had been sold out from under her, the dream of finding another such place had pursued her "like an ache." Over the years, she'd whittled the dream from a sprawling, surrogate Villan to its essential

63

Louise inside her wilderness Cabane, 1937

elements. Trees. Birds. Water. Wildness. A place that could never be taken from her.

Standing at last on her own few acres, among the soaring white pines that nestled her hand-built log house, cardinals clicking from the treetops, Louise must have marvelled at how unlike Svensksund this was, yet how like it was, too.

5
———

Hold Fast to This

At first glance, Leonard Lawrence seems an odd match for Louise. He was eleven years younger and considerably shorter, a wiry whippet of a man compared to her tall, Ingrid Bergman elegance. He had little formal schooling and had been earning his living as so many northern men did—even when I lived there in the 1970s and '80s—as a carpenter, road worker, handyman, jack-of-all-manual-trades. Louise was the goddaughter of a queen, schooled in five languages and all the arts of a debutante. She had travelled the world; he had never been beyond the district of North Bay. He was nothing like her father. Nothing at all like Gleb.

I don't know how Louise met Len, but I suspect it was in the Bennett camps that dotted the road being surveyed near her property on Pimisi Bay. There is a photo of Len, not yet thirty, in his lumberjack pants and high boots, with some of the men from the camp at Eau Claire, near Bonfield, where he worked as a commissary clerk, keeping the road gang housed and supplied.

Louise first mentioned Len in a letter to her sister. The Finns had finished building her Cabane by Christmas 1933, but it was an empty shell. She worried about leaving the building abandoned all winter and was looking for someone to act as guardian in exchange for free rent.

"I have the most marvellous man working for me," she enthused to Ebba in the spring. "He has looked after the place all winter. He is most wonderful as housekeeper and the place is spotless. He is awfully handy as a carpenter, gardener, roadbuilder, cook, and valet . . . and he takes as much pride in this place as if it were his own . . . He washes dishes, cooks the food, and polishes everything until it shines like the sun in Karlstad. If I didn't pay him, I think he would still stay. I cannot say anything else, but I have had the most wonderful luck with servants and the marvel with it is that they stick whatever happens."

By the time Louise resigned as nurse-in-charge of the Quints in June 1935 and moved into her Cabane, Len was a permanent fixture. He had panelled the walls and ceiling with pine and made chairs, tables, and built-in bookshelves, then constructed "a little house up on the hill behind my house in which he will live, so that I don't need to have him around here all the time when I have my friends visiting."

Len was an indefatigable builder, self-reliant and entrepreneurial in a way I used to think was unique to northern Ontario, traits I realize now are essential to survival in any economically challenged community. When I lived in the north, my neighbours' gateposts were laddered with homemade signs: *Haircuts. Fresh eggs. Firewood for sale. Taxes.* In the absence of steady jobs in factories and mines, people cobbled together a living cutting wood in winter, servicing tourists in summer, doing odd jobs for each other, growing their own food with a little extra to sell. This must have been even more true during the Great Depression Louise was living through.

It isn't entirely surprising, then, that in the spring of 1936, Louise and Len joined forces to start a poultry enterprise on her little plot of land. Although she was busy writing her book about the Quints, she was determined that "I will not be dependent entirely on the success of my writing," she declared to her mother. "If run properly, it is a very good way of investing one's money when one has the land and the *arbetskraft* [labour]."

On October 3, 1936, Betty the First laid the inaugural egg for L.K. Poultry Farm. Louise blew it out and sent it to her mother as a memento. Intent, as always, on learning everything she could about whatever piqued her interest, Louise attended a meeting of North Bay chicken farmers with Len. She was the only female, "a rather smart and elegant contrast to their, to say the least, plebeian figures. The crowd of North Bay poultrymen were not a toy to the eyes. However, I am one of them now, though I hope Len and I will beat them in every way soon. It seemed to us both—though this may be a little conceited of us—that not only the elegance of appearance but brains, in spite of our inexperience, are mostly on our side."

Louise recorded her daily harvest, determined to be the best egg producer the north had ever seen. By early November, she and Len were selling eggs. Every Friday, they'd drive the thirty-five kilometres into North Bay with ten dozen eggs that they sold for forty-five cents a dozen ($8 in 2020). Already the chickens were paying for their feed and Len's salary.

Over that first winter, Louise decided to triple the flock and add meat birds. By the time *The Quintuplets' First Year* was released in the early fall of 1937, she and Len were gathering a hundred eggs a day and had another 153 pullets almost ready to lay, plus dozens of roasting capons awaiting slaughter. Altogether, they were earning $100 a month (about $1,800 in 2020).

The next step was to eliminate the expense of buying day-old chicks by incubating eggs from their own hens. For Louise, the chickens were an ongoing saga, material for letters to her mother, and occasionally, articles for *Farmer's Magazine*. "Now I am running all around the house with my precious box of fertilized eggs to see that they have the exactly right temperature all the time. And if there are no chicks in them by the time they are due to come out, it is certainly not my fault, nor the hens, I know that. I'll blame it all on the roosters, Solomon and David. To make them very passionate, we shut them by turns into a crate, from where they can watch the other rooster make love to all the hens. There is a terrific crowing and cackling going on as you can well imagine, and we hope with good results. All is fair in love and war."

Her relationship with Len at this point appears to be all business. She paid him to cut her fuelwood and haul it to the house, to cut blocks of ice from the bay in winter and layer them in moss in the icehouse to last through the summer. He maintained the outhouse and the paths. He built the henhouses and looked after the birds. Len's financial investment in the chicken business was a truck with *L.K. Poultry* painted in large letters on the side. Even so, Louise was in it up to her elbows. Every evening, even Christmas Eve, she candled and packed about a hundred eggs. When Len took his holidays, she was "*solokvist,*" [a lone branch]. She mucked out the chicken houses, gathered the eggs from the nesting boxes Len had fitted into cabinets along the walls, and when a hen broke its leg, she set it with a splint. "Rather amusing to look after everything myself."

I wrote the same bright lines to my mother from the shack in the woods where I lived for nine years until my first husband and I built our house. I never told her about lugging wood all day to bring to a boil the huge cast-iron cauldron full of water, then dipping in the headless birds that moments before had been zigzagging among the trees, spouting blood that drove the birds waiting to be slaughtered crazy. The cloying stink of mucking out the henhouse; the horror of finding a hen on the floor midwinter, frozen to death, or a bird still breathing though its face had been gnawed to the bone by a raccoon. Instead, I told her about the pleasure of scattering fresh, fragrant hay and watching the hens scratch deliriously for the few dried seeds; the satisfaction of slipping a hand under a plump bird and sliding out a still-warm egg. For most of my adult life, until five years ago, I kept chickens. Now I hunt for *Farm Fresh Eggs* signs along the back roads, more than willing to pay $8 a dozen.

Like Louise, I knew to the penny how much I earned from selling eggs, how much the feed cost, how much I cleared in a month. We were, Louise and I, both of us new writers who had chosen to live in the woods, stretching every dollar to make ends meet. But that's where the similarity ends. She kept track of the hens as meticulously as she'd tracked every moment of the Quints' days. She gave each shipment of chicks its own group name—Annies, Betties, etc.—and banded each hen with a ring number that was hung on the henhouse wall when the bird died.

It is difficult to assess the relationship between Len and Louise during those early years. She hired him full-time; he took holidays and regular days off. On Fridays, when they went to North Bay to sell eggs, she drove home alone and he stayed in town, took in a movie or visited friends, then travelled by train back to Rutherglen, where she picked him up at the station.

Len with the LKL Poultry delivery truck, 1938

Their arrangement was clearly financial: after Len sold the truck (he realized too late the impossibility of delivering eggs in winter in an open pickup), Len made payments toward buying her car when she bought a new one in the spring.

In her letters to her mother, Louise praised him constantly.

"Len works like a slave at the chickens."

"Len is quite shrewd at bargaining."

"He cannot do enough for me in a thousand different ways."

Were they lovers too? They each had their own house on the property, yet they seemed to spend much of their time together, socializing, taking tea with friends. The way she wrote about Len by the fall of 1937 makes me think they were a couple. When a friend invited her to spend a weekend at a cottage, she told her mother, "Len thought the rest would do me good so he made me accept." And after she returned, "We are both glad that we are alone at home again, in peace working hard." When she heard the first review of her Quints book on the radio, it was Len she rushed to, dancing with joy.

I approach this part of Louise's life delicately, with reservation. Few contemporary writers have thought so deeply about the writing of other people's lives as Janet Malcolm, author of *The Silent Woman: Sylvia Plath and Ted Hughes* and *Two Lives: Gertrude and Alice*. "We know no one in life the way biographers know their subjects," she wrote in a 2019 *New Yorker* piece on Susan Sontag. "It is an unholy practice, the telling of a life story that isn't one's own, on the basis of oppressively massive quantities of random, not necessarily reliable information. The demands this makes on the practitioner's powers of discrimination, as well as on his capacity for sympathy, may be impossible to fulfill."

I feel those demands most heavily now, writing Len's place in Louise's life.

Louise's mother met Len in the summer of 1936. Louise had been urging her to come to Canada: "You will be much happier if you do and so will I . . . It is so gorgeous here that you can't but love it."

She sent her mother detailed instructions on which ship to take: the SS *Drottningholm*, a vessel named for a Swedish castle and one of the ships that had been in wireless communication with the *Titanic* as it went down. She advised her mother on how to avoid seasickness, exactly what clothes to bring—a warm coat, a smartly tailored travelling suit, light sundresses for Ontario, and an evening gown for the crossing, although "you must be sure not to wear it on the first night, which no one does." She should wear a mauve rosette in her lapel when she disembarked at Halifax so that the friends Louise had arranged to meet her mother would recognize her. "You'll have no trouble at the customs at all. Canadians are very good in that way." The friends would take her to the train, where Louise recommended a lower berth and a tip of twenty-five cents per night to the porter. Louise herself drove to Montreal to pick up her mother from the train, a trip of over five hundred kilometres—a very long day's drive in Henrietta. Louise was determined to do everything she could to ensure her adopted country and her rustic backwoods life made a good impression: "You must remember that you are coming to a very new country and it is not at all as in Sweden. People are very different in every way. One must not make any comparisons, simply take everything as it is."

Among the letters that Louise saved was one that Len wrote to her mother early in 1937, thanking her for the Christmas gifts she'd sent. He included a primitive sketch of their burgeoning poultry layout. His sentiments were sweet and kind. He expressed himself well, although he seems unaware of the existence of punctuation. He addressed Louise's mother as Madame and referred to Louise as Madame, too, as if intent on emphasizing his relationship as an employee. More than anything, he showed himself to be ambitious and hardworking: "I have been busy moving my old cabin we are going to use it for a Brooder house Madame did not think it could be moved without pulling it down but it was not much trouble one horse pulled it over the snow." In the spring, he planned to build a forty-foot-long chicken house with three rooms: one each for laying hens and broilers, and a breeding pen. And he had built himself a new cabin with two rooms, one a workroom. A man with a horse helped him haul the trees he'd felled out of the forest, "and then six men came with a saw and cut it up there is a great big pile Madame is splitting some up everyday for exercise I think it is good for her as long as she dont try and do too much I have strict orders that I must not touch any she cuts up as it is for next winter."

In Louise's 1938 New Year's Day letter to her mother she cast unaccustomed light on Len, her relationship with him, and her own character. She was commiserating with her mother about the bad behaviour of a cousin whose "exhibitions of insolence are nothing but a mad desire to gain attention." Louise continued, "That was the same trouble I had with Len. . . . If it is not checked and checked wisely and consequently, it can drive its victims to most regrettable dispositions and outbursts. With Len, I have at last through a great deal of awful struggles come to alleviate this quite remarkably. I began by building up little by little his own sense of worth by giving him great responsibilities which I shoved on to him despite some resistance. For those with an inferiority complex lack courage too. They dare not. Then I tried to make him not only know but feel his worth to me and to make him see that what others think of him matters nothing so long as he thinks well of himself and feels he is capable of doing things others could not do. Then when he lapsed, I fell down upon him hammer and tongs relentlessly so that he felt that he had let not only me down but himself. I fostered in him a healthy selfishness which at the same time acted as self-preservation. But if his selfishness became mean in any instance, I checked him there and then with a tremendous mental slap. It has worked. For you would not know Len to what he was when you were here."

Despite what she saw as his shortcomings, Louise clearly shared moments of tenderness and humour with Len and a love of the place where they had separately made their homes. Len had grown up in Ontario's northland. He knew nature the way a local does, by its nicknames. Woodpeckers were wood picks; the biggest one, a cock of the north. Cardinals were redbirds. And the shy grey jay—not the noisy blue one—was a whisky jack, a camp robber. When Louise got her first bird book, they walked together through the woods, giving official names to what they saw.

And they had their private rituals. Every fall, they made bets on when the bay would freeze over, Len getting thirty-five cents' worth of cigarettes if he won, Louise winning a packet of Kleenex, which might not seem like much, but paper tissues had been in the stores less than a decade and were still a novelty in the north.

As Len and Louise moved into their third year living and working in close proximity, the mutual pleasure in their friendship is evident. Louise cooked their meals, and they ate together. They relaxed together in the evenings, too, often paddling her canoe into the dusk. "It was lovely up the river. We slid along at sundown. The river was white with foam from the roaring falls, far out we paddled through it. The water rushed down in several streams and on the north side of the cliffs there were glaciers of ice that mirrored themselves in the black water. It was beautiful. It is very rare to have such lovely spring days without flies. And we are enjoying it sitting on the cliff by my bedroom window to drink our after-lunch and -dinner tea."

They shared the holidays in what can only be described as a picture of domesticity. The week before Christmas, Louise went into a rage of housecleaning, polishing the silver and copper, washing and starching the curtains, waxing the floors. "Len thought it very unnecessary but once it was done he silently made me feel his appreciation." Louise decorated the house with a small bushy tree, which she set in a brass pot near the fireplace and hung with coloured glass icicles and candles her mother had sent from Sweden. She arranged pine branches on the bookshelves, interspersed with red candles. Fruit in the silver basket and the pewter bowl on the mantle. In every window, a red wreath in what she called the Canadian custom. On Christmas Eve, the two of them dressed in their finest and sat down to roast lamb and graham cracker pie—"Not any traditional food for Christmas, but just the things Len and I liked best." Then they lit the fire in the fireplace and the candles on the tree and "sat down on the couch to smoke and to enjoy the beauty of the room at Christmas. It was so lovely and so peaceful. The flicker of the fire and the candlelight, the snow gleaming dimly without the windows, the dark furniture, and the gleam of the clean silver, the samovar, all the little brass things everywhere." Then they opened their gifts to each other and from all their families and friends. "Christmas Day we slept in, had breakfast only at eight. Then we went slowly about our chores . . . At three we were sitting peacefully before the fire looking at the coloured flames and with a coffee tray before us on the milking stool."

Through 1938 and early 1939 Louise and Len were yoked to the work of making a viable life in the woods. When the chickens failed to fully support them, Len suggested they add mink to their little homestead. I wonder if he got the idea from an enthusiastic *Maclean's* article, published around that time, promoting mink farming as "simplicity itself," with the mink in their breeding pens living "a life of comparative luxury." Mink, it said, bred like rabbits, and the richness of the harvest was "astonishing." Pelts, it claimed, were selling for $2,000 or more ($35,000 in 2020). Hundreds of Depression-weary farmers went into mink in the late 1930s—Alice Munro's father among them, a story she tells in *Dear Life*. Len set to work building mink cages, while Louise researched how to raise and pelt the animals. In the spring of 1939, she bought three breeders—Adam, Eve, and Lilith. To finance the new venture, she screwed up her courage to ask Dr. Dafoe to underwrite her application for a loan. "His money has come to him through me more than through anyone else. I figured it was not too much to ask for a small return." He agreed, and within a year they were reconciled, the Quints debacle finally put to rest for Louise.

By July, Louise and Len were devoting most of their time and thought to bringing the little homestead to the point where its profits would support Louise so she could write. Len enlarged the henhouses to accommodate even more birds—layers, roasters, fryers, and soupers. "We now have 750 running around in the bush, 200 laying hens already laying, and the rest capons and cockerels. Len is beginning to caponize tomorrow." Her small acreage on Pimisi Bay was dotted with nine sheds of various sizes for the chickens and the mink. Louise named all the buildings, calling one the House of Commons, another Venice. "Can you imagine me building houses? We tore down a shed and built a range-house in 2 weeks, Len and I. We are rather proud over that fact."

The farm work that summer was all consuming. Louise got up at six, had breakfast, cleaned her house, helped Len with mucking out chicken sheds, then a hasty lunch, followed by slaughtering in the afternoon, or trips to town to sell chicken and eggs or to buy provisions, and in between the constant building and rearranging, moving flocks, caring for the birds' health, and a thousand other things. "Can you wonder that I have not had a moment to write a letter, let alone any kind of other authorship," she wrote her mother. "In the fall we will get into a routine and I shall have the afternoons to write."

But by fall, the world had shifted on its axis. On September 10, 1939, Canada declared war on Germany. The following day, Louise and Len drove 160 kilometres east to the courthouse in Pembroke where, with strangers as their witness, they were married.

Louise waited a month before writing a long and careful letter to her mother.

"There is one thing I will have to tell you today that at first may shock you, but that I am sure when you have thought it over you will understand. I have married Len."

As if to forestall the storm she knew was coming, she shared what her friend Grace had said when Louise told her the news: "One may speak of one being superior to the other in education, but after all, what counts more in this life of ours is loyalty and deep conviction and as life goes on, it's not good to be alone."

Louise continued: "To me it is this, that of all the men who have and who do love me, and there are some of these yet and have been quite a few throughout the years, Len is the only one who has served his seven years for his Rachel. I am fully aware of the things he has not got, but I am equally aware of the great things he has got, immutable loyalty, a great gentleness and a devotion for me that is almost adoration.

"I felt when I did it that in putting my house in order it was imperative to count in Len, he has made himself too much of an item throughout these years. I felt that the only fair thing was to carry him. He is not the same man as you knew, though most of his inner being is the same. He has developed and grown, and now when he has rock under his feet, I have no doubt that he will not rest upon his laurels. Of all the eligible men that I might have wished for myself and others might have wished for me, perhaps he would not have counted as one. But if one sums up the inner qualities of each and the unselfishness of each, I wonder if not Len after all may have summed up the grandest total."

In addition to Dr. Dafoe's shy proposal, Louise had been courted by a New York news service magnate, a Montreal doctor who came to Mattawa every fall to hunt, and undoubtedly many others. Her enthusiasm and confidence were compelling. But like so many seeming extroverts, she was an introvert at heart, a woman who appreciated quiet companionship by the fire more than a night on the town.

"In the course of many years, as Len has lived with me, there comes into a relationship many fine threads like a weaving. It is an interlacing of little things of reciprocal taking and giving. Neither party can let the other one down without the destruction of something of value. To have severed this weaving of life between Len and me would have been equivalent to have knocked the ladder from under his feet and let him fall. I could not have done that and therefore I married him, heaved him up to take his place at my level.

"He will falter in much, I know that quite well, but then I will falter in much too. And as to the greatest giver, Len is without a doubt that. As to myself as an individual, my 'soul-mate'—I really hate that word but it is the best I can find for what I mean—died before we had almost started our real life together. I find it an utterly futile enterprise to search for his equal. Therefore I am losing nothing by marrying Len but gaining something that few men could give me.

"The success of any marriage, wherein lies it? How many well-matched marriages carry on to success? Perhaps this unmatched one will be the easiest to reach that height. Who knows? At any rate the one who depends on destiny and fate and circumstance to bring happiness is to my mind a fool. Happiness comes where and with whom you wish to make it."

Louise's mother did not respond. How confusing it must have been for this high-born Swedish matron to imagine her daughter marrying a man in order to heave "him up to take his place at my level." And how worrying that her precious Lolo had bound herself to a man who had "sullen spells" so intense that her daughter had often thought of letting him go, followed by months when she had nothing but praise for him. How like this reckless, adventurous daughter who had defied everyone to become a nurse, go to Russia in the middle of a civil war, move to the backwoods of a country an ocean away. This daughter who had lost her father, her true love, her home—was she about to lose her future too?

Ever since Hitler invaded Czechoslovakia, this eldest daughter had been begging her mother to come live in the safety of the Canadian woods. When her mother argued that there would be no room for an old woman in the log cabin if Lolo should marry, her daughter had been quick to reply: "And as to my eventual marriage! Leave thou the future to take care of itself! I have no plans or visions whatever in that direction. I am quite over any sexual urges and as to companionship—well, it is almost too late, my life is well-filled and adjusted to what would have been happiness but never mine."

Only two weeks later, Lolo married her hired man.

I eloped, too, although I was much younger than Louise—twenty to her forty-five. My mother was devastated, but in the moment, I gave her feelings scarcely a thought. A secret weaves its own chrysalis: I was revelling in the selfish joy of doing something no one in the world knew about but me and my love.

At the heart of my running off, I realized eventually, was a gut understanding that the man of my choice could never be stitched into my close-knit family with its skeins of aunts and uncles and cousins thrice removed. But why am I telling my story? Am I guilty of a kind of anthropomorphism—gynemorphism, perhaps—interpreting Louise's behaviour through my own experience raising chickens, living in the woods, eloping?

But I see the differences as clearly as the similarities. In the end, my marriage unravelled. But Louise never forgot the June day when Len confessed his love. He had kept working for her not because of the money, he said, but because he loved her. He had lived beside her, toiling his heart out, suppressing his feelings, enduring the hard labour, his humble position, her demands, all with an uncrushable hope that one day he would be able to prove his love to this remarkable woman, unlike any other he was likely to meet in the north. And she had lived through it all in complete ignorance. When he laid his love before her, Louise was shocked and horrified—not at his love, at her own blindness. Shocked, too, at the magnitude of his devotion and humbled by her own feeling that she didn't deserve such a gift. In that moment, her world changed. "There at my feet lay a perfect heart and I had lived for years and not known it."

After three weeks, when Louise still hadn't had a response from her mother, she tossed another letter into the silence: "Once I have leapt I don't think I can ever be accused of having shirked the consequences and its responsibilities. Neither will I this time. Accustom yourself to the thought that I have, in my own way, adopted an orphan son who needed much the basis of belonging to me. Things are now very peaceful and contented and, yes, I can say it, happy. So let us leave it at that—for now."

But her mother wouldn't let it go. Although she renewed the correspondence with her daughter, her tone was reserved. Reading

Louise's mother, Hillevid Neergaard Flach, in her Stockholm apartment c1940.

between the lines, Louise could tell that her mother was still allowing the shock of her elopement and her choice of husband to get in the way of their relationship. "Don't let me feel that it would have been better never to have told you which I could so easily have refrained from doing," Louise chided. "Why should you feel sorrow and be so desperate about it when Len is neither a bandit nor a drunkard nor a philanderer after women but only born with other inhibitions than we are and with a bit of a neglected education and when I not only feel I have done right by him and myself, but am quite content and satisfied?

"You saw Len at a disadvantage and even then you felt that there was something rather engaging and true about him, you said so yourself. Len is greatly changed since that time, he has kind of found himself, he has striven hard for something which has put his feet firmly on the ground and he is so good to me in every way. He saves me from too hard work, looks after me and would go to any lengths even to go to work somewhere to earn more money that I would be more comfortable. As to my old age, why should I, or you, worry about that when I have got one, a young strong one at that, who does not ask for anything better than to cherish me and look after me and see that I have everything I need . . . more . . . Hence I think it is a waste of time and effort and nerves on your part to fret about a *fait accompli* any longer. Buck up, my dear little mother, and accept him."

Len and Louise had less than four months of married life before Len enlisted in the army. Louise wrote to the Red Cross offering her services, either at home or at the front, but she was already forty-six, too old for active duty. Instead, she gave instruction to local women in the making of bandages, gave courses in war readiness, and became an aircraft observer, memorizing the shapes of enemy planes and watching the skies for bombers.

Just before midsummer's day in June 1940, Len was posted to Camp Borden for training. He was allowed home one weekend a month, but they both knew his transfer overseas was imminent. Louise would never be able to manage the livestock on her own, so they butchered the chickens, except for a few to supply her with eggs, and when the mink failed to breed successfully, she eventually pelted them. Her plan of self-sufficiency through animal husbandry had been replaced with an army paycheque.

On her first wedding anniversary, Louise wrote to her mother, "This year with him, despite all turmoil and changed aspects of life, has been an incredibly happy one. Len's devotion is beyond words and his unselfishness in everything that regards me is sublime. . . . My duty is simple and clear: to hold and adore his home here, the vision of which gives to his life all that he lives and works for and all that he is willing to die for. Looking back, I think to marry him was the greatest thing I have done simply because of its complete fitness. And I don't think that I shall ever meet the date of September 11 with regret."

Soon after, Len was posted to Nova Scotia, and from there, to England where he was eager to see action. Louise knew firsthand that war was ruthless; she had already lost one husband to its cruelties. After Len's final leave, she drove him back to Camp Borden. As they parted, she handed him a letter:

My Darling Husband,

I want you to keep this with you, if you can, until you come back.

It is my faith in you, the essence of my marriage promise, that single fundamental upon which the parallel of our lives is based. I like better the word parallel than union as it expresses more truly the indivisible running together of two integral lives, that is, two lives each complete in itself indivisible by virtue of their common basis of faith.

I could never doubt you. No matter what happens to you in the future or to me, my faith in you is indelible. There is no virtue of mine connected with this fact. It is simply you and the quality of your love which has made it so. Whatever you may do or whatever circumstance may force upon you, it cannot be changed. Remember this always.

When we met my life was half lived. I had already experienced much love, many periods of happiness and also sorrow. What you brought me was quite different to anything of all this. At first I thought you an ordinary man who would just touch my life at one point and then go out of it. But what you carried inside of you was not common. It was deep and strong and true.

It was inevitable that once it was at last revealed to me I should respond. Perhaps too I was the only one under the circumstances who could release it. And if I were to be true to myself I could not fail to give back in like measure. And it is this reciprocal giving and taking that is the essence of our marriage.

So I came to attain a happiness more real and lasting than anything I have experienced before. It has body and light and constancy. And you have kindled a love that I have not given to anyone else. It too has body and light and constancy. This is yours and mine alone, untouchable by anyone and anything and indelible in our hearts for the rest of our lives. If you should not come back it will remain with me as if you had not gone, and if I should not be here on your return it will not be taken from you by my going.

But you will come back and I will be here to wait for you. Remember the crescent moon and the two stars, you and I and our love. They did not come back with me last night, but stayed with you to bring you luck through whatever may befall you until you return.

Hold fast to this and neither of us need have any fear!

Your wife,
Louise

I found this letter at the bottom of a manila folder in Louise's archives—a small square of paper that had been folded and unfolded so often its creases were almost worn through, the surface grey with handling, although the words were still plain on the page.

6

This Gentle Art

What a singular situation Louise found herself in that spring of 1940. In an abrupt twist of fate, she was suddenly free of both financial insecurity and the burden of farm labour. The business of living still made demands, but once she'd yoked water from the Little Stream that flowed down Peak Hill and had split and piled her day's fuel wood by the cookstove, her time and her thoughts were her own.

In leaving for the war, Len had inadvertently given Louise a great gift—the gift of solitude. A certain relaxation comes with being alone. With silence. A space opens in the mind. Louise had built the cabin to fulfill an ardent wish to awaken every morning for the rest of her life with the sunrise in her face, to spend her days in quiet contemplation. Now at last she was free to follow her curiosity too—and what she was curious about was the natural world.

She and Len had set up bird-feeding tables a few metres from the kitchen window. They would scatter seed on the tables, toss breadcrumbs and kitchen scraps on the ground, and tie balls of beef suet to low-hanging branches. On the windowsills, Len had fastened narrow troughs to bring the birds close. She recognized only a few that came to feed, cousins of those she'd known as a girl in Sweden— woodpeckers, wrens, warblers, sparrows, and small chattery balls of fluff that reminded her of the titmice she used to watch at her father's feeders. Len had taught her the common northern species— chickadees, blue jays, whisky jacks—but the brightly coloured birds that winged through her forest and nested deep in its foliage, appearing now and then at her feeders, were a mystery.

One beautiful May day the spring before Len left, a new bird landed on her feeding table. "He is sitting outside now watching some big starlings gobble up the feed on the tray—with sadness," she wrote to her mother. "He is bright orange over the belly, breast, and under the wings, which are black and white. He wears a black cap over his head. He is quite big like a large *domherre* [bullfinch]. His wife is grey with a softer tone of yellow-green underneath and black and white on the wings. Not knowing yet his real name I call him Jelly-belly."

Louise had trained as a nurse. She was used to calling things by their proper names. A leg bone was a femur. A lump in the breast was a tumor, either malignant or benign. She wasn't content with "Jelly-belly," even though the bird did look as though it had nested in a bowl of orange marmalade. But who to ask for the scientific name? Not Len. And not her neighbours, who were farmers, trappers, and tree fellers. She knew no one educated in the science of birds.

A casual friend, hearing of her dilemma, loaned her a copy of *Birds of Canada* by Percy Taverner, a book that Yousuf Karsh, the Canadian photographer who created an iconic portrait of Taverner, called "an exquisite synthesis of poetry and precision." When Louise tried to return the book, the friend told Louise to keep it, the book was hers.

"You should see us now running around the bush at the twitter of a strange bird, at the flutter of wings, book in hand to watch and decide what particular bird is nesting or flirting in our bushes and tree-tops. The Jelly-belly I wrote about last time is a Baltimore oriole, quite a

rare specimen, beautiful to look at. They are nesting now and we don't
see them so often, but we hear their clear deep whistle every day. It is
amazing what a variety of birds there are now that we are beginning
to discover them, red like butterflies, yellow warblers, green tits, and
purple finches. We have made friends with them all."

Louise had few books at the time. What she had, she shelved
not alphabetically or by subject but according to literary merit and
their personal significance to her. And so she placed *Birds of Canada*
between a biography of Madame Curie and *Alice in Wonderland* on one
side, and on the other, H.G. Wells's *Science of Life* and Edward Lear's
Nonsense Songs and Stories.

My copy of Taverner's *Birds of Canada* sits with the bird guides of
Argentina, Mexico, Norway, Hawaii, Britain, Italy, countries where
my husband, Wayne, and I have travelled. An adult and a juvenile
red-headed woodpecker perch on the dust jacket. The endpapers are
a map of Canada, where long-tailed jaegers fly over Hudson's Bay, a
bird of prey feeds its young in northern Alberta, seabirds cruise the
Gulf of St. Lawrence, and a spruce grouse high-steps between the
Ottawa River and Lake Nipissing, through the place where Louise
lived. Inside the book, dozens of colour plates follow notes on hundreds of species—concise descriptions of plumage, field marks,
nesting habits, distribution, economic impact, and a brief, luminous
paragraph that could only be written by someone intimate with the
lives of birds: "In severe weather the ruffed grouse seeks shelter
beneath the snow or allows snow to drift over it. Should cold weather
follow mild, as often happens, it is frozen under a crust which it cannot
break and so succumbs."

With the help of Taverner's book, Louise soon identified most
of the visitors to her feeders. She carried it into the woods to name
the shyer birds. In the evenings, by the light of a coal-oil lamp, after
she'd written to Len, she read and reread the first thirty-six pages, in
which Taverner wrote personally about the value of watching birds.
"Few forms of life appeal so strongly to the aesthetic sense. They are

beautiful; they arouse curiosity; their elusiveness piques the imagination; and by constantly presenting new aspects they escape becoming commonplace."

How difficult it must have been to learn about birds solely from a book. I learned from Uncle Syd the summer I was nine, when he and Aunt Lizzie joined my family at a cottage in Muskoka. I'd perch on the arm of his big old wooden lawn chair, leaning in to study the illustrations in his *Field Guide to the Birds of Eastern North America* by Roger Tory Peterson. Published in 1934, the same year as Taverner's *Birds of Canada*, the Peterson guide was a quarter the size and fit easily into the pocket of Uncle Syd's bush coat. When he died, I got the book and put my blue checkmarks beside his pencil marks in the life list at the back.

Even so, there are some birds I never recognize. From the balcony of our bedroom in Mexico, Wayne and I watch a bird, brown as a sparrow but too chunky, its tail too long. I feel what I always feel when meeting someone who looks familiar but the name escapes me. I should know this bird! I see a flash of rusty rump and the name comes to me: canyon towhee, a bird I first saw at the Grand Canyon. William Beebe in his book *Two Bird-Lovers in Mexico* calls it a brown towhee. We watch it slip under the bougainvillea and over the adobe wall of the house, more mouse than bird, as Beebe says, though its persistent singing is as welcome as a nightingale.

A week before Len left for Camp Borden, he gave Louise a parting gift—Chester A. Reed's *Bird Guide: Land Birds East of the Rockies*, a pocket-size reference perfect for carrying into the woods; but it was *Birds of Canada*, compiled by the chief ornithologist for the National Museum of Canada, that she pored over every evening of her new solitude.

Taverner's intent in writing the book was deeply personal: "to awaken and stimulate an interest, both aesthetic and practical, in the study of Canadian birds." There was, he said, much valuable work to be done, by every sort of watcher, physiologist, behaviourist, and amateur too. "The ordinary nature lover can observe and note as painstakingly as opportunity permits; he may record information of scientific as well as popular interest, take pleasure in observing passing beauties, train his powers of observation, and acquire a knowledge that greatly increases his capacity for appreciating nature."

Louise must have felt Taverner was writing directly to her. For the first time in her life, at the age of forty-six, she was without a project, without a job, without anything that made her feel valuable in the world.

He laid out the best way to study birds, pointing out the personal and scientific value of such study, not only for the bird watcher, but for the nation, and most importantly, for the survival of the birds themselves. The distribution of birds in Canada was far from known at the time: bird populations of vast areas were based on assumption; many provinces lacked even an up-to-date, authoritative bird list.

"It is only by the study of many local areas that such broader lists can be satisfactorily written," he wrote, "and in such local studies as these, much good work can be done by the amateur. It must not be assumed that such local faunal work is easy; when conscientiously done it becomes one of the most difficult fields of ornithology."

Inspired, Louise bought a large black scribbler and on the first page printed in bold letters: *NOTES ON BIRDS AROUND OUR HOME.* She allowed one page per species, flipping to a fresh sheet each time she positively identified a new bird.

Her notes on these first sightings read like story fragments.

"Saw you love-making so close to me in the thickets that I could have touched you," she wrote of her first Canada warbler. "In fact you almost took off my nose in your ardor."

"I saw you feeding a young daughter today at the suet," she wrote of a hairy woodpecker. "Are you especially early?"

And of the ovenbird, "Well, now you are feeling quite at home very near to the kitchen window and bird bath."

On the back page of the scribbler, she ruled columns, and at the end of the year, recorded alphabetically the total number of each species she'd seen. In 1940, her first year of serious bird watching, she

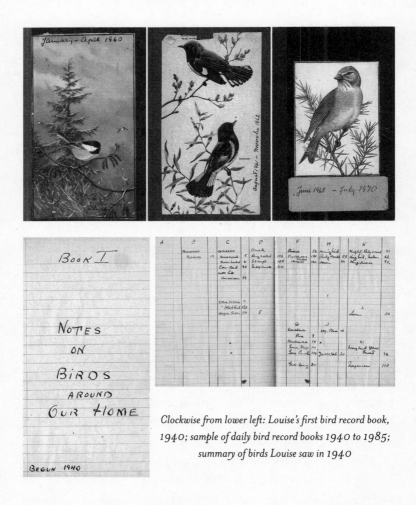

Clockwise from lower left: Louise's first bird record book,
1940; sample of daily bird record books 1940 to 1985;
summary of birds Louise saw in 1940

identified 73 species, including 14 rose-breasted grosbeaks, 92 king-
fishers, 34 American crossbills (now called red crossbills), 118 Arctic
redpolls, 66 Blackburnian warblers, 38 sapsuckers, and 10 blue jays.

But was she seeing ten different blue jays or the same blue jay
ten times? How could she know when they all looked and acted so
much alike?

Taverner would know. In *Birds in Canada* he wrote that the National
Museum of Canada welcomed enquiries from serious students of

birds. Would it be presumptuous to write to Taverner himself? Louise asked a summer acquaintance, Elsie Flett, a violinist who played in a string quartet that occasionally entertained at Taverner's home in Ottawa. The Dominion's chief ornithologist, Miss Flett assured her, was always happy to talk about birds.

In the first week of her solitude, Louise wrote to the great bird-man, never expecting a reply. "May I tell of a few things I have seen?" she began. She described the purple finch's "impassioned wooing of his demure little bride" and a male rose-breasted grosbeak singing so continually that she wondered "if he was neglecting his duties or whether he was a bachelor" still in search of a mate. She apologized for taking up so much of Taverner's time, but excused herself by saying that "the only drawback to living far away from other people was that one needs occasionally to find someone who knows more than oneself with whom one might be permitted to share impressions, crystallize observations and find guidance. Hence this letter, which I trust you will not look upon as a presumption . . . Meanwhile your book, excellent in a practical way and delightful in a literary sense, remains to me a prized guide and friend."

Taverner was sixty-five, ready to retire, but he had stayed on as chief ornithologist when the best of his potential successors went to war. He had grown up in the theatre where his mother was an actress, then trained as an architect, but more than anything, he loved birds. In 1912, although self-educated and entirely lacking in scholarly credentials, he'd been invited to take charge of the National Museum's new bird exhibits. He was thirty-seven. Over the next three decades, not only had he gathered a magnificent study collection of 35,000 specimens, but he'd been instrumental in convincing the Canadian government to sign the 1916 Canada-U.S. Migratory Birds Treaty, designed to "save from indiscriminate slaughter" birds migrating across the two countries. He'd also helped establish bird sanctuaries throughout Canada. Even so, in the face of another devastating world war, his work often seemed to him futile, picayune.

Louise's letter arrived at exactly the right moment. He answered almost immediately. "When I get such letters it makes one feel that life has not been entirely wasted."

Between June 1940 and August 1946, Louise wrote Taverner twenty letters. (He died in 1947.) He kept all her letters, and she kept his replies. Their correspondence spanned the duration of the war, when she wrote hundreds of letters to Len, too. His letters, carefully numbered to 206, are but a small stack compared to hers, he says, yet hers did not make it back from the war.

Did she tell Len about the appearance of a black-billed cuckoo the summer of their first year apart? Or the northern cardinal that lingered in the cabin clearing through the winter of 1941? With great excitement, she wrote to Taverner about her remarkable finds. "I have long moments of pleasure watching this scarlet vision against snow and evergreens. An old trapper came here the other day and as soon as he saw it, he exclaimed, *'Ah, mais ça c'est porte bonheur!'* [That's a harbinger of happiness!] He had never seen one in this bush before."

The delight of seeing a brand-new bird is a bit like the bliss of love at first sight. One Sunday, as I walked in the Charco del Ingenio, a wild canyon above San Miguel de Allende, a chunky grey bird with a thick mustardy beak landed on a cactus in front of me. Its crest was tall, brushed scarlet at the tip; around its beak, a splash of red that dribbled down its belly, as if it had just gorged messily on cherries. It looked at me and let out a thin slurring whistle, *what-cheer? what-cheer?* I stood rapt as it tore at the fruit of the cactus, just as the cardinals back home used to tear into late apples in our orchard. And sure enough, the bird was a desert cardinal—a pyrrhuloxia, cousin to the red cardinal that brightened Louise's winter.

Northern cardinals had been recorded at higher latitudes than Pimisi Bay, Taverner told Louise, but her sighting of a black-billed cuckoo marked the most northerly record of that bird. "This is one of the great things in bird study. There is always something new to look forward to, with thrills spaced evenly enough to sharpen the interest. If this gentle art is a relief from the sterner atmosphere that surrounds us, it is a blessing indeed. We need such relief these days. If I have had any hand in extending it, I can feel that I have been of some use in the world."

Wars, disease, personal tragedy: birds are oblivious to our human trials. Writing this during the Covid-19 pandemic, I feel the truth of Taverner's words. The song sparrows and Caspian terns outside my window are carrying on with their lives, trilling and screeching, nest-building and mating, the young hatching and trying their wings: stages in a life that remind us of the calm unrolling of our lives, too, regardless of the immediate upheavals we are suffering through.

"Blessed be these birds!" Louise wrote back. "With them it is quite impossible to feel one instant of loneliness or boredom."

Her first autumn alone, Louise woke one morning to find Lily-Pad Bay awash with ducks, more than a hundred of them paddling among the cattails. She wormed across the granite bluff on her belly, trying for a better view, but at the slightest motion, the ducks drifted away, their markings indistinguishable from the grey-blue waves. She was about to give up when she heard gunshots. She lifted her head to look and saw a wounded duck struggling desperately in the shallows. She scooped it up and raced back to the house to bind its blasted wing. "Perhaps it would have been better to kill it at once, but I felt a kind of sad duty to restore to it the dignity that my fellow species had so ruthlessly shattered."

The bird died, but examining its feathers, she was able to identify it as a female ring-necked duck. When she consulted *Birds of Canada*, she saw that little was known about the species, and so she reported it to Taverner.

"This salvaging wounded or sick wild things is perhaps misplaced humanitarianism," he wrote back. Everyone feels the impulse, he assured her gently, and rescuing "perhaps is worthwhile in our own development . . . as long as we do not let it obscure the real facts of life."

But Louise could not resist the urge to help. When she found a hatchling robin abandoned by its parents in a nest half-dissolved by torrential rains, she appointed herself "foster mother." She set the newborn in one of the nests she'd collected that lined her window-sills. For three days she hand-fed worms, shadflies, and raisins to the naked little bird, learning to touch a special spot on its throat to release the swallowing reflex. Typically, she took the front and back doors off their hinges in summer, creating what she called "her log tent," but she rehung the doors when the robin fledged, removing them again after it learned to fly. "Since then he has come and gone like a wild thing."

Not entirely wild. When Louise called, the bird answered and fol-lowed her through the house, begging for worms.

More than once, Taverner hinted that she was sentimental, and indeed, her enthusiasm in those first years seems so. She gave pet names to the chickadees she tamed to eat from her hand: "Joe, always black in the face from the ashpile, and Pete, thin and terribly indif-ferent to neatness in dress, with the air of a delicious gamin and always in the morning with a crooked tail that must have been crushed in the tightest corner of the chickadee dormitory, and Hesitant Mary . . . with a definite feminine look in the brightest of eyes."

Taverner provided a necessary corrective. When Louise told him she'd spotted "a scarlet vision," he suggested she write a detailed description that would convince a well-informed reader she had actu-ally seen a northern cardinal. "A statement of things as you see them," he insisted. She responded with a concise, precise paragraph, abso-lutely accurate, although not entirely shorn of the unique turns of phrase that made it recognizably hers.

Notes On Birds Around Our Home grew thick with detail. Soon, Louise was leaving four pages instead of one for each new bird. She advanced from recognizing a species visually to discerning its mating call, determining which tree it preferred for nesting, when it was likely to leave in the fall and return in the spring, and which birds were resident all year round. On Taverner's recommendation, she bought herself Frank Chapman's *Handbook of Birds of Eastern North America*—a book the size of a deck of cards, one page per bird, and squeezed into that small space a brief physical description, likely habitat, its song, nesting habits, range, and a colour portrait. Not as lovely and thorough as *Birds of Canada*, but like the Chester A. Reed guide Len had given her, much more portable.

"Using all three I have already found the answers to several questions. Chapman in particular gave advice on how to enter the woods. As a result I have been prowling around the bush decked out like a Jap sniper in ferns and branches . . . The effect has been marvellous with the birds without exception falling for the dupe."

Draped in ferns, she was able to discover which species was parenting the nest of naked hatchlings she'd found—certainly not the yellow warblers that attacked her as if the nest was theirs. "Detouring the persistent warblers, I sneaked within good view of the nest upwind, well camouflaged, where I lay watching amid buzzing flies. Reward came with two flycatchers coming unsuspectingly to feed the little ones." By observing details of colour, behaviour, size, and call notes, she was able to identify the family as Traill's flycatchers, a species originally named for Thomas Traill, a Scottish friend of John James Audubon, but which has now been split into willow and alder flycatchers, the latter most likely the birds that Louise saw.

By her second year on her own, Louise had positively identified eighty-four species in the woods around her cabin and learned their songs.

"Now as I stand in my kitchen making pies I can know without seeing whether the olive-backed thrush outside is frightened or happy, what youngster sits out there in the pine clamouring for food," she reported to Taverner. "I remember especially one summer night when six veerys, each in his tree-top close by the cabin, to borrow a line from your book, jingled their golden chains in a matchless serenade. Such beauty makes one forget the war and the violence of man."

Still, Louise was not content.

"I feel I need an aim," she wrote to Taverner. "I think what I want you to tell me is how, with what I have and what I can do, can I learn to learn more? How should I record what I see? How should I direct my observations? How can I do more, study better, and let it come to use for all our knowledge?"

"Why not take up banding?" was Taverner's reply. "That's the only way to get to know individuals. . . . I don't think that anyone can really know a bird until they have had it in hand."

Live-trapping and banding were still relatively new when Louise started in 1942. Bird enthusiasts in Canada had been banding privately since the turn of the twentieth century, but when the Migratory Birds Treaty was signed in 1916, banding became the official means of tracking an individual migrant bird's path. The United States Fish and Wildlife Service established its Bird Banding Laboratory in 1920, and three years later, the Canadian Bird Banding Office was set up.

To become a bander, Louise had to apply for a permit, proposing a banding project and providing references from an active bander or recognized ornithologist who could attest to her identification and record-keeping skills. Taverner agreed to vouch for her.

The Canadian Bird Banding Office sent her numbered aluminum bands in various sizes for the species she was likely to trap. Each band was impressed with a unique numerical code, which Louise typed onto file cards, along with a record of the leg that was banded (R or L), the sex of the bird (F or M), and the date and time it was banded. The band also carried a return address. Birds don't recognize national boundaries, and so Canadian and American banding offices worked together to receive news of the fate of a bird and pass it on to the bander.

Louise was dismayed by the diminutive numbers on the bands. To read them, she first had to make a workable magnifying glass, which she did by unscrewing a bottom lens from an old pair of field glasses. She had no trouble following the instructions to build a Beginner's Flat Trap—a shallow box constructed of a wooden frame covered with wire screening, about a metre square and fifteen centimetres deep, with one side hinged to flap up. "I must confess to a few bursts of minor profanities in the making of it."

She set the box open-side down on the ground and propped up the hinged side with a trip-stick. Attached to the trip-stick was a pull-string that she trailed along the ground to the house and up through the kitchen window. She scattered balls of suet and seed under the trap, then sat at her small red kitchen table, string in hand, watching and waiting. A chipmunk wandered in and she pulled the string, the trip-stick fell, and the side flopped down. The trap worked! Still, she couldn't quite bring herself to trap a bird. "I am delaying action, I hardly know why," she confessed to Taverner. "Perhaps I am a little afraid to use a precious band and muddle up its record, or perhaps I am afraid to catch Jackie, the chickadee, first and hurt him by my inexperienced handling."

The next day, she gathered up her courage and when a blue jay hopped into the trap, she gave the string a swift tug. She pulled on her coat and hurried outside. Remembering everything she'd read, she lifted the side and reached in, grasped the bird, and clumsily turned it on its back.

"I thought it was safer to start with a bigger bird. He was angelic once I got the right hold on him with the exception of a few pecks at my finger at first. I trembled getting the band on, but I got it on and the bird left my hand unhurt by either trap or handling. What a marvellous thing you have given me to do!" she enthused to Taverner. "I am thrilled beyond words."

Louise banded her first bird on October 14, 1942. By the end of the year, she had banded thirty-three birds, mostly chickadees and woodpeckers. She experimented with flat traps, house traps, water drop traps, and a drop trap over a salt lick. When winter came, she poked the pull-strings into her kitchen through tiny holes she bored in the chinking between the logs. She watched the strings out of the corner of her eye as she read and made notes, ready at the first tremble to yank the trip-stick and rush out to slip an identifying band on yet another bird.

"Each time I catch a bird I am thrilled," she wrote to her mother. "It is wonderful to hold them in your hand and to note the beauty of their plumage. The birds get quite tame some of them and I retake them and so can see which are staying and which go on further north. Of course as I band more and more birds it will be still more interesting, especially if I retake some birds year after year and so can follow their life."

As soon as Louise could afford it, she bought a Potter's trap, developed in the 1920s by Miss Jessica A. Potter, an avid bander in an industrial suburb of Los Angeles, California. A marked improvement over other bird traps, the Potter's trap is still the standard among banders. The frame is made from stiff wire and hinged so the trap is collapsible, a great advantage in the field. And it includes several compartments, each with a door that slides up and a trip-doorstep that triggers the door to fall when a bird steps inside to take the bait.

The following spring, Louise was rewarded when one of the song sparrows she'd banded returned to her woods. This was what she had been waiting for, "the thrill of holding in the hand once again a bird which has travelled many hundreds of miles since I saw it last. It has found its way back to the exact spot in this wide land of the north where last year it mated and nested."

Suddenly she realized how short a time "her birds" were with her— three months, a little more, to stake a territory, sing a mate to its side, build a nest and lay eggs, raise a clutch of young, then feed like crazy before flying south to rest before returning north to do it all again.

She wrote to Taverner, thanking him for so productively filling her solitary days while Len was gone to war. "I am glad to have my thoughts occupied. When I stop to think I get a little panicky." But she was not given to brooding. "Between my duties as bird-bander, official aircraft observer, mink breeder, writer of sorts and housewife, I have no time to get bushed."

Banding card for a female red-breasted nuthatch, 1953

Hundreds of index cards, arranged by bird species, are squashed into the shoebox that confronts me in the third-floor reading room of Library and Archives Canada in Ottawa. Beyond the wall of windows at my side, the snowmelt-swollen Ottawa River has burst its banks and is roiling downstream, milky with mud, ferrying tree limbs and islands of debris into the whirlpools that worry the edge of the lot where my car is parked, where I had an extended conversation with a male cardinal, me *phishing* through pursed lips, him cocking his head at the strange sounds from this giant, two-legged, red-coated creature.

I shimmy individual cards out of the crammed box. I am wearing white cotton gloves, careful not to leave a smudge or crease or anything that might say *Merilyn was here*. Louise typed these cards every evening from the notes she'd made during the day, watching in the woods. (She went to extraordinary lengths to procure a key with male-female symbols for typing up her nesting cards.)

Each card is black with information.

R-A, ♀

Hairy Woodpecker   *RED left*   *42-221205 Nov 22/1942*

This woodpecker was female. R-A indicates Louise put an aluminum band on the bird's right leg and a RED band on its left. From these two bits of data, Louise created the bird's name: Red RA. The number is the official designation on the aluminum band, supplied by the Canadian Bird Banding Office and unique to this bird, which was trapped and banded on November 22, 1942. The card goes on to list every sighting of Red RA over the next six years: at the feeding station, being courted, feeding her young. Reading the cryptic entries, a story emerges: the young female visited the feeder all through the winters of 1943 and 1944. According to Louise's weather records and snow charts, these were relatively mild winters with heaps of snow. In the spring of 1944, the female hairy raised a clutch of young, then disappeared again for a year. In March 1948, she was being courted by an unbanded male that was chased off by another woodpecker.

As Louise's studies intensified, her banding records became more detailed. She measured the length of the bird, bill-tip to tail-tip, and the length of its wing; she weighed it and scored its visible fat level. By 1944, the data was so overwhelmingly complex that she created an index, listing the various behaviours she was observing: Courtship, Call Notes, Flight Song, Distraction Display, Defence Behaviour, Feeding, Nest Building, Plumage, Predator Interaction, Territorial Behaviour, and more. Within each category, she noted every species from which she'd collected that particular information and where exactly it was stored.

This obsession with detail was nothing new. She'd kept scrupulous notes on the feeding, changing, and airing of the Quints, and again with her flocks of laying hens. She was punctilious by nature—a fastidious housekeeper, a list-maker and planner in her personal life, conscientious by medical training, when a life might hang in the balance, and now meticulous in her notes on the workings of the avian world. And yet she was never myopic, her eye always trained on the forest as well as on the trees and the nests in their branches.

Answers to her questions seemed within reach. Yes, individual birds returned year after year to her woods. Yes, a specific bird nested in the same tree where it had nested the summer before. Some species, she discovered, kept their mates season to season. She banded nestlings and tracked how far they dispersed from the nest, how many years they returned to raise their own families in her woods. She became interested in how long a bird in the wild might live: one of her banded chickadees lived for nine years; a Canada jay stayed ten years before it disappeared; and she monitored a female hairy woodpecker month to month until it reached the age of seventeen.

For seventeen years—1942 to 1959—Louise trapped hundreds of birds and fitted tiny aluminum bands around their ankles. Only eight of her banded birds were recovered, three within a few miles of her property. One of her evening grosbeaks, a male, was caught, rebanded, and released in New Hampshire; seven years later, it was found dead in Sorel, Quebec. Another was trapped and released in Connecticut. A merlin, one of a pair of nestlings Louise raised on dog food and raw liver after their parents disappeared, was found dead at Eagle's Nest Resort, Minnesota, on the western tip of Lake Superior. She banded only one wren, a perky little male that built nest after nest on Louise's property—in the wren houses she nailed to trees, in a cardboard box by the back door, even in one of her boots. He sang and sang, but no female returned his mating call. In the fall, he migrated alone. Four years later, Louise learned that her banded wren had been killed against a telephone pole in West Virginia.

In all, she banded 2,628 individuals, representing fifty species. That seems like a lot to me, but Louise was disappointed; through the magazines and newsletters she subscribed to, she knew of banders who trapped that many in a year or two. "I thought I would only have to set the traps and flap the doors on hundreds and hundreds in no time." But in order to know the birds, she had to catch them. And to catch them, she had to know enough about them to lure them into her traps: what they ate, whether they were tree creepers or ground feeders, shy or curious, all of which determined which trap to use and how to bait it.

"There is a trick to every trade and the same goes for observation," she wrote to Taverner. "To you, of course, all this is an old story of which you know all the chapters. To me it is just the very first paragraph in a fascinating fairy book which you opened before me."

Two years into her banding project, Louise wrote to the chief biologist at the National Museum. Percy Taverner had retired, replaced by Rudolph Anderson, a mammalogist rather than an ornithologist and a man whose tone was as snippy as Taverner's was warmly welcoming. Anderson was American-born, a veteran of the Spanish-American War that had brought Puerto Rico, Guam, the Philippines, and Cuba under American control. A desk job must have chafed this brawny soldier-explorer. In his letters to Louise, Anderson took every opportunity to criticize Taverner and blow his own horn for overcoming the inconveniences of wartime—so much space had been confiscated by the military that bird collection cases were stacked ten feet high and three deep. He needed a ladder to get to the ones on top, he complained. Even so, Anderson said, he had boldly scaled the mountain and found the specimens Louise requested—four evening grosbeak skins and one of a purple finch—which were being mailed to her parcel post to further her studies.

A year later, when Louise discovered a freshly built Canada jay's nest deep in the woods behind her cabin, she avoided Anderson and turned instead to Austin Rand, an associate zoologist at the museum, cast in the same mould as Taverner.

Rand responded immediately, with barely contained excitement. At the time, almost nothing was known about the reproduction cycle of Canada jays. They nested in remote forests, while snow was still thick on the ground, making them almost completely inaccessible to researchers. Louise's discovery represented a unique and rare opportunity.

"There are so many things we would like to know about it. Do the male and the female take turns at incubation? If so, how often? How long does each spend on the nest at a time? Does the male feed the female on the nest, and if so how often? What does he bring her? Does he carry it in his gullet or in his bill? How long does it take the eggs to hatch? For how long after hatching are the young brooded? By which sex? How long are the periods of each bird in brooding? Is there a ceremony when one adult brings food? Does this change as the young get older? How long do the young stay in the nest? Do the young have any down on them at hatching?

"These are some of the questions to which it would be well worth finding out the answers, and they would make a real contribution to our knowledge."

Within a year, Rand would become curator of birds at the Field Museum in Chicago. Had Louise hesitated, she would have missed out on his expert crash course in how to study a breeding bird.

Out for a walk on an unseasonably warm Palm Sunday in 1945, Louise's neighbour noticed a pair of Canada jays ferrying nesting material among the conifers on a rise above Lake Talon, near the chute where the Mattawa River is born. Three weeks passed before the neighbour led Louise and some birding friends to a bushy young white spruce and pointed a couple metres up to the nest. The birds had woven dry sticks between a fork of branches, creating a frame for the bowl they'd shaped from last year's oak leaves, strips of birch bark, bits of a wasp nest, and threads from tent caterpillar cocoons. Inside the bowl, a mass of dead grasses and strips of cedar bark formed a thick mattress overlaid with fine grasses, hairs, and feathers from a ruffed grouse and from the breasts of the jays. Five eggs, beautifully white and spotted with olive brown, lay with their small ends neatly turned into the bottom of the well-insulated nest.

It was only after Rand told her how little was known about the nesting habits of the Canada jay that Louise realized her luck in seeing such a nest so close by. On April 26, she hiked the four kilometres through heavy forest to the spruce. "Thus, armed with watch, mirror, and a blanket (how I wished I had thought of a groundsheet too that day because the best spot for observation happened to be all but in the little rivulet), I set out on my first nest-watching expedition with no previous experience but much enthusiasm."

The clouds hung low, pushed swiftly by a wind that blew from the northeast. The temperature hovered just below freezing. She set up a flat trap, baited it with suet, and settled on a stump within sight of the nest, holding the blanket close and sitting perfectly still, hoping the jays would accept her as part of the landscape. A loon called in the distance. A hermit thrush sang its fluting song. She smeared a nearby stick with peanut butter. The jays flew in, swallowed the peanut butter with a soft *xhrae*, and flew back to their·eggs. They ignored the trap. Without the certainty of holding one in her hand, Louise couldn't distinguish male from female, both dark grey above, lighter grey below, a distinctive white patch on the forehead and black at the back of the head. She assumed she was watching a mated pair.

"Uttering mellow notes, they stepped around the nest and over it, apparently undecided which one of them ought to sit down on it. They stretched their necks and opened their bills but no food passed from one to the other. In growing excitement both crouched and shivered their wings until finally one of them entered the nest and sat down on the eggs, carefully adjusting them under its brood spot. The other followed and sat down on top of the first bird, their bodies slightly cross-wise. The one covering the eggs, with only its head and tail showing, was embedded deeply under the long fluffed feathers of the one on top."

For an hour and a half the birds sat on the eggs, stacked like a double duvet. The top one would leave for two or three minutes and

Louise's sketch of 'stacked' Canada jays incubating eggs in early spring, 1945

when it returned, the bottom bird would get up and they'd switch roles. As they settled, they trembled their wings and made soft *miewing* sounds, turning to each other with open bills, sometimes ruffling the nape of each other's neck. Then they fell still for another hour or more. From above, it must have looked like a two-headed bird dozing on the nest.

A ruffed grouse stepped by. When a pair of slate-coloured juncos alighted in the spruce, the startled jays called *yoo-yoo* in alarm. Snow began to fall, dropping heavily through the air, then the wind picked up and Louise left, afraid she wouldn't be able to see to find her way home. She had sat by the nest for six hours.

The blizzard raged all the next day. In the afternoon, Louise waded to her watching post. Snow was piling on the top bird so thickly that now and then it had to get up and shake the snow off, strutting around on the branches close to the trunk as if trying to warm up. Louise lasted four hours.

"I wondered how they could stand such cold weather with so little nourishment. Keeping the nest and eggs warm seemed to be their only preoccupation. Each time they moved it would be accompanied by *miewings*, trembling wings, and opened bills. On the whole, it is impossible to imagine a more devoted and companionable way for a pair of nesting birds to perform the tedious chore of hatching young, especially in a snowstorm."

On the fifth day of watching, Louise arrived just before sunrise. The nest had been pillaged, all the eggs taken but one, which was still warm to the touch when she clambered up the tree to check. She searched the surrounding bush and finally found the parents, huddled together in a white spruce some distance away, *miewing* and trembling their wings and opening their bills to one another. Then the birds flew off. Louise caught glimpses of them at long intervals, farther and farther away, until they disappeared altogether.

Within two months, Louise had written her account of the nesting Canada jays, concluding after twenty-one hours of watching that winter-nesting Canada jays keep their eggs warm by both parents incubating together, stacked on the nest. She sent her report to Rand, along with the carefully boxed nest containing the sole remaining egg, which Rand tested and found infertile. He added the nest and egg "to the collections of the nation."

"The activities you describe, as far as I know, are unique," Rand wrote to Louise. "Let me congratulate you on the fine piece of observation and reporting. It is an excellent piece of writing."

She also sent a draft to Margaret Morse Nice, with whom she had just begun to correspond. Margaret Nice was the best-known female ornithologist in North America at the time, famous for her studies of the song sparrow and her theories of avian territoriality. She read Louise's Canada jay paper with a characteristically critical eye. As far as she knew—and she was extremely well read in the bird sciences—the only other account of nesting Canada jays had been published in 1899 in *The Auk*, the journal of the American Ornithologists' Union. The author, who was on a photographic mission, not a nest watch, claimed that only the female sat on the eggs. "Male incubation is exceptional in the Corvidae," Margaret wrote. "I suppose this difference from the rule is correlated with their extraordinarily early nesting. But does anyone have any explanation to offer for that? I wonder what they feed the babies."

Louise had no answers to Margaret's questions. She was confident in describing what she'd seen, but had she interpreted it correctly? Could both adult jays have been females, survivors "of a friendly triumvirate that were simply doing exactly what they were meant to do"? Or were these birds like the nuthatches that also nested in late winter—oddball corvids in which both the male and female incubate?

There were no other studies to consult. As Arthur Bent wrote in the entry on the Canada jay in *Life Histories of North American Jays, Crows, and Titmice*, "Few of us have been able to observe its nesting habits, in spite of the fact that it is an abundant bird over a wide range. Its nesting site is usually remote from civilization, the nest usually well hidden in dense coniferous forests, and extensive traveling on snowshoes is very difficult at that season. Moreover, the birds, though exceedingly tame and sociable at other seasons, are quiet, retiring, and secretive during the nesting season."

Louise's first foray into nest-watching had taken her into almost-virgin ornithological territory, alive with questions and controversy, rich with opportunities to make a contribution. How could she resist?

One of the birding friends who accompanied Louise to the Canada jay nest was Oliver Hewitt, an ornithologist she'd met just a few months before.

"His proper title is Chief Migratory Bird Officer, a somewhat cumbersome title for sure and meaning little to the uninitiated. The man is much shorter than his title and extremely nice. I did not know him before, but he had written . . . and asked if he might call, as he was doing a canoe trip down through the Mattawa River."

Hewitt had just joined the Dominion Wildlife Service and was keen on visiting the banders like Louise who were sending in regular bird reports. The two immediately hit it off. Four years later, he would become the first professor of wildlife management at Cornell University, and even then, he would continue to write to Louise, asking her to count all the ducks in her bay on a certain date or all the birds she sighted on Christmas Eve, or to write a special report on the nesting success of some species.

Hewitt arrived with his brother, a geologist, weary from shooting the rapids on the Mattawa. Louise fed the two, then brought out her records and spread them on the chesterfield in front of the fire. It was the first time she had spoken face to face with someone trained in bird science. No matter what question she asked, Hewitt had the answer.

For Louise, the meeting was momentous. "He felt that I was doing remarkable work, situated as I was in the midst of the woods and being able to make continuous studies like this and that I was getting all kinds of bird records in banding that they had very little of."

This was high praise from a man who had studied vertebrate zoology at Cornell with Arthur A. Allen, known as "America's First Professor of Ornithology." When Louise confessed she had no idea what she might do with such records, he assured her, "Notes such as you are now keeping often become of great value when one least expects it."

As he was leaving, Hewitt asked if he might return one day and bring a friend, George Miksch Sutton. Louise knew Sutton's name from his articles in *Audubon Magazine*. He'd been curator of birds at Cornell until he enlisted, but he'd continued to report on bird life from army bases across the continent. Sutton was a watcher and a scientist, but he was also a painter who had studied with Louis Agassiz Fuertes, one of America's best bird artists. Of course! Hewitt must return and bring Sutton and anyone else who would broaden her understanding of birds.

At the end of her first letter to Taverner, Louise added a postscript that became a frequent finale to her letters: "If ever you should pass by this log cabin would you stop and pay us a visit?" Without fanfare, quietly paddling down the Mattawa, steering their Model Ts up the road that had once been a dogsled path, loaded with binoculars and notebooks, tents and cameras, scientists arrived to tramp with Louise through her forest in search of birds. In return, as a kind of bread-and-butter gift, each brought some new tidbit of knowledge, some improved technique or unfamiliar ornithological publication, some link to another watcher engaged in a similar study, nurturing this solitary woman isolated in the woods, this ardent student of the gentle art.

7

————

Like the White Wings of Angels

Without warning, a rather short, blonde woman emerged from the winding forest path Len had cleared from the road. Behind the woman, a man who looked so much like Louise's long-dead Russian husband that her hand flew to her mouth. He was tall, with a black beret on his head, and he walked with a slight limp, like Gleb. His face had that same gentle, scholarly cast. He seemed much younger than his wife, who was a bit matronly but had such a fresh, smiling face that Louise, opening the door and stepping into the clearing thought, Here is a supremely happy woman.

The couple hardly noticed her. Their eyes were raised to the birds flitting in the canopy. They were listening, heads cocked, softly calling out names to each other.

"I was no little put out when the first thing they did was to discover the presence of four species of birds I had no inkling inhabited my very special and private region. I was blithely under the impression I knew every single bird that was here. That knocked me perfectly flat, ornithologically speaking."

Literally too. Within minutes the trio were lying on their backs in the clearing, watching pine siskins cavort through the upper branches of a tall poplar. Louise had never watched birds with anyone who knew more than she did, who could identify a bird simply by its song. For years, she had longed for such a companion and now—what a miracle!—here were two. Not a single word had yet passed between her and the visitors, yet already her pride lay in a heap at her feet, which was not in the least discouraging to her. In fact, she was ecstatic. For the first time, she could see what it meant to truly recognize birds in the wild.

The couple were Murray and Doris Speirs, by 1944 already fixtures in the Canadian bird world. Murray was a doctoral student at the University of Toronto, writing his thesis on the American robin. Doris was researching the life history of the evening grosbeak. The war had brought them to the air force base in North Bay, where Murray was assigned to the weather office.

The three became instant friends. Doris was born the same year as Louise—1894. Louise had turned fifty in January; Doris would follow in October. Both had come recently to birds. Murray was just thirty-five, fourteen years younger than Doris; Len was eleven years Louise's junior. By another remarkable coincidence, both couples had married in the same year—1939. Louise was a widow when she married Len; Doris was a divorcée with two children and a grandchild when she met Murray. And Doris had been born into a family not unlike Louise's. Her parents were personal friends of A.Y. Jackson, Lawren Harris, and J.E.H. MacDonald, founders of the Group of Seven who encouraged Doris's artistic talent. She took up painting, married an artist, and for a time was among Canada's notable art patrons, the first Canadian to buy a Georgia O'Keeffe canvas. But all that was behind her now. With Murray, she embraced birds, one in particular about which almost nothing was known—the evening grosbeak. As Taverner pointed out in *Birds of Canada*, the breeding grounds of the eastern subspecies had not yet been found, but the new

Doris Speirs, just before she met Louise in 1944

friends agreed: evening grosbeaks must surely be raising their young in Louise's woods, or very nearby.

All day they talked birds. Louise was in heaven. As the afternoon waned, they walked the paths through the forest, looking for EGs, as Doris called them. When it grew too dark to see, Louise laid out a buffet of cold salads and a lemon pie she had baked with her entire week's war ration of sugar. They sat in the living room with their plates on their knees, the conversation barely pausing long enough to lift food to their mouths.

Two weeks later, Louise started her first daily bird record, a practice she would continue for the next forty-two years. At the top of the first page she wrote: "This record is begun on June 11th, 1944, on the advice of Mrs. Murray Speirs. The Speirs . . . are the first real ornithologists I have had the pleasure to share bird experiences with, a pleasure that I have anticipated for years. For the encouragement and inspiration in further bird study which they imparted to me, I shall forever bear them the most deep-felt gratitude. Thus with their blessing, I begin."

Every morning, before the sun crested the trees on the far shore of Pimisi Bay, Louise walked the paths that wound beside the water, through the woods, up the hill behind her clearing, across the road, looping back to her log house. Binoculars hung from her neck; in her pocket, a little bird-count notebook, a pencil, and her two small field guides. She walked slowly, watching for flitting shadows, the telltale tremble of leaves. Every few steps, she stopped and listened, filtering through sounds of wind, distant loons, rushing water, the rattle of rock and chatter of squirrels, until she could hear the *tseet*, *vee-wit*, *meeyah*, *ʒree*, *churr*, and *tuck* of the songbirds. When she isolated a call, she followed it, scanning the shrubs and trees with her field glasses until she found the bird and confirmed its identity. When she was absolutely certain, she jotted the sighting in her notebook.

Back at the house, sipping a fresh strong coffee, she sorted her sightings into the order of the birds in the checklist published by the American Ornithologists' Union (the same order that Peterson, Sibley, and all North American bird guides use today). Then she sat down at her second-hand typewriter, her bearskin rug underfoot, and typed the names of the birds she'd seen that day. On that first dawn walk in June 1944, she saw fifty-six species, including three yellow-shafted flickers, eight cedar waxwings, four hermit thrushes and three olive-backed thrushes, twelve American crows, nine red-eyed vireos, four chestnut-sided warblers, one bobolink, six white-throated sparrows, one winter wren, and a lone chimney swift. She noted the weather—fair and very warm—and the mammals, reptiles, fish, and flowers she saw along the way (four chipmunks, one garter snake, one pickerel, and the first wild strawberry of the season). She also recorded the names of the observers: herself and Mrs. Murray Speirs.

As the weeks went by, her records became increasingly detailed. The weather at dawn, in the forenoon, and in the afternoon. The mating success of various singing birds; their songs and calls. "Hummingbird collecting cobwebs for a nest," she wrote. "Banded one chipping sparrow." When the daily bird record was complete, she punched two holes at the top of the page and slipped it over the rings of the wooden clipboard that hung by the back door—a page for every day of the year.

In the first weeks of January, she collated all the data from the previous year to create an annual bird list that included the number of species she'd seen, the first and last date each species appeared in her woods, and the "peak date" on which she'd counted the most individuals of that species in a twenty-four-hour period. The numbers are astonishing. On May 30, 1945, she counted fifty-five chimney swifts. On June 6, twenty-six Wilson's thrushes (now known as veerys). On June 20, thirty-three red-eyed vireos. On October 17, seventy-five American pipits. The thought of thirty-three red-eyed vireos singing in her small forest fairly makes me swoon.

In her photograph album, Louise pasted pictures of herself at the time, dressed in trousers and shirt sleeves, a kerchief knotted around her neck, stubby binoculars not much bigger than opera glasses in one hand, a notebook in the other—a rustic Katharine Hepburn. As much as she loved solitude, Louise easily attracted friends, mostly women left alone by the war. They exchanged visits, knitting socks for soldiers as they discussed the news from the front, books they were reading. They joined her on her tramps through the woods, trousered, fresh-faced women with suspenders and cigarettes, nurse friends, teacher friends, women who shared her love of the outdoors, although none of them had her stamina. Not even Doris could sit and watch as long as Louise. After they trekked back to the Cabane, her friends would lounge in the sun, while Louise sat hunched over her *Birds of Canada*.

Louise and a friend birding during Second World War

In the year she met the Speirs, Louise's annual species list for her property jumped to 133. It wasn't that more birds were in her woods, but that she was getting better at seeing them and identifying them accurately. She could have become a life-lister, always on the lookout for new species. But instead of breadth, she chose depth, focusing her curiosity on the songbirds of her home woods.

"Bird studying has such a scope that I feel one must limit oneself somewhere," she wrote to Taverner. She faithfully sent him updates on the progress of his "embryo bird student," although her letters were less frequent now. "From the things I have lately read about different ways of learning about bird-life, it seems that a well-conducted regional study for a period of years is yet a field that has been little explored. With this in mind and with the help and direction of the

Speirs, I am having my area properly mapped this spring as soon as we can get around in the bush and, from then on I shall be able to say exactly where whose territory is and how far so-and-so goes for food or fight or just meandering."

Whenever Louise went into town ("town" was North Bay; the "village" was Rutherglen, just a few miles up the road), she would meet the Speirs on the shore of Lake Nipissing to spend an hour or two looking through Murray's spotting scope at ducks, sandpipers, godwits, whimbrels, and other water birds. Back at the Speirs house, Murray would pull volumes from his impressive library of bird books to show Louise what he and Doris had seen since the three of them were last together. The Speirs visited Louise often on the weekends to watch birds and to hunt for evening grosbeak nests. Late one autumn day, they lingered through supper.

"We sat around the kitchen table, drawn out so that all of us could look out and watch the birds in the yard. When we finished, it had grown dark and then we went out for a walk on the highway to listen to the night sounds. That is Murray Speirs' specialty. Not only does he know every squeak and peep and where it comes from, but he also knows of nothing quite as fascinating. I share this opinion. But all was silent, not a sound. In the sky the stars began to gleam and all of a sudden Murray waxed eloquent about them. He used to teach astronomy in a university in the States so he knew every blinking star, every nebulous nebula and to listen to his discourse was a treat. In the midst of it, I was the only one who saw an enormous shooting star . . . I was sad I had not had time to wish on the star for good luck. But I just wondered, do we need good luck, isn't just living, seeing, breathing good luck all the time?"

A year later, in June 1945, Murray was reposted to Camp Borden, a three-hour drive south. Before they moved, the Speirs spent several days with Louise, and as if nature were bestowing a going-away gift, Louise finally spotted an evening grosbeak nest as she backed into a creek, intent on the faint cheeping of young birds. Doris and Murray showed her how to mark the nest's location and what to watch for in observing the parents and hatchlings so she could collect data for Doris. When, after the war, the Speirs moved even farther away to a small stone house in a forest east of Toronto, their friendship carried on. Louise continued to record evening grosbeak data for Doris, and the Speirs continued to open doors that Louise eagerly marched through.

Doris's education was artistic, not scientific, but under Murray's tutelage she had expanded her studies. She often visited the Royal Ontario Museum (ROM) in Toronto to examine specimens of evening grosbeaks, and she urged Louise to apply for a collector's permit so she could contribute EG specimens to the collection—not birds she shot, but ones she might find dead on her property or on the roadside. During one of Louise's visits south, Doris took her to the ROM and introduced her to Clifford Hope, who showed her how to prepare a study skin.

A study skin is just that—the skin of a bird with feathers attached but minus the skeleton, muscles, and organs. To prepare a study skin, the dead bird is laid on its back and the abdominal cavity cut open with a single incision, breastbone to cloaca, taking care not to pierce the abdominal sac that encases the organs. The skin is peeled back from the body and up over the skull, disarticulating the leg and wing bones from the main skeleton and severing the muscle attachments.

Louise watched as Clifford Hope set balls of cotton gauze into the eye sockets and stuffed the skin with a wad of gauze wrapped into a vaguely bird shape. Then he sewed the incision closed and fluffed the chest feathers to conceal the seam. He groomed the bird until it was restored to its life size and shape and its feathers lay naturally along the body. Finally, he tied the bird's legs together and wrapped the body in a girdle of cotton gauze, setting it aside to dry for several days. Properly prepared, Hope said, a study skin could last decades; the oldest in the ROM collection at the time was 150 years. Louise had already tried her hand at preparing a skin by herself, thinking her education would be advanced by having her own collection of specimens to refer to for comparison. "A terrible disappointment . . . I was all fingers." Hope encouraged her to send her dead birds to him for preparation; the ROM would loan them back whenever she asked.

At the ROM, Louise also met Jim Baillie, assistant curator of ornithology. Baillie was self-taught like herself, a man who, although he never finished high school, had been registrar, cataloguer, and custodian of the museum's ornithological collections before becoming assistant curator. I know his name from the Baillie Birdathon, the oldest sponsored bird count in North America, a twenty-four-hour birding competition organized each May by Bird Studies Canada to raise money for bird research and conservation. For nineteen years I've participated with a gang of writers in the marathon count on Pelee Island, where Baillie had often come to watch the spring migration.

Baillie was a big man, a burly redhead with enormous bushy eyebrows that in certain lights looked pink. Like Louise, he was a smoker; his brand of choice was Sweet Caporal because the pack had a lined space on the back that he used for bird notes. It was Baillie who told Louise that the Mattawa River region was a uniquely favoured spot for observation—a place where the southern reaches of northern birds and the northern reaches of southern birds met and overlapped.

They began a correspondence. In one of his letters, he warned her "to be skeptical of the reports of most untrained observers." He was obsessed with accuracy. Do not list anything of which there is the slightest doubt, he'd tell new birders. Don't believe anything you hear and only half of what you see. A man of deep integrity, he never tired of expounding on the potential of bird watching to improve the mind, enliven the community, and introduce a sense of responsibility in a person toward their environment. Taverner and the Speirs had taught Louise technique and given her confidence, but Baillie had a rarified moral compass that Louise responded to. He became her model of what it meant to be a self-trained scientist of integrity.

Baillie invited Louise to join his provincial network of naturalists who sent bird data and specimens to the ROM. He wrote the "Audubon Field Notes" that appeared in the *Federation of Ontario Naturalists' Bulletin* and asked Louise if she could provide a monthly summary of her observations. Louise was ecstatic. "What good are notes," she wrote to Doris, "unless boiled down to the marrow! I have got more knowledge accumulated in these few days [of summarizing] than in all the hours I sat on the spot watching. Imagine nest study added to nest study in this graphical way and tell me then if that is not material, MATERIAL (in large letters) for anything I might wish to write about at any time I wanted!"

Periodically, red crossbills, evening grosbeaks, purple finches, pine siskins, American goldfinches, and white-winged crossbills would invade Louise's woods by the dozens. While these members of the Fringillidae family generally live year-round in Ontario's Near North, they only entered Louise's territory in those years when the conifers were weighted with cones. Scientists call such an influx of birds an irruption—a sudden, sharp increase in a natural population due to some favourable change in the environment. But the abundance of pine and spruce seeds was not the only attraction. One cold December day when Louise was walking on the frozen bay, she counted scores of flocks flying high overhead. When she got to the road, it was dark with birds, especially the steep hill by her house where the gravel was heavily salted against ice.

The birds sat on the road in clusters, each species keeping to its own, although the red crossbills sometimes mingled with the pine siskins. When a car roared by, they rose like dark steam, then settled again to their salty feast. Several times a day, Louise walked the shoulders a half mile on either side of her driveway, picking up half a dozen dead birds or more on each trip.

By March, at the height of the breeding season, she counted sixty red crossbills on the road and at her salt lick by the house. She watched as they drank the salty snowmelt by resting their crossed bills side-ways in the liquid and lapping it up with their tongues. Why were the birds eating salt? How much were they ingesting? Was it the salt or the gravel or the snow melted by the salt they were after? Was there a connection between the need for salt and their reproductive cycle?

Louise decided to study the stocky, brick-red birds with mandibles like misaligned manicure scissors. It was April before the snow was melted enough that she could get through to crossbill nesting terri-tory. She found four nests, all of them so high in the pines and spruces that she had to hire a neighbour boy to clamber up and measure the distance—7, 8.5, 9.8, 10.6 metres off the ground. Each nest was sad-dled on a sturdy horizontal branch, midway between the trunk and the branch tip. Although the nests had been built in various parts of the forest, they shared one peculiarity: each faced a clearing.

Two had been abandoned, one with an egg in it. Another was tucked so deeply into the branches, it was all but impossible to see. Only one nest afforded a good line of sight. Louise set herself up between two windfalls to watch. "From here I had a fairly clear view of the nesting branch which extended in a long petrified dead end pointed in my direction and inside the canopied green vault I could discern the faint outline of the rim of the nest. I sat wrapped in a greenish steamer rug. It took me some time to achieve a way of steadying my binoculars on knees and elbows at the crucial moments, when shivers from cold and long sitting had a tendency to keep them wavering annoyingly."

On the day the young hatched, the temperature hovered at freezing. Every day Louise returned, often arriving at her watching spot at 4:30 a.m., an hour before the first blush of sunrise, and staying until after 7 p.m., snowshoeing home in the darkness after the female had settled onto the nest for the night. During her watch, Louise timed the comings and goings of the parents and the feedings of the young, noting how the pattern changed as they grew.

On the fifth day, Louise glimpsed the three hatchlings, light grey with silvery bills. Their gaping throats were the crimson of sweet william. Now the female left the nest, too, to forage for food, leaving the young alone. When the parents returned, they no longer chattered, but approached in silence, landing on the treetop and furtively hopping down branch to branch. On the seventeenth day, the young stood up in the nest and flapped their wings, calling *tchetetetetetet* for food so loudly that Louise could hear them from her observation post across the ravine. She was sure they'd be fledging soon.

She worried about the blue jay she'd seen scouting that part of the forest, and sure enough, one day as the female crossbill was descending to the nest, the blue jay called. The female immediately sounded the alarm, a whistling *lu* . . . *lu* . . . *lu*, and flew off. The male followed her, both birds calling loudly from a distance. The jay ignored them and landed in the conifer just below the nest.

"May the unscientific behaviour of this naturalist be forgiven, but at this crucial moment I could not endure so abrupt an ending to this fascinating crossbill story, a sentiment I could well have spared myself, leaving nature to take care of its own. I clapped my hands and chased the loudly protesting blue jay away from the nest.

"Twenty minutes later the crossbills returned. The female flew down and hopped around the nest in evident distress. I stood tense, watching until my neck ached. Finally, she flew into the nest—and out again—and at that moment both she and I realized that the young were gone."

But they weren't gone. They were hiding. The male found one fledgling tucked away amongst spruce twigs close to the nest. The second emerged from a hiding spot on another branch, and after much calling, the third appeared too.

"The next day I found the family in the lake area. One young, a small stubby-tailed fluffball, sat on a twig near the lake. I hid to let the adults point out the other ones to me. With no difficulty I captured one of them. Not expecting to find them again after the episode the day before, I had brought no banding equipment with me. So I carried the young one home where I could examine and band it in peace."

The bird was fully feathered, heavily striped in lighter and darker shades of grey, the wing and tail feathers etched with cream. Tufts of natal down still clung to its head and shoulders. Its bill was silvery grey, the mandibles not yet crossed.

Louise put a bright blue band on its leg then took the bird back to where she had caught it, this time bringing bands and a Potter's trap with several compartments. Using the fledgling as decoy, she set up the trap and waited. The female and the other two young succumbed. "But even with his whole family imprisoned, inducement enough one would think for any family father to let caution go by the wind, the male steadfastly refused to enter the one compartment open to him."

Louise went ahead and banded the others. The young showed no fear. "Two of them let me put my hand over them without the least protest. The third one dropped from its perch and crouched in the moss where I picked it up without further ado. Yet when the blue jay invaded their nest tree, they apparently knew enough miraculously to disappear out of sight."

The next day the weather turned. Sleet rained down for hours. When Louise finally ventured out, hiking through the sopping woods to where she had last seen the family, she found no trace of the birds with the bright blue bands.

The ROM in Louise's day was a bustling hive of information and connection. Phones rang, doors opened, mail rushed in and out. Serious birders loved the place and were welcome; it was where they went for help, where they gathered to share their latest discoveries. That vitality has now been formalized. Appointments are required; people speak in low voices, the atmosphere more church than town square.

I sit in the vaults, surrounded by ten-foot-high metal cabinets, each fitted with dozens of narrow trays, each tray holding stilled multitudes of birds. Pardon me: study skins. The ROM's collection includes over 140,000 skins, 45,000 skeletons, and 12,000 nests and eggs, all methodically catalogued and organized by species. Some of the skins are over two hundred years old, many arrived in crates from collectors who tramped through jungles and bogs and deserts in the farthest corners of the planet. The ROM collection contains one of the world's largest gatherings of extinct birds, including 132 passenger pigeon skins and one each of the extinct Labrador duck and the great auk. It also includes what the ROM terms "a significant collection" of North American wood warblers, New World vireos, flycatchers, and sparrows.

Late in the summer of 1945, Louise mailed Jim Baillie an evening grosbeak nest, most likely the one she found for Doris. It was the first evening grosbeak nest in the ROM's collection. Three years later, she sent four birds she'd found dead by the roadside—a white-winged crossbill, a pine siskin, and two red crossbills—as well as a red crossbill nest with an abandoned egg. She sent eight specimens in all, but the technician has found only four: the nest of a

Nest of a red crossbill (above left) and a black-throated blue warbler,
and skins of a white crossbill (below right) and a pine siskin, donated by Louise
to the Royal Ontario Museum, 1948 to 1952

black-throated blue warbler; the red crossbill nest that the hired boy climbed so high to retrieve; and the prepared skins of a pine siskin and a white-winged crossbill.

I lift the crossbill nest out of its small, hand-formed cardboard box and marvel at the interweaving of spruce twigs, cedar bark, dead grasses, and mosses, still soft after three-quarters of a century. A crackle of eggshells inside. I imagine the embryo slurped up by a rat snake that slithered up the maple trunk, or a chattering squirrel, or maybe a blue jay that happened by when both parent birds were taking a break. Weeks of establishing a territory, choosing a mate, building a nest, and incubating gone in a few egg-piercing seconds.

Only one other researcher sits at the study tables in the vaults, a young woman with a tray of what look like flycatchers in front of her. With miniature calipers she is measuring the length of each body, bill to tail, then each wing that she pulls to its full spread of feathers.

I can barely stand to look at the white-winged crossbill on my tray. The white-winged is much like its red cousin, except the red is brighter—coral, instead of brick—and it has two broad white bars on its black wings. Lying on its stomach, the bird is remarkably life-like, although when I prod it onto its back, the thin, bound legs make me think of folded hands in a coffin. I can't see where the prepar-ator made the incision through which he pulled the bird's organs, then stuffed the skin with cotton until it was as plump as a living bird. Overlaps of gauze bulge from the skull sockets in imitation of seeing eyes. The upper and lower mandibles are parted slightly, as if about to snatch a seed from a stalk. The tag confirms that this is specimen #75252, a female *Loxia l. leucoptera*, found on February 27, 1948, on Highway 17 near Rutherglen, Ontario, and donated by L de K Lawrence. Except for the crossed mandibles, the female of the species doesn't look much like the male: its plumage is streaky grey with yellow patches. The breast of this female is the fresh hue of buttercups, lightly barred with chocolate. The wings show a single splash of cream. On the back, just above where the wings fold together, a sunny patch.

A paper on the desk near the bird tray cautions *PLEASE DO NOT MOVE BODY PARTS.*

I am undone by all this death. More than a hundred thousand birds that once built nests and raised young, sang their hearts out at dawn, and soared through the flaming dusk are stuffed into drawers, unseeing and silent. I understand the rationale. Such collections allow scientists to study extinct and rare birds they might not otherwise encounter. A series of birds of one species, taken over time, can reveal much about environmental change and adaptation, leading researchers to a better understanding of the factors that affect birds' lives, thus enabling future preservation. All birds of a species share similar markings but individuals vary, so access to a range of specimens is important for positive identification too.

The birds are precisely arranged in their cabinets, but only by species. When I ask if there are more of Louise's donated birds, the technician opens the drawers of evening grosbeaks and pine siskins and invites me to search. Clearly, it is hopeless. It is a miracle that he found even that one poor crossbill.

In Canada, the Migratory Birds Regulations allowed banders like Louise to salvage birds that died in the course of banding or birds they found dead. The regulations gave specific instructions on how to record and preserve every dead bird that came into their possession and how to send it to the National Museum of Natural Sciences or to another qualified Canadian institution, such as the Royal Ontario Museum, for future study. Following their instructions, Louise would have placed a pinch of sawdust in the bill and throat and on any bloodied parts of the bird. She would have slipped the body with its data tag into a special bag, arranging the bird so its feathers were smooth and properly aligned. The bag would have been sealed and set on ice or, in winter, set outdoors to freeze. When the bird was frozen hard, she would have wrapped the bagged bird in newspaper and placed it in a box lined with crumpled newspaper and some dry ice to keep the body chilled. Where, I wonder, would she have found dry ice in 1940s northern Ontario?

I cup the crossbill in my hand. I've held birds captured in mist nets, felt their small hearts beating against my palm, but this is nothing like that. Seventy-five years ago, this bird was feeding on a northern stretch of gravel when a blow from a passing car snuffed out its life. A woman a decade and a half younger than I am now picked it up off the road and cradled it in her hands. She packed it up and drove to the Rutherglen post office, no doubt adding extra postage so the bird would swiftly make its way south, not under the power of its wings but in a train that picked up the mail every afternoon at three. And someone in the building where I am sitting now, someone with the initials C.E.H.—Clifford Edward Hope!—unpacked this small creature and set about preparing the skin so it would last forever, so I could hold it and marvel at the passage of life and the passage of time and the peculiar ways we humans have concocted to learn about the world that isn't us.

For as long as she could remember, Louise had felt an inclination toward what she called "self-expression." As her Cabane was being built, she had imagined herself living alone in the woods, writing stories. The vision never revealed what stories exactly, but publishers' interest in her Quints book led her to believe she had what it took to be a writer. "I was received by the editorial director of this publishing company who told me that I have got a talent for writing which I must not spoil," she'd written to her mother at the time. "You can imagine to what an extent I am encouraged to go on. He also asked for three more articles which I am to write some time when inspiration strikes."

Louise took to writing as she took to everything—with her whole heart. "This has always been a guiding principle to me: Whatever you do, do fully and completely, never piece by piece."

Stories of all kinds surged in her head; the challenge was to find the right form. She took heart from something she remembered about Hans Christian Andersen, who had yearned to write novels. "He never got anything out of that. He had to lay the novels aside one by one and take up his fairy tales, by which he won immortality." Not that Louise aspired to immortality. "Like success, and even more so, happiness, such things cannot be aimed at. They only descend upon you in their best forms—like the white wings of angels."

The year Louise began her correspondence with Taverner, she had discovered *Farmer's Magazine*, a bi-monthly tabloid that advertised itself as Canada's National Farm Magazine. Between 1942 and 1946, during the years she was alone, *Farmer's* published ten of her articles. Louise called them her "Insignificant Bird Stories": two to three pieces a year on the love life of a dove, the bachelor wren that never found a mate, her beautiful grey jays. The essence of her writing style is apparent even at this early stage: acute observation, keen insights, exacting language, and original phrasings (she called a blue jay a "one-time opera singer"). Yet these first efforts are both over- and under-written. Too much verbiage; not enough accurate science.

Writing filled the days empty now of Len and the demands of poultry and mink. By ten every morning, she was sitting at her typewriter by the window overlooking Pimisi Bay. She didn't leave until three or four in the afternoon, except for a quick break to grab a biscuit and cheese or heat up some soup and tea for lunch. By the time the sun set, she had split wood for the morning fires and taken the dogs for a walk over the frozen lake. In the evening, she read newspapers by the light of her coal-oil lamp, then knit soldiers' socks as she listened to her battery-operated radio, which pulled in programs from England, Germany, France, and occasionally Sweden, where she heard news of how life was unfolding for her family, whom she worried about endlessly, their letters often arriving late and blacked out by war censors. When the nights wore on and her fears swelled, she played endless rounds of solitaire, a game she'd played in Russia while Gleb was out on patrol, laying out the cards again and again, until they came out right.

Louise wasn't only writing stories. Like every well-born young lady of the late nineteenth century, she had undoubtedly received instruction in the visual arts, but in those war years, she started drawing in earnest. She began by copying photographs from magazines and enlisting her dogs and her cat as live (though sleeping) models. She sketched her own feet and hands, most often her left hand with a cig- arette burning low between her fingers. She drew the dead birds she collected from the roadside and the study skins she ordered from the Royal Ontario Museum. She sketched pages upon pages of the chick- adees that mobbed the feeding ledges on her windowsills: stick legs at odd angles, wings folded and outstretched, bills open and closed, heads cocked in every direction.

Nine of Louise's sketchbooks and several folders of her loose drawings and paintings are preserved at Library and Archives Canada's Preservation Centre in Gatineau, Quebec. Leafing through them inspires me to buy a sketchbook and a box of Faber-Castell graphite pencils, 2H to 8B, and a compact palette of thirty-six water- colours. I have no delusions about my artistic talent. But I know that drawing helps me see in a different way, makes me more inquisitive about what I'm looking at, a spiral into deeper understanding. Every drawing becomes an investigation, an opportunity to grasp some elusive detail.

I sit cross-legged on the bedroom floor in front of the window where cardinals, song sparrows, house sparrows, and finches come for the sunflowers we pour into a clear plastic feeder suctioned to the glass. I focus on the house finches that I insist on calling Mexican finches—their name, after all, is *Haemorhous mexicanus*. Original to Mexico, they were shipped to pet shops across the continent in the

1940s as "Hollywood finches"; escapees took up permanent residence as far north as southern Canada. They are among the few beautifully trilling birds that grace both my northern and southern soundscape. Despite intense desire and hours of sketching, my skill barely improves, but I persevere because I like the way drawing makes me look again, and again. Is that a white bar on the wing or just lightly tipped feathers here and there? Where exactly does that streaky brown on the belly start?

Drawing birds is making me a better watcher, honing the sense I've noticed in expert birders who can identify a bird from a flash of wing among the trees, a fleeting shadow on the ground at dusk. As Louise described it, "not only the all-seeing eye, but a special gift of understanding, a kind of lightning almost intuitive realization." Field ornithologists call it jizz, the knack of instantaneously grasping which bird has just darted by, not only by its colour, size, and shape, but by its habit, its personality—the "vibe" of the species. The word first appeared in print in 1922, when Thomas Coward in the *Manchester Guardian* used it to explain how we can recognize someone at a distance, but it was popularized in birding by Miss E.I. Turner, a frequent contributor to *Country Life* magazine who has since sunk into obscurity.

It was a Red Cross district nurse, Gladys Reed, who rekindled Louise's interest in sketching. Gladys asked to stay with Louise through the fall and winter of 1943 and 1944 while she made her rounds of nearby schools. Louise agreed with reluctance. "When somebody stays here all the time it is hard to get oneself into the mood of writing. Too much distraction of thought in a small place like this where one cannot go into another room and close the door for a couple of hours." Gladys was a painter, and on evenings when the weather was fine— and that year October was particularly warm—the two women would load the canoe with their sketching kits, Gladys's dog, and Louise's two canine companions and they'd paddle out to a rock in the middle of the river where they'd sit for hours, sketching the ruined log dam and the blasted pine beside it.

Louise began to draw as she sat by a nest, waiting for something to happen. The covers of some of the sketchbooks are watermarked, as if splattered by rain. Inside, renderings of a nest overhung with a leaf, a profile of a chickadee in full song, a fledgling beside a nest in a tamarack tree, a blue jay feeding its mate. Many of the drawings were clearly done from her kitchen window that overlooked the feeding station with its trays, smears of peanut butter and lard on the trees, hanging coconut shells filled with seed for the small birds. Ground-feeding birds would snack on balls of her special mix of rolled oats, weed seeds, and the used fat she bought by the fifty-pound pail from the Italian restaurant in North Bay. Closer to the house, Louise set out a small silver goblet of sugar water, which she replenished several times a day for the hummingbirds that she never tired of drawing.

The following summer, Doris encouraged Louise to take up brush and paint. They spent several days together at the Cabane, getting up at 3 a.m. to be at the salt lick Louise made by soaking a rotten log with

Various chickadee poses with a woodpecker, from Louise's sketchbook, 1940s

brine, watching the grosbeaks arrive, banding and taking long tramps through the woods, generally having "the grandest time. . . . We are fly-bitten, dirty, suntired, and burnt to a frazzle, but completely and gloriously happy." Partway through the week, Murray sent Louise a box of pastels. Her sketchbooks contain portrait after portrait of evening grosbeaks. The sketches are relatively unsophisticated, yet one of the pastels—I have no idea which one—Louise thought good enough to enter in the art exhibition of the Arts and Letters Club of North Bay, where it won a certificate of merit.

The sketchbooks are archived in the order Louise donated them. They are not dated, but if I line them up a certain way, I can see her progress. Proportions become more realistic, stances more authentic, the pencil strokes surer. Eventually, Louise took up a straight pen and what looks like India ink, which she sometimes thinned to a wash. When she visited the Speirs, she often brought her drawings "to get them criticized, which is a great help." Her friends didn't hold back. "If there is a 'bump'—well, we have said so. And if the drawing is sheer joy to us, we have said so too," Doris wrote after one visit. "But we could have kicked ourselves around the block for saying that your abstract drawing of the nest in the pine needles suggested the homely potato."

Louise's first bird story in *Farmer's Magazine*—"Such is life with the Birds," published in 1941—was illustrated with her own pen-and-ink drawings. "I am quite proud over my efforts," she wrote to her mother, "and am now trying to illustrate a little bird story for a magazine which just bought it. It would be fun if I succeeded, wouldn't it?" The nest with the roof-like leaf, the singing chickadee, the blue jay feeding its mate, they're all in that article. She illustrated her 1945 story, "The Grey Lady," too, including a drawing of her own strong hand cradling an injured bird. By the time *Farmer's* published "Satin Tails" in the spring of 1946—the last of her "Insignificant Bird Stories"—Louise was illustrating her popular articles not only with sketches of individual birds and trees but with scenes: a pair of cedar

waxwings by a nest in a conifer occupied by two gape-beaked hatchlings; a chicot with eight waxwings sitting upright as sentinels.

She was also illustrating her ornithological studies. In one of
her first letters to Louise, Margaret Nice complimented her on the
drawing in her red crossbill study and asked how she'd done it. Louise
explained that she sketched in pencil while watching the nest, then rendered the bird in pen and ink when she got home.

During the six years of the war, Louise published eleven articles
and had three more awaiting publication. She was nearing the end of
her incubation, both as a writer and as a watcher. Although she was
married by then, she signed all her magazine pieces Louise de Kiriline,
a name rooted in her past. But looking closely at the illustrations, I see
a different signature in the lower right-hand corner—offset, overlap-
ping Ls, for Louise Lawrence. A set of wings in flight.

8

Nothing Happens Haphazardly

In 1942, a letter addressed to *Nurse Louise* appeared in Louise's mailbox.

"Nurse Louise, Do you realize that you could write an amazing book about your bird experiences? Are you keeping notes?"

The letter came from Ada Clapham Govan, a weekly nature columnist for the *Boston Globe* who contributed reviews, notes, and poems to *Nature Magazine* under the alias "Of Thee I Sing," a nod to Walt Whitman. She had banded some four thousand birds in two years, with a record 580 returned bands. And she had created a bird sanctuary on the woodland connected to her backyard, saving it from development.

Ada's letter arrived tucked in a copy of her autobiographical novel, *Wings at my Window*, sent to Louise by Taverner. Birds had been a life changer for Ada. After suffering the loss of two children and the crippling of a third, followed by her own crippling illness, she had found comfort and hope in watching the birds in her backyard. Louise devoured the book. "So many familiar happenings, so many feelings of pure happiness and enjoyment recognized and shared, so many new possibilities to make my bird world limitless."

I don't know if Ada's letter was the stimulus, but within months Louise was writing what she called her "little bird book." The subject was indeed a little bird—a chickadee named Peet—but she also conceived of the book as small and precious. The way she spoke of it makes me think of *The Little Prince* by Antoine de Saint-Exupéry, who had met the tousle-haired boy who inspired that story while living in Quebec City in 1942. The slim classic appeared in bookstores everywhere in 1943, undoubtedly in Fosdick's bookshop in North Bay too.

Buoyed by her project, Louise took to getting up in the dark in order to get her chores over early and her daily bird walk done so she could get to her typewriter by the time the sun cleared the horizon. She strictly rationed her personal correspondence, which had become so voluminous that the green stone intended to hold it down teetered dangerously.

By November 1944, the book was finished. November 16 at 4 p.m., to be precise.

She sent the manuscript off to her friend Grace, dean of girls at a North Bay high school, who promised to read it with her teacher's eye, watching particularly for grammar gaffes and the peculiar phrasings that came from writing in a language other than one's mother tongue. At the same time, Louise sent the story to Doris and Murray for a scientific read.

Louise was what my first fiction editor, Ellen Seligman, would call "editable." When I met Ellen at our inaugural lunch, she leaned across the table and asked, "Are you editable?" "Of course!" I replied with enthusiasm, although I had no idea what she meant. Thirty years later, I understand. Some writers cling to their first-born words as if they were a gift from the gods. Others happily revisit their work, inspired by critique to deeper, clearer prose. Louise was not only willing to rethink and rewrite, she solicited comment from anyone who might have something useful to say.

While awaiting her friends' critiques, she worked on illustrations for the book. She sketched pen-and-ink portraits of the chickadees at her feeders; the kingfisher zipping along the shore; a thrush hidden in the woods; and the drawing she considered her masterpiece—the Mattawa River as it tumbled out of Lake Talon between the high cliffs of the chute.

All through January 1945, she revised and rewrote, "without ever thinking it is good enough. Some days as I read it I think it is all right, then I read it again and think it is terrible. So that or this chapter gets a new overhaul."

Louise intended to send the manuscript "out on the wild seas" sometime in the spring. When she warned her mother not to be overly optimistic, she seems to be warning herself too. "Now, because of all this enthusiasm and hard work, don't you go and have any hopes of its being accepted. There is a far cry between the spoon and the lip, or whatever the saying says. And as Murray Speirs says, 'Whatever happens, just imagine all you have learned!' And he is so right."

The winter of 1945 was particularly brutal. In January, the mercury sank to -44°C. Snow piled so high it reached to the windows in front of the house and to the eaves on the lake side. Louise had enough wood to keep the fires roaring, although she was endlessly sawing and splitting. The house fairly steamed from the heat that escaped through the chinking.

In the midst of her solitary labours, Louise received an invitation requesting her presence at a farewell reception for Her Royal Highness Crown Princess Märtha of Norway, the daughter of Prince Carl of Sweden. The princess had been a childhood playmate of Louise, their fathers close friends. As young women in the early 1920s, they had gone their separate ways: Louise to Russia in the footsteps of her aristocratic soldier-husband and Märtha to Norway with Crown Prince Olav. When the Nazis occupied Norway in 1940, the crown prince and princess and their three children moved temporarily to the United States, where they lived for a time in the White House. (Rumour had it that the beautiful and charming Märtha was having an affair with the womanizing FDR.) During those wartime summers, the Norwegian royal family lived at an estate in the lake district near Gravenhurst, Ontario, just two hours by car from Pimisi Bay. Louise had written to Märtha several times, hoping to visit, but had received no reply—until this invitation.

Louise professed an egalitarian spirit, but there was a distinctly elitist streak in her that revelled in the way of life she'd been born to: fine clothes, impeccable service, connections to power and influence. This may seem contradictory, but at the time, privilege came with noblesse oblige, the expectation that people of wealth and influence would act with generosity and grace, restraining the self in service of the good of the people and the country, values that fascinate North Americans in television series such as *Downton Abbey* and *The Crown*, whose characters we watch as we might an exotic species.

Louise and her teacher-friend Grace went into a huddle about what Louise would wear: her "smart dark grey suit, very tailored, VERY tailored" would be just the thing, "enlivened and softened by a frilly white blouse." In the middle of its lacy jabot, she sewed the Padda—a golden frog bequeathed her by her great aunt. "The hat, with some alteration, was found all right, it is one with good lines tipped forward on the nose, adorned with fur (I mean the hat, not the nose) and as a last piff, Grace leant me a most utterly chic little fur collar of fine Persian lamb round-cut, falling to the shoulder and with an upstanding short collar at the neck. The effect was dramatic, to say the least and I knew I would feel just like a million dollars in that exclusive assembly thus attired."

The day before the reception, Louise packed and preened, working to make her nails, roughened by chopping wood and fetching water, presentable. As dusk fell, a howling gale blew in from the east, the kind I always dreaded when I lived up north, for it never failed to carry a heavy burden of snow. Before going to bed, Louise went outside to shovel, thinking she'd get a head start on the morning's work, but the snow was coming down as fast as she could clear it. All through the night, wind and snow thrashed at her bedroom window. When she rose at six, she had to push the front door with all her might to open it against the bank of snow. The wind was still blowing, but the blizzard had stopped. She pulled on her parka and began clearing the drifts from around the bird-feeding tables and off the roof, which she worried might collapse under the weight. She fed the birds, carried water up from the hole in the ice that covered the lake, brought in the wood, stoked the fires, had breakfast, and was just starting to shovel the driveway when the sun rose. By quarter to nine, she was pulling on her finery, muscles aching. She eased her car out of the garage and backed down the road and onto the bridge across Pimisi Bay. Then she gunned the engine, taking the hill at a run. In a cloud of swirling snow, she pressed forward, up, up, up until she was on the flat road, heading west. In North Bay, she stopped long enough to pick up Grace and drink a quick cup of coffee, then together they headed south, as luck would have it, right behind a snowplow. The going was slow, but the driving was easy, and by three o'clock she was moving through the milling crowd at the reception, a tall, handsome woman heading for the beautiful crown princess, who was waving her forward from across the room.

Princess Märtha kept Louise close all afternoon and evening; now and then they snuck away to a back room for a tête-à-tête. During the supper, the royal party was seated at a head table, leaving their guests to perch where they could with their plates of food. From the buffet table, Louise spotted the publisher Doris had introduced her to just before Christmas when she'd visited Toronto; she'd sat in his office for more than an hour, talking about her new book. Looking around, she suddenly realized the room was filled with people she recognized: the photographer who had made movies of the Dionne quintuplets, the vice president of *Maclean's*, the editor of *Chatelaine*, all of whom she knew from her year with the Quints. But it was the publisher she walked toward, the man to whom she'd told Peet's story.

"Where is that manuscript?" Reginald Saunders demanded jovially, reaching out his hand. "I've been waiting for it!"

In May 1945, just as it seemed the war in Europe might finally end, Louise sent *The Loghouse Nest* to S.J.R. Saunders Publishing. "For myself, I am in the state of mind when I cannot think it is any good at all," she wrote to her mother. "I have worked on it so much and read it and re-read it so many thousand times that my judgment is all but paralyzed."

Unfortunately, Reginald Saunders died suddenly that summer. His wife, Ila, took over the business, but it was August before she was able to write to Louise. It was her husband's last wish, she said, that *The Loghouse Nest* be one of two books they would release that fall. And Ila would very much like to meet its author.

Immediately, Louise drove to Rutherglen and sent a wire to Doris: "Arriving tonight, prepare for a whirlwind." Within the hour she was ready to go, the dogs in the car to be dropped off at a friend's; the farmer down the road set to come feed the cat and check on the house.

The weather was awful; she always seemed to make that drive south in dreadful snowstorms or downpours. A summer storm had started the night before, rain rattling on the roof and lightning illuminating her windows in blinding flashes, followed by bone-rattling thunder. She had burrowed into her covers, thinking, If I am to die tonight, this is a good place.

By the time she was in the car, the thunder and lightning had subsided but rain was still pouring down. Just outside North Bay, she picked up a hitchhiker, dripping wet. A "little soldier," she called him in her letter to her mother. He was just returning from overseas, where he'd been in all the great battles, and for three hours, he regaled her with tales of war. She couldn't help but think of Len, stuck in England for the duration, eager for action, and if not that, then a troop ship home. Just as she was driving into Barrie, the news came on the radio of Japan's surrender. She pulled over to let the little soldier out and left him dancing on the roadside in the rain, tossing his beret in the air. Her heart lifted too: with luck, Len would be safely home soon.

Louise's meeting with Ila Saunders was more than she could have hoped for. The book would come out in October, which was perfect, since that was the time of year when Peet's story began. Ila told her that Thoreau MacDonald was already at work designing the book and he'd draw the illustrations as well. I expected Louise to be heartbroken after all the time she'd spent developing her pen-and-ink sketches, but she was philosophical: "I think that is a minor matter . . . I can always use them sooner or later."

Ila told her that Saunders intended to sell *The Loghouse Nest* in the United States, England, Switzerland, and the Scandinavian countries. Not only that, the contract included an option on her next two books and allowed her to keep radio and film rights. Louise was delighted. She had already decided to send the book to the Canadian Broadcasting Company for their nature series and to "Walter" Disney to make into a film.

No one could ever accuse Louise of thinking small.

Thoreau MacDonald lived alone in a small house in the middle of a four-acre garden near Vaughan, Ontario, a place he'd inherited from his father, one of the founders of the Group of Seven.

"A very queer duck, as most artists are," Louise reported to her mother. After the meeting with Ila, the Spiers had driven her north to meet the man who would illustrate *The Loghouse Nest*. "He is about the homeliest man one can imagine, without teeth (not even false!), a figure rather like a skeleton. His speech is very blunt, he says just what he thinks without embellishment and he has a kind of dry humour that is absolutely *skrattretande* [ridiculous]. When he comes out with some of this he looks at you from under his pale-blond brows to see if you appreciated it. If you did, he looks much encouraged and will soon again come out with another dry comment."

Louise assessed Thoreau to be a lesser talent than his father, the Group of Seven painter J.E.H. MacDonald, "but he still is all the same, a very good artist. His work is very decorative, mostly landscapes and the native animals which he depicts with just a few daring strokes. Very striking."

Like Louise, Thoreau MacDonald was self-taught. Because he was colour-blind, he worked mainly in black and white. His illustrations from the 1920s and '30s became iconic, particularly the endpapers he drew for books published by Ryerson Press. I have thumbed through a box of his ink drawings with my friend Beth, whose father was the editor of Ryerson Press in its heyday, and felt the kind of deep aesthetic pleasure Louise must have felt when she laid eyes on Thoreau's unique and perfect laddered skies, forests rendered in thickened spears and scoops, birds flying in stylized profile as if they'd taken off from an Egyptian glyph.

Louise expected the fall of 1945 to be filled with celebration. The war was over by mid-August and the peace signed in the first days of September. Her book would be out soon, and Len would be home.

But paper was still in short supply, and so was labour. Saunders pushed the printing of *The Loghouse Nest* forward to January. And although Louise wrote to everyone she could think of, still she had no idea where Len was or when he might return.

September 11, 1945, was Louise's sixth wedding anniversary. That morning, she was sweeping the last of her housecleaning into a dustpan when Buck began to bark. She glanced out the window. Walking up the path, a beret cocked over one eye, his uniform studded with coloured flashes, was Len.

They had lived apart for five years and three months.

Len and Louise on the front stoop of the log cabin, 1945

When Len left, they were newlywed poultry farmers just starting into mink and Louise was floundering for a way to be quit of the Quints. He returned to a full-time writer who was about to publish her first real book, dedicated to him; who had bird stories in several popular magazines; who was studying birds seriously, banding them, earning the respect of university-trained ornithologists. A self-trained amateur who had written a research report on the Canada jay that would soon appear in a Canadian peer-reviewed scientific journal. A woman who had sketched and painted and explored the woods for birds and nests with the top birders in the country. An individual used to being on her own.

Louise rushed out to meet her husband, falling into his arms. In the midst of their first longing kiss, a neighbour hurried down the path waving a telegram: Len would arrive that morning! They all laughed.

Louise had had such a welcome planned! She would be waiting on the platform of the North Bay train station, dressed in her crown-princess suit and a new hat, "elegance beyond words with which to slay him with amazement at the wife he was coming home to from the wars!" Instead, there she was in her oldest pants and shirt, an apron tied across her belly, and there he was, several days' growth of beard bristling his cheeks, tired and dusty from the ride he'd hitched in a dump truck. But the sun shone through the trees, the birds sang around them, and they were, just like that, beautiful to each other.

9

A Strong Wall around Me

Len came home to a woman with a deep sense of mission. Her days were filled with bird studies and observations; her evenings, with the stacks of correspondence generated by her research and her writing.

What place was there in this for an uneducated northern woodsman?

For the first while, Len busied himself with catching up on maintenance and repairs around the house. The government would keep him on their payroll for a year and a half, but eventually he'd have to find a job. With veteran benefits, he could go back to school and retrain: any job he wanted was his for the asking, since returning soldiers got first dibs. Louise's letters to her mother were full of ideas for what her husband might do: set up his own carpentry shop, where he could be his own boss, or maybe become a game warden, since he knew so much about the forest.

She sounds brave, and a bit defensive talking about these first months back with her husband. "Len is very much his old self. He has matured to some degree, but he always had a great deal of common sense and shrewd judgment. I feel very secure in his great devotion, which is like a strong wall around me wherever I go." Everyone seemed to like him. "It could not be an altogether easy thing to come back home to a wife with a whole set of new friends that he was not present to help make, but he is taking up his place amongst us all with remarkable lack of difficulty."

As always she was pragmatic, with a dash of idealism. "We could have more money, but I doubt if we'd be richer. We could have a bigger house, but I doubt we'd be happier. Len is fine to live with, he is not perfect, if he were I'd be bored to death. . . . We laugh a great deal, squabble some, and fight very seldom. We work from 5 in the morning until 7 at night, mostly, which is a good way of keeping out of mischief, and we have lovely evenings buried behind newspapers. Len loves to listen to the radio and all sorts of quiz programs, I don't, so I stop my ears and let him listen. I like to read at night in bed, Len doesn't, so he looks at pictures for a while and lets me read. We both hate to go to town and none of us crave so-called outside entertainment, because we both find our best pleasures concentrated in and around our home."

A domestic domain that for Louise was about to crack wide open.

The Loghouse Nest hit the bookstores in January 1946. Not only was the book beautiful, the precious volume she'd dreamed of, but the timing of its release could hardly have been better. George Orwell's *Animal Farm* and E.B. White's *Stuart Little* had just been published; *The Little Prince* was still a runaway bestseller. In the wake of the war, readers were clearly ready for a world in which flowers talked, boys were mice, pigs ruled, and birds philosophized with first-growth pines.

When I first read *The Loghouse Nest* in the late 1970s, thirty years after Louise wrote it, I dismissed the book as hopelessly anthropomorphic, a kid's story more than reading for intelligent adults. It is a memoir of a year in the life of a black-capped chickadee, told from the

The Loghouse Nest, *published January, 1946*

point of view of Peet, one of the first birds Louise caught in her drop trap. Peet was a spitfire the day she held him in her hand to slip the shiny band on his ankle, and his temper never improved, which endeared him to her. The charming, feisty bird leads the reader through four seasons in the Pimisi forest, from the icy bondage of winter through the spring fervour of returning songbirds to the fresh silence and solitude of late fall. The fictional talking birds are grounded in accurate avian behaviour and framed by their relationship with Louise—"She of the Loghouse Nest."

When I opened the book again a few months ago—seventy-five years after publication—it seemed a different book entirely. The book hadn't changed, of course. The world had. I had.

In part, I had dismissed the story because of the commonness of its main character. A chickadee? I sniffed. A bird so familiar it is practically invisible. My insistence on a more exotic protagonist strikes me now as a relic from a past that many of us have come to view with shame and regret—the colonizing mindset that drove the work of so many early naturalists, including Carl Linnaeus. He was obsessed with the new, desperate to know everything there was to know about the natural world, not for the sheer joy of knowing and not for the deeper pleasure of understanding. His goal was strictly utilitarian: to discover what in nature could be used. Nature as commodity.

A contrary view of the natural world as a living organism to be nurtured has always existed, mostly among Indigenous Peoples, but periodically it sows itself among the settler population too. In Massachusetts in the early nineteenth century, Henry David Thoreau celebrated the restorative effects of "wildness" on the human spirit. At the end of that century, the outdoor movement spurred the creation of city parks and wilderness preserves, as well as the more questionable "nature tourism." Similar movements after the First World War, and again after the Second World War, saw the war-weary searching for tranquility in untrammelled places. In 1954, Scott and Helen Nearing wrote *Living the Good Life: How to Live Sanely and Simply in a Troubled World*, a bible for those of my generation who moved back to the land in the mid-1970s—which was how I ended up in the woods near Louise.

The simplicity of her life on Pimisi Bay made Louise aware of the complexity of the natural world around her. No bird was too familiar to catch her interest. She wanted to know everything about it. Not the kinds of details gleaned in a laboratory—skeletal structures; digestive, respiratory, and circulatory systems—but the relationship of one bird to another of its kind, to birds of other species, to all the creatures in the forest, to the trees and plants and the lake, even to humans, those strange giants who walked on two legs like birds and built gargantuan, all-but-impenetrable nests that lasted hundreds of years.

Little wonder that she gave the leading role in *The Loghouse Nest* to a bird. Peet talks and yearns and succumbs to fear and love. Such anthropomorphism—explaining nonhuman behaviour in terms of human feelings and mental states—was an intellectual sin when I first read Louise's book. But research now suggests that from an early age, humans show a predisposition to communicate with nonhumans, quarrel with them, compliment them. Anthropomorphism may in fact be a fundamental aspect of human cognition, related to the development of empathy. Where anthropomorphism was once decried as the misattribution of human characteristics and abilities to nonhumans, it is now credited as helping to stimulate the exploration and fuller understanding of nonhuman behaviour—in Louise's case, the behaviour of birds.

When she wrote, "I learned his language, expressed eloquently by the inflection of his cheeps and twitterings," she was not seeing Peet as human. She was giving him the deepest respect as another creature that was moving, talking, communicating, and learning in the natural world the two of them shared.

I am not the first to wonder if Peet might be an offspring of the animal protagonists of Swedish fables. In one of the most famous, *The Wonderful Adventures of Nils*, written by Nobel Prize–winner Selma Lagerlöf and published when Louise was twelve, a lazy, mischievous boy who plays at torturing animals finds himself reduced to the size of a beetle and able to understand what the animals say. He redeems himself by doing good deeds as he flies around the country on the back of a chatty goose.

Fables have a much longer history than realistic animal tales, which only appeared in the early twentieth century when Sir Charles G.D. Roberts and Ernest Thompson Seton published stories with wild creatures (and not barnyard animals) as their heroes. In fact, the animal story has been called the one uniquely Canadian art form. As Margaret Atwood put it in *Survival: A Thematic Guide to Canadian Literature*, "English animal stories are about the 'social relations;' American ones are about people killing animals; Canadian ones are about animals being killed, as felt emotionally from inside the fur and feathers."

Realistic animal stories and fables, by the time Louise started writing them, tended to deprive wild creatures of their true identities. The virtues imposed on them were human and the narratives assumed that residents of the untamed world subscribed to such humanistic moral notions as right and wrong.

Louise abhorred anthropomorphism. In *The Loghouse Nest*, she was attempting something quite different—presenting birds in their environment acting like *birds*, true to their avian nature, as she observed it. She envisioned a new kind of bird story that was engaging, scientifically accurate, and no longer human-centric: a complete break with the bird stories that had gone before. A story that presented the world—nature, humans, houses—from a bird's point of view.

Whether or not she knew it, she had a foot in the same camp as Jack London. *The Call of the Wild*, published in 1903 and set in Canada's gold-rush-era Klondike, is narrated by a St. Bernard–Scotch shepherd cross named Buck, a pet who is sold into servitude as a sled dog and eventually joins a wild wolf pack (and perhaps the inspiration for the name of Louise's first sled dog). London's canine protagonist is very similar to Louise's chickadee: in both books, wild creatures speak excellent English, and they think thoughts and have insights about the world, which dogs and birds may or may not have. When *The Call of the Wild* was published, Jack London was accused by President Theodore Roosevelt of being a "nature faker" for the way he attributed "unnatural" feelings to a dog. In what became known as the War of the Naturalists, London defended himself: "I have been guilty of writing two books about dogs. The writing of these two stories . . . was in truth a protest against the 'humanizing' of animals, of which it seemed to me several 'animal writers' had been profoundly guilty. I endeavored to make my stories in line with the facts of evolution; I hewed them to the mark set by scientific research."

Humans, which London portrays as alternately loving and viciously cruel, are reduced to near invisibility in Louise's book. When "She of the Loghouse Nest" appears, it is at a distance and in passing, much as birds move largely unnoticed through human lives.

Less than a week after the book's release, Louise received a letter from the American Ornithologists' Union (AOU), a society of some two thousand men and women devoted to the serious study of birds. Hoyes Lloyd, superintendent of wild life protection for Canada's National Parks, was president and actively enlisting Canadian members. "Note from your press reviews that you have now joined the class of ornithological writers. Hope the book goes well. I am enclosing an application for membership, fee is $3, applications are acted upon at our AGM next fall."

For a self-taught amateur like Louise, the invitation was like a door flung open to the inner sanctum of North American bird science. And it came at a time when she felt that she finally had the credentials to join such a club.

Reviews of her book, on the whole, had been good. The *Globe and Mail* recommended it as "a delightful combination of shrewd observation and interpretive fantasy" for any nature-lover "who is not so prosaic as to boggle over feathered linguists." The *Ottawa Citizen* called it "the enchanting story of a bird's year, told with the insight that love alone gives, and with delicate humour." The *Toronto Daily Star* noted its "joie de vivre so quietly contagious that the reader closes the book feeling as though he had filled his lungs with a long breath of good Canadian air."

As well as publishing a book on birds, she had completed three scientific studies. Two for the Speirs—observations at the evening grosbeak nest she'd found with Doris and records of local and migratory movements of the American robin for Murray's PhD thesis—plus her study of Canada jays, which Austin Rand had forwarded to *The Canadian Field-Naturalist*, Canada's journal of natural history. Her first scientific article—"Five Days with a Pair of Nesting Canada Jays"—was scheduled for publication in 1947.

Louise's drawing of her wilderness cabin, published in Farmer's Magazine

And after years of submissions, she'd finally had a piece accepted by *Audubon Magazine*, the flagship of the National Audubon Society. "A Bird in the Hand" told the story of Louise's bird-banding adventures and included her sketches of the Loghouse Nest (formerly the Cabane), her Potter's traps, and a map locating her northern banding station between Lake Nipissing and the Ottawa River, with tiny thumbnail drawings of grouse, hawks, squirrels, and deer, a riff on the endpapers in Taverner's *Birds of Canada*.

A pattern was taking hold. Research, with its intense observations and note-takings, in the spring "when the great bird season is afoot" and writing in the winter—scientific articles that connected her to a network of ornithologists and popular articles and books that put food on the table, ribbons in her typewriter, and brought her an audience of ordinary people interested in birds.

After months of sending off job applications, Len took seasonal work with the department of highways, grading roads. He was posted to the northernmost part of the district, which meant he stayed in motels during the week and came home only on Sundays, leaving Louise alone all week to watch and write.

On Monday mornings, they'd walk together out to the highway to wait for the North Bay bus that passed at six. Some winter days, the temperature hunkered below -40°C, so cold that mist hung like frozen veils over the lake and the trees cracked like pistol shots. They'd wait together, marching in place to keep their feet from freezing, until over the hill they'd see the headlights of the bus, swinging like a searchlight, "then all of a sudden the noise of the oncoming bus broke loose like thunder in the frost-brittle morning, like a thousand trains at full speed . . . we flashed our torch then *pisht-pisht* went the air brakes and it stopped and swallowed up Len."

Louise took her typewriter with her when she went to Sweden in the fall of 1946, her first visit home in almost fifteen years. She'd gone back in 1932 to assure herself that she really did want to become a Canadian citizen. (She did.) This time, she was boarding a ship to soothe her mother, who was still unsettled by her daughter's marriage to Len.

No letters survive from this visit to Sweden. If she wrote to Len or Doris during that time, they didn't save the letters. Her mother was the person to whom she poured out her every thought and feeling, and for those precious three months, she could do that in person.

I feel a kinship with Louise's intense love for her mother, whom she addressed in her letters as Dearest Mother, Darling, *Min alskade lilla mams* [my dear little mama]. I was never that effusive with my mother nor as forthcoming in matters of love and literary yearning. But for most of my life, my mother was my most stalwart friend, someone I could always count on to be interested in what I had to say and to stand by me, the voice I most wanted to hear when I was down and the person with whom I most wanted to share good news. Twenty-five years after her death, our conversations continue, although they are decidedly one-sided now. After she died, I found my letters to her waiting for me in a large manila envelope in the drawer of her bedside table, my name across the front in her perfect penmanship.

I imagine this is how Louise's letters came back to her, at her mother's death, a living record of Louise's most intimate thoughts, her hopes and goals and frustrations, the details of her daily life reported every week without fail for almost forty years. Those same letters come to me in storage boxes, thick files of them arranged chronologically that I read in the same way I watch the birds: alert for nuance, scanning for a wisp of expression or behaviour that will reveal her true identity; a display, an interaction that will help me understand another facet of this woman as she moved through the world.

Louise returned to Canada by way of Buffalo, where she delivered her first bird talk to an audience of three ornithological clubs congregated in the library of the Buffalo History Museum. She was so nervous she didn't think she could go through with it, but as soon as she took the podium, "My nervousness vanished miraculously and I talked of my interest in birds, its birth with father, its growth through Len's showing me the common birds that he loved and then . . . I carried them on farther beyond the birds as it were, and how life and the art of living is learned and understood from the observations we make and the wonders we see . . . It was quite a successful evening judging by the great warmth and sympathy with which they all crowded around me to press my hand and ask further questions."

By the time Len picked her up at the North Bay train station on a snowy night in November, Louise had been gone thirteen weeks. She left before the leaves turned red and returned to drifts of snow.

"The house looked a bit small I must admit at first and it is taking me a bit of time to shake down into grooves of our life here, but it is all very wonderful." She fussed around the house, laying the Persian carpet she'd brought back for Len in front of the fireplace and moving the bearskin to the bedroom. On the narrow wall between the doors to the bedroom and the kitchen she hung the painting her mother had given her—Bruno Liljefors's pheasants.

Louise never made the transition from town to country easily. Human interaction stirred her emotions, often to an anxious pitch. She preferred the silence of the woods and the company of her own thoughts. With Len back at work and her relationship with her mother restored, she had expected to turn her attention to her typewriter. But she couldn't settle.

"I am not in a writing mood which irks me. I don't seem to be able to produce a thing worthwhile nor can I get started on the idea of my next book. Forms and material seem to be mixed together in an unholy mess with neither head nor tail to which to hang on for a start. In such a state of mind I lose completely my artistic self-assurance."

Some of the disruption was domestic. While she was in Sweden, Len's seasonal work had switched from grading gravel to clearing snow, which meant he worked nights, plowing when traffic was light. He'd been reassigned to the southern part of the district, so he was home every day. He returned in midmorning, just as she was sitting down to her typewriter. By the time he had eaten and was ready to sleep, her best writing hours had evaporated.

In early April, he switched back to working days on the grader. Louise no longer had to worry that the clatter of her typewriter keys would disturb his sleep. She turned her clocks forward an hour to a personal daylight savings time so she could be out watching the birds before sun-up and at her desk by ten, where she stayed until she had to stop to make dinner.

But even that routine didn't last long. The writing season was over. The birds were coming.

The winter had been cold with huge dumps of snow, and spring was late, wet, and stormy. On the first balmy Sunday, after a fine, leisurely breakfast, Len and Louise went out for a stroll and walked smack into a wave of returning songbirds. They stood rooted to the path, hardly able to identify the birds moving so quickly through the bush and in such numbers, more than a hundred all at once.

I can imagine what they saw. For eighteen years Wayne and I have been travelling to Pelee Island in May for the spring migration. The species don't vary much year to year, although the number of individuals does. Often the weather is chilly and damp, and we have to strain to spot an occasional warbler moving north through the island, feeding and resting up for the final push across Lake Erie to mainland Ontario. But in the spring of 2019, we stood awed on the forest paths of Fish Point, where the birds land after their overnight flight from Ohio, our heads swivelling with the calls of black-and-white warblers, red-breasted nuthatches, gnatcatchers, bluebirds, jays by the dozens, rose-breasted grosbeaks too. Every warbler we'd ever seen on the island was flitting past, not in ones and twos but by the dozens. Just as the sparse years drive us to despair that the birds are gone forever, these bumper years give us unwarranted hope that nature is bouncing back.

That May Sunday when Len and Louise stumbled into the wave of migrants, the ice finally went out of Pimisi Bay. They watched as the lake shed its hoary coat, the water "lovely and moving and alive again and the reflections marvellous . . . After dinner we did what we had longed for all day. We got the canoe in the water, we dressed warmly for it became quite chilly with the setting of the sun, and out we went on the lake for the first time up the river.

"Here and there the snow still lay in *skärvor* [shards] and sheets of ice hung down the cliffs. Ducks came flying over and settling with a splash in the water. Never have we seen so many *lommer* [loons], there were seven all told. I began calling to one of them, *whoo-ooo-ooo-ooo*, and he answered me back and he kept answering me until Len got tired of hearing us. The thrushes were singing, oh so softly and so beauti- fully their song floated over the lake. The river was at highwater and up near the falls there was half a mile of foam on the surface. It made such a wonderful pattern on the water according to the currents, swirls and whirls, and white lanes and circles on the black water and you can hardly imagine how perfectly *trolskt* [magical] it was. Len and I glided into the enchanted area and each time he dipped the paddle it made little whirlpools all its own, and the canoe made a black lane through the white foam. We couldn't go very close to the falls for the water was too rough and dangerous. But it sang to us in the dusk and shone white amid the pines and cliffs. And presently we turned back again and saw the moon shining red through some frilly clouds and after a while we glided back into our little harbour again."

Louise paddling up the Mattawa towards Talon falls

That day was a brief respite in a spring that continued to be wet and cold. People were flooded out of their homes by snowmelt pouring out of the forests. Farmers couldn't seed their crops. Despite the cold, Louise managed to trap a hundred birds in May, many of them returnees to her forest.

She dressed for winter, a cushion pinned to the hem of her parka, ready to flip under her bum to sit on sodden stumps to watch the birds. "You may imagine I made a rather droll picture walking about gazing at the birds with that cushion dangling by the corner to my coattails. And yet I have seen wonders and the time runs short even though my teeth chatter. And so you may behold me sallying forth soon after dawn with a substantial breakfast under my belt, with a lunch and a flysprayer and a bird book and one small mirror in a basket on my arm and one round mirror on a long pole trailing behind."

The mirrors were a trick she'd learned from the Speirs. For nests high up in the trees, she'd raise the pole mirror to the branch and tilt it to see the parents or the eggs in reflection. Other nests were so camouflaged deep in the undergrowth that she couldn't look directly at them without disturbing the birds, so she manipulated the small mirror until the nest was in view.

"I step carefully and sometimes stumble, for my eyes are not on my feet. I see a bird, and she is picking nesting material, birchbark from a tree, she disappears, I see her again, I stumble forth, follow her with my eyes. And I see her go into a certain place, and the leaves move, tremble a little with her movements. She nudges a spot on a branch, the crotch of a tree, high up, and she beds herself down into a half-made little nest, and out she goes again and I stand nailed to the spot not to lose it."

At first, Louise marked the position of the nests with strips of Kleenex. She worried that the endless rain would dissolve the tissue. That didn't happen, but one bird liked Louise's markers so much that it carried them off and built a Kleenex nest. "She spat on it and glued the stuff together with her spit and it sticks. So now I have *remsor* [strips] of coloured cotton with which I mark the sites of my nests . . . having 38 to look after just now, that is a necessary precaution."

The number of nests Louise had under observation at any one time varied. Through the 1946 breeding season, she kept notes on sixty-two. Each day the reproductive cycle of some avian household would be completed and the young would fly off, just as another mating pair were choosing their nest tree. Whatever she saw or heard, she jotted down, and at the end of the day, she typed up the scribbled notes, shaping them into something that made sense of what she'd seen. She typed sitting at her kitchen table, shouldered up close to the woodstove, otherwise "my hands would gellify on to the keys."

She witnessed the most intimate moments of the reproductive cycle—the courtship ritual, the laying of the eggs, the incubation, the hatching, the fledging, even the conjugal act.

"I have seen delicious little acts with the female crouching invitingly with her wings a-ripple and her bill full of nesting stuff and the male like a butterfly alighting upon her and the next instant she was moulding and modelling her nest as if the delicious intermezzo was nothing but a natural prelude. Which it is. And I have often thought, why should such an enchanting interlude as mating, such a natural, pure, sound sequence of life be so vilified by us unnatural scabbaloons that some of us can't even speak of the mating of a bird without becoming grossly shocked by the dirty insinuations of our nefarious mind? What hellish curse has made us so utterly unnatural? We who live and breathe and think dirt in a world so pure and so beautiful."

Despite such free-thinking attitudes, the mechanics of bird sex remained a mystery to her. After several years of watching birds in the act, she finally wrote to Taverner. "How exactly do birds mate? . . . What exactly takes place?" Taverner, as always, was kind. "With all the concealing feathers, the modus operandi is difficult to make out. Yes, some birds do copulate in the air, as do the swifts. Others in the water. The male has a retractile penis that folds away when not in use." He enclosed a rough drawing for clarification. The drawing is lost, but I presume he was explaining sex in water birds such as ducks and geese when he mentioned the retractile penis. Only three percent of bird species have externally visible penises. In most cases, both sexes have a cloaca, an internal chamber that discharges urinary and digestive waste and also holds the sex organs—testes or ovaries. During mating season, the cloacae of both male and female swell to protrude slightly outside their bodies. Avian sex is a matter of birds rubbing their swollen cloacae together so the male sperm is deposited in the female cloaca where it eventually fertilizes an egg.

"I am aghast at my lack of reasoning powers not even to have surmised such an obvious possibility," she exclaimed. "How involved we have become in our brain functioning when nature constantly has to point out to us the secrets of its utter simplicity and logic! . . . It has opened a new and most interesting angle to my bird observations."

Louise came upon the chestnut-sided warbler as it was lacing the bottom of its nest to criss-crossing canes in a wild raspberry patch at the edge of a break in the woods. A few days later she showed the nest to Hugh Halliday, an outdoor columnist for the *Toronto Star* and a wildlife photographer who sometimes supplied photographs to illustrate Louise's *Audubon* articles. When his wife spotted a Nashville warbler hopping about, trailing one wing on the ground, she tracked the little bird for over an hour until she spotted its nest, not far from the other nests Louise was watching.

She added the Nashville and chestnut-sided warblers to her circuit, immediately intrigued by the difference between the two nests. The Nashville built directly on the ground, shaping its nest from rootlets and fine fibres and hiding it under a thatch of dead leaves. The chestnut-sided hung her nest half a metre off the ground, using fine grasses and strips of birch bark to create a perfect camouflage in the dappled light. The nest in the raspberry canes contained four creamy eggs; the Nashville's held four small bluish-white eggs with cinnamon spots and one very large grey-freckled egg—a deposit from a brown-headed cowbird, a species that doesn't built its own nest but drops its eggs, up to forty a season, in the nests of other birds, often much smaller species such as warblers. Louise was no fan of cowbirds and their parasitizing ways. She was tempted to remove the oversize egg and save the parents' energy for their own offspring, but this time, scientific restraint prevailed.

The colouring of the Nashville female was so like the forest floor that Louise had a hard time seeing her, unless the gleam of an eye or a slight movement gave her position away. At first, the bird flushed easily, but soon she accepted Louise as part of the landscape. The chestnut-sided female, on the other hand, never moved even when Louise was close enough to reach out and touch the nest. The bird always faced south when she sat on her eggs, and always headed east when she left the nest, ducking through a screen of leaves. Regardless of where she took her break, she always returned from the east, too, flying into a sapling birch, hopping down into the lowest branches of an elderberry bush, then running sideways up a thin branch, tail spread and wings dropped, until, with a swoop, she settled back on her eggs.

Day after day, Louise watched as the females brooded, the males serenading from their perches nearby. The chestnut-sided eggs hatched without incident and once the female alerted the male with some intensive chipping, both parents took up the task of foraging and feeding. In the Nashville nest, the cowbird hatched a day before its adopted siblings, a naked giant that lay draped over the smaller eggs until three of them hatched. (One was infertile.) The Nashville parents fed all the nestlings, doling out food equally to the four birds, despite the fact that the cowbird was twice the size of the others. Even when the cowbird stretched its neck high and fluttered its wings, begging, still the parents kept to their egalitarian regimen. On three occasions, the parents pulled food from the cowbird's gaping mouth and gave it to their own offspring. Often the female stood on the cowbird while she fed her little warblers, throwing her whole body into keeping the giant in line. More than once, Louise watched and cheered as the little female tugged at a wing or a leg of one of her chicks, rescuing it from under the sprawling parasite.

Louise banded the young chestnut-sided warblers when they were eight days old, the day before they left the nest. She banded, weighed, and measured the Nashville chicks when they were seven days old and the cowbird was eight. The cowbird was almost twice as big as its nestmates. The next day when Louise arrived, all the young had flown.

Louise had been voted in as an associate of the AOU while she was in Sweden. Barely six months later, she sent her comparative study of the nesting behaviour of chestnut-sided and Nashville warblers to *The Auk*, the official publication of the AOU. Most manuscripts languished for months, but hers was accepted immediately. "It will certainly make my name more known," Louise wrote to her mother, "for this periodical is read by EVERYBODY that is interested in birds and nature from topmost to lowmost. It is also used for reference."

It wasn't until later that fall, after the songbirds had left and the daily burden of recording her observations and daily counts eased, that Louise returned to a project begun before *The Loghouse Nest* was tucked into the bookshelf beside the fireplace—a book for children called *Tales of the Green Woods*. The story was simple: a little boy meets a queen ant with lovely shiny wings that he admires, so she gives them to him, warning of their magic. With his new wings, he flies into the branches of a tree, which changes his perspective as surely as if he'd fallen down a rabbit hole.

It seems odd that Louise would turn to writing for children. She had no children of her own, although during the war, while Len was away, she'd taken in Roy Oddy, the nephew of a friend and a "war child" sent from England late in 1943. Strangely, Louise never mentioned the boy in her letters to her mother, Doris, or Len, although Roy lived with her for more than a year. She professed no particular fondness for children, yet the snapshots of Roy in her photo album convey a certain tenderness. Under one, in which he is feeding a chickadee from his hand, she wrote *Roy with a Chickadee, broad English accent, "a nuthaatch, Aaunt Louise."*

Perhaps she conceived of *Tales of the Green Woods* as a way of introducing city children like Roy to the natural world. At the time, Thornton Burgess was producing two, three, sometimes four books of children's nature stories a year, which must have been inspiring, as was the inexhaustible popularity of *The Little Prince* and *Charlotte's Web*, books written ostensibly for children, but richly appealing to adult readers.

Exhilarated, Louise flew through the first draft of *Tales*, typing the story on the back of a draft of *The Loghouse Nest*. The scenes came together easily, but the structure gave her trouble and the child's voice did too. She edited vigorously with broad strokes of her thick pencil, and by spring, had finished what she hoped was a respectable draft. But she was still uncertain, and so, before submitting the manuscript to her publisher, she sent it off to Margaret Houston, a friend whose literary taste she trusted and a woman she could count on to be frank.

"She didn't like it at all. In fact she did not find one good thing to say about it. The trouble with this one was that I was aiming to write to a certain reader. It is a mistake to write to anybody. Your heart can't be in that, though your purpose may. Some people have a *läggning* [orientation toward] and understanding of children that makes it possible for them to write for children. I was really talking down to the child, quite uncertain as to what actually his approach would be to the subject I had chosen. That made the whole thing artificial and untrue. So I burnt it."

I read the letter again, disbelieving. I have wanted to burn manuscripts, especially an embarrassingly bad children's story called *Drippy*, based on the life of a raindrop. I even opened the woodstove door, manuscript in hand. But I couldn't do it.

Louise was braver, or more impetuous. "I thought, what's the use of being a writer if you can't have the courage to destroy stuff you write that isn't first class. The next thing I write I shall have learned and shall, I hope, do better."

She had hung onto an earlier draft, but she had no heart for the story now. She was busy outlining yet another book. "To my joy I found my pen or rather my typewriter slide into stride as it did for *The Loghouse Nest*. I have thus the skeleton of a story in the raw, which promises rather well . . . for which I have not even a name yet. But it needs such loads more of material before I can even start to put down one chapter."

Louise's energy and optimism were irrepressible. In the same letter in which she admitted to burning a manuscript, starting another book, and writing several articles, she told her mother that she had made contact with Arthur Cleveland Bent, a Massachusetts businessman and self-taught amateur ornithologist who had spent decades compiling twenty-one volumes of *Life Histories of North American Birds*, published by the Smithsonian Institution from 1919 until he died in 1954—and for another fourteen years thereafter. He prepared the books in that series in collaboration with an army of ornithologists, amateur and professional, who submitted information about courtship, nesting, eggs, young, plumages, food, behaviour, voice, enemies, and more.

Bent was twenty years older than Louise, close to the age her father would have been. Not only had he served as president of the AOU, he was considered the chief biographer of North American birds. (His books are still a primary reference for bird biologists.) The tone of his writing was enthusiastic and his prose both scientifically accurate and literary, a style Louise aspired to.

She wrote to him, asking if he would put her on his mailing list for future volumes. He replied that contributors got first crack at new publications, to which she responded with reams of detail about the nuthatches, wrens, and thrashers that were his current subjects. "He sent back a lovely letter very pleased, asking for more and saying he would probably quote from my letters.

"So that too is a way of taking part in great work."

10

Ennobling Influence

L ouise had been in many fine hotels in her life; the liveried
staff, the bowled palms, and soaring, crenellated ceilings of
the Royal York Hotel in Toronto did not daunt her. But
milling around the check-in desk for the sixty-fifth annual meeting
of the American Ornithologists' Union were bird scientists from
across the continent. She spotted California, New Jersey, Alberta,
even Chile on the name tags of the people around her, almost all
men, though here and there a woman's hat poked through the crowd.

The AOU when Louise arrived in 1947 was a steeply hierarchical
organization. Associates had to be invited to join and voted in. An
associate could become an elective member only after making a significant contribution to ornithology. Fellows were ornithologists who
had made a sustained, exceptional contribution; they were elected by a
two-thirds majority vote. The number of fellows was limited to fifty;
the number of elective members to two hundred. When she joined,
the AOU had 2,138 members, just under half of them serious amateurs like herself. All the elected officers were men. Fifteen percent

of the associates were women, but there were only eight women elective members and one lone female fellow—Margaret Morse Nice. As one woman quipped, it was hard for a woman to be a fellow. Some may have bridled at such a rigid structure of power and influence, but Louise couldn't resist its challenge. The AOU was a ladder begging to be climbed.

What luck for her that a year after the AOU approved her as an associate member, the annual meeting took place in Toronto, only the fourth time in sixty-five years it was held outside the United States. Louise arranged to stay with Margaret Houston, the woman who had critiqued *Tales of the Green Woods* so brutally that Louise had tossed it in the fire.

Two weeks before the conference, Margaret died. She had long suffered from a serious heart and lung condition, so Louise wasn't surprised when the family told her Margaret had succumbed during a late-summer heat wave. Her daughter insisted Louise stay at the house anyway, and there Louise discovered the truth: Margaret had ended her own painful life. "She had lots of courage to do it. . . . Somehow her end fitted her dynamic nature."

Margaret's death cast a sadness over Louise's first immersion into the assembly of bird scientists. She felt an obligation to Margaret's family and tore herself away from the sessions to spend time with them in the house that for years had been her home away from home when she was in Toronto. But she caught the streetcar back to the ROM as often as she could.

Forty-three ornithological papers were presented, in subjects ranging far beyond local birds: North American migrant songbirds in Chile; African flycatchers; courtship displays of emperor penguins. Many papers dovetailed with Louise's particular interests: nesting territories of wood warblers; effects on bird populations of DDT.

Strangely, Louise's letters to her mother stop at the end of August that year and don't resume until mid-November, and so, although archives yield programs and proceedings for the meeting, I have only a scant idea of what this initiation into the world of bird scientists meant to Louise. The only clue is a brief note she sent to Doris immediately after: "A thousand thanks for having taken me under your wings at the AOU. It was so very worth while being there."

Louise had hoped to meet Taverner at the conference, but he died that spring. "The contact with you I count as the most important factor to my introduction into the bird world," she wrote in her last letter to him. "It has been a great privilege to have known you, although I have never seen you. You led me on, step for step, and I recall with gratitude the help it was to be able to check with you on my first little discoveries, the fox sparrow, the cardinal, the cuckoo, now all my long-established friends."

She'd lost the man she had always turned to for enthusiastic, considered answers to her bird questions. In his place, she now had access to thousands of AOU members, among them the best bird minds on the continent.

The flock of black-capped chickadees at Louise's feeders was steadily increasing. In 1944, her best one-day total was twenty-seven individuals; by 1947, it was seventy. The friendly little birds visited her feeding station year-round and in all weather, but their numbers typically varied with the season. Spring and fall would bring a sudden influx, almost as if migrants were passing through. According to the bird guides, chickadees didn't migrate, yet in several ornithology journals, she had noticed reports of chickadee "migrations." At the time, very little was known about the movements and behaviours of many species of birds, including the common black-capped chickadee. Were some of hers simply moving to other feeding grounds nearby? Or were they travelling a great distance in true migration?

She had no idea how to answer these questions until, sitting in the lecture hall at the AOU meeting, she listened as Albert Wolfson, a migration biologist at Northwestern University in Illinois, described his study of fat deposition and weight changes in white-throated sparrows and slate-coloured juncos before, during, and after migration. If she could measure the fat on her chickadees, she thought, maybe that would tell her something about how far they flew in the fall.

The next spring, when she caught returning chickadees in her banding traps, she palpated their bodies for fat deposits. It was hopeless. She had no idea what she was feeling for.

She wrote to Wolfson, and he immediately replied, explaining the method he'd developed to assess body fat: blow on the breast feathers to expose the area of the furcula (the wishbone) as well as the wingpits and lower abdomen and score the visible fat levels as none, light, medium, or heavy. He also shipped her a scientific balance on loan so she could weigh the birds she was banding. "We know so little about body weight and fat deposition in birds under natural conditions that whatever information you get will be a definite contribution." After a second spring of weighing, Wolfson suggested they write a paper together using the data Louise had collected. She accepted, despite her misgivings. "I feel very inadequate to have my name linked with so prominent a scientist."

Eugene Odum, a biologist at the University of Georgia, was conducting similar bird-weight research on white-throated sparrows. Often called the father of modern ecology, Odum introduced the word 'ecosystem' into the English language. His book, *Fundamentals of Ecology*, published in 1953, was the standard text on the subject for the rest of the twentieth century.

In 1949, after her second AOU conference, this one in Buffalo, New York, Louise corresponded with Odum, who encouraged her to increase the number of birds she was studying. "Although the chickadee is much banded, few weights are taken. What is needed is a large series from a single population or location." The weight differences would be small, he warned. She would need an extensive sample in order to approach statistical significance. And he advised against weighing birds before 11 a.m., since birds require several hours to recover from the weight loss of the previous night—a phenomenon human weight-watchers know well.

He also asked her to observe the timing and extent of chickadee moult—the replacement of worn, faded feathers that typically occurs in the lull between breeding and migration. "In regard to molt, you are in a position to make excellent contributions, since, as far as I know, nobody knows much about molting in this species, strange as it may seem. . . . Your notes on this over a period of years will be very valuable."

Odum's letters read like notes from a thesis advisor. He cautioned Louise against estimating fat deposition from what she could feel and see on a bird's body or even from measuring changes in body weight. In his own research, he used chemicals to extract the fat from a collected (i.e., dead) bird's body. He had concluded that visible fat was not necessarily a good indicator of actual body fat and suggested that Louise measure actual fat. But killing a bird to increase her understanding of it was an irony she couldn't live with. No, she replied, she would not move that far into the laboratory.

Louise weighed and measured every black-capped chickadee and white-throated sparrow she could get her hands on. She used two Potter's traps and two automatic trip traps; as soon as the birds got used to having the traps nearby, she left her feeding trays empty and offered seed only in the traps. Once she had a bird in hand, she'd slip a paper cone over its head and body to immobilize it during weighing. Then she'd dab some scarlet nail polish on the edge of the primaries—the long outer wing feathers—so she could tell which birds had been weighed. (Her record was seventy-eight chickadees in one day, although it wasn't unusual for her to capture between fifty and sixty.) She also weighed nestlings. Once, she managed to get a newly hatched bird weighed before its first meal. She wanted to mark it so she could tell it had been weighed, but the nail polish was too heavy and ink wouldn't stick to the natal down. Margaret Nice suggested tying a piece of silk thread to one leg, which worked perfectly.

Making sense of the data was frustrating. "Every time I believe I have found certain trends in the curve, I am all upset by the next day of weighing-in." To record enough useful data, she continued the weigh-ins for five years, capturing, banding, weighing, and releasing 340 black-capped chickadees. In all, she recorded 1,279 weights. A third of the birds she captured were residents; two-thirds were new to her woods.

Wolfson was impressed. His evidence for the relationship between fat deposition and spring migration in white-throats was published in *The Auk* in 1954, acknowledging Louise's contribution. Four years later, after a decade of weighing and measuring, without benefit of laboratory or funding, Louise published her own study in *The Auk*. A great many black-capped chickadees are migratory, she concluded, or at least extensively wandering, while a much smaller proportion is resident, locally wandering, or occasionally transient, following their food supply. Contrary to what she'd expected, it wasn't migration or movement that most influenced changes in the birds' weight; it was the temperature of the air. Her chickadees, like so many of us, put on weight when the thermometer dropped and shed it when the season warmed.

Several times a week, Louise extended her morning dawn walk beyond her own paths. She would paddle across the bay to the wild hinterland north of the Mattawa River, where she once saw a green heron, the most northerly record of that bird. Or she'd walk through marshes and black spruce bogs to the fields that lay between her forest and the northwest tip of Algonquin Provincial Park. Or she'd drive the rutted back roads into Grand Desert, where amidst the eroded land and abandoned farms she watched great migrations of swallows, pipits, and raptors that flew singly or in loose parties, sailing leisurely and stiff-winged on the winds.

One day, she crossed the causeway that separated Pimisi Bay from Beaver Lake, and climbed the slope of Brulé Hill. From a distance, she could see pigeon hawks perched in the blackened pines that punctuated the horizon; nearby she found their nest, forty feet up a branchy white pine that stood alone on a rock shelf. The nest wasn't hard to spot: a metre across, it was supported by a trio of stout branches on the south side of the trunk.

In the 1938 edition of *Life Histories of North American Birds of Prey*, Arthur Bent had published a full description of the nesting behaviour of pigeon hawks—members of the falcon family now known as merlins—but Louise still had questions, particularly about their feeding habits. She had assumed that an area patrolled by falcons would be avoided by the small songbirds that were a regular part of the merlin diet. Instead, she found warblers, sparrows, and robins all nesting close to the merlins without apparent fear or harm.

"The Nashville had a favourite singing perch not 50 feet from the hawks' nest; the myrtle warbler male had a feeding ground laid out through the red pines immediately south of the nest; the olive-backed thrush successfully reared two young in a willow just below the shelf where the hawks' nest stood; the white-throated sparrow conducted a party of young just out of the nest through the bushes in full view of the hawk perched on guard; the robins repeatedly attacked the hawks with such fury that the birds of prey wobbled on their lawful perches, without lifting a wing to counterattack."

Squirrels and chipmunks also seemed to have safe passage, although larger mammals, including humans, roused the merlins. As soon as they detected Louise's presence, they went on guard, screaming each time she dared move. They would not resume their normal lives, no matter how long she stayed. One day a female saw Louise coming while she was still quite far away and began screaming. "I dove into the bush and, thinking I could fool her, hid waiting for a while, then made a long and laborious detour through a swamp and a dense thicket until I came to a point where I could overlook the situation." When she peeked out, there was the merlin perched in a dead tree above the thicket she had just crawled through. A second later, the bird alighted in front of Louise, screaming. "My entire manoeuvre was as plain to her as if I had walked through the clearing."

In the study area near her house, she watched the falcons feeding on the same small species they ignored in their nesting area. A hatchling kingbird was snatched from a nest at the very top of a tall spruce. A female Blackburnian warbler, returning with a mouthful of mayflies, was literally nailed to the branch beside her nest. Once, Louise spotted a purple finch clutched in a merlin's talons. Another time, a scarlet tanager.

"The longer I watched the food habits of these hawks, the clearer it became what a surprisingly small quantity of food they actually required relative to their size and expended energy, probably due to the highly nutritious value of their diet." She did the math. At two birds a day for each adult and three birds a day for their young, she estimated the merlins killed some 450 songbirds during their seventy-five days at the nest. And indeed, the following year, Louise noted a marked decline in small birds, especially the brightly coloured, tree-nesting warblers.

Louise's drawing of a merlin, published in Audubon Magazine, *1949*

But which birds exactly were her nesting merlins eating? When they abandoned the nest, she climbed up to take a look and found buried under a heap of dried excrement, a midden of small bones. She knew exactly whom to ask to identify them.

Since the 1947 AOU meeting, Louise had been sending her year-end summary of bird sightings and nest records to a scientist she'd met there: W. Earl Godfrey, a biologist with the National Museum of Natural Sciences in Ottawa. His response to her first submission was pro forma. "By this kind of cooperation by observers we hope to build up a better knowledge of distribution of Canadian bird life." But then he asked a question. Other observers had noted a decline in black-capped chickadees that year. "Does this coincide with your records?"

And that opened the door.

Yes, she replied, the daily count at her feeding station had dropped from seventy to about twenty-five, a decline she attributed to the pigeon hawks nesting nearby. Could she send him a box of bones and debris from inside the nest for identification? The National Museum didn't have a good bird skeleton collection for comparison, he replied, but he'd take the bones to the Cleveland Museum of Natural History, where he'd worked before moving back to Canada. Within weeks, he sent his results. The nest contained one leg bone of a brown-headed cowbird, the right leg of a blue jay, the left leg of a yellow-bellied sapsucker, two left legs and a left wing of a yellow-shafted flicker. No chickadee bones at all.

Louise could hardly believe it. "If I had sent the fragments to the ROM, the little box would have disappeared in a deep silence for at least a year before I would have known any results at all."

Meeting Godfrey shifted Louise's scientific compass from the ROM to the National Museum of Natural Sciences (now the Canadian Museum of Nature); from the Toronto birding establishment reigned over by the Speirs to Ottawa with its rich resource of highly trained biologists on government payroll. She immediately sent Godfrey a trio of red crossbills she'd found dead on the highway and asked him to examine their stomach contents.

As it happened, Godfrey was especially eager to get material on red crossbills. Almost nothing was known about their breeding habits. Several subspecies had been identified, but no one knew which were populating Ontario's north. When Louise told him she had a nest under observation, he asked if he could come collect—that is, shoot— the parent birds to determine the subspecies they belonged to. "It is, of course, highly important this be done, and I would try to make the trip to Rutherglen in order to do this. I understand, of course, that you may have feelings in the matter. It certainly is not a pleasant duty to have to collect a nesting bird but occasionally, in an important event like this, it is necessary for us to close our eyes to sentiment in the interests of knowledge."

Louise sent a rush postcard by return mail, arguing vigorously against the veiled charge of sentimentality. Having spent seventy hours watching the crossbill nest, she couldn't see how killing her subjects would advance human knowledge of the species. "However, if you care to take a chance on *other* crossbills outside my study area, you are most welcome to come up."

In consolation, after the young had fledged, Louise sent him the crossbill nest, which he immediately added to a habitat display in the museum's exhibition hall.

Precise and analytical, a scientist and never a personal friend— they remained Mr. Godfrey and Mrs. Lawrence throughout their correspondence—Godfrey became the first reader of Louise's scientific studies for the next ten years. She revelled in his critique. He would send pages of notes, citing studies to support his points, and within days, Louise would respond with pages of her own, providing more details from her observations to prove her conclusion or agreeing that a revision was necessary and offering options for his approval.

Godfrey was extraordinarily patient and generous. He assisted Louise even when her study was destined for a journal other than *The*

Canadian Field-Naturalist, where he was ornithology editor. This was the case with the pigeon hawk study. When the editor of *The Wilson Bulletin*, Dr. Josselyn Van Tyne, helped her borrow essential literature from the Wilson Ornithological Club Library at the University of Michigan, "he inquired with such kind interest about my study that I felt encouraged to brave his reputation as the most difficult editor to please and submit the paper to him," Louise wrote to Godfrey. "To be published in *The Wilson Bulletin* would undoubtedly be an achievement, especially for an amateur." Godfrey agreed. All that mattered to him was the science and the sharing of insights through publication, however that happened.

Louise laid all her questions at Godfrey's feet. Why was the red crossbill breeding season so long? Why did black-capped chickadees start their courtship songs in December? What colour were sapsucker legs, usually? Did young hairy woodpeckers have a white eye-ring? Godfrey would check his reference books and examine the specimens in the museum's collections and answer as best he could. When he couldn't find the answer, she considered the subject "an open field for study" and set about filling the gap. Godfrey urged her on: "We know so little about these matters that one can only theorize, and it is only through work such as you are now doing that the answers can be found." And when, after long study and several seasons of collecting data, she still couldn't figure out why a certain behaviour or physical characteristic manifested as it did, he was consoling. "The answer may come to you some day through just such careful observations as you are making."

Louise was not naive: she knew how much she still had to learn. "Whatever faux pas, academically speaking, that my last letter contained, I regret none, since it elicited such exceedingly interesting comment from you. . . . It is becoming more and more regretful to me now that I am not academically trained; it would have given me a much better foundation for my present work which, I think I can truthfully say, has developed to more than merely an amateur's hobby.

On the other hand, it would almost certainly have led my life into other directions . . ."

Always, he pushed her for evidence. When she observed hairy woodpeckers displaying preliminary breeding behaviour in mid-winter, he asked her to send any dead woodpeckers she might find so he could examine the gonads. He always used correct terminology and insisted she do the same, sending her to dictionaries until she knew a covert from a speculum. When she asked what "wing-snap" was and did birds have collarbones, he explained the anatomy of avian clavicles—what most of us call wishbones. He was her laboratory, her library, her endless source of comparative specimens.

Godfrey sent study skins to help her with difficult identifications and to aid her understanding of the nuances of plumage. And when an erythristic brown-headed chickadee—one with an unusual rufous wash over its cheek patches, bib, and sides—appeared at her feeder, he sent her a sketch of a similar bird by Taverner for comparison. For each of her unique sightings—a wintering golden-crowned kinglet, a Cape May warbler, a Connecticut warbler—she checked first with Godfrey to see if the species had been recorded that far north, then wrote a "Note" for one of the bird journals so the record would be public. "The main thing," she wrote to Godfrey, "is that the record should be scientifically absolutely trustworthy and the judgment of that is in your very capable hands."

After meeting Godfrey, she sent all the dead birds she found to him. He showed her the correct way to refer to scientific papers in her studies, how to decide whom to acknowledge, the format for foot-notes. Bit by bit, he nudged her kindly and respectfully up to the bar of scholarly standards.

Godfrey was a born teacher. He received and answered as many as two thousand letters a year. But he must have seen something spe-cial in Louise. "So few people have opportunity or inclination to make such observations as are needed . . . You have the opportunity, ability, patience, and enthusiasm, a combination that is hard to beat."

They exchanged more than a hundred letters. In 1948 alone, they wrote back and forth, on average, once every two weeks. For some reason, the correspondence peters out and stops in 1959. There was no apparent falling out: Godfrey continued to praise her articles and wrote to congratulate her on her book releases. By then he had become curator of ornithology at the National Museum, following in the footsteps of Taverner and Rand; perhaps the job became too all consuming to continue his vast correspondence. At that time, too, he was working on a revised *Birds of Canada*, not just an update of Taverner's book but an entirely new edition that would show the distribution and clarify the taxonomy of every bird in the country. In the published book, he mentioned Louise in the section on red-eyed vireos and again with the crossbills, crediting her with distinguishing between the songs of red and white-winged species.

Or perhaps it was Louise who let this correspondence lapse as she became caught up in another massive undertaking. Whatever the reason, the intense conversation ended, although Louise never stopped feeling grateful to Godfrey, who had "indeed become a mentor of the kind Mr. Taverner was to me."

I don't know what prompted Louise in the spring of 1948 to package up her article "Five Days with a Pair of Nesting Canada Jays" and ship it off to Alexander Skutch in Costa Rica. For the past two years, since she started subscribing to *The Auk*, *The Condor*, and *The Wilson Bulletin*, North America's top ornithological journals, she must have been reading Skutch's remarkable life histories of tropical birds— marbled wood quail, golden-naped woodpeckers, turquoise-browed motmots. Detailed, evocative, and highly personal, these life histories show a flair for narrative that is matched only by Louise's.

"It was indeed pleasant to receive your letter . . . with the enclosed account of the nesting of the Canada jay," Skutch responded. "It is all too rare in ornithology to read a paper at once so informative and so agreeably written; although I read it on a warm afternoon amidst tropical verdure, it made me feel that I was actually in a northern coniferous woodland, watching jays in a snowstorm."

Alexander Skutch was regarded by scientists and amateurs alike as one of the world's great ornithologists. He is best remembered for his pioneering work on 'helpers at the nest,' a term he coined to describe a social structure in which male or female juveniles and sexually mature young stay close to their parents to help raise subsequent broods, instead of flying off to start families of their own. Until recently in rural Canada, this was a noticeable phenomenon among humans too: the spinster sister who stayed on the home farm to help raise her younger brothers and sisters. The practice is more common in birds than other animals: an estimated eight percent of bird species use helpers at the nest. (Ornithologists now use the term 'cooperative Breeding' to describe the phenomenon of several adult birds working together to raise nesting babies, a kind of avian kibbutz.)

Although a bird watcher from early childhood, Skutch studied botany and after graduating with a PhD, he joined the United Fruit Company to study the banana leaf in Central America. There, he became obsessed with tropical birds. Most of the species he saw had been named and classified, but as with birds in the Canadian hinterland, almost nothing was known about them. For the next twenty years he collected plants for museums and arboretums to underwrite his studies of birds.

Skutch wrote to Louise from Los Cusingos, the wilderness farm in the Río General valley where he settled permanently not too long after Louise retreated to her small acreage on Pimisi Bay. The *finca*, named for the fiery-billed aracari that nested there, produced most of the food for his table. Like Louise, he drew his water from a stream and lived without electricity. Periodically, but with no regularity, he rode his horse down the rough lane to the village post office fourteen kilometres away. When Louise first made contact with him, he was still earning his living by collecting plants, although his enthusiasm for botany was growing increasingly "feeble." When Louise contacted him, Skutch was writing his first book, *Life Histories of Central American Birds*, which would be published in three volumes through the 1950s. Eventually, he produced forty books and over two hundred papers on birds. His archive in Costa Rica is heaped with unpublished work, including more than fifty volumes of his nature diary; seven philosophical notebooks, entitled *Thoughts*; essays and book-length manuscripts on the subjects of metaphysics, religion, moral philosophy, axiology (the study of what humans value and why), environmental ethics, the philosophy of nature; and at least five unpublished works of fiction.

Louise found in Skutch an ornithological and literary soul mate. Both experimented with a range of literary genres in their quest to articulate their explorations of the natural world and the human place in it. (Louise's archive also contains several unpublished short stories and poems.) Their letters are an intellectual walk in the woods, meandering through birds, philosophy, religion, writing, the trials of living a simple life, and the unique pleasures and advantages of field ornithology. While Odum taught her much about laboratory science and its methods, Skutch was his opposite—a mentor who believed wholeheartedly in the necessity of learning about birds as they went about their ordinary daily lives in the place where they naturally lived. The watchers' challenge, he said, was to become an unobtrusive and non-invasive part of the bird's landscape.

Louise and Skutch were increasingly in the minority among bird scientists, focused as they were on documenting the lives of individual species from egg to death, devoted exclusively to prolonged observation in the wild. Ornithology was already well into its transition from descriptive natural history to a more theoretical avian biology that relied on laboratory technology and controlled experiments. Both kinds of research had always been done and would continue into the future, but the balance was shifting, and not in favour of these two watchers.

Skutch believed that naturalists had a responsibility to make their findings not only accurate and accessible to the general public but also a pleasure to read. In an essay in the American scientific journal *Nature*, he admonished nature writers not to minimize the harshness in nature in order to win sympathy for their cause. Louise took the criticism to heart. "Personally, I felt this very strongly, since I realize a tendency in this direction. The truth lies in the truth, and not beside it."

Like Skutch, Louise was a woman of strong beliefs. Through the 1950s, she wrote outraged letters to the editor under the pseudonym Blue Jay. She decried the practice of paying twenty-five cents ($2.44 in 2020) for every dead crow brought to the Sudbury Game and Fish Protective Association, pointing out that crows are mostly carrion-eaters and devourers of grasshoppers and May beetles, which made them a friend to humans, not an enemy. "By offering a bounty you are letting down the fence for the mass murder of a single species," she wrote. And she railed that the Hamilton starling shoot was undoing conservation education and triggering a killer instinct in young people. Their excuse for the hunt—the burgeoning population of starlings had become a public nuisance—mirrored the "pest-like proportions of the uncontrolled population increase of men and their fondness for aggregating in restricted areas, not without destructive effects upon their environment."

In their letters, Louise and Skutch puzzled over the ethical dilemma of supporting the conservation efforts of sportsmen's organizations: they applauded the marshes these groups preserved but abhorred the underlying intention—to lure birds to wetlands where they would be killed for sport. Skutch, who refused even to trap birds for banding, wondered "whether we were wise after all in joining hands with those whose principles we cannot approve. I would be glad to learn your views on this matter." By return mail, Louise sent a draft of an article on conservation she was struggling with.

Four years later, she dug out Skutch's letter and reread it when Ontario lifted its ban on shooting doves and grouse. Their conversation resumed as if no time had passed. "In both cases it was stated by what should be responsible spokesmen, that the shooting of the birds would be profitable (?) for the species, at any rate, not harmful," Louise wrote. She was "utterly disgusted and discouraged." She had started to write to the government in outrage, then "thought better of it because I cannot be unemotional about such things." Instead, she decided to quit every conservation club she belonged to, then thought better of that too. "I was suddenly convinced that quitting would be a negative approach by which no special good could be obtained. I could not stop the shooting of the birds. But I could stay by the guns, meta-phorically speaking, and continue to write and to think."

Louise and Skutch did not always agree, especially as his inter-ests veered into spiritual matters. She had been raised in the Church of Sweden and as a young wife still believed in God and heaven, but somewhere in northern Ontario, religious faith was supplanted by faith in Nature.

"Immortality!" she scoffed. "The concept still remains unrealistic to me. Death and dissolution seem to me to be neither loathsome nor depressing, since they represent a change so essential, logical, and nat-ural as to be inevitable . . . I shall be no longer, I shall vanish without trace though I was once alive."

Far from threatening their relationship, Louise found their dis-agreements invigorating. Few of her correspondents—and by then she had dozens—pushed her to think so deeply or gave her such con-fidence that she wasn't alone.

"Although our understanding of some things does not always coincide, I feel that quite outside your erudition and learning and my basic ignorance, we are in tune. To meet and talk of these and many other things would be a pleasant experience. This, unfortunately, is not likely to happen . . . But this I can say at a distance: that an ennobling influence is attached to the occasion whenever I think of you, either directly or through your works."

What a shame these two watchers never met. Both loved unspoiled forests and lakes and were unhappy when forced to be apart from them. Both valued precision in observation and clarity and candour in writing. Both were unafraid of new ideas, iconoclastic in their outlook. They both believed that birds thought and felt emotion. They both puzzled through and ultimately embraced the apparently contradictory notions of harmony and conflict in bird life. And they both came to condemn the killing of birds—not for food, but for sport and for science. When Louise decided against shooting her brooding Canada jays to determine their sex beyond all doubt, Skutch applauded. "I believe you have no cause to regret that you did not exercise a little of the 'collector's ruthlessness.' . . . Your evidence that both take substantial shares in the incubation is quite adequate as it stands."

Their correspondence continued for fifteen years. It would be another forty years before Skutch died (he lived to be a hundred), so it seems strange that they stopped writing to each other—or that she stopped saving his letters—especially given her comment that "There is no lack of other things I would so often like to discuss with you."

Reading the letters between Louise and Skutch during the first months of the Covid-19 pandemic has reconfigured my notion of isolation. Remote and reclusive do not necessarily spell detached. Louise, secluded in her northern wilderness, and Skutch, sequestered in his tropical valley, may have withdrawn from civilization, but they were not in the least isolated from intellectual currents. Widely read, inveterate correspondents, they were apart from the world, yet very much of it—on their own terms.

At the same time that Louise was communicating with some of the most respected professional ornithologists on the continent, she was drawn into a circle of serious and often eccentric amateurs doing field research on birds. One of these was Roy Ivor, who created the Winding Lane Bird Sanctuary near Cooksville, Ontario. Known affectionately as the Birdman of Mississauga, Ivor was sixty-five when Louise met him and, like her, a self-educated bird observer. They were introduced by Margaret Houston and started corresponding over birdseed. The cost of supplying her winter feeding station was breaking Louise's budget; next to her car, birds were her biggest household expense. Ivor fed his birds with gleanings from a local gristmill and he promised to get her some.

In many ways, Ivor was a model of the kind of bird observer Louise was determined not to be. He wrote hundreds of pages of notes, single-spaced, on long sheets of foolscap, "a lot of it useless," he admitted, and "much that should have been put down in writing is not." While Louise revelled in watching birds in their wildness, Ivor believed that "fundamentally there is no difference between a bird kept in captivity in a proper aviary and under proper care and a wild bird." He built a multifaceted aviary with winter quarters, an outside recreation area, and a large feeding room at the back. His house was scattered with cages inhabited by hatchlings and sick birds that needed special attention. Raising birds in captivity, he said, allowed him to study behaviour without introducing the fear of humans, which in his opinion tainted even the most careful observations in the wild. When he asked Louise if she might pluck a few Canada jays from a nest and send them to him to raise in captivity for study, she was reluctant, even after he sent her a prepaid shipping cage in which to post them. In the end, she decided she couldn't do it.

Ivor was sympathetic. "I must tell you that when taking a bird from a nest the only way in which I can bring myself to take it is to make myself realize that it may not be alive an hour after I leave if I do not take it. Perhaps I may add years to its life, for as you know, the lives of most of our birds are so extremely short. I doubt if there are more than two out of every ten that live a year."

Perhaps with Ivor's words in mind, Louise broke her own rule when the merlin parents disappeared, leaving their eighteen-day-old hatchlings orphaned. The little birds looked like goblins, bluish-grey natal down fluffing around feathers just beginning to sprout, their eyes set in a mask of bare skin, a dollop of yellow like egg yolk at the base of their beak. Louise scooped them from the nest while Len adapted one of the mink cages to become their new home. She fed them raw meat and liver, poking bits at them in a fast, jerky motion that mimicked the way she'd seen the female offer food, and the only way, Louise discovered, to release a gaping response in the little birds. When Louise had to leave for a few days, Len put a bowl of canned dog food into the cage every morning before he left for work. The birds accepted Louise, but when Len came home after a day's work, the birds screamed at him until he disappeared inside the house.

Merlin hatchlings, rescued, adopted, and sketched by Louise

After eight days, the merlin chicks were fully feathered. Not long after, when Louise opened the cage, one of the birds hopped out and flew up into a nearby tree. After that, she left the cage open. She caught deer mice and left her kill on top of the cage; then she removed the cage and left the mice and raw meat on the picnic table. Soon the young merlins were swooping low over the table to snatch up their dinner.

At five weeks, they were making training flights out over the lake. On one of these flights, some instinct took them to their home-grounds on Brulé Hill, where they perched in the same tree as their parents, returning to Louise only for food. Their visits became less frequent. Soon after Louise noticed them with prey in their talons, they left altogether. Without parents to teach them, the young merlins had learned to fly and hunt and defend their territory with all the posturing and screaming distinct to their species. They had even found the nest tree where they'd hatched. Louise wasn't a convert to the study of caged birds, but she understood now what could be learned through observation at such close quarters—and how little it affected the natural instincts of the bird.

Louise's correspondence with Ivor reveals a sympathetic connection between the two bird-lovers, an uncommon openness about the place of birds in their lives. Perhaps the intensity of their obsession had something to do with the fact that they both came to birds later in life. Louise was forty-six when she took up bird study; Ivor was forty-nine. In response to a very personal question from Louise, he wrote, "Yes, I do miss my birds as much as I would human friends. But I miss them too much. I have lost so many through the years, so many that have been very dear to me, that it has taken far too much out of me. Unquestionably, a great many birds have been closer to me than human beings in general could be. The trouble with many, possibly most, of those who do not see what we can in animals, is conceit, or as you put it, the over-development of the cranium. That very conceit is what troubles the world today. Man can see nothing above their own intelligence."

The two shared a skepticism, a crustiness that Louise seldom let show in her other correspondences, perhaps because Ivor was such a radical, so much an outlier. He lived alone in isolation, often in poverty, working on his theories. Despite his constant requests, the ROM never funded him, and neither did anyone else. Still, he persisted, and was among the first to explore the strange ritual of "anting" in which certain birds, including blue jays, song sparrows, crows, and robins, catch ants and rub them against their wings and tails, causing the ants to release formic acid, a powerful insecticide and fungicide.

In Louise, Ivor must have seen a fellow traveller. They were among the first Canadian watchers to notice the drastic decline in bird species and individuals through the 1940s and early 1950s, and among the first to write about the effects of roadside spraying of DDT. They shared their bird counts, their worries, and the articles they published. In one of his first letters, Roy complimented her on the release of *The Loghouse Nest*, and he closed his last letter in 1958 with "You are doing wonderful work with your articles."

Most of Louise's early professional correspondents were older than she was, often by a decade or two. The majority were iconoclastic thinkers; some such as Skutch and Ivor were radicals, their work marked by controversy. Almost all were men. Yet in all those thousands of pages of letters I detect scarcely a whiff of sexism. The university-trained professionals as well as the self-trained amateur ornithologists exhibited a genuine and eager interest in what Louise was doing and what she had to say. To a man, these scientists welcomed Louise and her endless, often naive, questions. They discussed theories and processes with her and encouraged and advised her without condescension.

Only once did I come across a male ornithologist referring in a derisive and sexist manner to women watchers. This was in a letter Doris sent to Louise, relaying a comment from the eminent Finnish ornithologist Professor Baron Lars von Haartman: "She [Louise] has the same very careful and thorough way to work as dear Margaret N. [Nice]. Women ornithologists do rarely have so much patience, they draw their conclusions quicker and with less material (and often with poor results!)."

Haartman, I suspect, reflected the prevailing attitude; Louise's scientific mentors were the anomaly. Why else, in an organization of over two thousand members, were there only eight women elective members out of two hundred? Only one lone female fellow out of fifty?

Seven years after being accepted into the AOU, Louise was voted in as an elective member, in recognition of the consistent excellence and volume of her bird studies. She wasn't able to attend the meeting in Madison, Wisconsin: the cost of travelling so far was prohibitive. Of the fifteen Canadians who did make the journey to Madison, five were women. I imagine them applauding wildly, whooping with unladylike enthusiasm as Louise became the first Canadian woman to stand on this rung of the North American ornithological ladder.

11

The Eyes of the Heart

Louise de Kiriline Lawrence is not the only eccentric woman to tramp the bush looking for birds. In her free-spirited love of nature, her strong opinions about humans, and her indomitable, ingenious resourcefulness, she is part of a lineage of self-taught women bird watchers and writers that stretches back two hundred years.

I mention these women because they were accomplished and fascinating, but also to right the intolerable imbalance in the books I've been reading on the history of bird watching—books written as if half the human population (the female half) never existed. When women ornithologists are mentioned, it is most often as "bird ladies" who sympathetically took in wounded robins from school children or as doddering crones who wrote overenthusiastically and sentimentally about their passion for the wild.

The truth is that botany and zoology were among the few sciences open to women in the nineteenth century. Plant collecting was included in a genteel young woman's education, but for the most part, those with an interest in birds had to tutor themselves. Even as late as the 1930s, little formal training in ornithology was available, for men as well as women, but especially for women, who were economically and intellectually hobbled by a society that still believed a woman's hand was best employed at the hearth and cradle.

The women who broke through this gender barrier were not dabblers casually commenting on the birds in their backyards. They were pioneering naturalists, women who developed their own ways of watching birds and their own ways of talking about nature. They were thinkers, interested in the relationship between humans and the natural environment. Through their letters, journals, and pamphlets, they were part of the discussion that slowly shifted the focus of bird study from observing singular species in isolation to an ecological view of birds interacting with each other and with their landscape. Perhaps this was a natural consequence of birding without a gun. The collector who shot a bird then removed it from forest or field in order to dissect it or stuff it was considered superior to the field naturalist who studied birds from afar through a spyglass or with only their eyes. But in his eagerness to collect, the shooter surely missed nuances of bird behaviours and relationships with its habitat and with other creatures—details a watcher would catch.

These early women watchers, often self-trained, were instrumental in transforming ornithology—human thinking about birds—from an exercise in naming, categorizing, and exploiting into narratives that combined fact and interpretation in a way that opened the avian world to anyone who could read.

This was the lineage Louise stepped into when, in 1939, she opened her eyes to birds.

I don't know if Louise had heard of the women who walked before her down the watcher path, if she took heart from them, or if she felt she was cutting a new swath through the ornithological forest.

I doubt she had read *Rural Hours*, a nature journal published in 1850 and written by Susan Fenimore Cooper, often called the mother of American nature writing. Susan was the daughter of the novelist James Fenimore Cooper and worked as his copyist and secretary. On her own time, she studied birds. She determined that birds preferred maple trees with their forked twigs to sumacs as nesting sites. Watching loons dive after a fisherman's line, she had the depth measured and found the birds would plummet as far as ninety-five feet to steal a fish.

Twenty-four years before Susan Cooper published her nature journal, Harriet Sheppard published "Notes on Some of the Canadian Song Birds" in *Transactions of the Literary and Historical Society of Quebec*, insisting that songbirds demonstrate melody in their songs. At about the same time, Anna Jameson brought a literary sensibility to nature writing in her *Winter Studies and Summer Rambles in Canada*. Catharine Parr Traill, who might be called the mother of Canadian nature writing, wrote twenty-four books on settlement life and the natural history of the Peterborough area in central Ontario. *Sketch Book of a Young Naturalist* and *Narratives of Nature*, both published in 1831, combined narrative with close observations of the natural world.

If these women represent the first generation of women watchers, Florence Merriam Bailey, whose life straddled the nineteenth and twentieth centuries, represents the second. Florence was born into privilege like Louise; her father was also a naturalist who nurtured his daughter's interest in birds. I mention the fathers with so many of these women watchers not because they were necessarily the most influential in their daughters' lives, but because the mothers are largely lost to history.

When she was twenty, Florence enrolled at Smith College as a special student; after four years of study she was granted a certificate—women were not yet granted degrees. While at Smith, she started one of the first chapters of the newly fledged Audubon Society, created in 1886 in memory of John James Audubon, the first organization in

North America dedicated to the preservation and study of birds. At the age of twenty-two, just two years after the AOU was founded, she became its first woman associate.

Struck by the "perplexities" of fellow students who came on the Audubon bird walks she organized, Florence wrote what is considered the first field guide to watching birds, *Birds through an Opera-Glass*, published in 1890 when she was twenty-six. It described seventy common North American species, classifying birds by locality, size, colour, and song, and included a colour key as well as lists of visible markings. She wrote five more books on birds and in 1929 became the first woman elected as a fellow of the AOU. Her advice on how to become a watcher is as on-point today as it was a hundred years ago: "Cultivate a philosophic spirit, be content to sit and listen to the voices of the marsh; let the fascinating, mysterious, bewildering voices encompass you and—hold your peace."

These women knew how to hold their peace in the marsh and forest, but thank goodness they didn't hold their peace—or still their pens—in public. They were not marginal writers, selling a few books out of their back kitchens. Neltje Blanchan De Graff Doubleday, a contemporary of Florence, wrote eleven books about birds, including *Canadian Birds Worth Knowing* and *Bird Neighbors*, which sold 250,000 copies. Her books were part of the educational movement that was instrumental in stopping the feathered hat trade. She made her purpose clear in the preface to *Birds That Hunt and Are Hunted*, published in 1898: "The point of view from which this Book . . . is written is that of a bird-lover who believes that personal, friendly acquaintance with live birds, as distinguished from the technical study of the anatomy of dead ones, must be general before the people will care enough about them to reinforce the law with unstrained mercy."

Harriet Mann Miller had already written several books for children under the pen name Olive Thorne when Sara Hubbard of the Illinois Audubon Society visited Brooklyn in 1881 and took Olive on a bird walk in Prospect Park. Suddenly, at the age of forty-nine, Harriet discovered a winged world that until then had flitted by unnoticed. She devoted herself to learning about birds and within four years, published *Bird-Ways*, the first of eleven books on birds. Her tone may strike us now as unbearably moralizing, but it served its purpose in late-nineteenth-century North America.

Mabel Osgood Wright, another second-generation watcher, published one of the first and most successful birding manuals, *Birdcraft: A Field Book of Two Hundred Song, Game, and Water Birds*, in 1895, a forerunner to modern field guides such as Peterson's and Sibley's. Her "Key to the Birds" grouped birds according to their colour and where they might be seen: "Brown or Brownish Birds of Various Sizes and Markings" and "Tree-Creeping Birds of Various Sizes seen upon the Trunks and Branches." Such categories might seem bizarre and impractical to an experienced birder, but for someone just learning to identify avian life, they were a godsend.

Mabel is one of the forgotten heroines of the North American conservation movement. All twenty-three of her books are now out of print, yet they sold consistently well when published; *Birdcraft* went into eleven editions. In 1901, she, together with Olive and Florence, became the first women voted to elective membership of the AOU. Mabel's credo was similar to Florence's: "Nature is to be studied with the eyes of the heart . . . and a pocket full of patience."

Few women in Canada reached the prominence of these American watchers, but that doesn't mean they weren't tramping the forest with their field glasses. Elsie Cassels emigrated from Scotland to Alberta in the early years of the twentieth century. She knew her birds, her neighbours said, "as mothers know their children." For fifty years Elsie kept detailed diaries on the migratory birds that passed over the Red Deer area and made life-history studies of both the barred owl and the white gyrfalcon, which she was the first to record in Alberta. Sadly, when she died in 1938, all her field notes and diaries—her life's work with birds—were destroyed by her husband.

I intentionally refer to these women watchers by their given names. In their own time, they were invariably referred to by their husbands' names—Mrs. Cassels, Mrs. Wright, Mrs. Miller, Mrs. Bailey. Their surnames, both after marriage and at birth, were attached to them by husbands and fathers; only their first names were truly their own, often handed down mother to daughter. I understand that calling a woman by her first name can sound condescending; men have often used this tactic to infantilize women. But I choose this style consciously for the intimacy it implies—and because it reflects Louise's habit. These women knew each other. They inspired each other. The way they looked at the world of birds was intimate, as if trying to get on a first-name basis with them.

Until I was an adult and my interest in birds dovetailed with my interest in women's lives, I had never heard of Florence Bailey, Olive Miller, Mabel Wright, or Elsie Cassels. But from the time I started reading novels, I adored Gene Stratton-Porter. (I was a grown woman before I realized Gene was Geneva, and not a man.) Unlike many early women bird watchers and nature writers who were born into the monied classes, Gene was an Indiana farm girl who grew up roaming the forests and fields, collecting wildflowers and bird nests, and making pets of fledglings.

At thirty-two, she received a camera as a gift, and within a short time, was producing expert bird portraits. Publishers asked for text to go with her photographs and her literary career was launched. When oil was discovered on her farm, she used the windfall to build a cabin on the edge of Limberlost Swamp and wrote her first book, *The Song of the Cardinal*—a genre she called a "nature story sugar-coated with fiction."

"Every fair day I spent afield," she wrote. "My little black horse and load of cameras, ropes, and ladders became a familiar sight to the country folk of the Limberlost, on the banks of the Wabash, in woods and thickets and beside the roads. Being so afraid of failure and the inevitable ridicule in a community where I was already severely criticized on account of my ideas of housekeeping, dress, and social customs, I purposely kept everything I did as quiet as possible."

In fact, she kept her writing so firmly under wraps that her husband had no idea she had completed a book until she asked him to sign her publishing contract. (At the time, women had no legal authority, not even over their own words.)

When Gene offered publishers the manuscript of her second book, *Freckles*, they all said the same thing: cut out the nature stuff.

But putting *in* the nature stuff had been the whole point.

"All the natural history I ever have put into a book has been the result of personal investigation, clean, straight stuff, scientifically verified in every instance." Verified not without difficulty: in her short memoir she describes how she "waded morass, fought quicksands, crept, worked from ladders high in the air, and crossed water on improvised rafts without a tremor." And so she remained firm until she found a publisher who understood that the nature had to stay.

Ironically, Gene died in 1924 in a traffic accident in the city of Los Angeles, California. She had published twelve novels, eight books about nature (including five about birds), four books of poetry, and four books of essays, including *Birds of the Limberlost*. Many of her books are still in print. A few years ago when I presented at a writing conference for grade four students, I mentioned that *Freckles* had been one of my favourite books. The front row of girls swooned. Gene Stratton-Porter's collective readership is now estimated at close to fifty million.

Like most of these women, Gene was an activist as well as a bird watcher and a writer. "I was very strong, vital to the marrow, and I knew how to manage life to make it meet my needs."

Althea Sherman was cut from the same no-nonsense, strong-minded, resilient cloth. Her father was an Iowa farmer who made a good living loaning mortgage money to his neighbours. Althea's brother became a lawyer, and her two sisters trained as medical doctors. Burning to be an artist, Althea earned a master's degree then studied at the Art Institute of Chicago and in 1885, at the Art Students League of New York. Her career was cut short when she was summoned home to care for her ailing parents. After her mother died, her sister Amelia returned, too, and set up a family practice in rural medicine.

The sisters lived the rest of their lives in the family home, taking on classic domestic roles: Amelia was the breadwinner and Althea looked after the house, doing all the cleaning, mending, cooking, preserving, and gardening—not without rancour. In a letter to fellow ornithologist Margaret Nice, Althea refers to her sister as "that lazy, shirking, domineering miser" who "dons her most charming mood and tongue-lashings in order to *do* nothing."

At the age of fifty-two, Althea became a bird watcher, first keeping company with the birds in her dooryard—robins, wrens, phoebes, swifts, and hummingbirds—then tramping into the meadows and swamps to study screech owls, thrashers, soras, and kestrels. After the round-the-world trip she'd been planning for years was cut short by the First World War, she set about her great life's work: a comprehensive study of the chimney swift. She'd spent many a summer evening standing on a box in her kitchen, tilting a hand-mirror up the cold chimney, squinting to get a glimpse of the night life of the swifts nesting there. What she needed, she decided, was a chimney designed specifically for watching.

In the summer of 1915 she hired three carpenters to build her a bird tower. The structure was the size of a small bedroom and as tall as a three-storey house, with four oak posts in the centre, set in cement to keep the tower from listing in strong prairie winds. Inside the tower, a two-foot-square chimney made of rough pine flooring extended down fourteen feet from the top of the tower, with a drain pan underneath to catch rainwater. Peepholes were augured periodically into the chimney wall and windows placed strategically for light, inset in a vee so Althea could put her head into the triangular space to get a clear view up and down. A winding staircase wrapped around the chimney top to bottom, with bookcases set into the tower walls. Small shelves and pegs allowed Althea to position kerosene lamps for night studies. Below a second-floor window was what Althea called her "opera seat," where she would sit at eye-level with the birds nesting in the trees around the tower. A ladder ran the full length up the outside so she could clamber up to open the chimney in the spring before the swifts arrived and close it in the fall after they migrated south.

Swifts soon found the faux chimney and built a nest a scant fifteen inches from one of the inset windows. "During numerous summers, with a lighted lamp before their window, I have frequently sat up in night-watching of the swifts. Not once has a swift left the chimney," she wrote, refuting the common wisdom that swifts foraged for food at night.

She observed other birds too. When a nest of phoebes in the barn appeared sickly, she climbed a ladder and held aside the young birds while her sister poured a tablespoon of sulfur into the nest. They removed the nestlings for weighing and discovered the birds were infested with lice. Amelia picked 118 lice from one tiny bird, its body half the size of her thumb. They scoured the walls around the nest with sublimate of mercury and sopped the nest with the solution too. Then they removed the hair lining from the nest, washed it and dried it with a flatiron, returned it to the nest, and set in the nestlings. For a week the sisters continued to hand-pick for vermin. The young birds survived.

By the time Althea ended her forty-year study of the chimney swifts, her day-to-day observations filled four hundred pages—91,000 words written in her cramped longhand. Just as no one before Louise had ever recorded the nesting cycle of the Canada jay, no one before Althea had ever witnessed the nesting cycle of the chimney swift, and her work still represents the most extensive study ever undertaken of the species.

Althea always intended to write a book from her copious notes, but she never did. She published a magazine story that reads a bit like *The Loghouse Nest*: a memoir by a nestling grey catbird of its first eleven days of life, in which Althea and her sister are referred to as "house-people" who save them from falls and bring them inside to weigh them and capture their portraits with camera and pencil. From this story, it is clear that the two sisters, despite their differences, were a team, with Althea crawling on her hands and knees, thorns tearing at her hair, until she found the little bird fallen from its nest, the warmth of her hand reviving it while she called for her doctor-sister, who determined that the bird would probably die, which it did.

Althea was what some would call a natural ornithologist, a self-trained amateur who studied the lives of local birds until she was eighty-three, filling sixty notebooks with detailed data on 162 species. In the summer of 1928, when she was seventy-five years old, she made four hundred visits to her tower, climbing stairs that she estimated would have reached over a mile into the sky had she climbed them all at once.

That year, Althea escorted 133 visitors up the tower, among them, Florence Bailey and Margaret Nice, women who represent the second and third generations of women ornithologists: Florence, who grew up in nineteenth-century, pre-First World War North America— before binoculars, before banding, when birds had to be killed to be studied, when knowledge could be gleaned only with one's own hands, eyes, and ears—and Margaret, whose career spanned the belly of the twentieth century, from the first binoculars and cameras to sophisticated spotting scopes, thermal imaging, and cassette players that could record and play back birdsong. Althea was the bridge between these two generations, climbing up her tower watching birds until the day she died at the age of ninety in 1943, three years after Louise started watching.

Louise may not have known of Olive Thorne and Gene Stratton-Porter, who died in the years immediately following the First World War, and she may have missed Mabel Wright, who died while Louise was nursing the Quints, but she certainly would have known of

Florence Bailey and Althea Sherman, if only from their lengthy obituaries in *The Auk*. And Margaret Nice became her closest friend.

Born eleven years before Louise in Amherst, Massachusetts, Margaret was among the first women ornithologists trained in scientific methods. She graduated from university with a degree in zoology and published a few articles on her graduate research into bobwhite feeding habits, but after she married and had children, her interests were diverted to child psychology, a relatively new field in 1915. She earned a second graduate degree and published eighteen papers in psychology journals, based on her observations of her five daughters.

One day, walking in the woods to escape her chaotic household, she felt a sudden reversal to her former self, the young woman who in university had set her sights on birds. "I saw that for many years I had lost my way. I had been led astray by false trails and had been trying to do things contrary to my nature. I resolved to return to my childhood vision of studying nature and trying to protect wild things of the earth."

Armed with Florence Bailey's *Handbook of Birds of the Western United States*—a woman's eye and a woman's mind to inform her own—Margaret went on extended camping trips with her husband and daughters in their second-hand Dodge throughout Oklahoma, where they were living. Margaret would shinny up tree trunks alongside her children, in search of bird nests. "I met birds that were entirely new to me; indeed, I had not dreamt that such existed. The absurd little bush tit, the sedate canyon towhee, the astonishing Lewis' woodpecker, the Cassin's sparrow with its exquisite refrain. All these birds were *mine*. For Oklahoma belonged to me in a way it could belong to few others . . . It was mine for I loved it passionately . . . most of all, its birds."

When Margaret met Althea Sherman at the 1922 AOU annual meeting, they had already been corresponding for a year. Margaret admired Althea's chimney swift studies, and Althea commented on Margaret's interest in the incubation dates of mourning doves. "I am glad to welcome another woman to our ranks," she wrote. "Too many women are dabblers." They commiserated with each other on the difficulty of finding time for birds given their domestic duties. As Althea wrote to Margaret, "When congratulating you upon your work done, I do not for a minute forget the greatest task, the rearing of a family of children. That alone seems too great a task for many women."

Althea was sixty-eight; Margaret was thirty-nine. Margaret was just rediscovering her love of birds; Althea was growing tired, feeling overwhelmed by the mountain of notes that she was struggling to transform into a definitive life history of the chimney swift.

"I loved and admired her and of course was inspired by her friendship, her example, and her appreciation of my efforts," Margaret responded when Louise made a passing comment about Althea's great influence on Margaret's bird studies. "But my training came largely through Clarke University where I first really learned about research and then my own independent labors on child psychology, particularly speech development. Some of this was good original thinking; all of it a great deal of persistence and patience."

Margaret published two monographs on the birds of Oklahoma before 1927 when she reluctantly moved so her husband could take up a teaching position in Columbus, Ohio. They bought sixty acres of tangled wasteland where song sparrows nested in profusion, and Margaret threw herself into a study of the irrepressibly musical birds. She banded birds and observed their breeding habits over several years and successive generations. Based on thousands of hours of watching, she developed original theories on the role of territoriality in song sparrow breeding.

Althea had warned Margaret "not to publish piecemeal" but to present her studies fully in a book, a lesson the older woman had learned from hard experience. The advice was not lost on Margaret. "It is a tragic thing that a woman of her intellect, gifts and character would have had to spend so much time in manual labour that she could not give her message to the world. This problem is an increasingly serious one in our civilization. Our highly educated, gifted women

Margaret Morse Nice, doyenne of American ornithology,
became a close personal and professional friend to Louise.

have to be cooks, cleaning women, nurse maids . . . We must follow
our path with the courage of our convictions, refusing to be diverted
by the clamour and confusion of less important demands."

Fifty years later, Margaret would pass the same warning to Louise.

No North American publisher would take Margaret's *Studies in the
Life History of the Song Sparrow*, although—or perhaps because—it
was both methodologically and theoretically revolutionary. Instead,
it was published first in Germany in 1933, and four years later in the
United States by the Linnaean Society of New York. In 1934, she was
proposed as a fellow of the AOU but did not garner sufficient votes, in
part because she wasn't particularly well liked and in part because she
was a woman, but largely because few of her colleagues appreciated her
work. Some were frankly hostile to any work that slanted toward the
new "Ecology," where "any loose statement goes unchecked . . . in
the meantime the work of the systematic ornithologist gets less attention," wrote one indignant AOU fellow. But her supporters were
determined. She failed the vote again in 1936 but was finally elected in

1937—still the sole female fellow when Louise joined the AOU a decade later. In 1942, when Margaret was put forward for the position of editor of the AOU's flagship publication, the president at the time demurred, saying, "We can scarcely pick a woman editor for *The Auk*."

At the Ninth International Ornithological Congress in 1938, Margaret met Konrad Lorenz, the Austrian ornithologist already renowned for his imprinting studies with the greylag goose. He invited her to visit his estate outside Vienna where he kept a menagerie of domestic, wild, and exotic birds. Margaret spent two life-changing months there, studying captive bird breeding with Lorenz, robbing nests to raise hatchlings in a flannel nest in a paper box, feeding them twenty-six times a day, learning how to raise the tiny, naked birds to healthy adults, discovering what to watch for in their development and how to distinguish innate from learned behaviour.

Margaret, whose research until then had been in the field, returned to the United States ready to raise baby song sparrows for study. A year later, she published *Watcher at the Nest*, the story of two male song sparrows who staked out their territories in her garden and whose boundary quarrels, mating, nesting, and relationships with their mates, their young, and the other birds in their community she had tracked over eight years.

Just months after her summer with Konrad Lorenz, Margaret presented at the AOU annual meeting in Washington, DC. Doris Speirs was in the audience. Doris was new to birds then and had just started watching evening grosbeaks—she hadn't yet seen the nest on Louise's property—so she was touched when Margaret, on meeting her, asked about her work.

Margaret was keenly aware of the importance of a network of women watchers. "I feel that the study of ornithology is a wonderful game in which strong sympathy and fellowship reign between the serious participants," she wrote to Doris. "We are friends and glad to help one another. We have high standards for our science and we want beginners to realize this."

In the summer of 1950, when Louise first glimpsed Margaret walking down the path toward the Loghouse Nest, the woman seemed tiny and frail. Louise at fifty-six was still firmly in middle age; Margaret at sixty-seven was beginning to feel the accumulation of her years. Still, the older woman's figure was straight and girlish, her hair only slightly streaked with grey, her skin smooth. "Her face was arresting. A wide mouth, a high forehead, eyes with a soft gleam that, nevertheless, suggested hard concentration, an overpowering wish to perceive the ultimate item of reality."

Louise took Margaret by the arm and led her down the rock-lined path to where a black-throated green heron was sitting on its nest. The two women felt they knew each other well, having corresponded for several years. Louise first wrote to Margaret after reading *Watcher at the Nest* to tell her what a help the book had been. Margaret already knew about Louise from Doris, who had forwarded her *Farmer's Magazine* articles, which Louise felt were insignificant but which Margaret applauded. "The more good bird articles we can get before the general public the better." Margaret had given up on magazines after several rejections and commiserated with Louise whenever she failed to place her stories. "It is too bad that the American public demands the *Believe It or Not* style in nature writing; they are nothing for the truth—only sensation . . . How discouraging for the outlook of American society that your birds are 'too normal.'"

In the beginning, Margaret and Louise addressed each other as Mrs. Nice and Mrs. Lawrence. They exchanged reprints of published papers and commented on their own experience with whatever species the other was studying. They shared observations from their watches, especially on birdsong. Margaret recommended books on bird science, sending boxes of them to Louise, who had quickly exhausted the holdings of the small public library in North Bay. To the encouragement of Taverner and the Speirs, the instruction in scientific methods offered by Rand, Godfrey, Wolfson, and Odum, and the ethical modelling of Baillie and Skutch, Margaret Nice added a course in directed reading.

What open territory there was for the wide-ranging curiosity and intellect of these two women! More than anything, they seem to me like lab partners, enthusiastic students of birds discussing their explorations in a way that was unique in Louise's personal and professional relationships. In so many of her correspondences, I sense a power imbalance, however slight—Louise overly awed at the accomplishments of others, too quick to downplay her own observations and conclusions. Yet, regardless of disparities in experience and education, Margaret and Louise spoke to each other as equals, their admiration in perfect balance. Of one of Louise's unpublished papers, Margaret wrote that it was "a beautiful thing. You have such a poetic imagination and you express yourself so beautifully. You see into the depths of things, whereas most of us just skim over the surface. We take the wonders of life for granted."

Through the summer and early fall of 1949, the women had exchanged long, lively letters on vireos, arguing for and against the methods and conclusions of the research papers they were devouring. Margaret had published on the Bell's vireo and Louise was doing research for a paper that would eventually appear as "Nesting Life and Behaviour of the Red-eyed Vireo" in *The Canadian Field-Naturalist*. Louise had five pairs of red-eyes under observation. She shared her insights into vireo loyalty to territory and suggested reasons why Margaret was seeing newly fledged vireos as late as September. She also wrote at length about her interpretations of vireo song, which they both loved. "I can listen to it for hours," wrote Louise, "and, as you, never find it monotonous, especially now since I have discovered all its variations and meaning." They both agreed that the red-eye was "a superior species."

In watching the parents, Louise noted that only females sat on the nest, although her friend Doris had told her that a renowned ornithologist claimed that the male took part in incubation too. Margaret told her to trust her own eyes. The expert Doris quoted, she wrote, although "a most delightful person and a fine ornithologist in many ways, was very careless in his statements as to which parent incubated. Time and again he gets it wrong. I've never known of a dependable instance of the male red-eye incubating."

Whether bolstered by her accumulating research or by this new friendship, Louise began to take on the ornithological establishment. For months, she waged a campaign against the inaccurate red-eye incubation data published by E.L. Palmer in *Nature* magazine and in his *Fieldbook of Natural History*. Politely but persistently, Louise pointed out Palmer's errors to him and to his publishers. Margaret was less circumspect: "If people are not sure of details in life history matters, such as which sex incubates, nor the actual length of incubation, they should say nothing about it, not glibly perpetuate ancient errors."

Louise worried that her red-eye observations had not been careful enough. But when Margaret had the opportunity to ask Palmer about his evidence for the male incubation, "he was much surprised that he had ever stated the male helps incubate. He says he has no evidence that the male does so. So apparently all such statements are merely careless assumptions from the fact that in most vireo species incubation is shared."

Margaret was so incensed that she carried out a detailed historical study of incubation data through the centuries. The result was a stinging critique of how faulty guesses from as far back as Aristotle had been perpetuated by scientists unwilling to engage in the prolonged watching that would have told them exactly how long birds sat on their eggs. Worse, they refused to trust the work of watchers like Althea Sherman and Louise who *had* put in the time to get accurate results. The manuscript went back and forth between Margaret and Louise until it was published in *The Auk*, where Margaret thanked Louise in her acknowledgements. Reliable records have since showed that red-eyed vireo males do sometimes incubate eggs, but the controversy had the happy result of triggering a landmark study exposing lazy science.

For Louise, the drawn-out fight with Palmer bolstered her faith in her own eyewitness and opened her perspective on what she was seeing. "It appears to me there are innumerable examples of the female's, I would perhaps not say dominant, [but] leading role in birdlife," she wrote to Margaret. "It is, after all, in most instances she that decides where the nest shall be built, she that in spite of the male's passionately aggressive wooing, in her own good time allows herself to be 'pounced' upon. And if the male tries to subject her too early or too late, she defends her body with all the power and tenacity needed to repulse him. I have good examples of this in a purple finch I once watched, in a pair of phoebes, warblers, vireos, rose-breasted grosbeaks, robins, mink, even, and red squirrels, particularly. Speaking of pouncing, the most amazing pouncing technique I have ever witnessed was between two phoebes. The time was between the completion of the nest and the first egg, one evening at dusk. The male hopped on a lower branch, then, of a sudden, he pounced on the feeding female, copulation took place, an instant and it was all over. This happened 5 times while I stood and watched. The violence of the act was amazing; to one ignorant of avian affairs it would have seemed the male was brutally killing the female. It impressed me so that I shivered, you know as one does when watching some particularly spectacular performance at the circus. The cry was most eerie, like an embodiment of all the earth's passions."

By the time they met in the summer of 1950, Margaret and Louise were addressing each other by their first names and signing their letters "affectionately" and "with much love." They wrote not only of their bird research and publication trials, but of personal matters. Margaret was shy to the point of inaudible in person, but forthright and forceful on the page. "I wish I had stayed with birds all my life," she admitted once, "instead of getting diverted for years into research on child psychology."

Louise lamented the need to set aside the vireo study in order to "get a few popular articles off my chest," and to tend to the constant stream of visitors that interrupted her work. "Happily, I am very little bothered now by people who waste my time," Margaret responded.

"You will just have to be ruthless with such empty, selfish people." She urged Louise to set priorities. "I fear that with all your work of *living* in such severe weather, your feeding shelves for birds and deer, and this weighing added, that your winter 'leisure time' for writing will dwindle to nothing. Of course the weighing is valuable, but is it as valuable as your life history studies? . . . There are so many fascinating problems to intrigue one that one has to constantly exercise choice."

They talked, too, about the endless juggling of science and domesticity. "As to housework," Margaret wrote, "you must remember that your mother had servants—as did mine. Life is a compromise. We can never do a fraction of what we'd like to." In her own house, Margaret admitted that "the housework is pushed off to a more convenient time. We may not wash the breakfast and lunch dishes until we are getting dinner. Cleaning is usually done at odd times in the afternoon . . . Most of the laundry is sent out; all we wash is underclothes and I *never* iron . . . Now that I have raised my babies and have a good amount of leisure, I'm determined to use it worthily. That is my goal. I feel that I can make a greater contribution by using my mind than my hands."

Margaret was a constant and loyal supporter of her friend. In 1955, *Audubon Magazine* published a letter she wrote in praise of Louise. "May I express my deep appreciation of the articles in *Audubon Magazine* contributed by Louise de Kiriline? They show a sensitive awareness of the beauty and wonder of wild things, a deep sympathy with birds and other animals, keen and conscientious observation, and insight into the significance of what has been seen. And, moreover, she is an artist with the English language. 'Irrepressible Nuthatch' . . . is such an important contribution to science that I have reviewed it for *Bird-Banding*."

Margaret continued to broaden Louise's circle of bird people, introducing her to other women watchers of her generation: Amelia Laskey, who was studying bluebird nesting, monogamy in brown-headed cowbirds, and the acquisition of song in a northern mockingbird called Honey Child that she kept for fifteen years in her house in

Nashville, Tennessee; Winnie Smith, a columnist and watcher in Two Rivers, Wisconsin, who was researching the influence of weather on bird migration; and Ruth Thomas, a nature columnist in Little Rock, Arkansas, who was a prolific bander and author of *Crip, Come Home: The Story of a Bird Who Came to Stay*, published in 1952. In the same way that Althea was a bridge between the second and third generation of women watchers, Margaret linked the watchers of the third generation to each other.

"This gift of communication was the reason why Margaret Nice gave so much in her friendship," Louise wrote. "To discuss an experience with her, to elicit her advice or her opinion, released answers that never dealt with only the minor details but somehow, partly as a result of her remarkable erudition, projected a whole picture of the natural web into which the details fitted perfectly. She had vision. She had enthusiasm of an inextinguishable kind. She had a generosity to share that was both disciplined and lavish. And she was endowed with that very rare kind of humility that is entirely pure."

Louise and Margaret did not meet often—in 1953, she visited Pimisi again with her husband, and in 1959 they were both made patrons of the AOU in honour of their distinguished contributions to the study of bird behaviour. But what was most precious to Louise was their correspondence. Over thirty years, she received 145 letters from Margaret and presumably wrote as many or more in return. Margaret was a very private person and left no personal letters in her archives, so I will never know the extent to which, for Louise, this correspondence was a "free exchange of thought and experience." But through their continuous contact, they came to know each other deeply, two women shoulder to shoulder in their quest for knowledge and the truth about birds.

In 1952, the Hungarian ornithologist Miklos Udvardy and his wife visited the Speirs in Toronto. After dinner, the men rose to go to a meeting of the Toronto Ornithological Club. The women stayed in their seats.

Udvardy looked at the women, perplexed. "Aren't you coming with us?"

Murray leaned in, explaining softly: the TOC admitted only men.

"Is this the fourteenth century?" Udvardy exclaimed, turning to Doris. "You must start a club for women!"

Doris immediately consulted Louise, who had been instrumental in creating a Nipissing naturalist club a decade earlier. She advised Doris to limit the organization to twelve members, any more and they wouldn't be able to hear the birds on their walks. As well, seven corresponding members—women from outside Toronto—were admitted, including Louise. Among the members were a poet, a photographer, an illustrator, and a wildlife sculptor, several conservation activists, international birders, a botanist, a nature columnist, experts on ferns, butterflies, and fungi.

"The 12 of us are mostly very busy women," Doris wrote to Louise, "and our day each month means a tremendous amount to us, to get outdoors, to look at nature, to listen and record the birds, to observe innumerable details of wilderness, from skunk cabbage to baby yellow warblers." They christened their women-only bird-watching society the Margaret Morse Nice Ornithological Club.

Louise attended meetings when she could, giving talks on her research subjects of the moment. She contributed regular bird notes to the club's monthly newsletter *The Niceia*: the snow buntings she found in mid-January, dozing in the sun, tucked deep into the toe of a snow print she'd made; the timber wolf playground she found late one February, "the whole story so vividly written in the snow" that she could see how the wolves had romped and raced, "a nose thrust into the snow for a large mouthful of the cooling stuff on their sweating tongue"; the March morning before dawn when she stood in the pale stillness to listen to wolfsong, "a wonderful full-throated sound, clear, rising and powerful, ending on a sustained thrilling long note"; the summer she spent tracking yellow-bellied sapsuckers through the woods "out of breath and stumbling through the undergrowth upon her clodhopper feet, forever too late to take in the whole development of those bizarre hitching antics and displays."

The club was devoted to birds, but also to philanthropy and especially to helping women watchers. Near the end of its first year, Doris wrote to Louise: "The members of the MNOC, being most appreciative of the great contribution which you are making to Canadian ornithology, want to express their gratitude to you in a tangible way. For some time I have known, and Margaret has known too, of your need for a better typewriter, or an extra one so that you could have your old faithful friend fixed and yet not be minus this most necessary tool for a writer . . . The idea came first to dear, dear Margaret . . . Her letter about you and your work brought tears to my eyes. How she loves and appreciates you. All the members of the MNOC do really value what you are doing."

And so Canada's first women's ornithological club, in their first act of generosity, bought a new typewriter for Louise.

12

A Limitless Capacity to Rebound

The spring of 1956 was slow to arrive. April had been cold with heavy snows; at the end of the month, the ice on the bay was still solid. The spring migration seemed off-kilter. Louise knew by then exactly when to expect each species to arrive, but even so, she double-checked her records. The few *flyttfåglar*—migratory birds—that landed in her woods were five to eleven days late.

On May 2, the weather warmed briefly and a thin stream of migrants trickled in: robins, flickers, geese, ducks, white-throated sparrows, even a few barn swallows. The vast flocks were stalled, Louise assumed, somewhere to the south. The birds that did arrive pecked in the snow for seeds and bugs, but the insects weren't there. It was still too cold.

The ice finally went out of Pimisi Bay on May 7, the latest date the lake had ever cleared. The next day was so cold that new ice formed along the shore. The mass of polar air that had moved in during the night hung over Louise's forest for almost a week; the snow stayed crisp and deep. She watched as a flock of swallows turned in the teeth of the cold wind and headed south again. "But I do not know how far they went, perhaps only a mile or two out of the worst rage of the elements. There is a lot in nature that you only think you know because it seems logical, but things may not happen as you think they ought."

Then on May 11, warm air flooded in and within hours the temperature soared to 28°C. The buds on the trees swelled. Insects hatched. Every morning and evening, Louise watched with anxious anticipation, but the wave of expected migrants did not appear. They were flying high above, she assumed, madly making up for lost time as they pushed farther north. On the night of May 15, when another Arctic cold front shoved temperatures back below freezing and covered the ground with snow, the birds came down.

"By nine o'clock in the morning a great mass of migrating birds overran the whole countryside. They came on this day, not through the trees but crawling, hopping stiffly from straw to dead leaf, covering the ground with their bodies. They wallowed in the snow looking for food that scarcely was there, or sat cold and shivering, trying to warm their freezing feet in the soft feathers of their bellies.

"Thrushes came in great numbers, fawn-coloured veerys, silent hermit thrushes in no mood for any characteristic light lift of their rust-red tails. There were gray-cheeked thrushes—never before or since have I seen so many of these rare thrushes that belong to the land from James Bay to Labrador and are glimpsed only occasionally on their passage through these parts. On this day they came down from the skies in a veritable avalanche.

"Ovenbirds walked all over the forest floor and in places sheltered from the snow turned over the dead leaves, one by one, looking for a snail, a mite, whatever edible thing the leaf might cover. Nashville warblers, bright yellow dots in the snow, fed ravenously upon the yellow stamens of the pussy-willows. And least flycatchers, feeling the cold badly with their utter dependence on winged insect life, hopped dismally from one grass-blade to another, close, close to the ground. They were too bone-cold to take any notice of me, stepping cautiously among them lest inadvertently I should trample one underfoot.

"At eleven o'clock the birds were still coming on, crawling northward along the ground. They covered the roadsides and the wires of the guardrails in great numbers, thrushes and more thrushes, white-crowned and white-throated sparrows, rose-breasted grosbeaks. . . .

"All through the day the birds moved slowly and laboriously northward across the Pimisi Bay region in the teeth of the piercing wind, hugging the ground, seeking what scant shelter there was to be found from the icy blasts. As night came, it grew colder and colder. A ruby-throated hummingbird, rebuffed by the wind, fell on the cold cement foundation of the house and clung there for a long miserable minute, then miraculously found strength to lift upon vibrating wings, hovering along our windows and then disappearing toward the north in the gathering dusk.

"It froze hard during the night. As dawn came, the flycatchers and the warblers had tracelessly disappeared. The greater mass of these birds that came into this region on that dreadful day, crawling onward dominated by the one urgency to reach their well-known breeding grounds, powered by their last ergon of energy, must have perished.

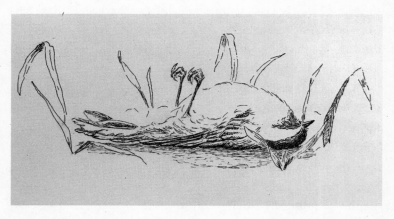

One of thousands of birds that died in spring, 1956, sketched by Louise

"But the thrushes and the sparrows, hardier than the insect-eaters, survived. They flocked to the feeding station . . . The white-crowned sparrows, proud birds of the far north, interrupted all their activities with song; they sang as they fed greedily on the ground, as they rested, as they preened, as they chased one another through the trees. Having thus come upon the same rigorous conditions they would undoubtedly meet on the tundra, the goal of their journey, perhaps they thrilled to the illusory feeling of having already arrived and expressed it in the most enchanting chorus of haunting plaintive melodies ever heard in these parts."

There was frost every night, and often snow, as one cold front after another pressed down on Louise's woods. By the third week in May, the trees were still without leaves. She spent most of her time making food for the birds—suet balls, peanut butter smears on the tree trunks, bread crumbs and seeds suited to the species that were invading her small wilderness, some of them quite uncommon. Many clearly had never dined on human-made food; they didn't even recognize it as food, but they were starving. They saw other birds devouring the tidbits, and having no choice, they ate it too.

Louise watched, horrified yet mesmerized by the irresistible migratory urge that had brought the birds to this crisis, by the behaviours the disaster provoked. "Some are adaptive to emergency situations and some are not, and those that are not do not survive. Thus those that have the power to live on—the gift of adjustment—endow their progeny with some of their adaptive abilities. And so the seven days of creation goes on eternally. Before our very eyes."

For ten more days the murderous cold persisted. And still the birds came. "They came in straggling groups through the days, always travelling close to the ground, never once ascending into the treetops, their habitual stratum. Low-flying insects grounded the birds more than the cold itself, and judging by the behaviour of the crawling birds, there were not many of these. At one time, I nearly stepped on a tiny orange-crowned warbler sitting huddled by a small tuft of grass."

Untold numbers of woodland songbirds died of starvation and exposure that spring. Members of Louise's Nipissing naturalist club picked up dozens of dead birds from around the lakes west of Pimisi Bay. Hundreds more were never recovered. "In the forest, they fell into the leaves as they reached the inevitable end of the journey, upon the beds of green mosses and forest debris. And nature took care of their tiny bodies and buried them, unseen and uncounted."

In 1956, the birds, quite literally, crashed.

In the spring of 1852, Thoreau saw birds so numerous that "when they lit on a tree, they appeared at a distance to clothe it like leaves . . . a thousand birds gently twittering and ushering in the light."

When Louise first starting watching birds in 1940, she witnessed the same spring parade, rafts of warblers "that filled every greening tree all of a sudden, poured in over the land with twitter and song, unceasing movement, uncountable in their great numbers."

Eighty years later, I stand in the Mexican jungle, on the lip of *el sótano de las golondrinas*, the deepest natural cave shaft in the world, as thousands of white-collared swifts, dark birds the size of small falcons, circle around the limestone walls, building momentum to hurtle up into the dawn sky in search of food. A gauzy mist hangs in the maw of the cave. If we squint, we can see the opposite wall, several stone-throws away, but not the pit that drops a thousand feet or more below us. We hear the swifts before they see them: a whirring drum roll of wingbeats under a thin, high-pitched *wheeeeee*, punctuated now and then by the ear-splitting shrieks of flights of green parakeets. We watch for over an hour and still the birds keep coming.

Such moments are increasingly rare.

Louise noticed a decline in bird life in her forest almost as soon as she started watching. In 1943, as well as making field records of nestings and conducting concentrated nest watches, she began to chart her local population of thirteen species of warblers. By 1947, nearly half were showing consistently reduced numbers. By 1951, all were on a slow but steady slide. The number of Blackburnian and Nashville warblers dropped by ten percent over that decade; the population of chestnut-sided, mourning, and Canada warblers fell by an incredible seventy-five percent.

Louise was puzzled. She knew that fluctuations in bird populations could happen for all kinds of reasons, natural and man-made: shifts in the food supply, an influx of predators, unforgiving weather. But the raspberry bushes where the chestnut-sideds built their nests were still standing and the mayflies they caught for their young were as abundant as ever. Nothing in her forest, as far as she could tell, had changed to make her warblers go elsewhere to breed.

Until that vicious spring of 1956, she still hoped the songbird populations would recover.

There is a hole in Louise's life in the mid-1950s. I can see the edges of it and glimpse shapes in the darkness that might serve as evidence, but mostly I can only speculate. That must be how the diminishing bird life appeared to Louise. Some facts were clear: the birds still arrived in her forest each spring and left again in late summer, although where exactly they went and how they got there was a mystery. And why were fewer songbirds returning each year? Why had some species all but vanished, while others showed only modest declines, and some populations, like those of brown-headed cowbirds and blue jays, were exploding?

Nothing in her fifteen years of bird study prior to that disastrous spring was more alarmingly provocative than the disappearance of the birds themselves. She felt she needed to observe more carefully, think more creatively, analyze her data with more precision, write more persuasively. Yet all she could do was weep, great paroxysms of sobs that she felt helpless to stop. She was alone much of the cold, hard winter that heaped snow as high as the eaves. Len was plowing for the Department of Highways, living once again in a motel near where his machine was parked. He came home late Saturday, and on Sunday, he did what he could to relieve the physical demands on Louise. But he wasn't sorry to return to the motel Sunday night: he could hardly stand this sadness of his wife that seemed to have no limit and no cause.

Work had always been her refuge, but she hardly dared touch her typewriter. "All I say and write seems to be wrong," she wailed to her mother. Even basic daily chores defeated her, leaving her weak, shot through with attacks of physical pain.

Her correspondence shrivelled to a trickle. When she resumed writing letters a year, in some cases two or three years later, she scarcely hinted at what had sent her to her bed in total emotional and physical collapse.

Perhaps it started with Hurricane Hazel, the ferocious gale in 1954 that killed 469 people in Haiti before making landfall in North Carolina, whipping north through the United States and up into Canada, where it was downgraded to an extratropical storm that left eighty-one dead. On the night of Saturday, October 16, Louise woke to what sounded like a train tearing through the forest. Whirling wind snatched at the branches outside her window, torturing the giant spruces before ripping them up by their roots and crashing them to the ground, into each other, onto the roof of the log house. When the first tree hit, Louise and Len dove for the dugout cellar under the living room, where they huddled amongst the baskets of apples, carrots, and potatoes, listening to the yowling wind, the shattering trees, the smack of bay water against the foundation. "I do not mind admitting that I was frightened," Len wrote a month later to Louise's mother. "I was in lots of air raids during the war and helped in carrying away the injured and dead but it never upset me as much as that storm did."

The next morning, they climbed out of the cellar to a scene of devastation. Sunlight poured down through gaps torn in the canopy where trees had once stood. Thirty-seven towering conifers had come down. Louise didn't even try to count the smaller trunks, criss-crossed like a chaotic game of giant pick-up sticks. The lake, already high from weeks of rain, had risen until the house was marooned on its granite outcrop.

Louise had lived in her Loghouse Nest for twenty years, almost to the day. She and Len had worked tirelessly to improve the simple rectangle of peeled and stained logs; they'd built a front porch with a peaked roof that gave the place a faintly Swiss look and an addition on the back that expanded the kitchen with a glassed-in sunroom where Louise had a clear view of her banding traps and feeding station. She'd carried pails of soil half a mile from the swamp and dumped it into crevasses in the granite that Len had split open to create a garden. They still lived without running water, electricity, or central heating. Everything they did—hauling water, cutting wood, growing what they ate, building what they needed—they had done with their own hands.

Little Creek, where Louise fetched her water in summer

How discouraging to see her nest so disrupted. To be thrown back into construction, this time by strangers who crawled over her house like an invasion of restless woodpeckers, hammering like crazy to get a new roof on before the snows came. And the forest! She knew every tree and bush like a friend, the thin ground where the lady's slippers bloomed, the pussy willows where the warblers took their first meal when they landed in the spring, the nest trees she had watched, the trunks she had shimmied up to see blue, buff, and dappled eggs circled in a nest. She had walked this landscape every morning for twenty years—all of it now a foreign wasteland of twisted, broken limbs.

I have an inkling of how she must have felt. In 1998, I lived in Kingston, the epicentre of the Great Ice Storm that snapped the canopy off every tree in the city. Trees grow back, people said, as if in consolation. But growing back takes years, even decades, and there is no fixing the hole in the heart that aches every time you walk through a ravaged landscape you call home.

For Louise, the physical ruin of Hurricane Hazel came at a time when she was already near the end of what she could bear. The demands on her time had multiplied until she had hardly a moment to breathe, let alone sleep. As well as pursuing her own studies into the life histories of the black-capped chickadee, red crossbill, red-eyed vireo, various warblers, and the pigeon hawk, she was collecting data for several scientists and maintaining lengthy bird correspondences with colleagues and friends amidst a constant stream of strangers asking for help with their bird work. Becoming an elective member of the AOU had filled her mailbox to the breaking point.

None of this earned her any income, and Len's salary working on the roads was not enough to keep them. She depended on the paying work she did for magazines, yet in 1953 she had published only one article, and in 1954, only two. Magazine editors were still clamouring for her popular pieces, but her time and energy were taken up with unpaid scientific work. Books had always been part of her financial plan, yet it had been ten years since *The Loghouse Nest*. In the meantime, she had burned *Tales of the Green Woods*, reworked it as *Jimmy Joe and the Jay*, revising it again and again and still no publisher wanted it. In 1948, she had started an adult book called *Birds Alive*, but she hadn't yet produced a decent draft.

"Responsibilities always seem to increase. There is always a back-log of contributions awaiting your doing as the weight of your work becomes increasingly felt. Will you please write something for our journal? Please give us a talk on the Loon! Do you know this? Do you know that? Information is lacking. What shall we do about this, your opinion would be valued. And so on," she complained to her mother. Then, struggling for balance, she found the silver lining she always searched for. "All this process is immensely educational and inspiring for me, no less. It is *outside* my own internal living, extensional, widening, contributional . . . An outpouring of the self and *it must be good.*"

Louise was sixty. In the months after Hurricane Hazel, her hair suddenly turned more white than russet; her skin was pale and creased. She felt herself slowing down: she couldn't run as fast or do the heavy work she used to manage without giving it a second thought. If she didn't get a good night's rest, she was insufferable, which she admitted had always been the case, but now with the financial worries, the demands of her career, her concern over the birds, and the sudden, random destruction of her beloved piece of wilderness, she scarcely slept at all.

It is wrenching to watch such a strong, smart, resourceful woman brought low. I want her to be Wonder Woman, to climb every mountain, ford every stream until she drops dead at her natural time. But she was human, after all. And that winter of 1955 she succumbed to the realities of her hard life, a life she had chosen over the soft privilege of her birth. Maybe what Len said to her was true—"You wouldn't like it so much if it was easy"—but her life had finally knocked her down.

She was weepy for months, with rounds of high fevers followed by aches, sweats, and chills. The illness, if that's what it was, reminded her of the sicknesses she'd nursed in the Volga, the fevers and brain-breaking headaches, the nausea and confusion she'd suffered in Moscow, just before she saw Gleb for the last time. Yet there seemed to be nothing physically wrong with her. She tried everything she could think of to mitigate the strange symptoms. She found some sulfa pills left over from one of Len's bouts of influenza and gulped them down. She swallowed cod liver oil by the tablespoon. In the end, she decided her aches and pains were more psychosomatic than anything. Nothing, she told herself, was seriously wrong. It was just some kind of malaise. Yet for a woman who believed *Man är sin egen lyckas smed*—you are the smithy of your own success—such desperate sadness must have felt like failure.

What lay closest to Louise's heart, more than Len, more than Pimisi, more than the birds, was her relationship with her mother, and that winter, it crashed like a frozen thrush. On January 9, 1955, Louise received a cable from Sweden: her mother had had a heart attack and was drawing her last breaths. For five days and nights Louise mourned her mother's death. She was too distraught to tell anyone but Margaret.

Then a second cable arrived: her mother had rallied and was doing well.

Felled by grief, Louise was now consumed with worry and with guilt at being six thousand kilometres away from the person she loved most in the world. Since her father's death, she had been her mother's closest confidante and advisor. Over the years, she had invited, cajoled, even begged her mother to move to Canada so she could look after her, but her mother had refused, choosing solitude in Sweden with its familiar comforts. Louise's sister, Ebba, had died of tuberculosis during the Second World War, and Ebba's two daughters, Anita and Lise (named for Louise), were young adults. They doted on their grandmother and were caring for her now, a role that Louise felt was rightly hers as the eldest daughter, the surviving daughter, the daughter who by nature was an organizer and by profession a nurse. Shooting through the grief and worry and guilt was hot fury at her nieces and cousins and aunts and uncles—all those at her mother's bedside—who had kept her in that awful purgatory for five days, believing her dear mother was dead.

Louise had always felt an outsider among the Flachs. They saw her as a tomboy turned adventuress who had left her homeland to travel into revolution; who espoused ideas of equality and sisterhood instead of the patriarchy she was born into; who had abandoned her mother for what they counted as fame and fortune on the other side of the world. She felt she had become the antithesis of all that her Swedish noble family stood for: privilege, loyalty, decorum.

That second telegram was a relief—her mother was alive—but at the same time, more cause for worry. The heart attack had been followed by a stroke. Louise broke her silence to write in a panic to Doris: "If Mother recovers I feel that Len and I should break up our home here and go over to make our home in Sweden and take care of her."

Doris gently urged her to reconsider. "Certainly we want you to be in your right place, wherever that is. I have not felt sure that your right place was Stockholm rather than Pimisi Bay. But it may be . . . You will know at the time what to do."

Margaret was more direct: "What a soul-wracking time you have been through! Never have I heard of such a thing before . . . Whatever happens I hope it will not seem best to you to leave the wonderful work you are doing here. It would be a terrible blow to those of us who love you so."

Heartbroken, guilt-ridden, and tortured with worry, Louise could not hold her tongue. She lashed out against the family she felt had failed her so miserably, especially Ebba's daughters. Those first sharp letters written during her mother's illness have disappeared, but not the ones that followed, awash with grief and remorse.

"I have never meant to hurt you," she wrote to her mother. "But it will soon be wrong even to say I love you. I can't write nothings to you, and when I write what I feel, I hurt you. . . This cannot go on. It has been too much. It has been abnormal. I am sorry about all this. I am sorry for whatever I have done that has hurt you. Sometimes I am even sorry that I am your daughter. You might have had a very much better one."

What had come between them, she finally realized, was Ebba's children. "The more you spoke for, the more I spoke against, and the more I spoke against, the more you spoke for . . . I have long known how negative it all was, yet was incapable of getting rid of it. But one night, not so long ago, I woke up and knew that I had acquired the Will to relegate this mischievous issue to its right place. It is like giving up smoking, a most easy matter once the will to do it has been created . . . We shall drop the little issue of the children beside us in its natural fold and we shall preserve the deep intimacy of our love for each other intact and direct . . . I am crying now again, but I must stop that."

She signed her letter, "My love for you is pure and simple and everlasting," then she added a coda that reveals her embarrassment, and how important privacy was to her, a trait that held even the most personal of her published writing in restraint. "Don't say anything to anybody about this. This is ours alone."

Her "Will" restored, she could even see a silver lining in Hazel's devastation.

Len and the Loghouse Nest, after renovations prompted
by Hurricane Hazel, 1954

"Looking back on the changes that the hurricane brought to our environment just a year ago tonight, we are glad. All those uprooted trees, all the destruction and ravage we found that early morning after the terrifying night. In their stead there are flowers and green grass and bushes expanding their volume to the new beams of light, and a host of seedling trees have sprung forth that were there but not seen before. And there is much more light in our house and more sunshine on sunny days. There is no disaster, we know now, that lacks the attribute which makes it into a blessing. This, the omnipotence, is the wonderful thing with life. It is never at a loss."

Late in the spring of 1955 Louise, no longer weepy but still weak, stepped aboard an airplane bound for Sweden. Her trip was not the quick jaunt it would be today. "Throughout a day and night and another day, I sat by the window spellbound," travelling from North Bay to Toronto to Montreal to London to Copenhagen to Stockholm. Even from the air, she saw the world through the eyes of a naturalist: "There is a particular kind of 'nap' to this Canadian landscape. It is like the nap of a coarse Persian carpet, strong, deep, and everlasting. To me personally it was significant that in only two of the six countries I flew over I should find the same kind of 'nap'—Canada and Sweden—two lands of the north, my adopted and my native country. That of the other four was like silk." As the plane neared Stockholm, "the clouds parted and dissolved. And there below, wedged between two deep firths of the Baltic Sea, like a picture illuminated by a giant skylight, I saw the place where I was born."

It had been nine years since she'd been home. Almost as if in welcome, her mother had moved back into her own apartment. "I can so well understand the blissfulness of your heart when you reentered the familiar place and sat down among your beloved things. There is something about one's own hearth that is indispensable to happiness."

She might as well have been speaking about herself and her own ravaged land.

Louise wanted two things from her journey to her homeland: to visit her father's grave and to see Svensksund once more. She had always dreamed of buying back the forest at Villan and building a small house on the very spot where she was born, then living there until her last breath. She felt at home in Canada, but her connection to Sweden was visceral. "There are so many who tear up their roots and think nothing of it; and they do not understand that they have cut off their anchor. My Swedishness is in my heart and mind and it is indestructible."

Stockholm was thirteen degrees latitude further north than Pimisi Bay, which meant that Louise witnessed two springs that year: she watched the birds return to her forest from Central and South America, and she was in Sweden when the birds arrived from their wintering grounds in Africa. Stepping off the plane, the first bird she saw was a *kaja*—a jackdaw, what Lorenz called "the Perennial Retainers" in his book *King Solomon's Ring*. "A crow bird's walk always reminds me of Mae West," Louise wrote in a short article about her trip, published in the *Toronto Field-Naturalist*, "a sedate swaying of plumes and body, consciously seductive in the lady, but enchantingly unaffected in the bird." As she walked toward her mother's apartment, an invisible bird sang a song that she remembered from childhood. "It had neither the spring-water quality of the winter wren nor the canary-like sequence of notes of the purple finch; rather was it like the brief splashing of a brook over wet rocks, a rippling short cascade of joyful notes," and then she spotted it—a chaffinch in one of the linden trees about to burst into leaf.

Louise got up early in the mornings and sat in the drawing room with her portable typewriter, working on *Jimmy Joe and the Jay*. Then she had a bath, a luxury after decades of winter cat-baths at her kitchen sink and summer swim-baths in the lake. When her mother woke, Louise brought her breakfast in bed and ate hers off a tea wagon while they chatted. Every day they took brief walks; sometimes her mother cooked one of Louise's favourite childhood dishes.

She could leave her mother only for short periods, mostly in the mornings. One day, she rose at 4 a.m. to join a bird walk organized by the Swedish Ornithological Society. On the way to the meeting place—a forested park jutting out into the Stockholm archipelago, surrounded on three sides by water—she saw fifteen species. Great tits took crumbs from her hand. Many of the birds she saw were similar to those she might have seen on her dawn walk back at Pimisi—mallards, herons, nuthatches, terns, doves, warblers, and robins—although the plumages and markings were just different enough to be enthralling.

Once, on impulse, she took a detour through a wooded park on her way back to her mother's apartment. "No sooner had I got into the woods before I was accosted by a small boy about eleven years of age. He had seen my [field] glasses and notebook and became vastly interested. When I explained that I had just come from Canada and that I had forgotten all about the birds here, which I used to know when I was his age, he then became my gallant guide." As they walked together, they watched the birds, discussing habitat and plumage, spending a long time identifying a European redstart, and enjoying the courting rituals that almost always involved shivery, long-drawn-out songs. "Junior Guide and I walked homewards. We said goodbye as if we had known each other all our lives and were to meet soon again. Neither of us knew the name of the other. We had not seen a great many species, nor any but the most common, nor had we heard so much birdsong. But because of our chance encounter we had trod together on common ground and shared in an understanding of what we had seen."

She arranged a short birding expedition with Sigfrid Durango, author of the illustrated Swedish guide, *Fåglarna i färg* [*Birds in Colour*], and with Bengt Berg, an old family friend who was author of thirty books and one of the world's first nature filmmakers, instrumental in saving Sweden's sea eagles, golden eagles, and mute swans. Like Louise, he brooked no obstacle in finding birds, once suspending himself from the basket of a hot-air balloon in the Himalayas to get a picture of a bearded vulture.

But it was a morning row across Lake Mälaren on the outskirts of Stockholm with Gunnar Svärdson that most moved her. Trained as an evolutionary biologist and renowned as a fisheries expert, Svärdson passionately defended curiosity-based research—and like Louise, what he was curious about was birds. He was conducting ornithological studies on Sotholmen, a little island long ago declared a wildlife preserve so the King of Sweden would always have ducks to hunt. On the bald-faced rock, they found nests of common gulls and common terns, with tufted ducks nesting between. At their approach, the gulls and terns flushed, while the ducks sat tight to their eggs, an effective strategy, Svärdson told her, since the aggressive gulls and terns would chase away predators, saving their own eggs and the ducks' too. She saw common gulls nesting in the tall pines: "How strange and delightful to see the big white birds perching in the treetops and walking about along the branches." Svärdson led her to Sweden's only nesting mallards. Here, the familiar duck raised its family under fallen trees, low branches, and bushes, one female often brooding the eggs of several others that would sit nearby, amicably taking turns on the nest. What struck Louise was the fact that these females returned to exactly the same spot every year, a phenomenon that Svärdson believed was due to long-range imprinting, the acquisition of a fixed impression of a locality so strong and persistent that it unfalteringly brought the bird back to precisely the same nesting place.

Louise returned to Canada at the end of June, having seen neither her father's grave nor Svensksund, but she sounds entirely herself again. "I love Canada and all I have there, beloved husband, beloved friends, beloved home," she wrote to Doris. "But my heart is sweetly, sweetly sad over leaving my darling mother. We have agreed to go through it positively, to put a comma and not a period at the end of the sentence. It has been a most wonderful time, a period to be framed in gold in the mind and memory."

A year after the deep freeze that devastated the spring migration, Louise watched the returning birds with anxious interest. She knew from her observations and from her own experience that life had "an almost limitless capacity to rebound." Natural disasters, however painful in the moment, were unlikely to provoke radical change in overall bird populations.

Yet when the woodland songbirds landed in her breeding grounds in the spring of 1957, their numbers were significantly reduced, especially the least flycatchers and the warblers. That dip might have been expected, but in the year that followed, there was still no rebound.

Louise was enough of a scientist by then not to jump to conclusions. "Sometimes it seemed an open question whether or not I was just imagining a meaningful change, a significant displacement of certain species whose disappearance ought to be deplored not only for aesthetic and sentimental but for biological reasons as well."

But her years of daily records spoke for themselves.

"Woodland songbirds still inhabit our forests but their former profusion is no more. Only here and there in little pockets of especially attractive surroundings, where there is water and a thick growth of forest understory and of trees of varying ages, where the sunshine penetrates through openings in the verdure and the shade is deep and humid among the rotting windfalls, can the sense of former sylvan opulence still be recaptured. So long as the benign spot is left in its wilderness state, untouched and untrodden by too many human feet, the exhilarating interaction of birds and other wildlife and the environment may still be found there . . . But although these places alone contain the germ of hope for possible future restoration, not all of them, scattered over this vast land, are now occupied. Here is the emptiness. Here and in all parts of the forest, marvellous woodland habitats now lie silent and lifeless each spring after the migration of the birds has come to an end."

Through the late 1950s, her correspondence with fellow watchers bristles with anxiety over the thinning flocks of migrating songbirds.

"Many of us here are worried over the lack of birds, except, of course, the residents," Roy Ivor wrote, referring not to resident humans but to the birds that stayed in one locale year-round. "I do think, as do you, that sprays are doing very great damage. The new spray for killing white grubs seems to be lethal to robins. I have heard of eight picked up around this district lately. The Banting Institute is trying to find out definitely if this spray is the cause. I am trying to get things organized not only to get the public aroused but to get after the large chemical firms. It will be a difficult if not an impossible job for they are making millions out of spray material. I think that both in Canada and the States all who value birds, not only from an esthetic viewpoint but from an economic should organize and get the public scared of what could happen. Picture windows are killing millions on the continent; other millions by cats. Spraying may prove the worst of all. The combination of natural causes with all the others . . . could prove as dangerous as atomic bombs."

In June 1958, Chandler Robbins, a field biologist at the U.S. Fish and Wildlife Service, wrote in alarm after receiving Louise's spring migration report. "We have had many reports of scarcity of birds during the spring migration period as well as numerous instances of heavy mortality in the eastern states as a result of the severe winter weather. Many of the birds that you report missing from your study area, however, are species that would not have been affected by winter weather in the United States. We are very anxious to know whether the decrease you report is widespread or whether it is a local condition. Unfortunately there are comparatively few people who take the trouble to conduct annual population studies of nesting birds."

Since the late 1940s, Louise had been concerned about the effects of roadside spraying to kill broad-leafed plants. In 1952 she published a piece in the *Federation of Ontario Naturalists Bulletin* in which she recorded the songbird population of a half-mile section of a hydro right-of-way before and after spraying. Initially, the area was home to five pairs of yellowthroats, four pairs of indigo buntings, two pairs of mourning warblers, and one pair of song sparrows. The area was sprayed twice over that summer, the second time heavily.

"In the spring of 1952, the reduction of birds taking up territory in this half-mile area appeared so abnormal that I felt the repeated sprayings must be taken into consideration as a possible contributory factor." Repeated counts showed only one pair of yellowthroats and a single male indigo bunting. No mourning warblers. No song sparrows. "Other roadsides and hydro cuts that hadn't been sprayed showed birds in their usual abundance." She closed by suggesting ways to control unwanted plant growth without using chemical sprays.

But the spraying continued. Two years later, in 1954, she wrote again in the FON *Bulletin*, this time with barely suppressed rage, "chemical odours pursue us out of the cities, into the country, along every road and country lane . . . the work of the spraying machine that ruthlessly, senselessly, passed along a few hours ago and doused every plant and shrub and wild fanciful growth with its invidious poison. Drooping blossom heads, seared leaves, some still gallantly withholding the effects of the death-dealer, which will show tomorrow when everything turns brown from the chemical fire, mark its passage. Is there, in all this world, no escape? Shall there be no nook or corner, no compound or precinct, in our environment, which we may leave untainted and unpolluted by our artificial necessities?"

Rachel Carson turned her attention to the consequences of pesticides in the environment in the late 1950s, prompted by a letter from her friend Olga Owens Huckins to *The Boston Herald*, describing the death of birds around her property after the aerial spraying of DDT to kill mosquitoes. Carson took up the challenge to prove the link. She was not the first to notice the decline in songbirds or to connect that decline to chemical spraying: an army of watchers quickly provided her with the data they'd been recording for fifteen years. Since Louise sent her population data to the U.S. Fish and Wildlife Service, it is possible Carson had access to Louise's numbers too. When Carson's book *Silent Spring* was published in 1962, it galvanized both seasoned watchers and the unseeing public and metaphorically christened the slow depopulation of the forests with a phrase that still resonates with its warning of a bleak, songless future.

Louise greeted *Silent Spring* with relief. "A kind of sad satisfaction adheres to the information that others beside myself also note the change taking place in the numbers of small woodland songbirds," Louise wrote to Doris. "It is such a difficult kind of change to establish as a fact, partly because its effects vary to such an extent from year to year and partly because so many different factors have a share in these changes. Life pushes one thing this way, another the other way, and the true trends are not apparent overnight, but take a long, long time to become discernible."

The silence in the forest, Louise believed, represented more than the loss of avian music. Song was a form of speech—the means by which a bird declared its territory, its eligibility to mate, its objection to intruders, its intention to drive off aggressors, its willingness to fight. After its stake had been successfully defended, song was a bird's great, lyrical sigh of relief.

"A sufficiently marked decline in the population eliminates many of the bird's motivations to sing. Living in an environment with few or no close neighbours of its own kind, the bird encounters no rivals to kindle its singing efforts. Nobody whose presence disturbs it threatens to encroach upon its territorial borders. The bird's domain has no other limits than those imposed by its own food requirements and safe nesting opportunities.

"This is what happened in our forest after the great disaster [of 1956], an improbable and strange thing in these forests that resounded with birdsong in former days. The birds are still here but in much diminished numbers. They still sing, but their need for expression in song arises far less frequently than it did two or three decades ago when so many of them established their mosaic patterns of territories, when space was at a premium and competition was strong. But while our spring of today may be silent in comparison with the dawn chorus of other spring seasons once experienced, at least the silence is not yet total."

I started bird watching in 1957, just as Louise was confirming the serious and permanent decline in the numbers of songbirds in her forest. I was a young girl, delighted to recognize a robin, a wren, a thrasher, birds pointed out to me by my great uncle, who could lure chipmunks into the palm of his hand, a magic trick that impressed me almost as much as his familiarity with all the birds that came to his feeders in the small village where we both lived. I would take a peanut butter and honey sandwich, wrapped in one of my father's handkerchiefs, down to the back of our yard, climb the split rail fence, and push into the undergrowth to my log, hidden deep in the forest that to me was as thick and ancient as Gene Stratton-Porter's Limberlost. I had no binoculars. I carried no notebook. I just nibbled on my sandwich, away from the prying eyes of my sisters and parents, and I watched. I listened. The chickadees came close, chattering like little buddies, and I chattered back. The blue jays squawked like my mother's clothesline. Once, a thrush passed so close I could see the spots on its chest. I remember individuals, but the forest seemed to me to teem with birds, a whole world I had discovered, like Champlain, like Marie Curie looking through her microscope, like Louise in her woods. It never occurred to me to imagine the tree limbs once lined with birds, their song an orchestra instead of the tiny chamber chorus I listened to with such awe, trying to pick out the notes.

Sixty-five years later, that thin chorus seems complex and rich compared to the solo notes that announce my dawns now. A solitary robin. A song sparrow. The ongoing trill of a treetop vireo. I close my eyes and feel the songs run together until they fill my heart, if not the woods, the wonder still and always fresh.

13

Visions of Woodpeckers

The downy woodpecker clung to the white trunk of a birch and announced itself with a whinnying call that rang through the forest. He drummed on the tree, then puffed up in full display—black-spotted tail feathers exposed, bill gaping, red nape spot as erect as a crown set atop his head.

A female answered from a distance. She postured, tail feathers spread wide. The two called and drummed, signals leaping back and forth between them. A bond was formed; the range of their territory set.

The pair was feeding among the tall poplars when a lone female flew into their territory. She made straight for the tree where the male was preening and hitched up the trunk toward him. Within seconds, the mated female took flight, heading for the interloper. She landed on the nearest branch and aimed her bill skyward, pointing right-left, right-left, jabbing the air and flapping her wings, her tail spread flat against the tree. The intruder didn't budge. The female heightened her attack. She flew directly at the encroaching female, chasing her high up

Downy Woodpecker aggressive-social display, sketched by Louise

into the canopy and down. The male slunk behind his tree trunk as the sparring females surged around him. When the trespasser landed, the resident female landed beside her and rose up on tiptoe, confronting her rival with head raised and bill gaping, wings spread wide to show the white feathers lining her wings and belly. Slowly, she turned her body this way and that, an alabaster monument of winged victory. The interloper flew off, and the triumphant female dashed erratically among the trees, screaming in sharp bursts, *khirrrrr! khirrrrr!*

Woodpeckers' attitudes toward other Picidae were usually tolerant, even during nesting. Louise had watched a downy alight in the nest tree of a hairy woodpecker: no response. She'd seen a sapsucker forage near a hairy woodpecker nest: the male had popped his head out of the nesting hole, preened a little, then hopped back in, seeing no threat. And she'd witnessed a red-breasted nuthatch peering into a downy's nest hole: the female came out, looked around, and went back inside as the nuthatch continued leisurely down the trunk.

But within their own species, Louise noted that woodpecker relations were always strained. Hairys threatened hairys with drumming challenges and displays. Northern flickers stalked and chased intruding northern flickers. Yellow-bellied sapsuckers screamed at each other. Only occasionally did the confrontation progress to outright fighting; more often, the birds flew off in opposite directions, shrieking, flying erratically among the trees, shaking their feathers in a dramatic release of tension.

I witnessed similar behaviour recently when walking with a friend and her dog, Charlotte, in a local nature preserve. The paths we took were so well hidden that we didn't expect to meet anyone, but on this day, a couple was approaching with their dog. Charlotte was off-leash. My friend murmured, "Good dog, good dog," as Charlotte moved tentatively toward the other animal, sniffing and wagging her tail stiffly. My friend kept up her quiet, crooning encouragement until we were well past the other animal. Suddenly, Charlotte shook all over as if she'd just jumped out of a pond and barked loudly at nothing at all. Louise recorded the equivalent behaviour in birds: after a tense encounter, a bird would sing lustily, the way I might shout *Woo-hoo!* after avoiding a close call.

"Nervous tension that builds up under stress seems to be one of the most vital instruments in nature's self-regulatory systems," Louise concluded. "It tends to direct the living creature into channels of behaviour that in the strangest ways counteract upsetting pressures . . . and thus ultimately subserve the restoration of harmonious balance."

Louise was researching a major article on woodpeckers: a comparative life history of the four members of the Picidae family that nested in her forest—the downy woodpecker, the hairy woodpecker, the yellow-shafted (northern) flicker, and the yellow-bellied sapsucker. (The pileated woodpecker also nested in her woods, but since their territories are vast, there were too few to include in her study.)

A comparative life history was a new kind of writing for Louise, the most complex task she had set herself yet. Over the past twenty years, she had tried her hand at a variety of genres: long-form nonfiction in the Quints book; creative nonfiction in *The Loghouse Nest*; personal essays and poems published in local newspapers; environmental essays such as "Harmonious Association" and "Roadside Spraying"; narrative natural history articles for *Audubon Magazine* and *Farmer's*; and short, narrowly focused studies for scientific journals such as *The Wilson Bulletin* and *The Auk* that explored specific behaviours in red crossbills, red-eyed vireos, and black-capped chickadees. She had already written a comparative study of the nesting behaviour of two species of warblers, but a comparative study of the entire life history of four distinct species made those other projects look like a walk in a meadow.

The internet creates the impression that everything is known about everything, but in the natural world, this is far from true. The imperial woodpecker that lived in the pine and oak forests of northwestern Mexico went extinct at the end of the twentieth century without anyone having documented its life; what is known about this magnificent bird comes primarily from a 16-mm colour film shot in 1956 and discovered just ten years ago. The famous ivory-billed woodpecker, second in size only to the imperial, likewise went extinct (most people believe) before its complete life history was written: no nest was ever observed for the full length of incubation. Arthur Bent had published life histories of the downy and hairy woodpeckers and the northern flicker in 1939, but Louise's observations often differed from his reports. And the yellow-bellied sapsucker's life history had never been written at all.

Woodpeckers were among the first birds Louise identified in her forest, in part because they were so instantly recognizable with their distinctive black-and-white backs and bright red patches on the napes and pates of the males. Unlike the flitting warblers and the shy thrushes, woodpeckers jerked slowly up a tree trunk, propping themselves on stiffened tails to twist their heads this way and that, as if posing for positive identification. Their rhythmic flight—dip-dip-dip-drift—was distinctive, even from a distance, as was the *tap-tap-tap* of their chiselling beaks. And the downy and hairy woodpeckers were year-round residents: hardly a day went by, winter or summer, that she didn't see several flashing through her woods.

In Louise's first *Notes On Birds Around Our Home*, the hairy woodpecker was the seventh species that she identified. It was not the most populous on her property. Her year-end record for 1940 shows 134 magnolia warblers, 140 nighthawks, and an astonishing 112 Arctic three-toed woodpeckers (now called the black-backed woodpecker), but only 9 hairys.

The records she kept during that first decade of watching woodpeckers were detailed, but insufficient for the kind of scientific life history she was embarking on now. What she envisioned was a comparative ethology along the lines of Lorenz's work on water birds or a behavioural ecology like Margaret Nice's on the song sparrow. She was not especially interested in how the woodpeckers differed from each other. "Rather it is their alikeness that interests me most, how this or that reaction in given situations has developed in each, how their movements correspond, and so on. I am trying to analyze the derivation of these things, to find their intrinsic meaning, to learn the laws according to which the birds function."

Louise had already made some unique observations. She'd noticed a hierarchy within the four woodpeckers: downys were subordinate to hairys, and both downys and hairys were subordinate to the yellow-bellied sapsuckers. Hatchlings didn't always recognize their parents—they happily took food from any bird that offered it—and woodpecker parents willingly fed the young of other species. Yet they refused to feed other woodpecker hatchlings, no matter how loudly they begged. Within the Picidae, it seemed, parents recognized their own offspring and remained loyal only to them.

Unlike Lorenz and Margaret Nice, who gave up observing birds in the wild for the control of hand-raised birds, Louise observed only wild birds in their chosen territory, what the Nobel Prize–winning biologist Nikolaas Tinbergen called the "natural experiment." She didn't hide behind a blind; she simply made herself as inconspicuous as possible. This was a conscious choice, as she explained in the introduction to her study: "For my purposes the use of blinds caused observations to be focused too closely on a single detail or set of details. This frequently screens out the more distant stimulati that often account for many important and interesting variations in the birds' demeanour."

The birds in Louise's forest seemed to accept her as part of their environment. She made observations at the woodpecker nests and at her feeding station, which was located within the woodpecker territories and was visited by as many as forty to fifty woodpeckers in a day. Watching the crowd at the feeding station, she believed, was as good as observing the interrelationships and reactions of captive birds in a cage, with the added advantage that her birds' freedom of movement was not in the least curtailed.

The only invasive study aid she used was banding. In all, she banded 150 study birds: thirteen sapsuckers, seventy-seven hairy woodpeckers, and sixty downy woodpeckers. The northern flickers were shy: they nested in her woods, but they never visited her feeding station—not once in twenty-five years. In 1945, she managed to catch one in a water-drip trap set up in the trees about sixty metres from her feeders. This gave her one confirmed study subject. She studied many pairs at their nests, but without bands, she couldn't always positively distinguish males from females as they flew through the woods. (Males have a black mustache stripe; otherwise the sexes are identical.)

Like the watching women before her, Louise extolled time and patience as "surprisingly reliable allies in providing the answers to many seemingly insoluble questions. It seems to me that the keys to accurate interpretations of bird behaviour are seldom extracted from disconnected samples of activities, but are found secreted deeply within sequences of events whose correlations may be lost with missed installments."

Over the course of the seven years of her field study, from 1953 through 1959, Louise spent more than eight hundred hours in concentrated, systematic observation of her woodpeckers, about half that time on yellow-bellied sapsuckers and the other half divided among the northern flickers and the downy and hairy woodpeckers. She watched eighty-nine nests, from excavation through egg laying, incubation, and hatching to the fledging of the young, with most of her watches lasting three to seven hours. When she did dawn-to-dusk observations, she enlisted a neighbour, Hazel Petty, to spell her off. She recorded the birds' habits and territories, what they ate, how they foraged, their ritualized movements, posturings, and vocalizations. She noted the arrival and departure dates of the migrant sapsuckers and flickers and the ongoing activities of the resident hairys and the peripatetic downys.

In 1955, when she travelled to visit her mother, she watched several pairs of hairy woodpeckers excavate their nest cavities in late April, but by the time the eggs hatched, she was in Sweden. Len checked on the birds every day, making notes. Murray and Doris Speirs pitched in too. Near Thunder Bay they discovered a pair of hairys and took a day off from their own research to do a dawn-to-dusk observation, recording every activity at the nest as the birds flew back and forth feeding their young.

Then came that strange spring of 1956, when winter held on until early June, killing migrating songbirds by the thousands and disrupting the breeding of resident birds. "My woodpeckers are getting very upset because their urge to bore their holes for nests is affected by the cold weather. [The urge] is not strong enough to keep them at it. They make other holes, they get excited about other things, distracted from what they should be doing. It is a good thing that the forming of the egg in the females also belongs to the same mechanism as the urge to bore nest-holes, so that it is also delayed in developing. Else how awful if she should want to drop her egg where there is no nest. But everything works hand in hand, even the delays of seasons because of the weather."

The hairys were still at the top of her research list that cold spring, even though the weather delayed her usual seasonal routines to the point that, once the days warmed, she could work from before dawn until long after sunset and still not get everything done. Thinking that the bulk of her nest watching would be finished by the end of June, she had scheduled an appointment to have all her top teeth removed and replaced with a dental plate. Then just as her bird work reached its peak, she was diagnosed with a gastric ulcer caused, she believed, by her months of worry over her mother. Her father had died of a perforated ulcer, so she immediately went on a strict diet and eliminated all but essential activity.

She promised herself she wouldn't accept too many visitors that summer. Her forest with its charming log house had become a mecca not only for friends and colleagues but also for strangers who knew her through her articles and knocked at her door, having heard that Louise never turned anyone away. All were keen to stay to hear the dawn chorus. To accommodate the constant stream of overnight guests and keep them away from the log house, Len and Louise had dismantled Len's small house on Peak Hill and reassembled it close to the water at East Point, installing a cookstove and an outhouse to encourage self-sufficiency.

Despite her best intentions, Louise entertained guests for two out of every three days through the summer of 1956. Sixteen groups of people stayed at the House on the Point, many of them uninvited drop-ins. Over the Dominion Day long weekend, a birding party of four from Buffalo showed up. They came prepared to camp, but it rained so hard that Louise let them stay at the Point and invited them to use her own kitchen. While she was leading them on a long brisk walk through the forest to Talon chute, another party of four arrived unexpectedly from Toronto: Margaret Houston's son Jimmy, whom Louise hadn't seen in fifteen years, with his young family. By the time she returned from her walk, the rain had stopped so she pointed the Houstons to a grove of trees behind the garage, where they hung their hammocks. Both groups had brought food, and they invaded Louise's tiny kitchen to make supper.

Louise (centre) with visiting birders, Ora Richter (right) and friend

"Ten people cooking, washing dishes, talking, running around. Len was marvellous. He did everything and was everywhere to keep things going smoothly. I gave up and let the others cook and fuss. When I talked to one group, Len was with the other; when I talked to the other, Len was with the first . . . We talked birds and nature and conservation so that the roof puffed." The visitors were still chatting at the end of the weekend as Louise jumped in her car to drive to North Bay to address a local women's club.

In the midst of the summer chaos, Louise tried to work on her woodpecker study, gathering and analyzing data and reading every scientific study she could find in order to discover which conclusions supported and which conflicted with her observations, where the gaps in the knowledge lay. Her desk was piled with woodpecker observations to record, a scientific study to edit, scientific correspondence to answer, and journals to review for *The Auk*. The magazine had asked her to regularly scour two French ornithological journals and one Swedish and write reviews of relevant articles and books. The work was challenging: she spoke French and Swedish fluently but was still learning the scientific vocabulary peculiar to birds. "It is added work but it is worth it for not only do I contribute to the collective ornithological work in this special way but it makes me read these works of others with special attention and thoroughness, which is all very much to the good. This is one of the difficulties with me, to get enough time to read all I should read."

The disruptions were never-ending. Louise suspected something was wrong with the floor of the house when a pair of skunks moved into the crawlspace to birth their young. After the family departed, Len took a lantern into the basement and discovered the floor didn't need replacing—the beams were rotting away. Len and Louise wrangled cement blocks into the crawlspace to act as posts, then brought in huge beams, hoisting them onto the cement blocks. "Len did it with much groaning and moaning and puffing and spluttering and me holding and steadying here and there the best I could. He did a splendid job. We now have a floor that is non-shake, non-shivering, non-creaking, steady, stabile, well-balanced."

Outside, Len removed the rotting bottom logs and built a foundation of stones and cement, while Louise made her annual trek to Lake Talon in search of reindeer moss to tuck around the windows against winter drafts. As she reached for a perfect clump on a rock ledge, she slipped, and grabbing a branch to save herself, dislocated her shoulder.

"Luckily, I was able to get it back into place again and after having two more experiences of the same kind, I learned just which particular movements to avoid," she wrote to Doris. "But with all this I got the best moss for my winter windows I have had for years. So who am I to complain?"

That fall they drilled for water, a costly process that ended in disappointment. But in November, they brought electricity to the house. Louise worried through the entire process. Did they have to take down so many trees? How would they get the poles and the wires from the highway to their low house without disturbing the landscape? Where would they put the big ugly fuse box? And how on earth would they pay for it all, not only the poles and wires to the house, but the wiring inside the house, the outlets, and the lovely brass wall fixtures punched with tiny stars. (In the end, her mother sent a cheque for $2,000, about $20,000 in 2020.)

On the last Sunday of November, Louise and Len got up early instead of lazing in bed as they often did on Len's day off. They lit all their coal-oil lamps and read the whole day, their last chance to see words, the world, and each other in the light of a soft, natural flame, free of the urge to flick a switch.

At ten minutes after noon on Thursday, December 6, 1956, the lights came on in the log house. "That was the Banner Day, the first Banner Day," Louise wrote to her mother. "The second one will be, as I told you, when we sit down for the first time on our very own flush *dass* [toilet]. . . . We have lights in the kitchen and in the bedroom and a *kontakt* in the kitchen where we can put in the little radio I gave Len two years ago. Such brightness! Such music! But the brightness was the most amazing. We could see everywhere. And may I tell you that never in my life have I seen so much dirt in one place. I, who prided myself on being a rather clean housekeeper! . . . Scrub, scrub, scrub! Did I ever scrub the first two days after! . . . We have a flood-light over the back porch which is switched on inside. So that when we want to go out in the evening, switch and the whole backyard is flooded with light. Imagine what a marvellous thing this will be when we want to observe the nocturnal wildlife out there!"

On Christmas day, Louise did her annual "illumination," not with candles, but for the first time with electric bulbs, "every light ablaze in the wee Loghouse under the pines. Seen from the highway, you have no idea of the enchanting effect with the flood-lighted pines, the new-fallen snow, the outline of the house against the soft snow, and those amazing shadows cast across the lake by trees in a remarkable *stjårnmönster* [star pattern] immensely elongated. I stood looking at it for half an hour, it was such a beautiful sight."

That same fall, Bell Canada finally extended the telephone lines as far as Rutherglen, and shortly after, down the lane and into the log house.

"It is good and horrifying at the same time. The insulated cable that now connects our little loghouse with the outer world is symbolic of two things: 1) the break of solitude 2) the liaison with each other when apart and with other people with whom we may have contact. Good and bad. Or rather, bad and good." When the telephone was in the house but not yet connected, Len and Louise played at how their life might change, pretending to receive calls from Louise's publisher and Len's boss, asking him to work on Sunday, which he refused, emboldened by the ability to speak without being seen. "We are perfect idiots about it, and have such good fun. Simple pleasure, costs nothing except a good laugh."

For twenty years Louise and Len had lived alone in the woods, the pattern of their lives hardly different from that of the birds and animals around them, except that their nest had doors and windows and they knew how to make fire to light their way and keep them warm. Now the Loghouse Nest was buzzing with electric wires, with light, and with a telephone that rang incessantly for others on the party line and, occasionally, for Louise.

Louise was sixty-six by the time the woodpecker fieldwork was done. She had regained her strength and stamina. She was out in every weather, plowing through drifts on her snowshoes, standing in the cold, the wind, and rain, among successive clouds of black flies, deer flies, and mosquitoes, hardly noticing the weather or the ravenous insects, staring at the birds as they mated and excavated their nests, waiting for the young hunkered in their holes to poke out their heads. She was desperate not to miss a thing. Even the tiniest detail might provide a vital key to some hitherto unnoticed or unexplained behaviour.

"Some rituals are hard to analyze, but one grows wiser from year to year as the variations emerge in different situations." But most often, she despaired. "Very seldom I feel that I might some day be successful. Others do such wonderful work, with such thoroughness, elegance, and beauty. I often feel that I lack the power in some way. I am not persistent enough, not attentive enough, not sacrificing enough for it . . . Sometimes I feel that all my arguments are terribly naive, at other times I am blissfully convinced that I am a perfect genius. And that is a very agreeable state of mind in which to be, only it does not last, never."

By the late spring of 1960, the first sections of the woodpecker study were finished enough to send to Margaret for a critical read. Louise promised a finished draft to Doris and Murray, too, but "with Margaret, the behaviour expert, I must discuss every detail of my conclusions and *uppfattning* [perception] of the various aspects of behaviour," she explained. "If the created foundation is fairly sound, the finished result should be at least passable."

Margaret's critique was encouraging. Other than a few grammatical errors, she mostly wanted more detail, and here and there, more clarity. "What a wonderful study your woodpeckers are! I think you are wise in treating them all together as you do. You have such an immense amount of experience; you interpret your observations so skillfully and you write vividly. You are making a very great contribution."

Buoyed by Margaret's response, Louise wrote to the editors of the magazines that had been publishing her for fifteen years. By then, sixty-six articles had appeared in popular magazines and scientific journals. Now, she told the editors, she was taking a break.

"I have put aside all distracting activity, storywriting, even to cutting down reviewing to the most essential, in order to write my comparative study of the behaviour of four species of woodpeckers," she wrote to John Terres at *Audubon*.

Chapter by chapter, Louise moved forward, sifting the enormous bulk of notes and analyses into readable form. "At the moment it threatens to become a monster," she wrote to Doris. "I have always been a very slow worker, re-writing endlessly. Nevertheless, the snail is advancing, at times pushed on by *joie, fureur de joie de créer*. My days and sometimes my nights are filled with visions of woodpeckers, how they move, what they do, and thoughts upon the reasons why, the meaning of every move and gesture."

She was remarkably unhampered by her isolation. Margaret and Doris, who both had access to university libraries through their husbands' work, sent her boxes of books, journals, and reprints of scientific studies. Godfrey sent specimens and news of recent research. Her growing network of American and European ornithologists responded immediately to her queries. By then, she was a member of more than a dozen ornithological and naturalist organizations, each with its own publication and members willing to help. Every year, Doris gave her a membership to the Wilson Ornithological Society for Christmas, which meant Louise not only received *The Wilson Bulletin* but had access to the Wilson Ornithological Club Library at the University of Michigan.

Resources arrived from unexpected places. A "dear old gentleman friend," an expert on the green woodpecker who had visited Louise often when he lived in Deep River, now lived in England and was one of her regular correspondents. In a letter she mentioned how she wished she had a copy of Edward A. Armstrong's *Bird Display*, the classic introduction to bird psychology. "Lo and behold," she wrote to Doris, "long before I had time even to think, much less say Jack

Robinson, I had a letter telling me he had sent me his own precious copy . . . I am having a wonderful time with it."

Her reliance on friends and colleagues as a resource was profound. Margaret schooled her in scholarly practice, urging her to publish "Notes" about her observations so that others could cite them in their work, thus adding to the literature even before her study was finished. When Margaret sent abstracts from the Darwin Centennial Celebration, Louise found the text as impenetrable as a foreign language. She listed the most puzzling terms on the back of a card she sent Doris: "Perhaps Murray would be good enough to jot down, legibly please, their definitions if he has time one day! . . . I also wonder if Murray would give me a short written explanation on his views on [scholarly] authority, his stand with regard to it, why and wherefore? Ever since he first 'murmured' something about it, I have thought of it, but never caught on to the exact gist of it. I think that it would be very helpful for my thinking."

When Lawrence Kilham, a New England virologist and amateur ornithologist, published a long woodpecker study in *The Auk* before Louise had finished hers, Margaret was consoling. "It is a pity, but Kilham's work is very superficial. You are just the opposite. Your thorough, long-continued, meticulous studies and your brilliant insights into the meaning of the birds' behaviour cannot help but convince your readers. Indeed, your conclusions are neither far-fetched nor untenable. Not in any way unscientific."

Still, Louise was constantly irritated by her own shortcomings. "My thinking is not well enough trained in clarity and preciseness, and without a rather perfect *stomme* [framework], it is difficult to create a perfect form. Descriptive writing I feel that I do much better and with greater facility, although also here the first drafting is always, always like a hard *lort* [muck]."

Louise had begun the woodpecker study thinking it would be an article for a scientific journal, but as the project expanded in length and depth, Margaret started referring to it as Louise's monograph. In

academia, a monograph presents primary research and original schol-
arship at length—an in-depth discourse on a single subject. Because the
readership is one's scientific peers, a monograph is an important step in
establishing scholarly credibility. In Louise's day, Canadian publishers
of monographs were thin on the ground. The Canadian Wildlife Service
began a monograph series in 1960, and the Royal Ontario Museum had
been releasing monographs for some time, but Louise wanted her work
before an American audience of scientists.

For years, Margaret had been encouraging her to present the
results of her studies at an AOU conference, but Louise demurred.
She was much more comfortable sitting in the audience, learning, than
holding forth on stage. But in 1961, when the Wilson Ornithological
Society held its annual meeting at Britannia Beach, just west of
Ottawa, she decided to present a paper on sapsucker drumming—a
dry run for the monograph.

Louise was in a state by the time she got to Britannia Beach. Had
she got the research all wrong? Would these international bird experts
accept her interpretation of the yellow-bellied sapsucker's thirty-six
distinct drumming signals? Or her description of its ritual tapping
outside the nest, a ceremony never witnessed in other woodpeckers?
Luckily, her square-shouldered Nordic bearing effectively countered
her lack of confidence, and her presentation was a success. "I clearly
see that I must make a point of coming to these meetings more often,"
she wrote to Doris. "The personal contact in work like ours is of such
great significance and inspiration."

Another winter rolled around with its welcome solitude as Len
worked away from home six days a week. Louise was up by five, at
her typewriter by eight, the table in the sunroom littered with papers,
books, and notes that could remain undisturbed until Len returned on
the weekend. In the morning, all she had to do was pick up the thread
of her woodpecker thoughts exactly where she'd left off. "The hours
of the day rush by. I see no living person, only the birds flying by the
window, half noted by me in my trance of concentration."

*Louise writing on her second-hand Remington
at her homemade desk*

Before she sent each chapter to Margaret, she polished, and polished some more, determined to make her study not only absolutely
accurate but also highly readable. It was the part of the writing process she loved the most. "Revisions are my meat, I love to manipulate
words and meanings ad infinitum. Often you make the most wonderful
discoveries how things can be said in the pithiest manner."

Louise was closing in on seventy. Margaret's cheerleading—
"Remember the enthusiasm you evoked at WOS!"—kept her straining
forward, while Time pushed at her from behind.

"Neither you nor I can afford to play around with time too much,"
she wrote to Doris. "My woodpeckers and your grosbeaks represent

our major contribution to science and must be accomplished. . . . There is much to do. Time is filled to the brim with the greatest experience of all, the doing of something worthwhile."

At the end of June 1962, Louise took time out from her woodpeckers to attend the thirteenth International Ornithological Congress (IOC), the oldest and largest international meeting of ornithologists, held that year at Cornell University in Ithaca, New York. Since 1884, bird scientists around the world had been gathering annually to share their studies and develop research collaborations, but this would be the first time the IOC was hosted outside Europe. Margaret was there, as were Doris and Murray Speirs, Earl Godfrey, Jim Baillie, Amelia Laskey—altogether, 869 ornithologists from thirty-seven countries.

Among the Europeans Louise met was Heinz Sielmann, the German biologist and wildlife photographer who had just published a book, *My Year with the Woodpeckers*, on the making of the nature film that had made him famous overnight and earned him the nickname Mr. Woodpecker. His film *Carpenters of the Forest* was a portrait of some of Europe's most elusive Picidae species. Sielmann had defied scientific advice and inserted cameras inside woodpecker nest holes, capturing unforgettable footage of the birds feeding their young. The conversations between Louise and Sielmann must have been mutually exhilarating: both were passionate and iconoclastic; both had spent long hours with woodpeckers, not in aviaries but in the wild, integrating themselves into the birds' daily lives. "So I am not that backward," Louise wrote to Doris later. "Sielmann's and that of two other Germans are the best works on woodpeckers at present."

On Wednesday afternoon, Louise took a break and joined Margaret, the Speirs, Lars von Haartman, and Sylvia Hahn, art director at the ROM, on an all-day excursion to birding spots around Ithaca. Late Friday, she caught a bus from Ithaca to Toronto, then

Toronto to North Bay, missing out on the last day of presentations and the Saturday night banquet in order to be home for Len's day off. Doris sent her a rehash of the last day of events. "I would have enjoyed myself very much indeed up to the last," Louise confessed. "I would have liked to have much better opportunity to talk more seriously with many more people, Lars for one, Godfrey for another . . . One becomes a bit confused the first time at such a congress of interesting people that one forgets to act with sufficient purposefulness to achieve the contacts one would profit from most. However, for a novice, I feel that I did fairly well."

"You were the high point of the Congress for us," Margaret assured her. "Such enthusiasm, such keen judgments, such a rare spirit."

Louise's only regret was that she hadn't dared to give a paper.

"That I should have done."

When Louise finished a full draft of her woodpecker monograph, thoroughly critiqued by Margaret, she sent it to Oliver L. Austin, curator of birds at the Florida State Museum, for a second read. She'd met Austin at the Ithaca congress and had heard him at annual meetings of the AOU, where he was first vice president. He had just published *Birds of the World*, a luscious coffee-table book illustrated with three hundred of Arthur Singer's stunning paintings of birds. Austin had travelled with the navy through the South Pacific and the Hebrides, collecting birds in every port. After the war, he'd joined Admiral Byrd on an Antarctic expedition, before he and his wife, ornithologist and author Elizabeth "Silver" Austin, settled in Gainesville, Florida. He'd also written books on the birds of Korea and Japan and was responsible for introducing Japanese mist netting to North America as a means of trapping birds for banding.

Austin was both an expert and an enthusiast, soon to become editor of *The Auk*. He sent back a rousing evaluation. "To relieve your mind, your manuscript on the woodpeckers is a corking piece of work, well-researched, well thought out, well presented."

He had suggestions: the title could be improved, the introductory chapter should be expanded to include more about how she trapped her birds and conducted her observations, and about the landscape in which she did her field work. Her writing was fine, he said "right up there in the professional class," although she did occasionally use Swedish turns of phrase that "actually lends a great deal of charm." He offered specific suggestions for correcting her use of verbs and suggested she "haul all the scientific names out of your text . . . There is no getting around the fact that they stop the average reader's train of thought.

"Your main problem now is to find a publisher and frankly I don't think you are going to have too much trouble." Her manuscript, he felt, had the potential to be a commercial success on the scale of Nikolaas Tinbergen's *The Herring Gull's World* or David Lack's *The Life of the Robin*, both highly readable books by esteemed scientists.

Austin advised her to send the manuscript to commercial publishers, and at the same time, to contact the editor of a new monograph series the AOU was setting up to publish bird studies too long for *The Auk*. "I am so sure that he will jump at it that the only question is not 'if' but 'when.'" And if the AOU couldn't publish soon enough for her liking, she should submit her monograph to a series published by the Nuttall Ornithological Club, the oldest ornithological organization in the United States. "Count on me for backing if you need any recommendations," he concluded, closing with his trademark signature of a chubby running bird.

Austin's words "fell like balm upon my anxious heart." Because he wasn't a behaviourist, he had forwarded Louise's manuscript to a colleague, Franz Sauer, to comment on the science. Louise had already sent copies to Murray Speirs and to Olin Sewall Pettingill Jr., the naturalist, author, and filmmaker who had just become director of the

Cornell Laboratory of Ornithology. Murray, in his quiet, precise way, sent back six pages of critique. Pettingill was less thorough but equally enthusiastic, judging her study "beautifully written, precisely worded, full of solid information." And he was adamant that it be published as a scientific monograph. "I feel that if you were to modify ('popularize') the present work for McGraw-Hill or any other company interested in a trade book, you would be attempting an unfortunate straddle, ending up with a book that might not be popular enough and at the same time hurting its reception as a scientific work."

Louise was torn. The royalties and wide readership that came with commercial publication were tempting. "On the other hand, I am asking myself: If the monograph has real scientific value, would this not be to sacrifice a comparatively worthwhile scientific contribution for dollars? As a semipopular book, at least some of the data important to ornithology would probably have to be excluded."

In the end, Louise chose science over financial security. She worked through another draft, then with Oliver Austin smoothing the way, she submitted the manuscript to the AOU monograph series editor. She waited through the winter and spring, without a response. Assuming the delay meant rejection, she fired off a copy to the Nuttall. The very next day, she received a letter accepting her manuscript for the AOU Ornithological Monographs series, despite a reviewer's guarded comment that "in my opinion the descriptions become a little too flowery, too colourful in spots: well expressed but needing a bit of judicious streamlining to suit the needs of a strictly scientific journal."

As it happened, Lippincott, the prestigious old publishing house where her former *Audubon Magazine* editor John Terres now worked, rejected the manuscript as a popular book. The Nuttall Ornithological Club turned it down too. So Louise signed with the AOU. After two more years of editorial back-and-forth, *A Comparative Life-History Study of Four Species of Woodpeckers* was published in the spring of 1967, No. 5 in the AOU Ornithological Monographs. It didn't look like much: no shiny illustrated cover, no picture of the author or blurbs from

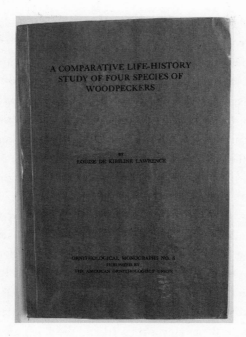

Louise's woodpecker monograph, published by the AOU, 1967

famous watchers. But between those soft, plain blue covers were 156 pages that represented twenty-five years of banding and daily records, seven years of focused scientific study, and seven years of writing. Her ideas, her methods, her conclusions had passed the acid test for original scholarly ornithological work. At seventy-three, Louise had at last made a permanent contribution to the science of birds.

Kudos poured in from ornithological colleagues and friends. Reviews appeared in every major ornithology journal, written by the most respected ornithologists. Godfrey, whose bird bible, *The Birds of Canada*, had been published the year before, reviewed it for *The Canadian Field-Naturalist*. Alexander Skutch reviewed it for *The Wilson Bulletin*. David Ligon, a young scientist who would go on to write *The Evolution of*

Avian Breeding Systems, concluded in his review in *The Auk*, "Perhaps the greatest contributions of this work are those dealing with breeding behavior. The descriptions and illustrations of the 'aggressive-social' displays of each species are highly useful and clearly indicate the relationship of aggressive and courtship behavior. As descriptions of actual pair formation are not often reported, Mrs. Lawrence's observations are important contributions . . . In summary, this work is an important contribution to the knowledge and understanding of woodpecker biology."

Other reviewers praised her interpretation of woodpecker communication through drumming and her theory, convincingly argued, that light, with its attendant warmth, was an important factor in choosing the location of a nest cavity entrance. Most of all, the study was a shining example of the value of prolonged bird-life studies.

At the AOU meeting held that fall in Toronto at the ROM, Louise and her monograph were the centre of attention. Its publication was announced to the assembly, only the fifth in the new series, and it was promoted in the books area. I am surprised she didn't present a paper. Perhaps she submitted and was rejected: the sessions that year were drawn heavily from the laboratory—studies of captive rails and caged scrub jays, zinc in mallards, a comparative study of avian hemoglobins. Not a single observational life history.

As usual, Louise didn't feel she took sufficient advantage of having so many eminent ornithologists in one room, even though she now knew many of them personally. "Thinking back, I am not very adept at making good use of the get-togethers of these meetings," she wrote to Doris. "I missed so many, saw them, thought I would see them again for a good talk. But that time never came in the constant circulation."

It didn't matter. They came to her. Inspired by the monograph, students from Canada and the United States arrived on her doorstep, keen to meet her. Ornithologists interested in woodpeckers wrote to ask her advice. Oliver Austin sent her thick manuscripts to referee. She was in demand as a book reviewer and as a manuscript reader, just as, a decade earlier, she had asked the same favour of Margaret, Godfrey, and the Speirs.

Fifty-three years later, Louise's monograph is still cited on Cornell's Birds of North America website. I suspect she would be surprised by that, and pleased. In the moment, however, she barely registered the acclaim, except for the boost it gave to her new project, a manuscript she'd been writing for twenty years, intended not solely for scientists—for everyone who loved birds.

14

With High Heart

On a chilly morning in late spring Louise entered her woods. It was 3 a.m., the hour of the wolf. For Louise, this time between the dead of night and the first blush in the eastern sky was the "most enchanting and mysterious moment" of the day. "A soft, misty light prevailed, the delicate luminosity of the night, not enough to see but enough to surmise the outlines of the trees and the opening in the woods through which the trail led."

A whippoorwill called once. Then again. And again. Louise counted the calls, then pulled out her notebook: thirty-seven *whip-poor-will*s. A faint streak of dawn appeared at the horizon; a light wind picked up from the west. A nighthawk made its final booming dive over the lake before going to roost on a horizontal branch of a tall poplar. The olive-backed thrush, the last of the crepuscular singers, gave its final, ringing call.

A pause, as if the curtain of night had been drawn, then the first notes of the dawn chorus, a symphonic roll call of the birds waking in the Pimisi woods. A veery, then a wood thrush trilled the light up into the sky. A purple finch flew past with "a burst of song sweeter than honey." In the distance, a rose-breasted grosbeak sang an aria. From the top of a green spruce, a robin. By four o'clock, Louise could see without her flashlight. A great blue heron flapped overhead, giving its sore-throat croak.

Exactly nine minutes before sunrise, at 4:22 a.m., the red-eyed vireo dropped its first phrase into the swell of birdsong. Louise listened and looked, guided by the song that never stopped, until her binoculars fixed on the bird in the crown of a trembling aspen, hopping twig to twig. "His bill opened and shut, his throat bubbled, and his crest rose lightly and fell with the rhythm of his melody." The bird sang and sang, a light pause between phrases, like a thoughtful robin.

Between five and six that morning, the red-eye sang 2,155 songs—at its speediest, seventy songs a minute. This bird wasn't monotonous; it was breathless. It sang and sang—6,063 songs in the first three hours. Although the vireo was somewhat nondescript, easily camouflaged and with a preference for treetops, it was easy to follow. Louise trailed after the music, whacking through the underbrush, hopping across snowmelt streams, clambering up the rocks of the Southeast Slope and through the Fern Dell.

The red-eye fed while it sang, often trilling with its mouth full. It stopped once to chase away another vireo. After four hours of constant singing, it stopped to preen and feed for half an hour, then started up again, although at a more leisurely pace—a mere thirty-eight songs a minute. By noon, the vireo had sung 14,027 songs.

The bird kept singing. At the height of the day, when the forest fell almost silent, Louise could still hear it, although the songs came more and more slowly. In the late afternoon, it rested again, then resumed its concert. By the time the sun was sinking, the bird was high in another aspen, moving perch to perch, dropping sweet notes into the still evening air.

"Lovely and clear, simple and eloquent, his songs and intonations continued to reach me from the top of the aspen. Hitherto his voice had been unaffected by his day-long singing. But now, as if he had reached the end and only with reluctance gave in, his songs shortened and were often just softly whispered. Between 6:00 and 6:13, my vireo sang 44 songs. Two minutes later, with wings closed, he dropped from the crown of the aspen into a thick stand of young evergreens. From there, like an echo of his day's performance, he gave six more songs. Then he fell silent and was heard no more."

1951 NEST D 1		Red-eyed Vireo	Area 3
Jun 22	HATCHING DAY		09.30 Nest found in Populus trem,
	EGG 1	YOUNG 2	the top of which last winter's
	NESTLIFE		snow had bent down to the height
			10 ft.
" 24	DAY 2		11.50 Female on nest.
" 25	" 3		10.35 Female on nest.
" 26	" 4	YOUNG 3	08.35 Checked.
" 29	" 7	" "	08.30 Checked.
Jul 1	" 9		Young have disappeared. Suspect
			predator Red Squirrel.

One of hundreds of bird index cards Louise used to track her study subjects

The sun set one hour and thirty-nine minutes later.

The vireo had been singing for six minutes shy of fourteen hours. Altogether, it sang a remarkable 22,197 songs. Just as remarkable was the woman who had tramped through the bush sunrise to sunset, nibbling on her sandwiches, squatting to pee, pumping her insect sprayer into the bush immediately around her to keep the black flies at bay, shrugging off the coat she needed at dawn, wrapping it around her waist at noon, and hauling it back up onto her shoulders as the sun sank, binoculars always at the ready, notebook in hand, ear cocked, counting, counting, counting . . .

When Calvert Noble-Rollin, the British amateur ornithologist and dawn chorus specialist, telephoned Louise to ask her to make an all-day study of some special bird activity, she immediately thought of the red-eyed vireo. Noble-Rollin held the record for an all-day bird-song count: a European blackbird he'd followed had sung 6,140 songs, dawn to dusk. The red-eye, she was sure, could do better.

The red-eyed vireo was one of Louise's favourite birds. Its smooth grey elegance appealed to her. As did the deliberate way it moved—not slow or sluggish, as it was usually described, but "with a fluid kind of sobriety." She took issue, too, with the descriptors applied to its song: monotonous, repetitious, preacher-like. She preferred subtle, trilling, tireless.

But how tireless, exactly? The bird seemed to sing all day, but when exactly did it start? When did it stop? What was the relationship between its singing and what was going on in its world? She detected nuance in its phrases where others heard monotony: what caused these subtle shifts of tone and phrasing? What was this bird saying? It was answers to these questions, not the breaking of a record, that drove her to the all-day count.

Louise had begun making notes on the red-eye in 1940 and had done a short nesting study in 1945, but in 1949 she decided to concentrate on the species. This was early in her relationship with Margaret Morse Nice. They discovered they both had nesting red-eyes under observation that summer, although the attempts of Margaret's two pairs had ended badly. Louise had five pairs under observation. One pair lost both their first and second clutches to predators and were working on their third; the other four pairs successfully fledged their young. When Margaret saw young being fed by parents in early September, Louise told her that her third-nesting pair was doing exactly that too. Margaret asked if she could use Louise's experience in the popular piece on red-eyes she was writing for the *Illinois Audubon Bulletin*; Louise asked if Margaret would critique her study before she tried to get it published.

"The more I am working with the red-eye," wrote Louise, "the more enthralled I am with this beautiful and interesting bird. When I first started really to concentrate on them, I did it with the thought of 'know thy most common birds first.' Now I would not have missed one hour spent with these interesting 'commoners.'"

Margaret sent Francis Herrick's *Wild Birds at Home* to Louise—it contained a description of red-eye nest-building—as well as a reprint of the only article she knew of on the red-eye, "and this doesn't give much." Louise described the bird's songs as she understood them, which prompted a conversation on individual versus species song that carried on through several letters.

The red-eye typically arrived in Louise's woods shortly after the middle of May, when the pin cherry and the trillium were in full bloom and the trembling aspens were just about to unfold their leaves. The males came first; the females a week or so later. Inevitably, they settled on the Southeast Slope, forested with aspens and birch and thickets of young growth. Within their chosen territory, each pair staked out a nest area for the female and a song area for the male, thick with tall deciduous trees with broad crowns.

Other observers had reported that both parents incubated the eggs, although no evidence was given for the claim. This intrigued Louise, given her experience with the Canada jays. Over the course of several years, she had watched nine red-eyed vireo nests, accumulating a hundred hours of observations. The pattern was always the same. When the female settled onto her eggs, the male withdrew like a nineteenth-century father. He travelled alone through his song area, singing and feeding, his singing during these days at its most persistent. Meanwhile, his mate sat in stillness on her nest. Suddenly, the male would sing very loudly, then stop. The female would perk up. She'd hop to the rim of the nest and fly to him in his song area, where he would feed her.

The song, Louise concluded, was not a musical overindulgence, some sort of virtuoso performance. The male's constant *cheer-o-wit*, *cheer-ee, chit-a-wit* was a means of staying in touch with his mate, like an endless series of texts saying, *I'm here, I'm here, I'm here*. His pauses were not a mark of exhaustion or a break to feed himself; they were a signal to the female to come, lunch was ready, let him take care of her for a while. Their roles were sharply defined, but interconnected: red-eye parents communicated through song, its sudden cessation a cue for courtship feeding—a behaviour never before recorded in red-eyed vireos.

There can't be many human records that have stood for more than half a century, but Louise's tally of 22,197 red-eyed vireo songs in a single dawn-to-dusk count has never been bested and is still cited in scientific literature. I recently came across a fulsome description in *Extreme Birds*, a glossy international anthology of avian feats.

An avian feat, indeed. But all prospective red-eye dads sing non-stop; only Louise charted their songs.

Like most of us, Louise was drawn to birds through their music: the sweet, orchestral dawn chorus; the pure, simple fluting of a wood thrush deep in the underbrush; the hilarious imitations of the catbird.

I, too, lie awake in the spring dawn listening. I have no more inclination to supply words to the music of a bird's trill than to the opening phrases of Beethoven's ninth. But Louise was driven to transcribe the vocalizations of birds into a written language that humans could read and reproduce. The red-eyed vireo's song invariably ended in *huit, huit*; its call was a whiney *meeyah, meeyah*. The red-breasted nuthatches, she said, "talked through their noses." Roger Tory Peterson had described their call as *ank* or *enk*, but Louise suggested *ein-ein-ein*, pronounced as in French (think of Proust's *madeleine*). The song of the black-throated green warbler was a memorable *cheese, cheese-little-cheese*. The boreal chickadee half-whistled, half-warbled *eet-tulu*, sung at about the same pitch as the song of the black-capped, "with the ending trill, quite musical and of a liquid quality, uttered rather like an afterthought." The downy woodpecker vocalized more than the *whinny* and *tchick* commonly mentioned by observers. Louise counted nine at least—location calls, a calling-out call that brought the sexes together, a challenging call, aggressive-social notes, courtship notes, contact notes, the musical twitters of the nestlings, a low-intensity alert call for when a mammal, say, wandered into their territory, and a high-intensity alarm for imminent danger, such as a merlin within hunting distance of the nest tree.

Too many Berries

Birds sketched by Louise as she watched and listened

To Louise these calls and songs didn't sound like indiscriminate chattering. Nor did she believe they were a bird's expression of joy or fear or loneliness, human emotions that birds may or may not share. Song, she believed, was language. Downy woodpecker calls that humans could barely hear and that pretty much sound the same to our ear are perfectly understood by woodpeckers. "Although the observer may have difficulty in separating one note from the other, the woodpeckers do not share this difficulty," Louise wrote in her monograph. "The recognition of the calls is essential to understanding the downy woodpecker's behaviour under varying circumstances." Louise developed her own phonetic renderings for the calls of the downy and dozens of other birds in her woods, setting out to learn birdsong language, just as she had learned the language of their ritual displays of bill-lifting and head-shaking, the shivering at coitus, and the zipping among the trees for no apparent reason other than the release of tension.

She recorded five distinctly different songs in the red-eye vireo repertoire: A courtship song "a mellow warble that reminded me of the song of the rose-breasted grosbeak. Sometimes it was quite prolonged, at other times abbreviated, and every time I heard it, it was given *sotto voce*." And four song-phrase themes that were sung so distinctly that she classified them separately: the advertising song, loud clear and slow in tempo; the alert song, also slow but with long intervals between the notes; the contact song, sung at high speed for long periods to stay in touch with a nesting mate; and the signal or nest song, a loud invitation to the female to leave her nest.

When *The Canadian Field-Naturalist* published her observations on the red-eyed vireo, it was the first detailed nesting study of the species, the first to accurately document incubation dates, the first reliable account of male and female roles at the nest, the first parsing of its song, and the first explanation of the so-called monotonous singing of this remarkable bird. Bill Gunn, an avian acoustic expert, told her, "this study will always rank in the forefront of life-history and behaviour studies. [Your song breakdown] strikes me as a brilliant piece of observation and deduction that could only come as the result of a tremendous amount of intensive observation and study."

For twenty years, through more than a dozen studies like this one, Louise had been working on a book manuscript with the working title

Birds Alive, which eventually evolved to *The Lovely and the Wild*. Louise referred to it simply as *Lovely*.

Today *Lovely* would be called a memoir: a personal tale of one woman's love affair with birds. But in Canada in the late 1940s and 1950s, memoir hardly existed. The first-person narratives that were published tended to be about war, politics, or travel. Books about nature were rare; personal accounts, even rarer. When Louise wrote the woodpecker monograph, Margaret Nice's song sparrow study was her exemplar. But for *Lovely*, there were no models for what she envisioned: a nature book that was scientifically accurate and authentic, but not at the expense of story, for it was narrative, she believed, that would expand her specific observations into universal truths about the workings of the natural world.

The Lovely and the Wild opens with Louise's first memories of birds, watching them through the dining room window of her family's Swedish villa, tramping the fields with her father and his conservationist friends, then settling onto a piece of land in Canada that in many ways was that Scandinavian estate in miniature, land where she began to notice Canadian birds, learning their names, recording her observations.

Louise worked on *Lovely* alongside the woodpecker monograph. At the same time, she was indexing her twenty years of daily bird observation records. "A necessary chore," she told Doris who had been with her the day she began that daily practice in June 1944. "A great amount of good material therein entombed has been brought to light again, some good writing, some fine records, some startling novelties that I had forgotten entirely." As well as reminding her of her apprenticeship as a naturalist, thumbing through decades in a matter of weeks gave her a broad perspective on the changes in the bird life of her forest.

In the spring of 1964, John Terres, now a book editor at Lippincott, wrote to Louise asking for biographical data for an encyclopaedia of American women in ornithology he was preparing. (Louise was the only Canadian woman he contacted; she suggested he also include

Doris Speirs and Margaret H. Mitchell, the first professional woman ornithologist in Canada, who had worked at the ROM.) Terres was a dedicated conservationist. In 1958, he had convinced the managers of the Empire State Building to turn off its huge spotlight between September and November to protect migrating birds. And in 1955, after he spotted a pair of ivory-billed woodpeckers in Florida, he had told no one, in order to give the birds a chance to reproduce in peace. When he and Louise renewed their correspondence, he urged her to write about the decline in woodland songbirds in their northern breeding ground at Pimisi Bay.

"I am thinking of incorporating some of my data on the vanishing of the warblers into the new book," she told him. "But it would be impossible to pinpoint the cause, for there seems to me to be a great number of them, man's own expansion not the least, with all its implications and altering every last corner of this earth."

Louise at the launch of The Lovely and the Wild, *1968*

By the mid-1960s, every time she watched an ovenbird or least fly-catcher, she couldn't help but think, Is this the last? Am I like the person who unwittingly witnessed the last passenger pigeon or Carolina parakeet in the wild? Her annual summaries clearly traced the decline; in *The Lovely and the Wild*, she pondered what those losses might mean.

"Whatever dies and disappears releases new space and opportunity for other forms of life," she wrote. New species arrived to take up the territories emptied of warblers, flycatchers, and thrushes. European starlings, never before seen in her forest, had suddenly appeared; the number of blue jays was on the rise. "Twenty years ago, one or two pairs nested in our forest in the summer and hardly more than half a dozen wintered in the area. Nowadays forty to fifty of them commonly converge upon the feeding station during the winter and noisy companies of six to eight families course the forest in the summer after the first broods fledge." Evening grosbeaks, which had been sporadic visitors, had become permanent residents. Red-winged blackbirds and brown-headed cowbirds, once seen only in clearings, "overrun the forest in large noisy parties, disturbing the peace."

Yet even with these raucous, tuneless invaders, Louise questioned her own responses. "If I had never seen the unassuming elegance of the red-eyed vireo, the vivid guise of the Blackburnian warbler, the redstart's ethereal displays or heard the singing of the veery and the hermit thrush; if I had never known the vast variety of woodland birds—might I not have looked quite differently upon these other innocents, the red-wing with its scarlet epaulets, the grackle in its rich iridescence, and even the cowbird in softest beaver brown and shiny black? Might I not then have thought them birds of striking beauty and overlooked the stridor of their voices? And having no others to compare them with, would I not then willingly have conceded their roles to be as important as those of any other birds?"

I try to think like Louise in the early morning when the Caspian terns squawk over our roof like tortured feral cats. It is a beautiful bird, the largest of the terns, porcelain white with ink-dipped wings, a startling tangerine bill, and a stunt-flier trick of taking high dives into the lake and swooping straight up with a fish pinched in its bill. These birds used to be unheard of on Lake Ontario, but a breeding population has established itself on top of our city's entertainment complex—their nests are little more than a random collection of sticks— and in the fall, dozens fly overhead morning and night, squawking their strident call, juveniles trailing behind, begging in high-pitched whistles. I want to love them as much as I love the song sparrows, but it's not easy.

"Change and evanescence, constant and continuous! Who am I to protest or to wish it differently? How can I judge which bird, which beast, is best, the worthiest, the blessed? . . . Who is the good, the bad, the one with claim upon survival more rightful than another's? Are these relationships not all dependent on proportion rather than identity?"

Louise was at her happiest immersed in this book. "I love to think of you 'writing with high heart' on *The Lovely and the Wild*, with all your beloved birds about you," wrote Margaret. Yet toward the end of *Lovely*, the writing is tinged with sadness and not only because the decline of the songbirds was breaking her heart. In the fall of 1964, the road that bordered her property was widened. Len and Louise lost a swath of forest to the project; they were forced to demolish their garage by the roadside and build another closer to the house. "What they have done to the Green Woods defies description," she wrote to Doris, "and what has happened to my beloved Beaver Lake where I would go to see the birds that once were, but are no longer where they used to be, I hardly dare contemplate. Going along the highway, I now find the edge of the forest far distant." When work on the new highway began, Louise moved with her writing to the House on the Point. "The noises were hair-raising and too disturbing for words. But down there the quietude of the forest reigned and I was able to do fairly good work, I got five chapters on the book finished and the sixth started.

"It is a good thing to be old, for the greater devastations, which are bound to come in spite of all our efforts of so-called conservation, we shall not see—in toto at any rate."

Contrary to her usual habit of sending draft manuscripts to colleagues for review, no one saw *The Lovely and the Wild* before she sent it to a publisher. She had heeded Sewall Pettingill's counsel about keeping the woodpecker study strictly scientific. As well as being director of the Cornell Lab, Pettingill was also author of ten nature books and a reader for the McGraw-Hill Book Company in New York. When she finished *Lovely* in the fall of 1966, she sent it first to him.

"I can say in all honesty that your manuscript has thrilled me to the core. The way you make words flow, the pictures you create, the feeling you engender, and the solidly factual information you work in! Realizing that English is not your native language, I marvel at what you have accomplished. Indeed, you make me feel most humble for I could not achieve in fifty more years your mastery of English even though it is the only language in which I can speak and write."

Pettingill sent the manuscript to Corton Garruth, an editor at McGraw-Hill, with his endorsement: "This is the finest manuscript of its kind that I have ever had the privilege to peruse. Beautifully written, an absolute joy to read, and chock full of good natural history! Mrs. Lawrence is one of Canada's eminent ornithologists. I truly believe that we have a prizewinner!"

Almost immediately, McGraw-Hill offered Louise a contract. Pettingill was chuffed. Privately, he confided to Margaret Nice: "The editors at McGraw-Hill and I think we have another Rachel Carson."

The comparison with Rachel Carson is not surprising. Publishing houses, cursed with eyes in the backs of their heads, are always looking for repeats of yesterday's bestsellers. Since the release of *Silent Spring* in 1962, they'd undoubtedly been trolling for a Rachel Carson clone. And Pettingill was right: Rachel and Louise were alike in many ways. Both women were early ecologists. Both bore witness to the beauty and integrity of the natural world. Both believed passionately that humans are only one small part of nature, not masters of it, and both were convinced of the dire consequences of the chemicals humans had been indiscriminately dumping in such quantities into the biosphere since the Second World War. Louise had noticed species decline fifteen years before *Silent Spring* was released. As early as 1950, she had linked roadside chemical spraying to the demise of songbirds. Fundamental to most of her articles through the 1950s was the notion that nature's interacting and interdependent systems were essential, with an intricate logic all their own. And Louise agreed with Rachel that "there can be no separate literature of science" because "the aim of science is to discover and illuminate truth," which is also the aim of literature.

Where Louise and Rachel Carson differed was that while Louise was radical in her thinking, she was no social revolutionary. Perhaps it was the natural reticence of her breeding or her years alone in the bush, but she was not a person to thrust herself forward in a crowd, let alone take to the hustings. Rachel Carson's *Silent Spring*, on the other hand, was a call to action, a challenge to the chemical industry and to the public to question the assumption of human dominion over the Earth. *The Lovely and the Wild* arose from a similar philosophy and scientific underpinnings, but its message of impending environmental disaster and its plea for human awareness was delivered through a poignant, personal account of vanishing bird life on one small piece of land.

Walter Clemons was assigned as Louise's editor at McGraw-Hill. Clemons was a skilled editor and a fiction writer himself, author of a collection of stories that had won the Prix de Rome. According to his lifelong friend, Eudora Welty, "he was filled with appreciation of what writers were trying to do." He returned the edited manuscript to Louise with a detailed note: "You will notice that Chapter IX is hardly marked at all—a comma added here and there, a change of one or two words—and this is typical of all the earlier chapters. You have a beautifully pure and precise descriptive style that needs no editorial tampering." He noted that she used commas rather too sparingly, something I admit I find irritating in her books, but Clemons was right that the practice "gives an effect of swiftness and lightness most appropriate to your notations of the birds' behaviour." Only the final chapters needed work, he said. "Here I sometimes found longer sentences confusing and syntax difficult to follow. I believe that the urgency of your feelings about what is happening to the region you love has sometimes led you to overload too many thoughts into a single sentence."

Louise welcomed Clemons's comments. As always, she grasped with pleasure any advice that might improve her scientific method or her English usage. "The blue pencil has therefore seldom disturbed me, quite the contrary. It has often annoyed me by showing up the rough passages and the overloaded sentences which I then feel I should have been able to see and to polish off myself before they got to the editor. To write descriptions is like painting. To write more or less abstract thought I find difficult. I become terribly involved, and in the excitement all too often unconsciously fall back upon the idiom of my native language, which makes for confusion."

But oh, she did love the English language. "There are many languages the sounds of which are far more melodious; Russian, for instance as I have known it in Pushkin's poems and Dostoyevski's prose; far more elegant, like the French, in whatever way it is spoken and written; far more heroic, as contained in some of the manful Scandinavian and Icelandic epics. But none of them is distinguished by the extraordinary pliancy of English, this flexibility that allows for the finest nuances, for the perfection of meaning, for ways to turn a sentence into a work of art."

After their initial spate of enthusiasm, months passed without a peep from McGraw-Hill. Then suddenly, Louise was informed that an artist had been hired—a young, unknown Canadian. She was devastated. She'd hoped her stories would be illustrated by the likes of Louis Agassiz Fuertes, maybe Francis Lee Jaques or Arthur B. Singer, renowned American wildlife artists who ensured the fame of every book they undertook. Even more distressing was the news that the publication date had been moved from the fall of 1967 to the following spring, leaving her without income for yet another year.

Clemons was consoling: *The Lovely and the Wild* was scheduled for release in the season when people were most aware of songbirds. "I would not like to see so sensitive a work lost in the flood of pre-Christmas publishing."

Louise gave in on the publication date and eventually on McGraw-Hill's choice of illustrator, too, although reluctantly. "I believe that a book by a Canadian author to be published in the States would gain by being illustrated by one of the many outstanding American artists," she wrote to Clemons. "To me the American public is the most important, and it is really for this reason that I submitted the book to an American publisher in the first place."

But Glen Loates was a prodigy nature painter. At the age of eleven, he painted the iconic yellow daffodil that would represent the Canadian Cancer Society for forty years. At eighteen, he produced the Federation of Ontario Naturalists' Christmas card, which led to a colour spread of his paintings in *The Canadian* magazine. In the fall of 1965, the Royal Ontario Museum mounted Loates's first solo exhibition, which drew the attention of McGraw-Hill. Their choice of Loates proved prescient: in 1968, just as Louise's book was released, the Canadian Broadcasting Company (CBC) aired an award-winning documentary on the twenty-three-year-old Loates called *Colour It Living*. That same year, he won the Royal Philatelic Award for Canada's first full-colour postage stamp, the "Gray Jay."

When Louise received Loates's sketches for *Lovely*, she rather liked his style, which reminded her of the drawings of Francis Jaques. But the illustrations were impressionistic, and Louise was a stickler for authenticity. She complained that his squirrel was too big for a pine squirrel and the pose of the white-winged crossbills was off. The weasel should have a short tail; the long-tailed didn't live in her woods. There was a bird with a dark head and neck that didn't look like either a robin or an oriole, or any other recognizable species. And the birds at the feeder were much too close together. "They would surely fight and be fully occupied with chasing each other instead of eating. The creeper, a very shy and diffident bird, is altogether out of place in the midst of such a mob." Was it too late to find another illustrator? she asked Clemons. "It is tempting to give a talented young man a chance," she wrote to Pettingill, "though not at the expense of the book."

But McGraw-Hill held firm. Louise met with Loates to discuss the most egregious errors. He was young and cocky; she was old and demanding, more than a little querulous. His sketch of the Ottawa Valley should be a scene of the Mattawa River where she paddled almost every day, she insisted. When she got home, she sent Clemons photographs of herself in a canoe on Pimisi Bay, along with her detailed critique of his drawings and comments from Sewall Pettingill and George Miksch Sutton, the Cornell curator and bird artist Hewitt had brought to Pimisi in the mid-1940s. Sutton praised Loates's style, which he found "decidedly free and deft and I wouldn't want to rob it of these qualities," although he noted that Loates had a tendency to make his birds big-headed or thin-bodied or both, "and when it's both, it can be really objectionable." Louise included a sharp note to Clemons urging him to insist on the corrections.

Alas, her registered package never made it to New York. The mailbag was stolen, and the post office held out little hope that the contents would be retrieved.

By the time she realized what had happened, it was already the end of October and production was moving swiftly. Loates refused to make more changes since, in the absence of receiving the promised references from Louise, he had already produced final drafts. Clemons suggested they eliminate the most problematic drawings and publish the others as "impressionistic sketches rather than scientific renderings." In the finished book, the weasel is still long-tailed and the dark-headed bird remains a mystery, but no feeder shows a mob of birds and two figures that I can imagine are Louise and Len paddle placidly upstream between what look for all the world like the cliffs of Talon chute.

On March 8, 1968, Louise finally held *The Lovely and the Wild* in her hands. "A beautiful book," she wrote to Clemons.

For the first time, her work was enthusiastically reviewed in more than twenty American newspapers, as well as the *New York Times Book Review*, where Brooks Atkinson, a retired theatre critic notorious as the conscience of New York theatre, compared a trio of nature books, including Louise's. "One qualification for distinction in bird watching is a good mind. All three of [these] bird watchers would achieve distinction in any field that interests them." Louise was, he wrote, a "bird watcher of conspicuous skill . . . Among many perceptive observations

The Lovely and the Wild, *winner of the 1969 John Burroughs Medal*

there is one in which Mrs. Lawrence describes the loss of self that is involved in bird watching. The silence, the stillness, the attempt to be invisible over a long period of time changes the proportions of her life and gives her access to another world: 'I am out, far out,' she writes, 'a small speck in an immense field.' In her selflessness as well as in the keenness of her eyes and mind, Mrs. Lawrence is an extraordinarily integrated human being."

What tickled Louise especially was Brooks's comparison of her work with that of Isak Dinesen, "who was also an indomitable woman." Dinesen was the pen name of the Baroness Karen von Blixen, a cousin of Louise's mother born half a century before Louise and famous for her memoir, *Out of Africa*. Both Louise and Karen were the black sheep of their ancient families, adventuresses who found home thousands of miles from where they were born. Both were extraordinarily resourceful and realistic, what Nietzsche would call "yea-sayers." Karen was also deeply attached to her mother, addressing her in the same loving style as Louise, which makes me wonder if this was common to their class and culture. And both wrote in English rather than the language they were born into, their prose exhibiting a similar striving for the most accurate word, perfectly apt, but often not a choice a born English-speaker would make.

In the first month, *Lovely* sold almost three thousand copies in the United States. Letters poured in from friends. "Your book is truly an inspiration," enthused Dorothy Luther, who had studied ornithology at Cornell and was chief naturalist at a state park in Indiana. "A perfectly wonderful book," Margaret wrote. "Your dedicating it to me came as a perfect and thrilling surprise. It makes me very proud and happy, beloved friend."

Clemons arranged a full-page ad in *Audubon*, to be run in the same issue as the review, featuring endorsements from top Canadian and American nature writers and ornithologists.

"A remarkable book by a remarkable woman," wrote Roger Tory Peterson. In the letter that accompanied the blurb, Peterson admitted to Clemons, "I had known of her conscientious ornithological work, but I had not realized what a splendid writer she is."

Fred Bodsworth, who had just stepped down as president of the Federation of Ontario Naturalists, had made his name as a literary naturalist with his novel *The Last of the Curlews*, published in 1955, and *The Sparrow's Fall*, which came out just before Louise's book. "I read [*The Lovely and the Wild*] with envy as well as delight," he wrote privately to Louise, "and I guess from another writer that is about the ultimate in praise."

It is always a blow to a writer when an editor departs before a book is fully launched into the world, especially an editor such as Clemons, whom Louise found congenial, skillful, and entirely trustworthy. Yet just as Louise's book was poised to reap the harvest of fall sales, he left to become an editor at the *New York Times Book Review*. And once Clemons was gone, McGraw-Hill's promised promotions fell by the wayside. The ad scheduled for *Audubon* never materialized; the powerful endorsements from Roger Tory Peterson, George Sutton, and Fred Bodsworth remained trapped on the pages of private letters.

Louise's book was released through McGraw-Hill subsidiaries in England, Australia, and Canada. The Canadian office did not discuss promotion with Louise; in fact, they didn't seem to realize that the author of *The Lovely and the Wild* was Canadian. Complaints came to her from all over the country: Where is your book? Why isn't it in the bookstores? Reviewers wrote that they couldn't get copies. Even the *Bulletin* of the Federation of Ontario Naturalists, where Louise had served as president, ignored *Lovely*, not even listing it under new releases. There were no interviews, no reviews. When one of Louise's friends asked for the book in Eaton's flagship store in downtown Toronto, the manager shrugged and said, "Never heard of it."

Frustrated that a book she'd spent twenty years writing might not find its readers, Louise wrote to the head of the nature books division of McGraw-Hill in New York, to see if he could light a fire under his Canadian colleagues. When she received no reply, she wrote to every executive she could find on the McGraw-Hill Canada letterhead, and when no one answered, she set up her own promotional tour to Toronto and St. Catharines, Ontario, and Niagara Falls and Buffalo, New York—anywhere she had friends who could arrange bookstore signings and interviews and host luncheons where she could talk about her book. She contacted Lotta Dempsey at the *Toronto Star*, an editor who had worked on the serialization of the Quints book in *Chatelaine*. Through other contacts she was able to schedule three newspaper interviews and one on CBC-Radio. When a fan from Niagara Falls, New York, wrote to the author and television celebrity Pierre Berton, telling him he should have Louise on his television show, he immediately contacted her with an invitation. The appearance was frustrating. Onscreen, she was identified not as Louise de Kiriline Lawrence, an internationally award-winning ornithologist and nature writer, but as *The Quints' Nurse*. When Berton brought up the Dionne quintuplets, she tried to make light of her time with them, but he would have none of it. He pressed her to talk about the babies, about Dafoe, about what it was like to be at the centre of that drama. Birds barely entered the conversation.

After the Berton show, Louise visited the offices of McGraw-Hill Canada. No senior staff was available to meet with her. Instead, she was directed to the general manager of the trade division and some people from the promotion department, who told her that a four-month-old book would no longer be stocked by bookstores and, anyway, the publishing company was out of funds and didn't have the staff to undertake any further promotion.

She was furious. As soon as she got back to her log house, she wrote to the president of McGraw-Hill in New York City, reporting her treatment at the hands of their Canadian subsidiary. "The Vice President is apparently under the impression that I am some kind of forest freak not worthy of his august attention."

What is it about life that it so often knocks us down only in the next instant to swoop us up? Six months after her frustrated tirade, Louise was in New York at the American Museum of Natural History, standing in a room full of admirers (including the top executives of McGraw-Hill) to receive the John Burroughs Medal, the most prestigious nature writing award in North America. Louise was the first Canadian to win the medal and only the fourth female recipient in the medal's forty-year history.

Named for nature writer John Burroughs, the literary naturalist who helped found the American conservation movement in the nineteenth century, the medal was awarded annually to the author of a book distinguished in the field of natural history. The list of winners was a who's who of North American nature writing: William Beebe (the inaugural winner in 1926), Florence Jacques, Frank Chapman, Roger Tory Peterson, Rachel Carson, who was the last woman to win it before Louise.

The award finally stirred the Canadian media. William French wrote apologizing that the *Globe and Mail* had overlooked her book and promised to review it soon. A Canadian Press story appeared in 143 newspapers. She was interviewed on a CBC-TV evening show that was aired seven times. The City of North Bay named her Citizen of the Month and gave her the inaugural Chamber of Commerce Award of Merit. Margaret Mitchell wrote to ask if Louise would mind if she gave the book to Adrienne Clarkson, then a freelance reviewer for *Maclean's* and *Chatelaine* magazines and cohost of the popular CBC-TV show *Take 30*. Grace, her long-time schoolteacher friend who had accompanied her to New York, promised to contact school libraries to get the book into schools. Louise received heaps of mail, including a congratulatory telegram from Prime Minister Pierre Elliott Trudeau and one from the premier of Ontario. Friends wrote, and acquaintances, and total strangers, "completely unknown letter-writers, all expressing in particular their pride and gratification over winning this award for Canada." Louise answered every one.

Mistrustful of her Canadian publisher, Louise wrote to the vice president: "Are you in any way prepared to meet a possibly increased demand?"

They were not. Louise might have been an award-winning writer and recognized as a leading world authority on the behaviour of forest songbirds, but in Canada, the ride remained rough for *The Lovely and the Wild*. The book was out of stock soon after the award was announced and remained unavailable through the entire summer of tourist traffic into northern Ontario. When Louise protested to McGraw-Hill executives in New York, she was told a second printing of six thousand copies was on order. It arrived in bookstores the week before Christmas, too late to benefit significantly from holiday sales.

Meanwhile, sales in the United States had reached 4,880 copies and the book was selling steadily, even in its second year. The executives were optimistic, predicting a long and profitable life for *Lovely*. But Louise was realistic. "For a prize-winning book one might reasonably have expected a great deal better when offered to a market of an estimated 20 million people in the States interested in nature."

The following spring, *The Lovely and the Wild* won the Sir Charles G.D. Roberts Special Award from the Canadian Authors Association, which created another puff of publicity. Louise was selling boxes of books at the bird talks she gave across Ontario, and she encouraged McGraw-Hill to send a display to the 1970 AOU meeting in Buffalo. The book was released in Sweden and Germany.

One year later, however, in November 1971, a memo tucked into a shipment of books informed her that the book was now officially out of print. Books would no longer be available from the publisher. She couldn't believe it. Her royalty payments certainly didn't reflect the sale of twelve thousand books—six thousand in each of two printings. Yet, this book, which had won the top international prize in its field and had been showered with both critical and popular praise, had disappeared from booksellers' shelves and publishers' lists after only three years.

Louise bought all the remaining stock she could afford, but that did little to salve the sting. Discouraged, she retreated to her log house and waited for spring, when once again the red-eyed vireos would scatter across the Southeast Slope and trill their lovely, persistent song.

15

A Fine and Baffling Interplay

The pileated woodpecker was hard to miss. His resplendent scarlet crest shook lightly as he drilled at the old aspen, the tree's crown still voluminous despite the bristle of dry sticks above the leaves that signalled rot at the core. Louise watched from afar, fixing the big glossy bird in her binoculars. The woodpecker stopped and laughed a loud *cuk . . . cuk . . . cuk.*

Far away to the west came an answering call. The pileated took off. Louise waited, and sure enough, he returned, beating the air with glossy wings. Not far behind, a female.

For days Louise watched the pair take turns drilling the hole he'd started. The eggs were laid; the young hatched and fledged; the family zipped through the forest together.

Late that fall, Louise noticed the male excavating a winter dormitory for himself three metres below his nest hole. Through the winter, immediately after sundown, she'd see him fly in from some distant feeding place, slipping so quickly and unobtrusively into his snug that she seldom caught him in the act.

When the weather warmed, he blazed a fresh nest hole in the old aspen above the one he'd drilled the year before. The woodpeckers were incubating their eggs when a pair of yellow-bellied sapsuckers chose a hole the pileated had started then abandoned; the male sapsucker went to work finishing the excavation, scattering billfuls of brownish chips into the air with quick shakes of his head. The young sapsuckers had just hatched when two northern flickers, their first nest robbed by a pine squirrel, came to the door of the pileated's winter snug, inspected the cavity, and moved in. The pileated family on the third level, the sapsuckers on the second, and the flickers on the first lived in harmony, even though by then the pileated young, stretching their long grey bills and striped necks out of the nest hole, looked like a den of vipers.

Through the next winter, the male pileated bedded down in his first nest hole, and the female roosted in the flicker hole. Come spring, the male hopped higher in the tree and excavated a fresh hole—his fourth. Starlings landed in the aspen and expropriated one of the lower cavities by staring down the pileated woodpeckers until they became so agitated they resettled in a nearby tree. The flickers took up residence in the topmost hole, while a hooded merganser moved into the bottom.

The merganser and the flickers returned the following year, joined by a new tenant—a female American kestrel that took over the pileated's winter snug. Two weeks after the kestrel brood left the nest, a violent storm sent a twister through the forest. In the morning, amidst the havoc, Louise found the top half of the old aspen crashed to the ground, splintering the high-rise apartment that had been home to eight pairs of mating birds and their thirty-six young. Six species had occupied that nest tree, raising their families without incident—predator next to prey, in harmonious association.

In the summer of 1968 Louise sent the story of the bird apartment to *Audubon Magazine*. Since 1946, Louise had had a close relationship with the nature periodical: they took everything she sent and were always keen for more. This time, she got no response.

Louise was flummoxed. "Such things get you down," she wrote to Doris. "It is a very mixed joy to be a writer."

When she finally heard from the editor, he rejected the piece, explaining, "we have been trying to steer away from our birds." How odd, thought Louise, from a magazine that focused on nature, with an avowed special interest in avian life. When she paged through the sample magazine he'd sent, she understood. The magazine had been redesigned, the title shortened to the punchier *Audubon*. "This is no longer the intimate informative bird-lore and nature-lore of past times, but a handsome over-luxurious affair, aiming at satisfying the kind of nature lovers who drive into the parks in droves and require hot- and cold-water taps at the campsite," she railed to Doris. "The ideals and enthusiasm and unadulterated inspirations that bore it . . . have been replaced by something too sophisticated and shallow."

Audubon eventually published "The Apartment," and Les Line, the amiable editor who had taken over the magazine, continued to publish Louise sporadically. But ornithology was undergoing a sea change, one that rippled through the study of birds and through Louise's life, eating at the foundations of the career she had built with such persistence and zeal.

By the time the 1960s eased into the '70s, ornithology had become professionalized. The number of universities was expanding rapidly to accommodate coming-of-age boomers; students curious about birds were graduating with a background in evolutionary biology, ecology, and animal behaviour, with the scientific training and tools to test life-history theories and the consequences of behaviours described by amateurs like Louise.

The idea of the amateur goes back to the ancient Greek Olympics where athletes were not allowed to compete for financial gain. But our English word comes out of the French Enlightenment of the late eighteenth century. Amateur—a person who does something for the love of it—was originally coined in opposition to 'professional,' which at the time implied rigorous training and established standards.

The earliest bird watchers were all amateurs, including the explorers who mapped the continent they'd stumbled upon and the colonizers who expropriated it for their own use. Indigenous people, of course, had a close relationship with birds long before Europeans arrived; their belief systems often feature birds as emissaries, cultural heroes, and wise advisors. Early settler Europeans like Humphrey Marten knew this. Marten was second-in-charge of a fur-trading fort on James Bay in the 1760s and is considered the first European ornithologist in Ontario (Rupert's Land in those days). He built nesting boxes for swallows around the fort to study the birds, and when he couldn't make bird observations on his own, he sought "the best Indian intelligence I could get."

Until the early part of the twentieth century, amateurs were admired as the epitome of undiluted passion in perfect harmony with an open, sharply focused mind. Calling someone an amateur was not a slur, although increasingly, the word carried a whiff of the dabbler, an odour that intensified as professionalization took over most human pursuits. By the time I left adolescence in the late 1960s, amateur was a definite put-down.

The AOU had never been sure what to do with amateurs. In 1884, when the organization discussed launching a journal, they proposed a special department reserved for "the amateur element," which greatly outnumbered university-trained members for the first thirty years of the organization. After the First World War, however, the balance slowly tilted. In 1925, field-trained amateurs comprised half the AOU's elective members; by 1980, they accounted for only sixteen percent. In 1920, almost half the papers given at the annual meeting were by amateurs; by 1965, that fell to a mere three percent. Proposals from the bumper crop of university-trained biologists would almost certainly have been more numerous than those from self-trained ornithologists; presenting at an AOU conference was a definite career-booster. University-affiliated scientists would have their expenses paid, while Louise was typical of the nonprofessional, always struggling to make ends meet, able to attend only those meetings that were close to home and where she had friends with whom she could stay. Self-trained ornithologists continued to publish—for a time. In 1950, around the time Louise published her first paper in *The Auk*, almost half of the studies were written by nonprofessionals; by 1980, that had slipped to eight percent. Louise published her last paper in 1968, but already she worried that as a self-trained amateur, her conclusions would be deemed "backward."

Louise's dwindling roster of publications, it could be argued, was not due to her age or to a waning interest in the serious study of birds: she was simply the wrong kind of researcher for the times. Apart from her nursing certificate, the only degree she ever received was an honorary doctor of letters, conferred in 1971 by Laurentian University in Sudbury, Ontario, a commendation that she called "my most precious award." But in the world of ornithology, that did not confer on her the status of "professional."

At about this time, a debate was simmering within the AOU. A formal mentoring program was proposed that would encourage serious amateurs by pairing them with professionals. A core of members feared this would lead to an influx of nonprofessionals— backyard birders and taxonomical hair-splitters keen to add more species to their life lists—who would dominate union votes, a "travesty" that could ruin the organization. Others welcomed the move to "democratize," pointing to self-trained ornithologists such as Louise who had benefitted from an integrated organization where birders of all backgrounds rubbed shoulders—amateurs learning scientific method from professionals and professionals supported by the data amateurs collected.

At issue, really, was the word 'amateur,' which among ornithologists could be applied equally to neophyte feeder-watchers, aggressive life-listers, dedicated banders, and self-trained naturalists undertaking unique, observational studies of birds—a continuum custom-made for misunderstanding.

Ernst Mayr, one of the twentieth century's leading evolutionary biologists, preferred the term 'nonprofessional ornithologist,' which he used when he praised the amateur in his presidential address at the International Ornithological Congress in Ithaca, New York, in 1962: "The precision of their observations, the imaginative and highly original posing of problems, and the lucid informative recording of their researches, which characterize the work of many nonprofessional ornithologists, would dispel any notion of their work being that of dilettantes. . . ." In fact, he went on, "it is not always easy, or even possible to distinguish members of the two groups; actually it is not really necessary as the serious amateur is a professional without a prestigious position or supporting salary."

Louise, sitting in the audience at Ithaca, surely basked in such praise, which both bolstered her sense of the value of her life's work and reinforced her conviction that only through long and consistent watches could she fully appreciate "the fine and sometimes baffling interplay that constantly takes place" between a living thing and its environment.

Louise was seventy-five, and she hadn't slowed down a bit. She had two new works in progress and at least two more in gestation. As soon as *Lovely* was accepted by McGraw-Hill, she had turned again to the children's book she'd been writing on and off since 1945. After so memorably burning her first draft of *Tales of the Green Woods*, she had resurrected the story as *Jimmy Joe and the Jay*, which the Speirs declared a classic akin to *Alice in Wonderland*. Publishers did not agree; their rejections had convinced Louise to slip the book back into her file drawer, where it languished for twenty years.

When she went back to *Jimmy Joe* in 1967, she knew she needed a new approach. She had reworked the story so often that the simple fairy tale she originally envisioned had been lost. Hoping to find her way again, she sent the manuscript to Eleanor Pettingill, a writer-photographer who had just returned from the Falkland Islands where, with her husband Sewall, she'd been gathering footage for a Walt Disney nature film. While reading the manuscript in a park, Eleanor overheard a circle of mothers complaining that books didn't offer their children enough good, solid material. "The women felt that we underestimate the ability of children to understand," Eleanor wrote to Louise. Based on the mothers' comments, Eleanor had given *Jimmy Joe* to an eleven-year-old neighbour with a passion for reading. "He brought it back today, eyes shining: 'I loved it,' he said."

Heartened, Louise rewrote the story again, this time aiming not at young children but at ten- to fifteen-year-olds—a nature book in the tradition of Gene Stratton-Porter. She sent the new draft to McGraw-Hill, but they declined, saying they had just signed a very similar book. To Louise, the rejection smacked of expediency. She pressed them for a detailed critique and when they agreed, she asked them to wait, she'd send an updated manuscript.

Before embarking on yet another revision, she solicited one more opinion, this time from Oliver Austin's wife, Elizabeth, who had worked in children's books. Elizabeth was blunt. No child over nine would read fairy stories; a book with magic must be written for children in grades one, two, or three. The large cast of characters was confusing. Learning new words was school work; a child would discard a book after the third trip to the dictionary. An ideal book for children, she said, should be no more than eight to ten thousand words; Louise's was four times that.

"One of the most delicate tasks in the world is to mix fact and fiction," Elizabeth wrote, trying to soften the blow. She suggested the premise would make an excellent series of board books: "Just let Jimmy Joe walk out to a spruce tree and meet a gray jay family and a few other wild creatures. Then the next book is *Jimmy Joe and the Red Squirrel.* Let him talk to his friends in each book without any explanation." If she did this, Oliver would take the manuscript to Simon & Schuster for its Little Golden Books series.

Louise was not interested in short books with large print. She already regretted the year she'd lost to *Jimmy Joe* and resolved to "not waste any more time on it." But she had a hard time letting go of anything. She went through the manuscript one more time and sent it to McGraw-Hill. Their critique was swift and devastating: the child-hero was "wooden"; the frequent interjections by the author "keep the reader at bay"; the dialogue was inappropriate to a child; there was too much telling and not enough showing; the mix of fact and fantasy, "one of the most difficult forms of writing," was simply not believable.

Another five years passed before Louise picked up *Jimmy Joe* one last time to see if there was any point in trying again. "Rewriting it probably ruined whatever wee merit it possessed," she wrote to Doris. "Essentially, my talent does not encompass writing for children, whatever else it does or does not encompass."

She boxed up the drafts and stored them away—this time for good.

Louise's mother had died in the spring of 1958, three years after Louise's last visit. After a lifetime of weekly letters, emptying her heart to this woman no matter where in the world she was, the loss was profound. Louise had no lack of correspondents—the stack of letters to be answered under her green stone was constant—and she had Len to talk to, but none of her colleagues, friends, or family could take the place of the woman who had given her life and who knew her better than anyone.

That fall, Louise returned to Sweden to process her mother's estate. There wasn't much money to inherit, and what there was, Louise left invested against the time when she could no longer work. She shipped a houseful of heirlooms back to Canada: seventeenth-century rugs, chairs, escritoires, quilts, and jewellery from her great-grands, her grandmother, and her mother. A few years later, when she decided to sell some of the rings and broaches to pay the bills, she sent them to Tiffany's for appraisal. The emeralds and diamonds were glass, the jeweller said, the gems replaced no doubt by ancestors who had fallen on hard times long before Louise.

Len in 1976, the photo Louise kept with her always

By this time, Louise was supporting both herself and Len, who had retired without a pension at the age of sixty, worn out by the stress of wrangling enormous graders and plows. (He'd spent time in hospital, diagnosed with mild neurosis.) Louise's various incomes didn't add up to much. When she turned seventy in 1964, she qualified for a monthly Old Age Security cheque of $75 ($616 in 2020). She still received a small annuity from a trust established by her grandmother, which paid for her journal and magazine subscriptions and her memberships in more than half a dozen national and international ornithological societies. Royalties were a trickle. She wrote one paying article in 1960 and not another until 1970, although she continued to earn income from earlier pieces now being anthologized.

Given her paltry, unpredictable income, Louise was elated when the Swedish ornithologist and ecologist Kai Curry-Lindahl asked her to be his English translator—not just for one book, but for three major works and three smaller books, all scheduled for publication in the United States over the next few years. She had no idea what was involved in the translations—she hadn't seen the books—and no idea what to charge. "It would be good to have steady work like that as a side income," she wrote to Doris. "But I also want to do my own work for what it is worth and I do not under any circumstances want to spend my time for another too cheaply."

Translation was a touchy subject between these friends who referred to each other affectionately as "almost-sister." Their relationship had nearly collapsed over it, starting in 1958, the year Louise's mother died. Doris was in Sweden at the time, travelling with von Haartman, who was a poet as well as a noted ornithologist. She had picked up some Swedish, and for practice, she said, she was translating a few of von Haartman's poems. She sent one to Louise to try her hand too.

"I was thrilled with Lars' poem, wrote and told him so," Louise responded. "And have since had a wonderful time trying to translate it and whether my translation is good or bad I do not know. . . . I do not understand much about poetry or rhyme or cadence. And very few poems 'speak' to me, either because they are not strong enough or true enough or, the other way about, because I lack enough imagination, mysticism, and subtlety. But this one of Lars' 'spoke' to me forcefully, inspirationally. . . . I would love to see some more."

At the time, Louise was deep into writing both the woodpecker monograph and *Lovely*. The poems were a distraction; the translation a literary challenge, a word-game she and Doris were playing together, for fun. "I think that your translation of 'Fallen Heroes' is quite amazing," she wrote to Doris. "It is far more literal than mine . . .

I cannot understand how you understand Swedish so well. All three first verses seem to me perfect. With the fourth, one realizes that you had difficulty and no wonder . . ."

Doris sent more poems and some short reviews. Before long, Louise was spending all her spare time translating. Then suddenly after two months, she stopped. "I may as well say it first as last: I am no longer interested in doing these literary chores either for you or for Lars. Enough is enough. My time and whatever ability I have in language or otherwise should rather go to my own work."

Clearly, Louise had sensed that this was no longer a word-game between friends. Doris caught the irritation in her tone and immediately sent a cheque for $25 (about $250 in 2020).

Louise erupted. "I do not want to accept the cheque because I do not want my English version of Lars' *poems or any part of them* used at all. I did them *for you*, not for publication. Also another thing apparently needs to be explained. When I want to do a thing badly enough, I *always* can afford it, for the simple reason that Len and I never want to do anything we cannot afford."

A testy detente held for more than a year. Then, just before Christmas 1962, Doris wrote to say she was sending Louise a copy of her translation of the von Haartman poems, newly published by University of Toronto Press. This letter, like most of Doris's to Louise, was written by hand on tinted notepaper of high quality. She had intended the book as a Christmas surprise, she said, but Murray insisted she write ahead, in case Louise bought herself a copy before the holidays. Doris went on: "I told the Nices about it at Ithaca and they vowed secrecy. Lars did want you to be surprised. Sylvia promised she wouldn't tell."

Louise was mortified. "I was shocked and hurt by the so-called 'secrecy' in which you involved my two friends, Sylvia and Margaret. I fail to see the necessity of it and find that it was not only insulting but also exceedingly stupid. . . . No one needs to think that I did not know what was in the wind or that I am or was unaware of being taken for a ride . . . You will gather that I resent it.

"Can you not imagine how incongruous it seemed to me that you with your very sketchy knowledge of the Swedish language should take upon yourself the task of translating a collection of highly sophisticated poetry? In spite of this, had you told me frankly of your true intentions, I honestly believe I would have understood and supported you. Instead you gave no explanation until much later, and then not a completely honest one. You let me work on a lot of translations which I in all innocence thought you just wanted help with for your own personal satisfaction and enjoyment. What an utter fool I was! You even criticized some of my versions as if I did not really get the meaning of some of the Swedish words. Can you blame me for feeling not only deeply cheated but also that my knowledge and talent had been used in an exceedingly unethical way? Mark well, that not before I wrote and asked point blank what you were up to, did you mention anything about the ulterior motive behind the whole thing. That, Doris, is where the shoe pinched."

Instead of apologizing, Doris wrote to Louise's friends warning them that she might react badly if they mentioned the translation. The friends, of course, showed Doris's letters to Louise. One of those, Hazel Petty, was the neighbour who spelled Louise during her marathon dawn-to-dusk watches. "I know that Louise is naturally impetuous (and she knows that I think so)," Hazel wrote to Doris, "but there is certainly no vindictiveness in her nature so your fears that I might run into a 'hornet's nest' are quite groundless . . . There is only one thing I might add. 'Soft answers' get nowhere with Louise if they avoid the issue at hand. I know from experience that if she misinterprets or misjudges one's attitude or reactions and one faces her squarely, she really enjoys being set right . . . if you feel that she has been unduly harsh in her judgment of your intentions and frankly discuss the whole matter with her, Louise is a big enough person to admit that she has been in the wrong if that is the case."

Louise typed several sharp responses to Doris, which she never sent. She kept only the last one, scrawling across the bottom, "I am keeping it as a statement of the origin of the whole dreary controversy, which Doris does not acknowledge."

In the end, Louise simply dropped the friendship. How hurt she must have been to make such a heart-breaking decision. Doris had been her personal and scientific confidante for thirty years; there is a hardly a letter from Louise that doesn't contains news of EGs, information that Doris incorporated in her study of the eastern evening grosbeak, published in Bent's Life Histories of North American Birds series the year after Louise's woodpecker monograph appeared. But for the next two years, whatever communication she had with the Speirs was addressed to Murray and was conducted in a strictly professional, if slightly chilly, tone. Eventually, Doris wrote with warm wishes for Louise's seventieth birthday, Louise reciprocated, and slowly the friendship was taken up again, although never with its former warmth and open trust.

Now Louise was asking Doris's advice on becoming a translator herself. Doris suggested Louise ask for a fee of two cents a word, twice as much as the publisher was offering. Curry-Lindahl agreed to send the first book chapter by chapter, which suited Louise, as she planned to fit the translation between her own writing projects. With those first chapters, she must have realized the amount of work that was involved. When she withdrew from the project, Margaret applauded. "You are wise to decline the translation unless you can get well paid for it. Your time is precious."

Louise found other paying work. Godfrey suggested she inquire at the Canadian Wildlife Service, and in 1973—the year before she turned eighty—they commissioned her to write five segments for *Hinterland Who's Who*, a series of sixty-second nature clips for public television. Louise wrote five mini life histories—on the Canada jay, the black-capped chickadee, downy woodpecker, ruby-throated hummingbird, and the whippoorwill, plus a piece on feeding birds.

My sons and I, sitting in our little house in the woods not far from Louise's log cabin, watched those vignettes so often we could recite the text along with the voiceover. Half a century later, *Hinterland Who's Who* still survives, relaunched in 2003 on a dedicated website. Now the distinctive loon flute-song segues to upbeat music, and footage of birds is interspersed with a young woman narrator. A new generation is watching the videos and reading the updated pamphlets posted at hww.ca, where Louise de Kiriline Lawrence is still acknowledged as the writer of her original text—a larger audience for her bird studies than she could ever have imagined. She was more prescient than she knew when she wrote to her mother thirty years before: "Whoever writes more about the Canada jay will have to quote me for what I found out about them. My name will have its own little niche amongst those who have added to the human knowledge in ornithology."

Since the release of the woodpecker monograph, Margaret had been after Louise to write a popular account of the yellow-bellied sapsucker, the least well known of the North American woodpeckers. This sapsucker was the only fully migratory member of the woodpecker family, travelling to wintering grounds that stretched from the American south into Panama. In the north, the bird was commonplace: its breeding range extended from Pennsylvania to James Bay and Alaska. This appealed to Louise. As she wrote in the foreword to *Mar: A Glimpse into the Natural Life of a Bird*, "The dramatic and the sensational seldom yield the treasures of enlightenment that the commonplace and the unpretentious often harbour unsuspected."

Mar was among the first of the migrating sapsuckers to take up summer residence in Louise's woods. As others landed and chose neighbouring claims, he drummed frantically to establish his borders. He raced from drumming post to drumming post—dry twig to metal road sign to chimney cap to an especially resonant hank of bark—each situated strategically within his territory.

Such drumming can be deceiving. The first morning in our house on Calle Ánimas—Street of Spirits—we were wakened shortly before

dawn to deep poundings in the water pipes. We called our house manager, who sent her master-of-all-trades handyman, but by the time he
arrived at a decent hour, the pounding had stopped. It wasn't until
later in the week when I went up to the roof with my morning coffee
to watch the sun rise that the mystery was solved. A golden-fronted
woodpecker was clutching the plumbing stack that rose from the roof,
pecking as if its bird life depended on it. Our plumbing stack was the
highest branch-like object in the *colonia*, and it resonated better than
any piece of wood. Once, I took a walk while the bird was drumming:
I could hear our *carpintero* three blocks away.

The first year, when Mar was an inexperienced yearling, he happened upon Louise's spade hanging from a nail she'd pounded into
a tree near her garden. For half a minute or so he clung to the trunk
of the tree, inspecting the wooden handle. Then he leaned over and
rapped out a signal that carried far into the forest. The next day,
Louise moved the spade. Mar dashed in pursuit and rapped out one
tattoo after another. Again she moved the spade, inching it toward
her woodpecker trap, an oblong wire box attached to a tree not far
away. Again Mar found it, unconcerned that his drumming post was
on the move. She shifted it once more, directly below the trap. "With
his usual flourish he alighted upon the handle and played a vigorous
tattoo. And then, in accordance with long established habit, he hopped
upwards. With a faint click, the trap closed upon him."

Mar took his turn brooding the eggs his mate had laid in the nest hole
they'd excavated in the old aspen. After the long flight north and the
rigours of the territorial joust and attracting a willing female, incubation was a quiet interlude. The pair performed its rituals *sotto voce*—a
murmured mewing that told Mar his partner had arrived to relieve
him. She clung silently to the doorway, flicking her head side to side
across the opening until he nudged her softly aside and flew off.

When the eggs hatched, the parents shifted into a new routine. Forage. Fly to nest. Stuff food into gaping gullets. Brood briefly to keep the hatchlings warm. Forage. Repeat. The sapsucker female had taken the lead in incubating the eggs; now Mar did most of the feeding and brooding of the chicks, although she helped, too, a syncopated rhythm of parental care.

Then, suddenly, the female was gone. Louise watched as Mar missed feedings and forgot to brood, apparently discombobulated without his partner's cues. Finally, the plaintive mewing of his famished newborns sent him speeding into the forest, and Louise breathed more easily.

He managed well for five days. Then, when the nestlings were eight days old, Louise noticed he was calling and drumming more, foraging and feeding less. His timing couldn't have been worse: the young were growing rapidly, more ravenous than ever. Just as Louise considered rescuing the hatchlings and raising them herself, Mar settled down to the responsibilities of being a single dad. By the time the baby sapsuckers were seventeen days old, he was bringing food every four and a half minutes, mostly mayflies from the swarms that lifted in clouds over Pimisi Bay. The young no longer needed to be brooded for warmth, but even so, Mar roosted with them at night, clinging to the inner wall of the nest cavity.

When an unattached female landed on his nest tree and peered into his doorway, Mar didn't chase her off, but neither was he welcoming. He pushed past her into the nest, fed the hatchlings, and left with a fecal sac that he deposited on the tree he had designated as his sanitation site. He continued his routine, though at a more frantic pace, darting about, nervous and anxious. He reacted to ordinary threats—a red squirrel in a nearby pine—with exaggerated, frenzied alarm.

The new female must have heard the hatchlings squealing for food, but she didn't respond, which Louise found strange. The sound of begging young usually provoked a feeding response not only in their own parents but in other unmated birds. She'd seen a female Blackburnian warbler, her beak full of insects, hastily stuffing the gaping mouths of a nestful of baby myrtle warblers she happened to pass; a sapsucker female so eager to feed that she insisted a red-breasted nuthatch take the food she was offering. But this strange female remained unmoved by the cries of Mar's motherless family.

According to Louise's calculations, the fledglings would leave the nest hole on day twenty-six. On day twenty-seven, Mar was still bringing them food. Then on day twenty-nine, the young sapsuckers climbed out of the hole and took their first flight. Within hours, the family was gone.

For four weeks Mar had worked double shifts, caring on his own for his naked little chicks. He'd taken three days longer than usual to fledge his family, but he'd remained faithful to his nest and successfully raised two young into the world.

"The quick response to change," wrote Louise, "is a natural balance—self-regulating, salutary, efficacious." "It directs and shapes the lives of every living plant and creature, begets them, supports them, drives them, and eventually annihilates them. It is the fundamental device that moves the microbe as well as the galaxy."

The story Louise wrote about Mar moves through the daily events of the sapsucker's life, his new loyalty to a telephone-pole drumming post and the nest tree where he mates twice, the second time with near-disastrous results. It is also the story of a forest community of sparring sparrows, an operatic winter wren, and the other sapsuckers with whom Mar negotiates, through displays and drumming, to secure the safety and privacy of his family.

After her debacle with McGraw-Hill over *Lovely*, Louise swore she would never again submit to publishers on her own. Instead, she found an agent, Corton Garruth, her original contact at McGraw-Hill, who was now with a literary agency in Pleasantville, New York.

Garruth submitted *Mar* to all the major publishers. One by one they turned it down.

He suggested Louise excerpt it for a magazine to stimulate interest. Or perhaps she could de-emphasize the sapsucker and expand on the other creatures in the story. "Its reception so far suggests that major revisions are in order," he wrote gently to Louise. "Publishers are so reluctant to take a chance on the 'odd-beat' book that I fear we shall not place it. What do you suggest?"

Louise had devoted four years to *Mar*, yet she had no qualms about setting it aside. She asked Garruth to return the manuscript, saying she couldn't think about revisions just then, she had a new project on the go. Maybe that was the secret to her abiding optimism: she always had another book waiting to be written.

Louise was almost eighty. Her mind and her will were as strong as ever, but physically she was starting to lose steam. A week after she received her copy of *The Lovely and the Wild*, she had suffered a minor heart seizure. A year later, she was diagnosed with trigeminal neuralgia— tic douloureux—that caused stabbing nerve pains across one side of her face. Both were controlled, though not cured, with medication. "I can generally take such things in my stride," she wrote to Doris, but the dissipation of energy rankled. "Planting, raking, watching, counting, observing keep me too busy to achieve much else these days. I do, sometimes to my surprise, get around in the bush, if not as far nor over as rough a trail or as often as heretofore and as I would wish. As time goes on, one cannot keep up [one's] former pace."

Most upsetting was the loss of her hearing, which had been steadily declining for years. By the time she was seventy-five, by her own estimation, she was missing about two-thirds of what she ought to have heard. "Luckily Len has very good hearing and knows the birds well, so I hear also with his ears, especially the thrushes which I cannot hear unless they are close."

Even without sharp hearing, she was still a crack birder. One day, she heard a *chuck* almost at her feet and looked around, expecting to find a hermit thrush, a species that had been absent from her woods for many years. But the bird she spotted was definitely not a thrush. "It is a finch, of all things, short, chubby, grosbeak bill, a blue evening grosbeak, blue, no, not possible, dull blue, with a lightish bill, distinctly lightish," she wrote to Godfrey. She was just about to send him a sharp-shinned hawk that had died when it hit her window, so she asked him, "Do blue grosbeaks have lightish bills?" Yes, he replied, their bills would appear lightish and their note was indeed *chuck*.

I've often seen blue grosbeaks in Mexico, where they perch in shrubs with lesser goldfinches and red Mexican finches, like bright Christmas ornaments. But my first blue grosbeak was a female that landed on Pelee Island one spring; like Louise's grosbeak, it was hundreds of miles beyond the northern limit of its breeding range. Suddenly the island was crawling with birders and photographers hoping to record the unusual species. In Louise's day, no one but Louise saw the accidentals that drifted into her region. Her personal records were largely private pleasures: the Cape May warbler that travelled with a flock of chickadees to spend the winter at Pimisi; the pair of golden-crowned kinglets she spied bathing at the spring on a frigid February day; the western meadowlark that returned to her area for three summers; the blue grosbeak she heard and saw for just half a minute. "The longer you study nature, look for things and find them, the more convinced you become that nothing indeed is impossible."

By the time Louise could afford hearing aids, it was almost too late—but not quite. "My great delight now is to find a singing bird and to be able to listen to the song in its full variation and intonations, not scraps, a tone here and there. At first I was afraid I would no longer recognize the songs . . . But I find that this is not so, for the memory of the songs I learned to know in long past years rises like a dawn sun."

Louise was so accomplished in so many ways, and yet there was an underlying modesty to this woman, a modesty verging on insecurity, that seems to deflate every accolade.

In 1975, in honour of the first United Nations' International Women's Year, the National Museum of Natural Sciences mounted an exhibition called *Canadian Women in Natural Science: Why? Why Not!* Nineteen female scientists were featured, eight of them no longer living. Among the entomologists, herpetologists, astronomers, glaciologists, botanists, geologists, and astronomers, were two ornithologists— Louise de Kiriline Lawrence and Doris Speirs.

The exhibit was scheduled to open in Ottawa then travel across Canada for three years. Louise was invited to the opening and asked to give a lecture. It must have grieved her to decline. Instead of a lush hotel and a rose corsage pinned to her gown, she spent the weekend in Toronto, undergoing an operation for cataracts. But she didn't miss out entirely. In November, the travelling exhibit made its first stop at the University of Western Ontario, where she appeared together with seven of the scientists. In her photo album, she pasted a picture of herself seated with the other women. Underneath, she penned the caption, *How I got to be in that illustrious company is still a mystery to me.*

The year before the women in science exhibit, Louise had lost her dearest friend and kindred spirit. Margaret Nice was a prolific correspondent: she spent mornings at her desk, writing to people around the world, mostly other women researching bird behaviour. But her connection with Louise was special. They exchanged letters on every topic under the sun for almost thirty years, addressing each other in their final decade as "Dearest Beloved Friend." They egged each other on and supported each other in their single-mindedness. Just as Margaret had encouraged Louise to write *Mar*, Louise urged her friend to write a memoir of her life with birds. When Margaret died at the age of ninety-one, she was still working on *Research Is a Passion with Me.* Four years earlier, she had submitted a draft to Sewall Pettingill, who deemed it unpublishable. He'd sent the manuscript to Louise, asking if she would take on the job of rewriting it. "Your request puts me badly on the spot in that I should sincerely wish to help my beloved friend. Were I twenty years younger I might well have plunged into it, in spite of my inexperience and almost total professional incompetence to tackle a specialized job like this . . . I can so well imagine all the re-writing, condensing, shaping up that it needs. Yet the material is precious."

In the end, Louise declined. (Eventually, Doris Speirs revised the book, which was published posthumously in 1979 by the Margaret Morse Nice Ornithological Club.)

Margaret, Doris, Louise: they all knew each other and told each other news of the others, a web of female influence that included Amelia Laskey, Ruth Thomas, Winnie Smith, and Dorothy Luther, who wrote on Margaret's death, "Dear Margaret has encouraged us all, hasn't she? Margaret gave all her women friends the same advice: 'Do everything you can before you get old. Don't be at the beck and call of your family and friends but get to *writing*. Be determined, even ruthless!'"

16

Lest Living Lose Its Zest

W hile Louise was still nursing the Quints, she bought herself a used Remington typewriter, upright and solid, with a carriage that dinged at the end of every row and a ribbon that turned with each stroke so the letters printed crisp and sharp. The keys were like glass buttons with chrome rims, black letters on white. I have a pair of steampunk earrings made from keys just like hers. In the 1920s, Remingtons were sold with the slogan *To Save Time Is to Lengthen Life*.

The typewriter was not an idle purchase. From the moment she discovered her husband's fate in Dafoe's library, she felt a need to tell Gleb's story—a story so powerful she had to become a writer in order to bring it to the page. As soon as she moved into her log house in the fall of 1935, she set to work, pounding out the tragic tale. She was on her own then, her year with the Quints behind her, no love in her heart for anyone except her lost husband.

By the end of the winter, she had finished *My Life*. She contacted George T. Bye, a New York agent who represented people in the news and amateur authors with a sensational story to tell. (His client list included Charles Lindbergh and Eleanor Roosevelt.) Bye took Louise on and submitted *My Life* to Doubleday. The company quickly decided, as they delicately put it, "to step aside."

Louise dove in again. For the next four years, with only a short pause to write *The Quintuplets' First Year*, she worked on her Russian story. The Quints book she saw as her apprenticeship; this was her "real book." When her mother visited Canada in 1936, Louise asked her to bring the letters she'd written from Archangel and Moscow, thick with detail. She knew nothing about the craft of writing, other than what she might have gleaned as a reader, yet with a beginner's optimism she told her mother, "I will be writing on it all summer and early fall to try and have it ready for spring publication perhaps."

In 1937, she incorporated parts of the book—the children's hospital in Petrograd, the victims of famine she'd nursed in the Volga—into a speech she delivered in North Bay. The audience was rapt. Their enthusiastic response powered her through another year of writing and in the final weeks of 1938, she submitted a fresh draft, now titled *Red Sun at Dawn*, to publishers in Canada, the United States, and Sweden.

When the media was flocking around the Quints, publishers were clamouring to read Louise's story. But by the spring of 1939, with a new war on the horizon, interest in the Russian Revolution had waned. But the problem was bigger than that. Macmillan of Canada was direct: "It is a terribly tragic story, quite unrelieved of its somber quality throughout, but it is an amazing document . . . it would require to be more or less rewritten for the writing at present is labyrinthine and even, I feel, florid, and yet as I think of it I don't know quite how it is to be altered without its being completely re-written by somebody else."

I find it hard to believe that such a personal rejection was not devastating. But Louise was realistic. "I am afraid you feel it far harder than I do," she wrote to her mother. "I take it with great equanimity. How could I expect to have the path rose-strewn for my first attempt at literature? As I have developed during the creation of this my first work, I have quite naturally mastered the point that Mr. Allward touched upon when the baby-book came out."

Louise had met Walter Seymour Allward, sculptor of Canada's Vimy monument, through her friend Margaret Houston. Allward had worked from 1921 to 1936 designing and completing his stunning testament to the First World War. Louise's Quints book had come out the year after the cenotaph was unveiled in France. "You must completely detach yourself from the work you have achieved," Allward said to her. "You have done your best and it is no longer yours."

"But how can one?" Louise responded. "Do you mean to say that you do not still live with Vimy that has been your life for over fifteen years?"

"I never think of Vimy any more," he said.

"And I never think of my book any more. Only when it comes back from the publishers and has to be sent out again."

Before MFAs in creative writing, before workshops and retreats, before how-to books and mentors-for-hire, a person wanting to learn the craft of writing could do so only through the luck of a generous editor or a professional friend like Frazier Hunt, a print and radio journalist who had published several memoirs and biographies. Louise met Hunt when he arrived in Bonfield to cover the Quints. He encouraged her writing, so when *Red Sun at Dawn* was rejected again and again, she sent it to him. Like Macmillan, he suggested a complete rewrite.

"Now the question is," Louise wrote to her mother, "when shall this be done? [Hunt] wants me to try at once—I feel I must lay it aside for a time and take up this work later. Meanwhile, I want to write small things during this summer to improve my style and composition, I have lots of material in mind, surging in my head, with which I shall sit down for a few hours each day and work at my type-writer."

For five years, *Red Sun at Dawn* lay dormant while Louise honed her writing skills on magazine articles. After *The Loghouse Nest* was published, she felt ready to tackle it again. As an experiment, she excerpted a section she called "In the Name of Gleb Nikolayevich" and sent it to *The Atlantic Monthly*. The editor deemed the story "well written in a curious shadowy way" although the attitudes of the main characters were "foreign to American sensibilities." He suggested what she already knew: the material needed the scope of a book.

The manuscript languished for another decade, then two, Louise picking it up sporadically, only to set it down in favour of her birds. "It will come in its own good time," she told her mother.

In 1968, after the critical success of *The Lovely and the Wild*, Louise returned to her Russian story. Although she never mentions it, I can't help wondering if the film *Doctor Zhivago*, released in 1965 and based on the novel by Boris Pasternak, influenced her to tackle *Red Sun at Dawn* again. If nothing else, the movie was evidence of a public appetite for a story about the Bolshevik revolution.

Or maybe Louise just had to wait for the world to cycle through the giddy post–Second World War boom years into another period of political unrest. In 1968, when Louise returned to her story of revolution and repression, the United States was fighting the Tet Offensive in Vietnam; 750,000 Warsaw Pact troops were invading Czechoslovakia to suppress the reforms of the Prague Spring; the Baader-Meinhof Group, also known as the Red Army Faction, was setting off bombs in Germany; a million students were marching in protest through the streets of Paris; in Rio de Janeiro, the March of the One Hundred Thousand was protesting the military government; a student demonstration in Mexico City ended in a bloodbath; in Canada, separatists were rioting in Montreal and planting bombs in government buildings; and with the assassinations of Martin Luther King Jr. and Robert Kennedy, the American civil rights movement looked ready to erupt into civil war. "This particular episode of anti-Bolshevik resistance," she noted, "bears a curious history-repeats-itself resemblance with recent historical events."

Louise described *Red Sun at Dawn* as "autobiographical writings." In its next iteration, titled *Nothing But This*, the point of view shifted from first to third person and the project became an "autobiographical novel." Then, in the wake of the success of *Lovely*, she arrived full circle and referred to the story again as memoir.

"I know that you have done an honest book—one that has been pulled by the roots out of your heart," Hunt had written back in 1946. "To work it over, you will have to dig deeply once again into your soul. And you have done so much of that already that I wonder if it is right to ask you to start it all over. But if you can do it—if you can make it even a more searching and life-story book than you have done here—I feel you may have a very great work."

In 1973, when she sent a new draft to Garruth, he said much the same thing: remove the mature-woman storyteller so the reader can be in the moment with young Louise. With Garruth's skilled and sensitive nudging, Louise produced yet another "final draft" that he sent around to several New York publishers. Again, the book was rejected. Out of respect for Louise's negative experience around the publication of *Lovely*, Carruth had not submitted to McGraw-Hill, but with all other options exhausted, he took a chance. Within weeks, a McGraw-Hill editor, Fred Hills, offered Louise a contract.

How much the life of a book depends on a single reader! Over the next months, Hills encouraged Louise to further pare away the family chapters until her cultured, leisurely upbringing served mainly as sharp, dramatic contrast to the main storyline—her epic tale of escape. At his urging, she tightened and focused, reining in her impulse to editorialize and poeticize. Hills travelled to Pimisi Bay for a six-hour visit that Louise pronounced "a harmonious meeting of the spirits." Even after she submitted her final version, he took a heavy blue pencil to it. And he suggested a change of title that alluded to Louise's overarching love of nature: *Another Winter, Another Spring: A Love Remembered*.

She had written a life history of herself.

A month after McGraw-Hill accepted the Russian story, Clarke, Irwin & Company bought *Mar*. Seven years had passed—the lifespan of a sapsucker—since the first round of rejections. In that early incarnation, Louise had intentionally left humans out of the story. Now Garruth encouraged her to put herself in. "The intimate life of a bird, or any animal for that matter, are things ordinary people know too little about," she responded. "I feel sad that 'human interest' is not a broader kind." Nevertheless, she complied. Just as she finished the new draft, she was hired to write the text for a Canadian nature calendar, published by Clarke, Irwin, and so on a whim, she sent them the draft.

Mar: A Glimpse into the Natural Life of a Bird was published simultaneously in Canada, the United States, and Britain in the spring of 1976. Ten months later, in January 1977, *Another Winter, Another Spring* was released.

Some reviewers found the "sudden transition from froth to fervor, dance time to death march" unbelievable, but most devoured the story. "This book is deceptive," the *Winnipeg Free Press* wrote, "not in the sense of deceptive-disappointing but deceptive-surprising. And the surprise is a rich, rewarding, even exciting one." Another noted, in mentioning Louise's earlier award-winning book, *The Lovely and the Wild*, that "if she hadn't used that title then, she could well have used it to describe her own younger self." *The New Yorker* declared: "The knockout is the love story. These young people felt and lived a blazing romantic passion of a kind that people nowadays either do not feel or do not admit."

Louise had just turned eighty-three. From that distance, the events of her early life seemed to her like beads on a single thread: that she should become a nurse, be drawn to Denmark through family connections, that she should meet Gleb, that he should die for the country he loved, that she should come to love Russia, too, so much so that she found its equivalent in Canada. Her younger self had railed against the horrific unfolding of history. Her midlife self had regretted the loss of so great a love. But by the time her older self wrote *Another Winter, Another Spring*, she saw her brief time with Gleb as "not to be lamented, never to be regretted, but to be lived intensely, forever treasured."

Louise's first phoebe was as stubbornly persistent as herself. The plump little grey bird with the velvet grey plumage and teeter-totter tail arrived in early April, announcing its name over and over. The chickadee sang its name, too, but its tone was convivial; the phoebe's was an impatient demand. *Phoebe! Pheebee!*

Louise had noticed two phoebes, a male and a female, flying around the house, the garage, the old chicken sheds. They travelled together, but it was the female that tested each site, looking for the perfect place to raise her brood.

Louise's account reminds me of the pair of mallards that decided our collection of townhouse condos at the junction of Lake Ontario and the Cataraqui River was an ideal spot to raise a family. For three springs now, the male and female have waddled along the brick path by our front window, hopping up into the planter across the way, where they raised their first family, then into our next-door neighbour's planter where, in the second year, the female sat for ten weeks on barren soil supplemented by the dried tops of my potted daffodils and tulips. Roofers working nearby left corn and cut-off Coke bottles of water. Everyone tiptoed past. My writing room looks out on the rooftop where an American crow perched every morning, waiting for the mallard hen to leave her eggs for a walkabout or a dip in the condo pool. Alerted by the mobbing call of grackles, I'd fly shrieking down the stairs as the crow swooped toward the planter-nest, my banshee cries driving it off. Day by day, the crow grew bolder until it stood its ground beside the duck eggs so long I had to flick its stiff black feathers to get it moving. But on the day the chicks were due to hatch, I slept too long: I woke to a shatter of eggshells around the planter and ugly greenish smears on the ground.

Phoebes are better nest-builders than mallards. Just hours after Louise witnessed a courtship on the sill of her bedroom window, "a thrilling little affair full of phoebe grace and low twitterings," the female began to build her nest. She gathered mud and wet moss and dropped it on a narrow ledge above the window of a nearby chicken coop. The slimey goo slid to the ground. The phoebe made trip after trip, escorted by the male, each billful of nesting material slipping off her chosen site. After two days, Louise took pity on the birds and nailed a strip of wire mesh to the board. "She fluttered to the ledge, dismayed at the sight of the wire, and dropped her mud and moss on the ground. She made several more fruitless trips, obviously expecting to see the ledge resume its familiar appearance."

The next day, Louise found the female by the garage, hard at work placing her muddy moss on a triangular shelf under the eave, sculpting the clay with "a snuggling movement, then a half-turn, then again she burrowed her breast into the nest-cup. When she finished with the moss and mud, she collected fine sticks and tendrils and frilly weeds." Five days later the nest was done, and four days after that, the first egg was laid. Louise posted a sign for visitors approaching the driveway: *Please pass around the corner quickly, quietly, and without looking!*

Louise knew something was wrong when she saw the birds once again at her bedroom window, examining the eave of the house. Sure enough, a predator had eaten three of the eggs in the garage nest and pierced a fourth, leaving only one intact. For the third time that spring, the female chose a nesting site, tucking her construction materials into the farthest corner of the ledge above Louise's window. "The male stopped singing as soon as the work on the nest began, but sang a few songs after the female stopped working for the day. After that, she came and crouched in the nest as if she could not bear to be away from it too long."

This sounds so much like Louise that it would be easy to conclude that she was imparting human values to the bird. But it could also be stated the other way around: Louise's attachment to her Loghouse Nest was no different than a bird's.

The phoebe lined its nest with threads pulled from a piece of felt Louise tied to a pin cherry tree. Three days later, the bird laid her first egg. That evening, Louise witnessed a remarkable performance. "As the two birds sat close together on their favourite look-out, he suddenly flung himself into the air above her with a long, loud whistled note followed by a string of rapidly uttered *phoebes*"—a flight song so seldom heard that it would not be audio-recorded for another fifty years.

The female was on the nest almost constantly, while the male perched in front of her on the tip of Louise's open bedroom window. Even after the young hatched and the adult birds set to foraging, they rarely let the chicks out of their sight, and neither did Louise. "The day the red squirrel ran up on the peak of the roof and peered over the edge of the eave, and the day the garter snake chased the leopard frog into the grass under the nest, were days of painful dread for me. Had the squirrel seen or smelled the young phoebes? Could the snake climb the walls? I wanted to surround the little nest with a protective screen against the dangers of the world, but I could not. I believe that for all wild things, the natural interplay between failure and success, safety and danger, must not be eliminated lest life for them lose its edge, and living its zest."

Sixteen days after the chicks hatched, they stood up and stretched their legs. The next day, the young phoebes—the parents' third attempt at raising a family—fluttered one by one from the nesting shelf into a tangle of honeysuckle as Louise cheered at her window.

Louise never wrote a life history of the eastern phoebe—Bent had published a reliable account in 1942—but she wrote two pieces for *Audubon*, one in 1951, the other in 1978. She chose the latter—a story of nesting tenacity—for what she felt might be her final book: *To*

Whom the Wilderness Speaks, a collection of eighteen *Audubon* articles that had been published originally in the United States but had never appeared in Canada.

Louise edited the pieces heavily, updating them with new information from her later studies. She arranged the articles not chronologically but gathered into sections that traced the evolution of her relationship with birds: first insights, what she called "the opening of the portals"; her research into birdsong, bird ecology, predation, and the display and response behaviour of particular birds that led her "from ignorance to revelation"; and the stage she reached in later life, "acutely aware of knowing far too little of all there was to know."

To Whom the Wilderness Speaks appeared in October 1980. At last, Louise was launching a book in the thick of the fall publishing season, perfectly timed for Christmas sales. She had an autographing party at the North Bay Public Library, where she signed more than a hundred copies. But elsewhere sales were modest. Having so long set her sights on the American market, she was mostly unknown in Canada except as nurse to the Quints. National media largely ignored the book.

And the world had shifted. That fall, Canadians were preoccupied with Terry Fox and his Marathon of Hope and with the repatriation of the constitution. Acid rain, water pollution, and hazardous waste were in the news, but more for their impact on humans than for their consequences to other species. Conservation and environmentalism, movements spawned by naturalists, had morphed into a fight over corporate practices. People were talking about endangered spaces, but endangered *species* would not rise into public consciousness for another two decades. In 1980, the daily lives of individual birds were, as the *Quill & Quire* reviewer put it baldly, "a crashing bore."

To those attuned to the natural world, however, *To Whom the Wilderness Speaks* was not just a sequel to the insightful, graceful prose of *The Lovely and the Wild*, but as the reviewer for *Seasons* noted, "a better book. There is a richer, darker side exposed as Mrs. Lawrence talks about the tensions of competition and predation, of vibrant life and sudden death. But she sees life as it is, not as we might wish it to be: she knows that she must not choose between the insect-eating warbler and the warbler-eating hawk. Life leads to death. Death sustains life."

After initially rejecting the manuscript, McGraw-Hill in New York took two thousand of the Canadian edition to distribute in the United States. And the book won the Canadian Authors Association Frances H. Kortright Outdoor Writing Award, named for conservationist Frank Kortright and sponsored by the National Sportsmen's Fund, an organization that supported wildlife conservation in the interests of hunting and fishing—an irony not lost on Louise.

Louise had set up her first feeding station for the pleasure of the company of birds, but also as her own small contribution to conservation—offering food when nature failed to provide. Her feeding tables gave her material for dozens of studies and articles, but by the time she wrote *To Whom the Wilderness Speaks*, she had come to see feeders as a "contrived artificiality" that did more harm than good. "Wildness, the wild creature's most vital asset of self-preservation, is lost. Lost is the daring, the spark that fires the successful escape, blunted is the instinct to avoid the too-close approach of a stranger."

Increasingly, she puzzled over what it meant to conserve nature. By the 1980s, 'conservation' had become a buzzword, much as 'sustainability' is now, used to sell everything from laundry detergent to plastic flooring. The word irritated her, and so did its meaning—to keep intact, to maintain existing conditions.

"It is high time we rethought these concepts in a profoundly penetrating way," she wrote to Doris. "What is conservation? Is it a realistic concept? How can anything be preserved in an unchanged or at least only slightly altered state when the essence of all existence and all life is continuous change? Is it realistic to try to make live again near-extinct species, the whooping crane for instance, other than for

aesthetic and perhaps scientific reasons and to ameliorate our feeling
of guilt that man, not evolution, all but pushed it over the brink?"

The "conservation" of wilderness spaces was especially galling
to her. She watched in horror as Algonquin Park—7,600 square kilometres of untrammelled lakes and rocks and trees half an hour south of
Pimisi Bay, established as a wildlife sanctuary in 1893—was degraded
by mining, lumbering, and tourism. "What are we doing with these
previous wilderness areas? We are letting into them the earth's
most destructive creatures with their cars and asphalt roads, their
unspeakable garbage and dirt and corruption, polluting the gorgeous
landscape and changing it unrecognizably. People need parks—but
parks do not need people. Every last one of them will eventually be
destroyed, annihilated, unalterably changed and worn out by the mass
of people and their inordinate requirements for elbow room and roads
and running water. This is what we call conservation."

During Louise's first years alone in the log house, she had noticed
cars slowing as they crossed the bridge that separated Beaver Lake
from Pimisi Bay, where hundreds of ducks would pause to feed during
their migration south. Men would take potshots at the ducks from their
car windows, not bothering to retrieve the birds they maimed and
killed for sport. Soon, at the first sound of a slowing car, Louise would
stick her 303 Savage out her bedroom window and shoot into the air,
scattering the ducks. She was a hunter, then. She stalked deer every
fall. She shot squirrels, enraged at the songbird eggs they stole: she
once caught a red squirrel sitting on its haunches, "twirling the head
of a nestling junco between its paws as if it were a delectable nut." But
she had given up guns as soon as she realized nature was fairly efficient
at keeping animal and bird populations in balance—with the exception
of *Homo sapiens*.

"I am tending to believe that all effort along these lines [of conser-
vation] is horribly futile if the control of man cannot be intelligently
achieved . . . We are too many. For populations gone wild the consequences are inevitable."

Ecological balance was the goal, she decided, not conservation. 'Preservation' was a better word, meaning to protect, to keep safe. Instead of humans acting the saviour, heroically keeping species alive, preservation acknowledged humans as part of the problem— preserving the natural world meant keeping it safe from humans too.

Louise was closing in on ninety. She was still abstracting ornitholog- ical papers for *The Auk*, as she had been doing since 1971, and she was reviewing for both *The Auk* and *Bird-Banding*, now the *Journal of Field Ornithology*. She regularly sent her bird sighting notes to the American Birding Association, the U.S. Fish and Wildlife Service, *The Canadian Field-Naturalist*, the ROM, and the National Museum of Natural History in Ottawa. And she was still labouring over articles.

Louise continued her daily bird walk until she was ninety-three

At eighty-eight, she wrote a piece called "A Plea for Reassessment," published in *Park News*, in which she argued passionately for ecological balance and the reining in of the human population and its excessive needs and desires before every corner of the planet was compromised.

When *The Living Bird Quarterly* edited her study on the courtship rituals of downy woodpeckers so heavily that she no longer recognized her own words, she demanded they send it back and rewrote the piece herself to their specifications, a gruelling and discouraging process. In 1984, the year she turned ninety, *Living Bird* published "From Hostility to Amity," her last scientific article. The following year, *Audubon* published "A Springtime Affair," her final bird story—what she called her swan song—for the magazine that had been publishing her for forty years.

The editor's notes described Louise as "one of Canada's most distinguished nature writers." It was a small group: the naturalist John Livingston, R.D. Lawrence, the West Coast riverman Roderick Haig-Brown, the novelist Fred Bodsworth, the wildlife photographer George Calef. No other women, although a new generation of women and men—Bridget Stutchbury, Candace Savage, Peri McQuay, Adrian Forsyth, Wayne Grady, Michael Runtz—were just getting started.

Visitors continued to flock to the Loghouse Nest, more than ever after the release of *To Whom the Wilderness Speaks*. Strangers made pilgrimages; old friends came for what often felt like one last visit. Louise made sporadic attempts at a guest book, but inevitably gave up after a month or two. When the chair of the Archives Committee of the U.S. Fish and Wildlife Service wrote to ask for her memories of ornithologists who had visited her woodland, she replied, "Many ornithologists have visited Pimisi Bay in the course of the years . . . But I have no photographs or even snapshots to commemorate these signal occasions. The talks, the discussions, the birding superseded all else."

Many of the visitors who came now were writers: Deborah Strom interviewed her for a chapter in *Birdwatching with American Women* and Andrea Lebowitz included her in *Living in Harmony: Nature Writing by Women in Canada*, both books published in 1986. Jack Cranmer-Byng came to talk to her about Taverner for his biography, *A Life with Birds*. Marianne Ainley, a graduate student at McGill University who was working on a history of North American ornithology, sent Louise a long list of questions. She had just finished her master's thesis, *Professionalization of North American Ornithology*, and had been invited to co-author a history of the AOU to mark their centennial in 1983. She would be contributing chapters on women ornithologists, Canadians and the AOU, and amateurs and the AOU. Louise fit all three categories.

The green stone that held down her correspondence teetered higher than ever with letters from students wanting information for papers they were writing on various species of birds, and sometimes on her. One wanted to know if Louise had observed parasitism in nesting woodpeckers. A young graduate student observing the birds of Manitoulin Island wanted her to write a preface for his book. Both the Canadian and American wildlife services were still asking her to partake in their research. As depleted as it had become to Louise's eyes and ears, her bit of boreal forest was still one of the most northerly songbird breeding territories under research scrutiny. And there was still so much to know.

In the fall of 1976, midway between the release of *Mar* and *Another Winter, Another Spring*, CBC-Radio aired an episode of *Between Ourselves* devoted to Louise, called "She Is One of Us." The title was taken from a speech by an undergraduate at Laurentian University in Sudbury, Ontario, in 1970, when Louise was awarded an honorary doctor of literature: Louise was a lover of forests and lakes, a northerner like the Laurentian students and profs. Barry Penhale, the CBC producer who came to Pimisi to interview Louise for the documentary, adopted the title, expanding its meaning. Louise was not only a northerner, she was one of us—an iconic Canadian, a lover of birds.

Penhale spent several days talking with Louise, recording their conversation on a reel-to-reel player. The tapes spill from boxes in his basement, an impossible jumble, although I find an undated transcript stuffed in a cardboard box. As well as interviewing Louise, he spoke to her neighbours in Rutherglen and Bonfield, travelled to St. Catharines, Niagara Falls, Toronto, and Ottawa to speak with colleagues, friends, publishers, and the curator of the *Women in Natural Science* exhibit, then on to Cobble Hill to speak with Doris and Murray Speirs. As Doris wrote to Louise, "He feels that he has been recording three 'love stories'—the love story of you and the Russian officer, the love story of you and Len, and the love story of you and Nature."

Penhale was surprised at Louise's vigour: before he arrived on that cold February day, she and Len had cleared snow from the forest paths, rising at dawn to do it. And he was touched by Len's tender relationship with Louise, his adoring demeanour, the small things he did to make her life easier: serving the tea, tending the fire. "She's a little outspoken," Len told him. "Not everyone loves it, but I do. She's eleven years older than me but otherwise she's younger than me, I have to run to catch up with her, she goes through the bush like a deer. I look at her sometimes and say to myself, It's a shame that a woman like that has to get old."

Louise had reservations about the radio profile. On paper, she revised endlessly to ensure her words conveyed exactly what she meant. Radio was so off-the-cuff. Which bits would be used? How would Penhale frame what she said? Would he prove to be another Berton, blind to her accomplishments beyond a year of nursing five famous babies forty years ago? She was on pins and needles until the documentary aired. When the evening came, Len sat in the living room and Louise sat in the sunroom, each listening on their own radio. When it was over, they admitted it was better than either had dared expect.

And here I must make a confession. As part of my research for a profile of Louise for *Harrowsmith Magazine* in 1989, I listened to a

*Photographer's portrait of Louise, dressed in furs and her
sapphire earrings from Gleb, feeding a pine squirrel*

recording of "She Is One of Us," and used Doris Speirs's colourful
phrase "barefoot in sapphires" in print. To my chagrin, the phrase
was picked up from that profile and repeated by several scholars over
the past thirty years. It is a captivating but utterly false image. Had
I known Louise better, I would have realized that she almost never
went barefoot—anyone who has walked on pine needles will know
why—and she would certainly never greet guests without shoes. Nor
would she wear sapphire earrings about the house. Those earrings
were all she had from Gleb's family, and she saved them for only the
most special occasions. This image of her in such deshabille, flaunting
her wealth like a half-mad "forest freak" was a fantasy, one that, like
the tagline "Nurse to the Quints," threatens to overshadow her work
as a serious watcher of birds. Far better to remember her with spruce
boughs shoved under her hat and a cushion pinned to the hem of her
coat, a pump sprayer in one hand, poled mirrors in the other, pockets
stuffed with notebooks, binoculars tugging at her neck.

Even more disconcerting, in the radio program Doris implied that when they met, Louise was resistant to learning more about birds, that she had to be convinced to take a more scientific approach, that it had been Doris who persuaded Louise to focus on the birds breeding in her forest with a view to making a contribution to science. But Louise was already actively studying birds when she met the Speirs. Their influence was profound in leading her to more scientific record-keeping and scholarly writing, but Louise had many scientific mentors, each significant in their own way. Hearing Doris's final judgment of her friend, I feel defensive on Louise's behalf: "Things are black and white with her . . . she feels very, very strongly."

Louise's thousands of letters leave no doubt that she was a person of strong opinions, but she was far from rigid. In fact, it was the grey areas, the subtle shades between black and white that most often caught her exploring eye.

Two years after producing "She Is One of Us," Penhale returned to Pimisi for a second interview, this one commissioned by the Ontario Medical Association for an oral history project. Louise's memories of her years as a nurse were detailed and precise, but she was also honest to an extent few of us achieve. She sugar-coated nothing, never rearranged history to make herself look more important, always gave credit where it was due. When Penhale declared that she was the Dionne quintuplets' first nurse, she corrected him, "I wasn't the first nurse, the first nurse was Yvonne Leroux. She was a young graduate, so she did pretty well with what knowledge and experience she had."

Louise talked about the difference between nursing in Sweden and in Canada in the 1930s. "[In Canada, the doctors] did not consider the nurses as a part of the medical team. They considered the nurse a little below, and I had a little difficulty understanding that . . . Why should not the nurse, a very highly trained nurse, be considered exactly on the same level as the doctor? Her knowledge is a different kind of knowledge than the doctor's knowledge but as a medical team they shouldn't be a great deal below or above." This egalitarian foundation in her

Swedish training explains in part her ability to approach ornithologists with doctorates as easily as watchers like Roy Ivor and Jim Baillie who never finished high school. Knowledge and expertise impressed her, however it was gained.

Penhale stayed in touch, and when he left broadcasting to become a publisher of natural history books, he contacted Louise again. Would she allow him to reprint her books? She agreed, and in 1986 a soft cover edition of *Mar* was released, followed by *Lovely* and *Another Winter, Another Spring* in 1987, *The Loghouse Nest* in 1988, and *To Whom the Wilderness Speaks* in 1989, just after Louise turned ninety-five. In a life filled with second chances, Louise had never imagined her life's work would get a second chance too.

The phoebes left Louise's woods, as always, at the end of August. By late summer, migrants were flying in from the north—swallows, warblers, flycatchers—to feed through the day, and when they carried on with their journey, the parents that had raised their families in Louise's woods joined them. The resident jays and woodpeckers gave the migrants little notice as they passed through, but the chickadees escorted the departing birds with chatter and song. By the time the sun set, the phoebes were gone and the other travellers too. Although she watched keenly and listened for the chickadee escort song, Louise never witnessed a phoebe farewell.

17

As Long as It Lasts

It was a finchy winter, the conifers heavy with cones. Red-breasted nuthatches flocked in abundance. Not normally aggressive, the small rust-bellied birds sat on their heels at Louise's feeding table, wings and tails spread in sharp fans. The chickadees gave way, and after that, the two species of small, energetic birds associated harmoniously, taking turns at the seed.

Louise had noticed that red-breasts generally stayed with their mates not just through the breeding season but all year long. Several pairs were feeding amiably when a lone male appeared, causing a great fuss. The locals hopped along nearby branches, posturing with wings dropped and stubby tails held high, *yanking* loudly, the equivalent of a sharp request to the bachelor to take himself elsewhere. The intruder *yanked* right back.

"Ridiculous to behold, these demonstrations often went on from 10 to 15 minutes, before the desire for food toned down the nuthatch feelings. Then, absorbed in their feeding, the established nuthatches allowed the newcomer to come to the seeds and suet."

On another occasion, a lone female joined a trio of male nuthatches at the feeder. For three days Louise had watched her zipping amongst the trees, making herself familiar with the surroundings before she settled down to become the most persistent diner of the red-breast quartet at the suet sticks. Louise banded the males, but the female resisted the baited traps. Instead, she perched on the telephone wire and looked around. A male alighted on the wire nearby. She dove at him, he flew off, and she sat herself exactly in his place. He landed in a thick white spruce and she followed, supplanting him once again. Twice more she shifted him off his perch until she ended up on the tip of a high branch, where she lifted her bill and pointed side to side, stretching her head and neck until her whole body was on a single horizontal plane, the stark black-and-white eye stripes like the tip of an arrow. In a final message to the male, she raised her wings in a shoulder lift and beat them rapidly.

"From this moment, the female was no longer seen without being closely attended by the male. Wherever she went, he escorted her, apparently trying always to keep her in sight, defending her 'personal territory' vigorously."

Louise was working on the last draft of her final *Audubon* story that spring of 1984—another account of ritual displays that bridged the gap between hostility and amity in the wild, this time between a male and female ruffed grouse. Birds, she concluded after a lifetime of watching, were not naturally cruel or aggressive. She had witnessed many examples of cooperation and collaboration in her woods, especially during nesting season. And they were good at conflict resolution, using song and ritualized displays to settle disputes, negotiate boundaries, and communicate with each other about sources of food and imminent dangers.

Louise had just turned ninety. "The indecent age," she called it. "All but obscene." Her birthday had lasted for days, with overseas phone calls from her Swedish nieces and extended family, visits from friends and neighbours, a mountain of birthday cards and letters, framed congratulatory wishes from the prime minister of Canada and the premier of Ontario, and a personal gift from the Swedish ambassador. Robert Nero, a specialist in great grey owls with Manitoba Wildlife who dropped in on Louise whenever he came east, wrote her a poem called "Woman by the Shore."

The previous summer, she'd hired a French-Canadian couple to "do" for her and Len. She'd known them since her days working at the Bonfield Red Cross Outpost Hospital, when they were school children and she was Madame de Kiriline, the district nurse. The couple came once a week to clean the log house and tackle the outdoor chores that were beyond Len now: bringing in the wood, clearing the paths, renewing the chinking.

Louise's handwriting was still firm, but words sometimes eluded her reaching thoughts. "Lots of things are now as if running away from me," she wrote to Doris, who was about to turn ninety too. "So many other things, thoughts, pursuits, are crowding in to squeeze these out, so to speak. And so it goes as time goes on, for nothing ever remains on the same point."

Her typing was terrible, she said; the composition of her sentences, odious. She never sealed a letter now without composing several drafts, fragments scrawled on scraps of brown paper as she struggled to get the phrases right before committing them to type. It was exhausting being old. And disconcerting.

But even though she found herself easily distracted and slow to accomplish much, still she watched her own deterioration with interest. "It is," she wrote to Doris, "logical and natural."

Len was eleven years younger than Louise, yet his decline was much more rapid. His spine was crumbling; arthritis made it painful for him to move. He was almost blind with cataracts, and his memory was failing badly. The depression and mood swings that had always plagued him had intensified with age. Recently, his rages had turned violent.

It was hard enough for Louise to watch Len lose the active life that had given him such satisfaction, but to see his mind go and his character shift must have been excruciating. The man she loved was disappearing: the partner who had helped create their forest paradise, who had made living in the woods not only pleasurable but possible. For forty-five years they had lived together in "deep harmony." She had worked hard to keep their relationship close, accumulating a hefty bag of effective tools, but no matter how she tried now to convince Len of her love and understanding, he raged.

Were his violent outbursts some sort of displacement behaviour? She'd seen it often in birds, most memorably in a male slate-coloured junco. Whenever the female he was pursuing rebuffed him, he'd droop and with great intensity peck at the ground or at the aluminum band on his leg. Pecking the ground was typical displacement behaviour: under stress he was reverting to the innate motor pattern of feeding—like heading for the refrigerator every time you feel depressed. But pecking at his leg band was different. The junco had never shown any interest in the band until the female refused his advances. It was a purely acquired response. Was the pain in Len's body causing him to lash out at Louise? Possibly, but with birds, aggressive display was almost always enough to sort out their issues: they rarely resorted to physical violence.

Len was admitted to the hospital in North Bay to determine if there was a physiological trigger for the psychological changes—a brain tumour, perhaps—but the tests showed nothing. The psychiatrist concluded that Len had a rapidly cycling chronic depression. His grasp of ideas was fading, but there was no evidence of hardening of the arteries or senile dementia. He was sent home with a prescription for Valium to control the rages and with the prognosis that while his condition might be managed, it would not likely improve. In the doctor's opinion, the best place for Len was with Louise, in familiar surroundings.

A firm believer in second opinions, Louise phoned a doctor who had treated Len before and who was now medical director of a psychiatric facility in St. John's, Newfoundland. He suggested an anti-depressant instead of Valium, which is an anti-anxiety drug, and gave Louise instructions on how to administer it, given Len's sensitivity to medication. "I do admire your courage," the doctor wrote to Louise, "and your ability to carry the extraordinary burdens of your life with such devotion and so well."

The Newfoundland doctor offered to work with her North Bay family physician on Len's case, but the local doctor refused. Len was kept on Valium and given Percocet for his back pain, which made him not only dizzy and nauseated, but wild with anxiety, and increasingly aggressive. On one occasion he ripped the photographs from the two "life albums" that Louise had painstakingly assembled, with typed notes on opposing pages. Across a glaring blank space she scrawled in frustration, *Len has ruined everything*.

Louise felt Len's rages as a personal failure. "Suddenly I discovered that the usual cheerful attitudes do not fit," she wrote to the Newfoundland doctor, the only person who knew the depth of her crisis. "A better way for caring is obviously needed; in whatever way, these sudden feelings of anxiety and stress are to be avoided. I have very little success."

Icy calm, Louise discovered, was the only possible response to her husband's irrational behaviour and threats—"to control every gesture, the tone of voice, every word that so easily provokes a tantrum, far more devastating to him than to me." How this must have grated on a woman who treasured honesty, authenticity, and forthrightness above all else—except, as she discovered, love.

In between Len's rages, there were good moments, sometimes whole hours free of outbursts. Louise clung to these, willed them to expand and return to her the man she'd known. She was determined to avoid ending up in a hospital. "I dread the hospitals. I understand that deep down Len does, too." Her aversion was not just to institutional care. What worried her was the failure of the medical establishment of the time to accept that death was, paradoxically, an integral part of living. As a much younger woman, she had written in 1945, "I deplore the idea of the sanctity of human life, which cannot allow a body to be gently let out of life . . . I think that is breaking the laws of all reason, and of life itself."

In the spring of 1985, desperate for a solution, she left their family doctor in North Bay. "One should act when circumstances demand a change, even if with regret," she wrote to him. She put herself and Len in the hands of the doctor at the Bonfield Medical Centre, next door to where she had served as district nurse almost sixty years before.

"We, Len and I, are living," she wrote to family back in Sweden. "We are learning even more deeply and seriously about living and life. What would life be without death? Life is change. Behind that word I would put Period."

Little wonder that a tone of sadness like a mourning dove's keening runs through Louise's letters from this time. Louise was a realist. She understood more deeply than most that death was "the only event that is universal and inevitable, though not predictable." But despite her best efforts to adjust, to adapt, to manage, a kind of grief was settling into her. Her sadness was not that she or Len would die, but that she would soon have to face the end of life as she had known it on the shores of Pimisi Bay.

Louise had moved permanently into her log house in May 1935. If there was a celebration of her half-century on Pimisi Bay in May 1985, it must have been private, perhaps nothing more than raising her cup of well-brewed coffee to the predawn chorus that had been the soundtrack to her life.

Although she wore hearing aids to magnify the sound of the birds and sometimes carried a cane against falls, still Louise took her dawn walk, as she had every morning since Len left for the war. She believed in John Burroughs's dictum: "To learn something new, take the path you took yesterday." She had been doing exactly that for sixteen thousand yesterdays.

When she started, the second-growth evergreens were still relatively young, the spindly birch, aspen, and ash interspersed with fresh green balsam firs. The canopy was sparse; light penetrated to the forest floor, where maple seedlings, hazel shrubs, and honeysuckle bushes sprang up to feed the deer. By the mid-1970s, the evergreens had grown to fifteen metres, broadening until their tips met to form "a vaulted roof full of skylights." Soft maples angled up as far as they could, starved for light. As trees blanked out the sun, shrubs on the forest floor thinned, and low ground covers took over: crawling lianas, wintergreens, lycopodium. After a brief bird walk with Murray Speirs one day in 1974, she "thought of one long ago birding together here in a younger forest, full of birds and we ourselves young and nimble of foot. Those were blessed days."

Now, a decade later, the forest had stumbled past maturity. Blister rust was bleeding the tops of the white pines dry. Giant trunks blown down by the wind lay scattered on the forest floor under a skin of moss and lichen. On her morning walks, she often had to clear fallen branches from the path.

Even so, there was a comforting sameness to her morning excursion, a thousand times stepping over the same roots, the same rocks, up to East Point to look out over the bay, down into the Dell still leafy with ferns, over to North Point where if she strained, she could hear the rush of Talon chute, back past the spring where water still bubbled up from the earth even though pipes now fed it to her kitchen taps.

"Imagine the privilege accorded one of my age, the happiness, of passing into another, still another spring with its matchless sights, sensations, experiences, and sounds!"

Louise's walk was never a morning tramp, never a tick-tick-ticking of a list of bird names. It was a Morse code of stops and starts, punctuated by listening, watching, interpreting the sounds of the forest as

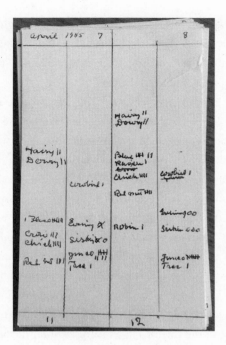

Louise's last bird count notes, spring 1985

it awakened around her. Once, while she was waiting to hear the birds announce themselves, she heard the hollow sound of water hitting an upturned leaf. She looked up to see if was about to rain but no, the sky was a clear, dark silk. She strained to listen. *Plop. Plop.* And then she understood. "This was the dew falling, a sound impossible to detect except in a solid silence where no birds were singing, no twigs were cracking, no wind was moving."

Every season, every month, every dawn revealed its singular surprises. In April, a lone hermit thrush sang for a few days then, having found a mate, settled into silence until the chicks fledged and the moult set in and it sang its most lyrical songs of the year. In early May, she saw a tiny kinglet, its ruby crown brilliantly on display as she heard "one rippling song follow upon the other the whole day long, almost without cessation. Loud, rounded, amazingly full-toned for so tiny a singer, his notes fell leisurely, unhurried, almost languidly upon the air." Then one sunrise, five days short of two months later, the kinglet sang two songs and vanished. After that, a silence "that made our green world appear singularly empty."

She never tired of listening, never grew immune to the intense beauty of the birds, the trees, the weather, the land. She'd be up at four in the morning to listen for whippoorwills, the last singers of the night. Once, she almost stepped on a whippoorwill sitting on its white eggs in a makeshift nest of leaves in the forest duff. Wanting to see more, she'd hung an old green blanket from a fir tree not ten feet away, with eye-slits cut here and there, and set up a folding chair tight into the fir, boughs arranged to cover her back, an insect pump sprayer at her side. As she watched, the male flew in like a huge moth and settled in front of his mate, his breast pressed to the earth as he edged up to her "until bill met bill and he became a perfect looking-glass image of her." Louise stayed all night and just before dawn, an ovenbird flung itself above the treetops in a magnificent flight song "moved by some special exultation."

Most mornings, she'd sit on top of Peak Hill by a hydro pole, the land falling away in front of her, listening in the perfect stillness before the cars disturbed the air with their noise. "The song of the mosquitoes was loud in my ears. Twenty-one minutes passed before the robins broke the silence, for years there have not been so many of them nesting. Then came the wood thrush—and the veerys—and then all the others."

Every now and then, a wave of migrants would pass through like a memory. "On the tail of a cold front, came a warbler migration almost to put you back into the pre-50's days," she wrote to Doris late one August, "if it had not been for the extreme brevity, only one or two days, and if the flocks had not been so small. But the illusion was there, with the bushes and trees suddenly full of flitting 'confusing fall warblers' for a minute or two—then gone, quickly in great haste, to be followed with nothing except an odd straggler at long intervals. But a migration it was and exciting for all its littleness. And for a very short while, as compared to other years, I spent my dawn walks from 05:15 to 6:00 in a world of exquisite music. This was my best summer experience—and most poignant because, perhaps, never to be heard again."

She was forever amazed at "what can be gleaned from a micro-environment like mine." The blush on the tree bark that was the cue for the thrush to hush, leaving the white-throated sparrow to sing its solo, "clear as the sound of purling spring water. Far back, a red-eyed vireo began its broken tone poems." The solitary vireo no longer visited the woods of Pimisi Bay, but once, in late summer, just after the sun rose, "with the fragrance of warming conifers strong in my nostrils, I stood spellbound listening to the exquisite notes of a chance duet. It was the solitary vireo giving his full, emphatic, slightly slurred phrasings, blending beautifully with the loud full-length warbling song of a purple finch. An occasion as rare as violets in snow, a moment brief as the fall of a raindrop, never again to be repeated.

"Do you know of any season, any moment, observing nature that does not bring forth something new, exciting, the thrill of behind-the-scene glimpses?"

How could she miss a day?

By the fall of 1985, both Len and Louise were in hospital: Len in the North Bay Psychiatric Hospital for his worsening moods; Louise in North Bay General with exhaustion. She had been prescient twenty-five years before when she mused on the occasion of her wedding anniversary, "What impresses me most is the closeness with which one life weaves into another in a good marriage, to create an interdependence that is both deeply satisfying and somewhat disturbing. Disturbing in the sense that it cannot continue forever."

Louise and Len would never live together again. Len remained in the psychiatric hospital. When Louise was discharged from North Bay General, she was assigned a nurse visit twice a week and a homemaker two mornings a week to clean the house and prepare meals. But even with that help, it soon became clear she could no longer live on her own in her Loghouse Nest, especially with winter coming. Reluctantly, she moved into a room in Leisureworld in North Bay.

I used to drive past Leisureworld when I went into town for groceries. The name struck me as oddly optimistic, more appropriate to a fun park than a residence for those in the final years of life. Applied to Louise, it seemed ridiculous. The woman had never indulged in leisure in her entire life; I couldn't imagine her starting at ninety-one. Not long before, in a letter to her friend Hartley Trussler, a local historian who was turning eighty-five, she'd mused, "That the accumulated years are so full of beatitude as some say to become 'golden,' I think is an exaggeration. We are so apt to seek with words to deceive ourselves and others. While I think it naive to clamour for a 'long life,' it is well to continue to use all the power of one's energy to the hilt, come what may. It is, in fact, the only way to exist."

Louise's room in Leisureworld looked out over placid Lake Nipissing, where almost four hundred years before, Champlain had paddled in search of a passage to the Far East. Occasionally, she heard the laugh of a loon. One of her biologist friends, Iola Price, arranged for a bird feeder to be placed outside Louise's window, and a few sparrows came to feed. But the sound of traffic was a constant dark noise, and the only trees were the stunted nursery conifers that hugged the building's foundation. The place was about as distant from her idyll on Pimisi Bay as any landscape could be.

"One should not live too long," she wrote to Taverner's biographer, Jack Cranmer-Byng.

In the spring of 1986, Louise dictated a letter to friends and colleagues, informing them of her change of address and sharing the news that her new publisher, Natural Heritage/Natural History Inc., had just released *Mar* in paperback. The letter was cheery and closed with a reassurance: "Life will unfold as it must and, after all my life experiences, I am not afraid for anything."

At the bottom of the copy she sent to Dorothy Bishop, a book reviewer for *The Ottawa Journal* who had become a close friend, Louise scrawled a personal message, urging Dorothy to search in the letter for "what I would have written and extract what is me."

Dorothy was a smart, deeply compassionate woman, the best sort of friend for Louise at this point in her life. She was never sentimental, never pitying: she didn't deny how difficult life had become for Louise. "Such a torrent of response comes to me as I read and reread your letter. I had so often wondered how this winter had been for you both. I picture dear gentle Len and what his confusion of mind must have been to you in your effort to care for him."

Dorothy understood what this move meant for Louise, and she didn't mince words. "For both of you who have been the most natural woodland people I have ever known, first hospital and now a nursing home are a kind of prison. . . . I know your references to your view out over Lake Nipissing from your room, and the aural company of loons and white-throated sparrows is your wish to reassure all of us who picture the Loghouse Nest and shared even briefly your life there—reassure us that the woodland connection is not and certainly cannot be broken."

She sympathized with Louise having to dictate her correspondence to a stranger after a lifetime of writing letters with the same care she had devoted to her published articles. Letters, for Louise, had been the meatiest of conversations, small bits of herself drawn out of her soul, placed tenderly in envelopes and entrusted into the receiver's hands and heart. Instead of thoughtfully writing, rereading, and revising, Louise's words were now filtered through the hands of an intermediary. "I know these first efforts must make you feel self-conscious and constrained," Dorothy wrote. "But oh, how glad I am that you have taken this step. I hope you will often make use of your typing service for your friends as for your business acquaintances. It is a treasured link with you, however reshaped by your present circumstances."

But Louise was too private a person to be comfortable with a secretary. As soon as she recovered her strength, she returned to writing her own letters. She had many visitors in Leisureworld that first spring, including Marika Ainley, who confided to Doris that she thought Louise looked well enough to attend the centennial International Ornithological Congress that was about to take place at the National Museum of Natural History in Ottawa. Doris urged Louise to make the trip: "It would be a wonderful experience for you and you would again realize that you have prestige as the most honoured writer, or one at the very top. No more gloomy pictures of yourself which came into your two letters to me and nearly made me cry and did make Marika."

Prestige meant nothing to Louise. And those massive gatherings had been a trial even when she was thirty years younger. At the IOC there would be a thousand ornithologists from sixty-five countries delivering 250 symposia papers, 150 oral presentations, 380 poster presentations and, by the looks of it, not a descriptive life history of a single species among them. She might have enjoyed the president's lecture, which extolled ornithology as an interdisciplinary science. Already by the mid-1980s, the disadvantages of the specialization that came with professionalization were becoming apparent. She would have been heartened to hear of the bridges being built between field and laboratory, between professionals and the unschooled public: ornithologists, concluded the president, had "a worldwide responsibility to global society to demonstrate that our concern, knowledge, insight, and scientific passion are more than idle curiosity."

Louise did not attend the conference, although she received phone calls from many who did, including Baron von Haartman. "I can imagine how wonderfully pleased he must have been, having travelled so far to be in Ottawa, to be able to hear your voice," wrote Dorothy. "The human voice, like the bird voice to which both you and he have become so sensitive, carries rich messages."

The letter from Doris encouraging her to go to Ottawa marked the end of their almost fifty-year correspondence. (More letters may have been written, but no others survive.) Perhaps Doris's cheery optimism no longer struck the right note. Or perhaps Louise needed a friend now without ties to the ornithological world, one who knew her as a person, not as a researcher or as a public figure. Someone she could rely on to keep her business private. Louise had been party to the circles of gossip that swirled around Margaret Nice's decline and death. She must have anticipated with horror a similar gossipfest around how aging was reshaping her life.

Dorothy Bishop, on the other hand, offered a discreet and non-judgmental ear for the new dilemmas facing Louise. Despite crippling arthritis, Dorothy drove to North Bay to visit her friend as often as possible. She kept Louise's room supplied with fresh freesia. And she wrote sensitively about "how precious each day becomes when you are aware there is no 'forever after' about the life you so love living. All the more I dearly admire the adaptations you are now making to this new and not chosen phase of your own life."

The truth was, Louise was miserable in Leisureworld. She was closer geographically to Len, a mere taxi ride up Thibeault Hill, but the seniors' home was stifling, a hive of inane chatter. She dashed off a note to Dorothy in angry protest, then apologized for taking up her time "for nothing."

"I know I cannot fully enter into the daily confinement that so oppresses your lively mind," Dorothy responded. "Would it be a help to you if sometimes, as often as you felt the need, you wrote—to me, to other good friends, letters of protest, letters that cry out. Tell me about your visits to Len. Tell me about anything you are finding to read that engages your interest. Such letters or notes, even short ones, would drown out for a time the meaningless noisy voices around you and would fulfill a friendship that—the phrase suddenly comes back to me from Thornton Wilder's *The Woman of Andros*—shares all living, the bright and the dark."

Louise wrote neatly across the bottom of the page: "Yours was a good letter, a reality, something one could understand. The sun, thru a little."

In the course of her life, Louise had lived with two very different men. Both those relationships changed her. With Gleb, she existed "on the wings of youth with all the impulsive abandon to do and to live and to love fully and with all one's might. It never got the chance really to be tested. That came 19 years later, when I came to love another man, finally to be shocked into the realization of his total unselfishness and love. It was then I learned what faithfulness really means, how inextricably related it is with a love that is true."

Len was still living in the North Bay Psychiatric Hospital. Louise, in her faithfulness, asked to be admitted too.

The Psych, as it was called by locals, stood on a clearing amid ten acres of forest at the end of Roy Drive, a narrow road that veers off Highway 11 after it climbs the hill out of North Bay on its way to Kapuskasing. Built in 1957, the sprawling complex of five long three-storey buildings was less mid-century modern and more like the psychiatric asylums of the late nineteenth century, designed as imposing monuments to civic progress and prosperity, and typically situated apart from the town. The facility was declared surplus in 2011 when the Northeast Mental Health Centre (formerly the Psych) merged with the North Bay and District Hospital to become the North Bay Regional Health Centre. For a time, it seemed as if the old psychiatric hospital would become a prison, but after it had sat empty for two years, it was reduced to rubble in a spectacular implosion.

When I first moved to North Bay, I lived across the road from Roy Drive. Police would periodically park their cruisers nearby to comb the woods for a patient gone walkabout. I was a stay-at-home mother with two young sons. The forest drew me, but the three of us never walked very far along the narrow road. Just a glimpse of the long rows of blind windows in the distance made me shiver and turn my back.

But for Louise, the place had clear advantages. The building was outside the bustle of the small city, distant from highway traffic. The forest was close. In the autumn, from every window, she'd be able to see the woods blazing orange and red. If she was lucky, a visitor or one of the staff might take her outside where she could hear the birds. Len would be on a different floor, but just a brisk walk away. And she had already made friends among the staff during her visits with him. The geriatric ward of the psychiatric hospital was, she believed, the best she could hope for.

And so she moved into a room on Ward 3A, one of the few private rooms in the place. Barry Penhale and his wife, Jane Gibson, recall visiting Louise there. "Bleak, that's the only word for it," Jane says. "What I remember are the corridors. You had to walk up long stairs, then someone on the other side unlocked the door and you were faced with a long hall, women with all sorts of afflictions wandering there. When the door clanged shut behind you, you felt a sense of dread, as if you might never get out of that place."

Louise's room was small: a narrow bed, a chair, and a side table filled the room to capacity. On the table, her correspondence: a diminishing pile as the months and years passed. Yet the staff were as caring as she'd hoped, tucking her precious sapphire earrings into her handbag so they wouldn't go missing, making sure her hearing aids were cleaned, sending her hairpiece and Len's out to be washed and styled.

In the spring of 1988, shortly after she turned ninety-four, Louise sent a second open letter to her friends and colleagues.

"I am delighted, after a long period of silence, to be back in contact with you again." She had good news for everyone, she said. Four of her books had been reprinted by Barry Penhale's publishing company and *Another Winter, Another Spring* would be coming out in Swedish the following year. An award for northern Ontario nature writers was being established in her name. And arrangements were being made to get secretarial help for her in her new residence; she would be in touch with everyone individually very soon.

There is something off about the letter. It doesn't sound like Louise. Close, but not exact, like a piano key shifted out of tune. As if she's been coached, or someone has taken her words and forced them through a filter that removed the fire and grit from her voice along with her peculiar Scandinavian turns of phrase. Tilted her from realist to optimist.

Less than a year later, Len died, one week before Louise's ninety-fifth birthday. He had just turned eighty-four. In recent months, he'd had more bad days than good. She sat beside his bed, holding his hand and kissing him until he stopped breathing. She didn't cry. The next day, she reverted to speaking Swedish more often than not.

Louise had always thought of her life with Len not as a fixed union but as a parallel along which their two lives evolved. What she had written to Len when he left for the war remained true to the end: "At first I thought you an ordinary man who would just touch my life at one point and then go out of it. But what you carried inside of you was not common. It was deep and strong and true. . . . I came to know a happiness more real and lasting than anything I had experienced before. It has body and light and constancy. And you have kindled a love that I have not given to anyone else. It too has body and light and constancy. This is yours and mine alone, untouchable by anyone and anything and indelible in our hearts for the rest of our lives."

And so it was.

Louise's correspondence dwindled. Robert Nero, the Manitoba ornithologist, stayed in touch, their relationship deepening when he wrote to Louise of his depression, so like Len's. Perhaps because they shared these intimacies, she was honest with Nero about her move to the psychiatric hospital. "Len is here. We are together. But my spirit is broken now without Pimisi Bay, Len's lovely house, the realities of nature . . . Nothing is entirely gone. But it hurts. It still hurts."

Her last letters to Nero are handwritten, the lines wobbly, the letters shaky, the words rambling, ending with "But I am sleepy, tired, for what reason I cannot tell. Don't look at what I have written, I cannot even think straight. I cannot write any better than this. Duller and duller are the letters I write. The words do not want to come as they used to do. Make of this letter what you can and will. I'll think of you often, but not bother you with my letters. They are not worth it any more."

Louise stopped writing to Nero in 1987, but she continued to correspond with Mary Moore, a botanist from Deep River, and Dorothy Bishop, who still made her annual visit to North Bay to see Louise. "What a lively ninety-four-year-old you look—just as you are in that eager spirit of yours." Dorothy sent letters about the birds she saw, such as the horned larks she happened upon in the middle of the Experimental Farm that lies within the city of Ottawa. "Just once I heard a bit of that small tinkle of a voice" like the "tinkly drip of water from the tip of an icicle. All of this, the sun, the lengthening days as February becomes March announce in a phrase borrowed from you and always conjuring you up in mind and heart, *Another Winter, Another Spring*."

Dorothy's last letter arrived on Louise's ninety-seventh birthday: "My keen wish is that in this quiet time you should be receiving the same gentleness that for so many decades you gave to the natural world you lived in at Pimisi Bay, to the world of birds especially from which you learned so much and taught us to learn. I never pick up one of your books without discovering all over again how happily deep in my own debt I am to your patient skill in looking and listening and recording. Yours is a love beyond all measure."

And then silence.

Dorothy was so alarmed that she became convinced Louise had died. She wrote to Louise's publisher, Barry Penhale, who assured her that Louise was very much alive, but Dorothy insisted on seeing for herself. She drove up to the psychiatric hospital and went to Louise's room, where her friend lay on her narrow bed, asleep. Dorothy watched for a while. Then, reassured but no less alarmed, she turned and left.

The Loghouse Nest continued to stand among the trees, exactly as Louise and Len had left it. Now and then someone would write to

The path to the Loghouse Nest, emptied of Louise and Len in 1987

Louise, asking if she might sell the property—a neighbour, a friend, a tourist who stopped at the Rutherglen Red & White to find out if Louise was still alive.

But Louise would never sell. "This is, was, will always be where nature is alive to me," she wrote to Nero. What she had always hoped was that her small wedge of forest would continue to be what it had been while she was alive—a sanctuary for birds.

The notion of a bird refuge must have felt to Louise like a family imperative. Before she was born, her father had helped create one of the world's first conservation areas on the Karlsö islands east of Svensksund. When she wrote to Taverner that she wanted to do more than simply identify birds, she was considering setting up a sanctuary.

Instead, she got involved in banding and research, but a few years later, when her mother asked if she knew Jack Miner, famous for his duck and goose sanctuary near Kingsville, Ontario, Louise replied that she'd heard him speak and greatly admired his success in attracting migrating waterfowl. "I have just been thinking that why couldn't we do the same here. I would like to turn this into the Pimisi Bay Bird Sanctuary in time. Doris says it is already 'on the map' through my recordings and banding activities."

On the day that Len returned from the war, Louise received a packet of information on bird sanctuaries from Doris. Louise and Len sat on the front steps together, reading the pamphlets aloud, imagining not only their future but a future for the woods around them.

Two-thirds of the migratory bird sanctuaries that exist in Ontario today were created in the 1950s and 1960s. Essentially, bird sanctuaries are government-designated places where migratory birds can rest and eat and breed without falling prey to hunters or collectors of nests and eggs. For a piece of land to be designated a sanctuary, the owner has to apply for a permit and prove that the property will in fact provide food and nesting areas for the birds they intend to attract. Permits are allotted by the provincial government and overseen by the Canadian Wildlife Service. It's not clear what the process was in 1945, but certainly, creating a sanctuary would have involved more than simply deciding to make their woods a safe place for birds. Permissions were required; plans would have to be drawn up and submitted.

Louise talked to Oliver Hewitt, the chief federal migratory bird officer for Ontario and Quebec, about what her proposal should entail. She approached the local game warden, who was enthusiastic and gave her a big box of wild rice to sow in the bay. The sanctuary seemed "to be going through like a roller coaster."

While Len was in Toronto being officially demobilized from the army, Louise met with the deputy minister charged with wildlife sanctuaries. "To my surprise the interview started not very auspiciously, the opposite to what I had expected from the correspondence," she told Doris. "Too many sanctuaries all over Ontario started by cranks and resulting in nothing. So I buckled my belt one notch and said to myself: 'Now or never forward in battle for your own!' I talked fast and furiously. In the end the gentleman thought my scheme had merits, asked me to write a book about birds for his grandchildren, promised to look at Len's application as a game warden, and bowed me out with a positively warmish cordiality. Between now and the spring I shall have to do some more talking to the district superintendent, Games and Fisheries; he is definitely in favour but a little hard of hearing."

In Louise's mind, the sanctuary was already a reality. But despite the deputy minister's warm farewell, he must have thought Louise a crank after all. The subject of a sanctuary disappeared from her written conversations as suddenly as it had appeared (as did the notion of Len becoming a game warden). It flared briefly in the mid-1950s when the knob of land across from Lily-Pad Bay came up for sale. Murray used his influence to raise the possibility of buying the property and its twenty tourist cabins with the idea of setting up an outdoor education school, but nothing came of it. Louise's dream of a sanctuary must have come to mind again in 1987 when the pastor of the Svensksund parish church informed Louise that the wetlands of Svensksund—the place where, at her father's side, Louise had taken her first steps as a naturalist—had been designated a nature preserve.

Instead of creating a sanctuary, Louise and Len did what they felt was the next best thing: they bequeathed their property to Swedish bird-watching friends, Lars and Svanhild Öhman. They were friends of only a few years, but the Öhmans' Swedish appreciation for the place touched Louise. Lars was an aeronautical engineer who worked as director of flight research at the National Research Council in Ottawa. He was thirty years younger than Louise: young enough, she thought, that the values with which the property had been husbanded for fifty years would be perpetuated into the foreseeable future.

In her usual careful and thorough way, Louise made a list of the jewellery and furniture she had inherited from her mother, her grandmother, and great grandmother and designated the nieces, nephews, and friends who would inherit each item. The Liljefors painting was to go to Ebba's son, Per-Olof; her sapphire earrings from Gleb's mother, to Ebba's elder daughter, Anita; and the large oval garnet brooch surrounded by diamonds—her father's gift to her mother on the occasion of Louise's birth—to Ebba's younger daughter, Lise. She listed a few cash donations in the five pages of bequests, most significantly to the Ottawa Field-Naturalists' Club, to be used, ironically, to establish a 'conservation' fund in her name.

Just before her ninety-first birthday, Louise wrote a living will even though such documents had no legal weight at the time (and as of 2020, still do not in Ontario). "Death is as much a reality as birth, growth, maturity, and old age. It is the one certainty of life," she wrote. She asked that she be allowed to die naturally, not kept alive "by artificial means or heroic measures. I do not fear death itself as much as the indignities of deterioration, dependence, and hopeless pain." She asked that medication be "mercifully administered" to alleviate her suffering, even if the drugs might hasten the moment of her death. Her living will, she declared, was made with the intention of relieving her family, her doctor, and her lawyer, and whatever medical facility or people were caring for her, of the responsibility of making end-of-life decisions "and placing it upon myself in accordance with my strong convictions." She asked that her body be cremated and the ashes buried near her bird-feeding station.

The future of her property, her family heirlooms, and her body taken care of, all that remained was her literary and scientific estate. In 1970, she had made the decision to bequeath her manuscripts, books, journals, and medals—the John Burroughs Medal as well as the Swedish Red Cross and the Nansen Mission medals for her work in Russia and the 1935 Jubilee Medal from King George V for her role in saving the Quints—to the North Bay Public Library "in recognition of the warm interest and encouragement that the people of North Bay have always shown me in my various endeavours." The library was delighted to accept. But then, in the early 1980s, Marika Ainley became her friend. As a student of the history of ornithology who understood the importance of archival research, Marika highly recommended Louise donate her papers to a more central and focused facility, specifically, the Blacker-Wood Library of Zoology and Ornithology at McGill University. There, Louise's archives would join a collection of more than three hundred manuscripts and over three thousand folders of letters written by naturalists, mostly from the nineteenth and early twentieth centuries. McGill's letter of interest arrived just days after a similar solicitation came from the Public Archives of Canada in Ottawa (now Library and Archives Canada). Because her focus had always been the art of writing as well as natural history, she chose the national archive. In what sounds a bit like a consolation prize, she bequeathed two bird illustrations to the Blacker-Wood collection, both painted by Roger Tory Peterson and given to her by Margaret Morse Nice.

Although her wishes condense neatly into a couple of paragraphs in her will, the arrangements took great thought and effort. What a relief it must have been, once the moment came when she had no choice but to leave her log house forever, to know that the future of her papers, her heirlooms, and her house was assured. In 1991, she relieved herself of the demands of letter-writing, too, consigning that chore to the staff at Barry Penhale's publishing house.

Her own future was less certain. One of Dorothy's last surviving letters to Louise describes the bumpy process of aging—of life itself—which rarely proceeds smoothly but rather in jerks and glides, taking a pause now and then before hurtling on. "You have been along variations of this road long before me and your philosophy of acceptance has long ago taught you that aging comes most of the time by gradual stages, like the learning process itself, holding at certain plateaus. It's the sharp shift from those plateaus that can at first be dizzying."

"I adjust," Louise said, with her usual stoicism. "Old age is the ultimate time of learning. And so it goes for as long as it lasts."

One by one Louise's loved ones were leaving her. Within two years, Len died, and Doris died too.

As a legacy, Doris had set up the Doris Huestis Speirs Award to be presented annually to an individual who had made an outstanding lifetime contribution to Canadian ornithology. In 1991, the award was presented to Louise at the annual meeting of the Society of Canadian Ornithologists, a group founded to host the 1986 International Ornithological Congress in Ottawa. Louise was ninety-seven, unable to travel to receive the award. Had Doris been alive to personally hand it to her, she might have found a way.

It strikes me as astonishing how many naturalists live to a great age. Margaret Morse Nice, Doris Speirs, Althea Sherman, Earl Godfrey, all lived into their nineties. Alexander Skutch lived to a hundred. Ernst Mayr to 101; when he was ninety-three he published *This Is Biology*, a marvellous book that ranges through a lifetime of thought. Murray Speirs lived to 112.

"When once I die, I shall have no quarrel with life," Louise wrote. "It has demanded much but it has repaid in full."

On a bright May afternoon in 1992, Louise's ninety-ninth year, a friend telephoned me to say her daughter had just driven up Highway 17 to North Bay and noticed a heap of furniture and boxes of books at the end of Louise's driveway. I called Barry Penhale in a panic. What happened? Louise had died a few weeks before, he said calmly. Lars Öhman had taken over the log house. Shaken, I called my friend back: ask your daughter to salvage whatever she can.

By the time she returned to the driveway, the boxes had been picked through. All that was left was a small table, the table on which I write this now. It is a kitchen worktable, no more than a metre square, with a pullout drawer divided for cutlery. It is obviously handmade, the work of Len, I imagine. The legs are square and heavy, but they are connected by a nicely shaped yoke of hardwood. The top is stained a deep red. I try to remember if I saw it in her house. I would be fabricating if I said I did. I never stayed in the House on the Point, but perhaps it ended up there, part of her attempt to turn the little cabin into a self-contained guest house that would siphon visitors away from her study area and her prime writing times. I imagine the table began life in Louise's tiny kitchen, before it was enlarged into a sunroom, before her mother died and left Louise the elegant furniture she'd grown up with in Svensksund. In my imaginings, this is the table at which Louise sat, holding the trap-strings that passed through drill-holes in the chinking of the log house in her first days of banding birds.

I have carried this table with me from house to house for almost thirty years. It is really too small for a writing desk, so it has sat in various corners of my life until this winter when we set up a proper reference library. Now it sits in an alcove framed by shelves of dictionaries, encyclopaedias, and bird reference books.

It looks like it feels at home.

18

Never a Day Alike to the Other

"We were so happy here." Louise pauses on the winding path through the woods, halfway between the garage by the highway where I parked the car and the house we can barely glimpse in the distance through the trees. She pauses the way the prince does at the sight of Snow White's castle. Or Alice as she steps through the looking-glass. It is a mythic moment, fairy-tale perfect, or it would be if I weren't so terrified that she'll trip over a root and fall in a brittle mess of arms and legs that I won't be able to lift. But Louise is sure-footed. She insists I carry her cane and only once does she lay a hand on my arm to steady herself.

Birds rustle through the underbrush and across the canopy as we make our slow way toward the house, a place she hasn't seen in I don't know how long. "I am here. I am here," she coos softly in a Swedish accent that has thickened since we last spoke. She responds to the faint chirps, tweets, and churrs with delight, calling out the names of the birds as if greeting old friends.

She hears the wheezing *oh-weee, oh-weee, oh-weee, oh-weee* of the yellow-bellied sapsucker before she sees it. "Ah! That's a voice I recognize," she exclaims, scanning the trunks of nearby pines for the jazzy black-and-white back of the woodpecker. She spots the bird nosing up a branch that protrudes from a fallen maple. She takes the cane from my hand, and bends to knuckle a sharp tattoo along its side: two firm raps, then a staccato roll, and a triple ritardando. The bird cocks its head, digs its talons deeper, and drums a responding *ra-ta-tatatata-ta-ta-ta*.

"You see," she whispers, "we still understand each other."

Louise and I have six precious hours together. I drove from Kingston the long way, through Algonquin Park and up Highway 11 to North Bay, so I could pass the little white frame house with the sign *Home of the Dionne Quintuplets* that was moved from Corbeil to the verge of the Trans-Canada Highway years ago. Louise was waiting for me in the foyer of the psych hospital when I pulled up in my little red Toyota. She was thinner than I remembered, a bit frailer perhaps, which I was prepared for. She is ninety-four, after all. What I didn't expect was her still-prodigious energy, the kind of stamina that propels migrating birds across continents.

"I hope I'm not tiring you," she asks with a concern that should be ironic, given that she is more than twice my age. As it is, only my pride and a perverse interest in the limits of her vitality keep me from suggesting we stop to rest.

The path meanders and I think of the pact Louise and Len made early on that "our imprints were to mar the surroundings as lightly as possible. We cut no trails but like the deer and snowshoe hare wore our paths over the rocks, around the trees and bushes. We left the thickets to grow in their own way, the undergrowth to remain dense and tangled to protect the resting places of the birds."

Using her cane as a wand, she pushes aside the branches and bracken that droop across the path. She points out the globules of resin that ring a sapsucker nesting hole, shining like a giant eye to scare away predators, its gossamer curtain in shreds, and the teacup nest of a warbler hanging in a patch of wild raspberry. I think we are meandering until I realize she is visiting the houses of the birds she studied, the way someone returning to the town where they grew up makes the rounds of the places where friends once lived. She stops at a crumbling stump, a stand-in for the remains of the tree that was once an avian co-op.

"Why? . . . why? . . . *why?* . . . that was mostly what I was interested in," she muses. Her lilting Swedish accent shifts every statement to a question. She speaks slowly and thoughtfully, as she always has, at least in the eight years I've known her, as if she is editing her sentences before she lets them out of her mouth.

The planters by the front door are still bright with fall asters; someone has been looking after the place during the years she's been away. Inside, kindling is stacked by the hearth; a half-finished sock stretches between knitting needles stuck into a ball of wool beside the chair that Len made for her.

I've brought a picnic lunch. I find blue plates in the sideboard, each decorated with a flying white gull. "Bing and Grøndahl," Louise murmurs. "A wedding present from my godmother, the Queen of Denmark." I offer to find other plates, if these are too good to use, but Louise waves away my concern, saying, "They are happy to be with us." She directs me to her parents' sterling silver cutlery, decorated with the Flach crest of her father and the Neergaard crest of her mother.

I lay out a Swedish smorgasbord: pickled herring, cardamom bread, marinated cucumbers, gravlax, pickled beets, Västerbotten cheese. I couldn't find lingonberry jam; I had to make the Swedish tea cookies with my own strawberry preserves dropped into the thumbprint. And Marabou chocolate: that was impossible. But I did bring a thermos of the good strong coffee she likes. I spread the plates of food between us on the small table in the sunroom so we can watch the birds as we eat. The feeding trays are empty, the coconut halfshells and hummingbird goblet gone, but the chickadees still land on the windowsill and we see a flicker, a hairy woodpecker, and kinglets playing in the shrubbery. We hear a loon, some scolding phoebes, the clothesline screech of a blue jay, the *chip-chip-chip* of chipping sparrows. A brown thrasher breaks through the underbrush and flies like a chestnut arrow across the clearing.

"Late for him to be here," Louise says. "And has the red-eye gone yet, I wonder?"

When we see a downy woodpecker, the smallest, most demurely reserved of the woodpeckers, I think of Louise's next-to-last article, the one she wrote and rewrote, and rewrote again for *The Living Bird Quarterly*, until it was a series of condensed, elegant paragraphs punctuated with Aleta Karstad's drawings. A male excavating a nest hole. His mate rising on tiptoe, bill gaping and pointed in the air, her body turning like a weather vane to ward off an interloping female. The female perching, tail up, motionless, waiting for her mate. The split-second consummation. The drawings are competent; the writing that opens a window into the bird boudoir, unforgettable.

It was not unusual for Louise to count seventy-five species in a day. I worry that she'll be disappointed by the handful we are seeing, but her face is wide with pleasure and curiosity. I've seen that look before, on Roger Tory Peterson, when we were watching gulls together on the shore near his home in Old Lyme, Connecticut. All we saw that cold, blustery November day were gulls and a few terns, but he was as entranced as if the entire brilliance of a tropical aviary were flying arabesques before our eyes. Neither of these watchers ever said to me, as I have said to myself, "Oh, it's just a gull," or "Nothing but sparrows." Every bird is worth knowing by name.

Some days, Louise says, she thinks there might be another book germinating. Other days, it's all she can do to recall the past as anything but fragments that bob to the surface, debris in the backwash of a life. I think of something she wrote twenty years before: "Now is the time neither to look forward nor to look back, but to fashion out of each day its own empire."

Before dessert we have a little walkabout through the house. Louise opens her bedroom closet and shows me her gowns, floor-length black, midnight blue, and jade green dresses, beaded and tucked, hanging beside her stout bush jackets and wool bird-watching trousers. She introduces me to the Bruno Liljefors painting of pheasants in the living room, the sweet portrait of herself at the age of five, the blue-and-white quilt her great-grandmother made from her two wedding dresses, still spread on the bed Louise once shared with Len. Above the bed, a pencil drawing of her great-grand-aunt Sophie von Knorring, a pioneering Swedish novelist, and on the walls, four tapestries embroidered with ninety-five medallions, each stitched by one of Sophie's ninety-five friends. The elegant eighteenth-century chairs and tables that came to Louise from her great-grands should seem out of place in this log cabin, but they don't. The bookshelves, the chesterfield and chairs in the living room, and the table in the kitchen were all made by Len; they are sturdy and functional, not without a certain grace. When she opens the drawer of a small table by the front door, black-and-white eight-by-tens spring out, rows of babies on a table, in prams, saying their prayers. She snaps the drawer shut.

It is growing cool and Louise seems tired. I don't want to cut short our time together by even a moment, so I suggest she sit in her chair by the hearth. "I'll make a fire," I say. The kindling has been set, not in the usual teepee arrangement of crumpled paper topped with sticks that rise to a log on top, but in log cabin style: a few layers of larger firewood squared on the bottom, some dry needles and tinder cupped inside, then smaller sticks to complete the 'roof.'

I am used to making fires. I have been cooking on a woodstove and heating my house with split maple and birch for more than a decade. I light a match and poke it in between the logs until the tinder catches. Smoke billows into the room. I am sure I opened the draft but I fiddle again with the knob, trying to make the smoke rise up the chimney. The air in the room is thickening at an alarming rate. I help Louise up and out of the house, settle her in a chair on the porch, then madly rummage through the kitchen for baking soda, my heart pounding. I find a box and dump it on the fire, poking the larger logs, which haven't yet caught fire, out of the way. I throw open the windows and wave my jacket madly to clear the smoke. Every few minutes I check on Louise, who looks bemused.

"Perhaps a bird has taken over the Loghouse Nest with a nest of her own," she says calmly, eyeing the smoke billowing out the front door.

The stories Louise tells me are not the same versions she wrote to her mother, not the same versions she shared with Doris and Margaret, not the same versions she laid before reporters and the people who came to hear her speeches, not what she honed so diligently for publication. The stories she told at forty often changed by the time she reached into her eighties and nineties. Listening to Louise, and now, reading her letters, her drafts, her notes to herself, I am aware of how much stories are shaped for their audience. And how much the way a story is crafted determines which details are retained, brought to the fore, and which are allowed to drop away.

Which version is true? As I tell Louise's story, I am constantly looking for 'the truth.' Not necessarily the factual truth, but the emotional truth, the version of the story that best reveals Louise for who she really was, insofar as I can know such a thing. Each version is true, of course, in its own way. I'm inclined to put my greatest faith in her letters to her mother and to Margaret, which seem frankly written, from the heart. Louise holds back in her published writing: some things are not meant for the public, for strangers. She has a sense of privacy that I associate with nobility. I think of her cousin, Karen Blixen, who wrote under a pseudonym, but even so, she chose to omit or mask details that weren't essential to the story or simply weren't, to her mind, anybody's business. Such reticence seems charmingly old-fashioned in today's tell-all anti-privacy culture. Louise didn't hold back with her mother, but most of the early letters are in Swedish, which I don't understand. Reading the translated pages, I worry about the nuances I am missing.

But I knew Louise. I spent time in her house. We drank good coffee together. I cling to that.

Thirty-two years later I am back in Louise's log house, which I did not burn to the ground, thank goodness. I am here for the month of September, to finish this book and to watch the fall bird migration.

When I heard that the new owners had extended a driveway up to the house, I was aghast. But Craig and Michelle, who operate the commercial centre of the village of Rutherglen—Home Hardware, Red & White grocery store, gas pumps, heavy equipment rental, and liquor store—are sensitive and discreet. The driveway mounts Peak Hill behind the house and circles within a screen of trees. Louise's path still winds through the Green Woods between the house and the garage, a path lined with her scavenged stones, now thickly mossed over. A large deck extends off the north side of the house, built by the woman who owned the property before Craig and Michelle. It is impossible to imagine Louise there. When would she have found time to sit and stare at the lake? She was far too busy watching the birds in the trees.

On my first morning, I wake before dawn and walk the paths in the scant light. Pine squirrels scold me from the treetops. The second-growth conifers that reached maturity under Louise's watch are tumbling now. Craig had to shoulder one up off the path before we could get to the house; it was so riddled with rot I could have lifted it myself. Thickets of skinny maple, birch, and aspen strain toward rends in the canopy. At first, the woods seem silent and my heart sinks. Will there be no dawn chorus? Then I hear a northern flicker. A chickadee. A blue jay. Half the trill of a white-throated sparrow. A broad-winged hawk dips overhead to see what might be for breakfast. There are American black ducks in Lily-Pad Bay. Three crows land outside the back door, and after a cawing conversation, start tipping over rocks in a complicated shell game.

As the sun warms, a myrtle, a Nashville, and a yellow warbler work their way bush to bush through the clearing. According to Louise's records, the last date for the departure of the yellow warbler was typically the first of September. I am grateful it waited an extra day and wish it farewell. In any ordinary year, sans pandemic, I might see them again in Mexico, tourists among the cacti and mesquite, or maybe that's not true for those of us who make two places home.

I'm too late for most of the warblers and the phoebe, too, I think. But then an eastern phoebe lands on a low branch, flicking its tail, pausing as if to make sure I get a good look. On my way back to the house, I prowl around the garage, the shed, the house, checking the eaves for phoebe nests and I find two, a fresh one on an old piece of lattice leaning against the wall of the house, and another, an elaborate three-tiered affair, on a ledge just outside Louise's bedroom window—evidence that phoebes have been raising their families around this house for eighty-five years.

I make myself a Swedish coffee and sit on the front porch beside a row of bottles Craig and Michelle dug out of a midden they exposed while making their road. Swedes are coffee fanatics; they are among the top three coffee consumers in the world. And they like their coffee strong—boiled with a raw egg to create a smooth, thick slurry that is astonishingly delicious. I no longer drink coffee, but it seems right to do so here.

According to Louise's cumulative "Last Fall Date" sight records, the flycatchers, swallows, brown thrashers, and some of the warblers—Blackburnian, chestnut-sided—should already have left, but there are dozens more birds I hope to see. I try to scale back my expectations. Decades have passed since Louise made that list: the birds might have moved to other breeding grounds; climate change may have shifted their departure dates; natural disasters akin to the wildfires raging in California may have culled their numbers.

Over·the weeks, I watch the dozen or so regulars. I buy birdseed, hearing Louise's sharp critique: "Wildness, the wild creature's most vital asset of self-preservation, is lost." But, I silently reply, it's fall. I'm just helping the birds put on enough fat for the winter or for the long flight south, okay?

I fill Louise's old feeders, and those left by the three owners since, including a trio of modern metal cylinders positioned over a rock cairn outside the sunroom window where I can watch the nuthatches and white-crowned sparrows as I work, my desk aligned with Louise's as she worked on *The Lovely and the Wild*. Blue jays and white-crowned sparrows make quick work of the seed I sprinkle in the remains of Len's birdbath and on the artful arrangement of stones that conceals Louise's ashes. I check the tips of the high branches for cones, but they are sparse. This isn't going to be a finchy winter like the one that brought the golden bird to our feeding stations, something we never talked about, although I am certain from her notes and mine that the same bird flew between our woods. "Can you imagine one dressed *totally* with the exception of the primaries in the deep golden of the male's eyebrowline?" she wrote to Doris. "Len saw it first, then I saw it to take in the details. It was also seen elsewhere, even at North Bay. A beautiful strange sight."

I spot a brown creeper inching headfirst down a soaring red pine. I am pondering the tree trunk, trying to figure out how to get a smear of peanut butter high enough to attract the creeper, when I notice a homemade, moss-covered ladder propped on a granite boulder and leaning against the tree. Red pines can live up to 350 years, reaching thirty-five metres in height and up to seventy-five centimetres in diameter. They do most of that growing in their first six decades. This pine is at least sixty centimetres across and soars above the canopy; it must have been young when Louise was here. I test the ladder rungs: only the top one is rotted. Gingerly, I climb up and lather the bark with organic crunchy peanut butter mixed with bacon fat. The next day the smear is gone.

The woods are eerily silent. I blame the road that bounds Louise's property, now widened into the Trans-Canada Highway—a constant three-lane race of logging trucks and tractor-trailers, air-brakes chuddering as they speed down the hill and over the bridge between Beaver Lake and Pimisi Bay. Silence is so rare that I time it with my iPhone stopwatch: on average, night and day, the lull between vehicles is a mere ten seconds.

In my boxes of files lined up in the sunroom, I find the photocopy of Louise's list of the birds that should still be in residence. I listen, but I hear no loons, no kestrels, no whippoorwills, no kinglets, no cedar waxwings, no thrushes, no woodpeckers. No. No. No. I make small red crosses beside the names of the absentees, then checkmark the species I see. Three song sparrows. A swamp sparrow. A pair of slate-coloured juncos.

I hear Louise's voice in my ear, "Because you see a bird, you do not know it."

Watching the birds and writing Louise's life in her sunroom, 2020

For two days I stalk a slim, pale-bellied bird as it flits through the canopy, diving into bouquets of bristling needles and dangling leaves. When at last it hops into the open, a ray of sunlight hits its garnet eye. A red-eyed vireo! And then I realize the error of my thinking. It's autumn: the birds are here, but they have no need to stake out a territory or attract a mate or stay in touch with a partner as she incubates her eggs. No need for song. All their energy goes into feeding now, building up fat for their long flight south or for the cold winter ahead. The traffic hasn't shut them up or driven them off. It bothers me, but to them it's no different, I suppose, than a rushing waterfall.

I am sorry there is so little birdsong but delighted by the unfamiliar juveniles. I hardly recognize the juvey red-winged blackbird with its bronze feathers, a nervy lipstick smudge on each shoulder. The young song sparrows seem undressed without their stickpins. The bibs of the adolescent white-throated sparrows are grey, as if they've been dumpster-diving in ash.

Louise is everywhere I look. Inside, the Liljefors is gone, the blue-and-white wedding quilt, the Empire chairs, Len's hand-crafted furniture, and the portrait of Louise at the age of five. But her royal-blue leather key fob with the shining *K* is on the window ledge, the key still inserted into its sturdy German padlock—a relic from when her surname was simply Kiriline. Beside the key fob, a handmade cribbage board with wavering lines of holes. Her bellows sits by the fireplace, near the three-legged milking stool a friend made her for Christmas in 1937. I recognize both from photographs of Louise in the living room a few years after she moved in. Above the table where I write at night, light shines down through delicately punched stars—one of the copper fixtures Louise bought in 1956 when electricity came to the log house. In the morning, I waken to the sun on my face, the same sun that woke her, that has wakened these woods for centuries, these granite rocks for eons.

It occurs to me that what fascinated Louise and became the focus of her studies—mating, nesting, communication, loyalty to place, and the constant righting of emotional balance—were also the forces that dramatically shaped her life.

I look out her bedroom window and see the phoebes launching from their nest into the honeysuckle bushes that still tumble toward the shore. When I walk the path to the road, I see her pushing her wheelbarrow full of groceries, chickadees fluttering around in escort, perching on her paper bags, on her shoulders, begging for sunflower seeds. I see Len approaching the house, the adopted merlins screaming at him to be gone. The log walls he stained deep brown each fall, whitewashing the chinking so that from a distance sunlight seemed to play across the walls, seem unchanged, although the roof is now red metal instead of cedar shake. Even so, the house still looks like a nest, low-slung and compact, tucked among the trees and underbrush. "We have made use of everything that extends naturally on our piece of rocky land without destroying any of its essence," she told the *Toronto Star* in 1968 when *The Lovely and the Wild* came out. "We live in harmony with all the life around us. If you saw it you would understand how rich such a life can be in the wilderness."

"I don't think I can ever give up this house," she said. But of course she could. She had to. She did.

Four years ago, I almost bought this place. My husband and I walked through the log house with its second owner, a woman in midlife. She and her partner had planned to retire here, then her partner found a new love, and this woman couldn't bear to be alone with her broken dreams.

When a friend in the area emailed me to say Louise's Loghouse Nest might be for sale, I wanted it with an ache that surprised me. I would turn the property into a bird sanctuary. I would start a nature writing school. I would complete the life that Louise couldn't.

The woman was a fan of Louise and took her legacy seriously: she had restored the paths and dug out the Little Stream that we crossed on our way from the garage to the house. But some things made me wince. The birdbath that Len made for Louise out of cement and stones from the shore, his "work of art," had been moved behind the shed. The woman called it a monstrosity, which I suppose it was, although lovely in the way that memories are. And overlooking the clearing, a statue of the Virgin Mary reached out in embrace, unaware that the god of this land is Nature.

We were leaving for Mexico in a matter of weeks, but I rashly made an offer. The woman wasn't sure. Someone else was interested, she said. Maybe she shouldn't be too hasty; the break-up was still fresh. She and her partner might get back together. She was in crisis, not the best time to make a life-changing decision.

For several months, we wrote back and forth. I felt in my heart that I was meant to be custodian of Louise's land. But the roar of traffic was constant. Across Pimisi Bay, the discreet row of cottages was now a campground; jet skis whizzed across the bay. I tried to be practical: we lived five hours away and spent half the year in another country.

In the end, I withdrew the offer. The woman couldn't make a decision; her future was too uncertain. And I was living in the past.

The last time Louise and I are at the log house together, we linger by her desk in the office bedroom, looking out the big windows that give onto Pimisi Bay. Her book of bird notes lies open to her last entry, dated April 30, 1985.

"You cannot imagine how it feels to have one question after another solved about how birds live," she says wistfully, fingering the notebook's pages. "When I think of it now, I realize what a mammoth job it was. It is a pity I couldn't finish it."

Understanding how birds are—the task Louise set herself—will never be finished. According to Robert Montgomerie, a bird scientist and one of the authors of *Ten Thousand Birds: Ornithology Since Darwin*, published in 2014, "There are 'modern' life histories for maybe one-third of the world's 10,000 bird species, but I would guess that only half of those, or less, are anywhere near comprehensive. I think it would be reasonable to say that only about 10 to 20 percent of the world's bird species have been well studied."

When Louise started watching northern songbirds in their breeding grounds in 1939, almost nothing was known about many of the species she studied. Since then, bird research has exploded, especially so in the last decade. According to *Ten Thousand Birds*, as many papers on birds were published in a single year—2011—as in the century between Darwin's *Origin of Species* and 1955. Birds, it claims, "have contributed more to the study of zoology than almost any other group of animals." Louise subscribed to a stack of ornithology journals in her struggle to keep up with the literature, but researchers no longer even try; there's just too much of it. And whereas Louise could know all the leading researchers of the day personally and be connected with the most interesting women ornithologists of her time, the world of bird science is simply too crowded now.

Many of today's studies are built on the foundation of life histories such as Louise's. The behaviours she recorded and puzzled over are being investigated and interpreted by scientists who, using technology that would have astonished her, are proving true what she deduced from observation alone.

Birds, it turns out, are the great communicators of the animal world. "Birds talk all the time, while they fly and fight and court and travel, they speak with their voices, their bodies, and their feathers, gestures, displays," writes Jennifer Ackerman in *The Bird Way*, a brilliant roundup of recent research. "They may not have facial expressions, but they have expressions nonetheless, subtle, and effective in communicating."

Birds have local dialects; species can distinguish between birds of their own flock and those from away. A bird isn't born with a repertoire of calls, notes, and songs: it learns them through a process not unlike the way a human child learns language. And calls that sound simple are actually acoustically sophisticated and nuanced in their meaning. The seemingly mundane and repetitive *chickadee-dee-dee*, for instance, is an alert call that contains coded messages about the size of the predator and the level of danger, based on the number of *dee-dee-dees*. There is a different sound if the danger comes from above or from below, so that the listening bird knows where to look. Different inflections indicate different threats. I used to see this in my chickens: they'd screech at an owl or a merlin; gurgle menacingly when a raccoon appeared. There are calls that ask birds in the neighbourhood to collectively mob an intruder, calls that tell them to flee. Birds sing duets that function like conversations. After generations of bias that assumed all avian singers were male, scientists have discovered (as Louise knew from watching) that females sing too. The newest research suggests that songbirds possess an ability to combine tones to create meaning, not unlike the way humans join words to create phrases, a skill we think is ours alone.

Louise carefully logged the specific food that birds brought to their young, but she didn't know where they got the larvae and flying insects or how they found so many amongst the trees. Using cameras fitted with special filters, scientists can now see the canopy as a bird does—not as a flat green ceiling but as a detailed three-dimensional world, more like a labyrinth than a painting, an avian food court that birds navigate with ease.

Researchers are dismantling conventional wisdoms that have been passed down and accepted by generations of ornithologists with the same lazy faith that led them to accept Aristotle's incubation dates—and so infuriated Margaret and Louise. For instance, scientists took avian lack of smell as a given until a scientific illustrator named Betsy Bang, working in the 1950s, provided anatomical evidence that most birds have olfactory systems. Since then, studies have confirmed that birds use smell to choose nest materials, locate their nests, choose mates, avoid predators, search for food, even create olfactory maps to guide them during migration.

Louise watched black-capped chickadees cache their food and retrieve it, surmising that they followed some kind of mental map to locate the hidden seeds. Now we know that birds do indeed have memories. Recently, researchers in Algonquin Park studied Canada jays, which cache berries, fungi, insects, carcass meat and other foods in the nooks and crannies of trees through summer and fall, remembering where they've stored tens of thousands of food items scattered throughout a territory as large as 160 hectares. The stored food helps birds survive the winter and makes breeding in mid-February possible—thus answering the question Margaret Nice asked Louise. The jays cache mostly in black spruce and pine, where the resinous bark has antibacterial and antifungal properties that help preserve the food. These are also the trees where Canada jays nest, as Louise discovered.

"It's clear that birds are thinking beings," writes Ackerman, "even if they are thinking about different things in different ways than we humans do."

As Louise watched her young merlins flying over the lake, it never occurred to her that their acrobatics could be anything but training flights. Contemporary scientists, however, have discovered that birds have a sense of play that includes flying contests. There's also a theory that play reduces stress, and this is something that Louise noted often: screaming woodpecker chases through the forest weren't aggressive so much as a safe way to let off steam.

One phenomenon that Louise noticed—the safe zone for small songbirds under the merlins' nest—has been explained by ornithologist Sue Healy: when predators such as hawks take up residence, smaller predators like jays forage higher up to avoid the hawks, creating a cone of safety for small songbirds under the hawk nest.

Matthew Louder answered another of Louise's puzzles: why does a baby cowbird, hatching in warbler's nest and imprinting on its adoptive parent, not sing like a songbird? How does it learn its birth mother's language? Louder discovered that the cowbird mother produces a chatter call in the vicinity of the surrogate parent's nest that acts as a kind of 'acoustic password' to unlock the brain so the young bird is receptive to learning the song language of its own kind.

At the time Louise was observing her sixty-five nests, scientists believed that parental roles were fixed: if a female disappeared, the male would carry out only his usual share of the work, even if it meant the young died of neglect. In *Mar*, Louise recounted the story of a male that took over all the feeding, brooding, and sanitizing when his mate disappeared, successfully raising his brood as a single parent. Researchers have now shown experimentally that if one member of a pair is removed, the other often compensates, working harder to make sure the job gets done, implying that each parent monitors the other's role, an interplay that Louise had recorded and analyzed forty years before.

Questions that never occurred to Louise have now been answered. I suspect she'd be amazed to learn that the tongue-tips of her beloved woodpeckers are capable of independent movement, allowing the birds to lap up insects deep inside the holes they drill. A gland under the tongue secretes a sticky fluid that glues the food to the tongue, yet the tongue is so hard it can impale grubs and caterpillars. The tongue is controlled by a complex system of bones and muscles that create "horns" that sweep behind the tongue and wrap around the skull, protecting the brain from the shattering percussion of the woodpecker's drilling and drumming.

The mystery of migration—one of Louise's ongoing puzzles and the one that closed her final book—is now at least partially understood thanks to Bridget Stutchbury, a Canadian ornithologist who fitted migrating wood thrushes and purple martins with miniature backpacks carrying geolocators the size of a dime. She discovered that the birds could fly more than five hundred kilometres a day, far more than the 150 kilometres a day estimated by earlier studies. One bird took just under two weeks to return the seven thousand kilometres from its wintering grounds to its breeding grounds. On the way south, the birds often made extended stopovers, sometimes as long as a month, to feed before making the long crossings across the Gulf of Mexico and the Caribbean on their way to South America.

Compared to the specificity of such research, the question that guided Louise's watches was broad: How do birds live?

"There is still a need for descriptive life histories," says Robert Montgomerie, who trolls decades-old observation studies for examples of bird behaviour relevant to his research. "Those old life histories still contain information of value to researchers because they are facts. Interpretations are subject to change, but facts remain."

More and more, scientists are navigating the boundary between the naturalist tradition of close observation and theory-driven biology. How Louise would have revelled in this new research, both for its conclusions and for the fact that it is based on how birds actually behave, rather than on assumptions that birds are just like humans. "Scientists traditionally have little use for anecdotal evidence, demanding data that can be replicated or manipulated statistically," Jennifer Ackerman observes in *The Bird Way*. "But a single observation by a competent and honest observer of a bird doing something exceptional can offer a rare window into a bird's flexibility of mind. Their reports are anecdotal to be sure, but together they produce plentiful evidence of the ability of birds to solve problems or discover new and better ways to accomplish daily tasks."

I sit in Louise's sunroom, watching the chickadees snatch up one sunflower seed after another, giving each a brisk tap with their beak, then flying off with the nutmeat to stuff it under a curling piece of bark or between two twigs, or in the fissure of a knot in a tree trunk. Louise banded birds just like these and plotted where they stored their fall harvest. In the winter, she told me, they returned to their scattered larders—in order, not randomly as scientists once thought—all of them emptied come spring.

At first, Louise had held a sunflower seed in her outstretched hand until the chickadees were so conditioned they'd sit on her nose or eyeglasses to pluck the seed from between her lips. When she went inside the log house, they'd hover at the windows, following her room to room, sitting on the sills, pecking at the panes. Eventually they learned that it was the door that returned this mobile seed-supplier to them, and they hovered there, waiting for her to come outside with more seed. She started to hide a sunflower seed behind the cream jug or sticking out from the pages of her books, leaving the sunroom window open to see how quickly the birds could find the food. In endless experiments, she canoed into the bay to measure how far the chickadees—birds typically reluctant to cross open spaces—would follow her for the sake of a seed. Most would venture only seven to fifteen metres, but Peet, her first and boldest banded chickadee, would fly forty-five to sixty metres to land on her head for his reward.

No matter how Louise stood or crouched, no matter what she wore, no matter whether she went into the house or emerged from her car, they came flitting for her seeds. The chickadees even recognized her lying down, plucking seeds from her forehead as she napped on the front porch. Only once were they deceived. When she wore her blond muskrat coat with the dark collar, even though she held out a generous handful of seed, they refused to come close, mobbing at a distance, loudly scolding and flicking their wings, darting branch to branch, chasing each other madly to relieve the tension of this perceived threat in their midst.

Chickadees don't live long, usually three years or so, although one of Louise's banded female chickadees returned through nine summers. Louise never knew how Peet died; he simply disappeared, "a lovely way for a friend to take his leave—to be there and then just to be gone."

From Peet and *The Loghouse Nest* to the mating grouse of her last study, what mattered to Louise, and increasingly matters to contemporary bird scientists, is the bird's perspective, not the researcher's. Getting a bird's-eye view isn't easy; it involves breaking down human assumptions and risking ridicule. Technology helps. Tools that Louise never dreamed of—cameras, microphones, and delicate digital sensors—can now record bird behaviour in the wild without a human ever stepping foot on the scene.

Louise called herself an amateur ornithological naturalist. She would have welcomed the rise of citizen science—a fancy synonym for amateur that embraces anyone interested in watching birds. A kind of avian crowd-sourcing of bird location data has effectively made banding obsolete for migration studies: millions of watchers all over the world record the birds they see, then submit their digital bird lists through the eBird app. As of 2018, some 600 million observations had been collated to create highly accurate maps of the range and migration patterns of more than six hundred species. During the 2020 Global Big Day bird count alone, eBird users submitted sightings of over 2.1 million birds. Data like this is analyzed to answer questions such as whether protected areas are really supporting biodiversity and if there is a link between migration timing and seasonal vegetation.

The reams of handwritten nest cards and bird study data of early watchers are also being digitized for the benefit of contemporary researchers. Just a few years ago, I had to make a trip to the Royal Ontario Museum and the Canadian Museum of Nature (formerly the National Museum of Natural Sciences) to find out how many of Louise's study skins were in their specimen drawers. Now, a few clicks of my mouse and I can see the entire list—eight donations to the Royal Ontario Museum and twenty-one to Ottawa—through the wonder of VertNet, a global collaborative database that provides free access to the vertebrate collections of hundreds of natural history museums around the world.

Public interest in birds has never been higher, especially since the Covid-19 pandemic made human interaction risky and sent people out of doors into nature, sparking a desire to know more about what they were seeing. According to Cornell University, in the fall of 2020, 22 million people visited its All About Birds website. Conservation films were viewed over 21 million times, and photographers contributed nearly seven million digital specimens to Cornell's Macaulay Library.

Given this boom in both research and public interest, Louise would have been disappointed, I suspect, by what prompted an exhibit mounted in 2018 by the Canadian Museum of Nature called *Courage and Passion: Women in Natural Sciences*. Just three years before, in 2015, Nobel Prize–winning biochemist Tim Hunt had remarked that "girls" were a problem in science because "you fall in love with them, they fall in love with you, and when you criticize them, they cry." That same year, Statistics Canada reported that women made up only twenty-two percent of the science, technology, engineering, and mathematics (STEM) workforce, a mere two percent increase since Louise's day. And women in the sciences were still being paid, on average, 7.5 percent less than men in the same jobs.

And yet women have persisted.

Jennifer Ackerman first tuned into the issues around women in ornithology at a roundtable on female birdsong at the North American Ornithology Conference in 2016. "In researching the book, I did not consciously set out to look for women in the field," Jennifer told me. "Wherever I turned, they were there in abundance and often considered among the best in the business."

What Louise accomplished as a self-trained ornithologist was remarkable, but as she would be the first to tell you, hers could be the story of any number of amateurs scattered across North America in the last century, standing in forests, meadows, and swamps for hours at a stretch, lifting their binoculars to watch.

"I know of no occupation so fulfilling as that of becoming a watcher. The observing self is pushed into the background and obliterated except for a cramped leg or an aching muscle imposed by enforced immobility. The present is dominated by the natural stage and all senses are focused upon the amazing events that are constantly taking place."

I am feeling sentimental, even though as Louise liked to say, "Nature has no use for sentimentality."

At Louise's cabin, I have to stop myself from checking for coloured bands on the legs of chickadees, from trying to tame them to eat out of my hand, to take a sunflower seed from between my lips as they did with Louise. I have to quell the urge to wonder which of the chattering red squirrels pitching cones on my head from the tips of the pines is a descendant of Louise's rascally Kicki. I collect scarlet maple leaves and press them between the pages of her books, gather fairy tufts of grey-green lichen from fallen branches, thinking I'll make a wreath—or something, some kind of memento of this place. I stumble across windfalls and through dense thickets, searching for the foundation of Len's first cabin on Peak Hill. I find the stony rectangle with the signature double row of rocks where he planted his roses, and behind his cabin, the foundation of the chicken coop. When I squint, I can see the line of boulders that bordered the trail he walked between his cabin and Louise's log house for years before she realized he stayed for love.

I try to keep in mind what Louise said. "Our lives, which seem so important to ourselves, die with us."

But do they?

Craig, the new owner of the Loghouse Nest, used to bicycle from Rutherglen to the log house to deliver groceries to Louise. He was ten; Louise was eighty-six. In winter, he and a buddy would show up to shovel her paths. Now he and Michelle keep Louise's books and relics by the fireplace in the Loghouse Nest that they are caring for with respect, knowing firsthand what the place meant to her.

Well into her eighties, Louise would be stopped on the streets of Bonfield and Rutherglen by people who said, You don't remember me, but I remember you; you used to come to our school. People around here still recall her walking with her cane along the highway, binoculars swinging at her neck, pausing now and then to stare into the trees. They called her the Bird Lady of Pimisi Bay.

Across from Lily-Pad Bay, on the knob of land where Murray tried to convince the provincial government to set up a nature school, is a provincial picnic area where a plaque to Louise was placed in 2016 by the Ontario Heritage Trust in partnership with the Nipissing Naturalists Club. No matter which direction you drive on the Mattawa–North Bay section of the Trans-Canada Highway, you are exhorted to stop and take a look. Every August, the Louise de Kiriline Lawrence Nature Festival takes place there. The Louise de Kiriline Lawrence Nature Writing Award is still given each autumn to a book by a northern Ontario author. The Louise de Kiriline Lawrence Conservation Action Fund, set up by the Ottawa Field-Naturalists' Club with a bequest from Louise and others, continued until 2017, funding the conservation of forests, defending wetlands, saving greenbelts, purchasing natural areas such as Gillies Grove in Arnprior and a threatened alvar on Manitoulin Island. Laurentian University still offers a $1,000 student scholarship in her name.

Mexicans have a saying: a person dies three times, first when they retreat from the material world, next when their body dies, and finally when no one remembers them. Clearly, Louise isn't dead yet.

What would Louise think of me, I wonder, sitting in her house, trying to resurrect her life? She was open and often confessional in her letters, but in her published work there is a distinct lack of personal detail. She seldom enters her own stories except as a distant narrator. Some inbred reserve or lack of self-esteem held her back, forcing me to comb through her letters and diaries and studies for hints of how she moved through the woods, what she carried, what she wore, the mundane, quotidian detail. As she wrote to a Swedish publisher: "I have far, far more interesting topics to write about than my own self, which frankly does not interest me one bit. Somebody else can write about me sometime if they think the subject worth while."

I do think the subject worthwhile. I have read everything she wrote, even the reams of unpublished pages. I have read most of the books that she read, the ones I know about at least. It pains me to think of the lost library in those boxes dumped by the side of the road. Did she underline passages or write in the margins, something I can't bring myself to do although it would tell me so much about Louise: Was it ideas or language that stirred her most? What novels did she read? Graham Greene? Nadine Gordimer? The stories of Alice Munro? Biographies of Dag Hammarskjöld? Was there a secret stash of mysteries or romances amongst the books of philosophy and science?

A person's library is a snapshot of the inside of their mind, and that's a picture of Louise I will never see.

I could convince myself that Louise is watching over the house, watching me. But Louise was not religious in any conventional way. She called herself an "unbeliever." As a young woman she was religious: "I had a feeling, a needing to worship. There was something unrealistic in this I was glad to be rid of." When she moved into her log house in the bush, she lost her faith in god and an afterlife, a source of conflict with Doris, who was a Christian Scientist. "The replacement has been my study of nature. I can't see just at the moment—I have to see the whole thing. I have to see the universe. I can feel so strongly the matter of balance, the matter of interwork. It seems to me so obvious, so right. I don't need sin."

Nature was where she found the deepest expression of what it meant to be alive. What she believed in was loyalty. Authenticity. Truth. In work not for gain, but for its own sake. In honesty and forthrightness. She didn't look away from what was before her. She did not allow herself to be distracted, to exaggerate or diminish. She watched not in judgment but as a witness. She pushed back hard against self-delusion. In her bird studies, in her writing, and in her life, she constantly grappled with ethics, with the nature of goodness and evil, and how best to be human—all the fundamental questions that organized religion addresses in its manuals for human behaviour. But it was questions that intrigued Louise, not answers. Perhaps spending so much time looking into the sky and watching birds flying through the air like angels lends itself to such musings.

What she strove for and what she believed in most fundamentally was harmonious association. "To the naturalist who spends much of his time in studying the laws of life and in observing the living world, harmonious association soon becomes a strong reality. He finds it everywhere, in the complementary relationship of one species with another, in the ecological significance of environment, in the chains of inter-dependency between all living organisms, from the lowest to the highest."

And yet, here we humans are, still contributing to the planet's pain, altering every last corner of the earth as if the wildlife we are destroying has nothing to do with us. In 2019, it was reported in *The State of Canada's Birds* that since 1970, North America has lost almost three *billion* birds—for every four birds that flew when *Lovely* was published, only one flies now.

In the past forty years, shorebirds have declined by forty percent, grassland birds by fifty-seven percent, and aerial insectivores—vireos, flycatchers, nighthawks, swallows—by fifty-nine percent. The picture is brighter for waterfowl (up 150 percent) and birds of prey (up 110 percent). In 1970 these two categories were on the brink of extinction, but now, as a result of the ban on DDT and dedicated habitat restoration (often by sporting organizations), they are recovering. We never used to see osprey at our end of Lake Ontario, but now their cries rend the air.

One in three birds in Canada depends on the forest. In both their Canadian breeding grounds and in their southern wintering grounds, forests are rapidly disappearing. Resident forest birds like blue jays and black-capped chickadees are holding their own, but warblers, grosbeaks, flickers, crossbills, and others that winter in Central and South

America are declining precipitously. In 1970, there were forty-five birds for every person in the United States. Today, there are twenty.

Make no mistake: these percentages are cumulative. In the nineteenth century, watchers reported skies blackened with birds for hours on end. Over the fifty years that Louise watched birds, populations in her forest dropped by at least twenty-five percent. Since then, their numbers have diminished by forty percent of that reduced number. The decline that was once a gentle slope is now a cliff.

Eighty percent of the species declared endangered or threatened in the last decade have been grassland birds and those that catch insects on the wing. They are endangered not only because their habitat is disappearing but because their food is too. The red crossbill, a species that drew Louise through waist-high snow to record the details of its nesting cycle, is now endangered. So is the Kirtland's warbler, loggerhead shrike, Acadian flycatcher, barn owl, and twenty other forest birds, several of them common to Louise's woods.

Humans used to look at the entrails of birds to read the future. Now we can know our fate just by looking at the empty sky.

It is September at the Loghouse Nest, and the nights are cool. I make a fire. The stone chimney has been replaced with insulated stainless steel and a Jøtul has been inserted into the fireplace. Smoke rises properly into the night. After almost a month, I am living once again in my body, telling the temperature by the air on my skin, telling the time by the passage of the sun. My phone no longer sits by my bed, ready to give me the morning news of the world. News of Louise and of the birds is all I care about.

It was bothering me that I hadn't seen any woodpeckers. Then this morning, I saw two hairys hacking away at the dying white pine by the back door when I went out to fill the feeders. A pileated was beating its way through the mist higher up Peak Hill. When I walked out to breathe some fresh air in the noonday sun—fresh air, sunlight, soap, and water—I came upon a downy, its tail pressed for balance against one of the swinging metal feeders. She knew I was there, how could she not when the red squirrel was reared up on his hind legs, scolding me vociferously. I took a chance and moved a little closer, my eyes averted. Intent on the seed she was working through the hole of the feeder, she shimmied around to the other side of the metal cylinder as if it were a tree trunk, as if I didn't have eyes in my head, and I went on my way, secretly cheered that she held her place.

The sapsuckers and vireos and thrushes that came back year after year, generation after generation to the same piece of land, often to the same tree, displayed a loyalty to place that Louise felt deeply. I sit on the couch in her log house, before the blazing fire, in exactly the spot she sat every evening for fifty-five years. I, too, feel connected to the north in some visceral way, but I have never been faithful: I have called more than two dozen places home. Maybe I wanted this house because I hoped to graft onto Louise's steadfast roots.

My month is almost over. Within this shell of logs, I have reshaped this book, as Louise reshaped hers. I kept my files in the wooden filing cabinet she bought second-hand in Toronto in 1945. The place feels indestructible, but I know that's not true. Powderpost beetles leave evidence of destruction on the darkly stained logs. Pine squirrels race across the attic above my head, gnawing through the night. There is a definite hump to the kitchen floor; the bookcases on either side of the fireplace slope dramatically. In another century, Louise's Loghouse Nest may well be a scatter of logs or simply a stone foundation in the woods, like the one I found up on Peak Hill.

For as long as I can, I'd like to come back. First to Pelee, to watch the birds as they make their first landfall on Canadian soil, then north to Pimisi Bay, where some of them will build their nests—or not.

"In the field," Louise reminds me, "there is never a day alike to the other, never a season that follows exactly the same pattern as those of the past."

Louise in her forties, looking out on Pimisi Bay

Source Note

Books beget books. It was reading Graeme Gibson's *Bedside Book of Birds* that returned me to Louise and my unfulfilled promise of thirty years to write her story. Slowly, I gathered the resources she used: the pocket-size Chester A. Reed and Frank M. Chapman bird guides and the 1934 edition of Percy A. Taverner's *Birds of Canada*, which stands as a fascinating record of human knowledge and attitude toward birds in mid-twentieth-century Canada. I also read the 1966 edition by W. Earl Godfrey, which cites her studies.

I was inspired by memoirs of passionate watchers, especially women: *The Watcher at the Nest* by Margaret Morse Nice; the posthumous collection of Althea Sherman's writings, *Birds of an Iowa Dooryard*; *Homing with the Birds: The History of a Lifetime of Personal Experience with the Birds* by Gene Stratton-Porter; *A-Birding on a Bronco* by Florence Merriam Bailey; and *Birding on Borrowed Time* by Phoebe Snetsinger, who was the first person in the world to see more than eight thousand birds.

That listing impulse seems more typical of men. *Wild America: The Record of a 30,000 Mile Journey around the Continent by a Distinguished Naturalist and His British Colleague* by Roger Tory Peterson and James Fisher and *Kingbird Highway: The Biggest Year in the Life of an Extreme Birder* by Kenn Kaufman beautifully illustrate the competitive watching of birds—a valuable contrast to the patient observations of watchers like Louise.

Most histories of North American bird watching were disappointing, with their tendency to overlook or trivialize the contributions of women. The exceptions were those written by women, such as *Birdwatching with American Women* edited by Deborah Strom. Among contemporary writers, Jennifer Ackerman brilliantly rights the balance in *The Genius of Birds* and *The Bird Way*, both exhilarating reads.

Although reading about the bird-rich past was often discouraging, I found it strangely motivating, too, like visiting a vanished world and returning with renewed vision. *Thoreau on Birds*, compiled with commentary by naturalist Helen G. Cruickshank, offers astonishing glimpses of the massive flocks that filled the skies 150 years ago. *Two Bird-Lovers in Mexico* by C. William Beebe records the bird life of the country of my heart a century ago, although it is Beebe's intrepid wife, Elswyth Thane, who intrigues me most. *Ten Thousand Birds: Ornithology since Darwin* by Tim Birkhead, Jo Wimpenny, and Bob Montgomerie traces not avian life but the study of birds through the centuries, parsing the relationship between birds and humans that so nagged at Louise.

All of this provided context, but the core of the story that is *Woman, Watching* came from archives across the continent, most of them closed during the pandemic that coincided with the research and writing of this book. In the months before the lockdown in Ontario, I spent many happy hours in the tall-windowed, high-ceiling reading room of Library and Archives Canada in Ottawa, sifting through the twenty-six boxes of Louise de Kiriline Lawrence's letters, scrapbooks, research notes, drafts of her books, and reviews. Louise wrote thousands of letters, including a weekly correspondence with her mother from the time she left home in 1918 until her mother died in 1958. Not all have survived, but enough to provide a portrait of Louise's evolving inner life.

She wrote letters to other amateur watchers, to scientists, to just about everyone she met who intrigued her. Sometimes, but not always, she kept her own letters as well as theirs, typing carbon copies that seem as ancient now as Egyptian scrolls. With my assistant, Astrid Mohr, I combed the archives of Louise's correspondents for the missing pieces of the story: the archives at Cornell University in Ithaca, New York; the Smithsonian Institution in Washington, DC; the Florida State University Archives; the Thomas Fisher Rare Book Library at the University of Toronto; the Archives of Ontario; the Ontario Medical Association archives; and even my own archives at Queen's University, where I found my notes and the tape recordings of the interview I did with Louise thirty-four years ago. I spent weeks at Library and Archives Canada, which, together with the Canadian Museum of Nature and the Blacker-Wood Collection ornithological library at McGill University, has preserved the correspondences of Canada's great naturalists. A treasure trove lay in the archives of the University of Northern British Columbia, which holds the papers of Marianne (Marika) G. Ainley, former principal of the Simone de Beauvoir Institute at Concordia University in Montreal and dean of women's studies at the University of Northern British Columbia, and a remarkable researcher who secured the place of the amateur and of women in ornithology in *The American Ornithologists' Union: The First Century, 1883–1983*.

From magazine archives, the holdings of small journals like the *Toronto Field Naturalists Newsletter*, and online resources such as SORA (Searchable Ornithological Research Archive) and the Biodiversity Heritage Library, Astrid and I painstakingly gathered copies of Louise's popular articles and research studies. Last bits and pieces were found in the personal papers of Barry Penhale, Louise's last publisher and literary executor, until my library of her work was as close to complete as

I could make it. I read her writing as I wrote her life, and watched her grow before my eyes and under my pen.

All of our gathered research materials will be deposited at Queen's archives, where others might continue to know Louise and her work.

Author's Note

A biographer begins their work already hobbled by impossibility: as Elizabeth Hardwick put it, we are the quick pursuing the dead. And yet that doesn't stop us from trying— with family, with lovers and friends, with strangers who intrigue.

I knew Louise, but only for a short span of her long life. Even with a person like Louise, who left wads of evidence of her outer life and a thick trail of clues to her inner life, much is a matter of interpretation, of fitting the woman into her social, cultural, economic, and political context. The papers that I pored through at Library and Archives Canada were well organized, as I expect her files were in the wooden drawers built into the narrow hallway between her living room and her bedroom office. I don't know if she spent months sorting and pitching, as Margaret Nice did, but it doesn't seem so. The gaps feel more like oversights than purges; she had no interest in controlling the future any more than she did the present or the past.

In *Woman, Watching*, I have tried, as much as possible, to allow Louise to tell her own story—through copious quotes from her letters and her published works. To avoid the constant repetition of "she wrote to her mother," readers can assume that unattributed quotes are from her weekly letters to Sweden. Actual quotes from her written works—books, articles, diaries, and personal correspondence—are framed in quotation marks; dialogue that appears without quotation marks is extrapolated from stories Louise tells in her writing.

At first, I was hesitant to braid my own story into Louise's, yet our lives so naturally intertwined—knowing her in the north; knowing birds in that northern breeding ground and in their wintering grounds in Mexico, where I winter too. A biography, I decided, is a testament, proof that something exists, and so I made myself and the biographical process visible, made my efforts to observe Louise part of the record, in the same way that she documented the particulars of each watch in her observational study of a bird.

Louise was a debutante, a nurse, a wife, a daughter, a recluse, but above all, she was an observer, and at midlife she turned her observing eye on birds. The recreations of her watches—her first foray into bird study with the Canada jays, the dawn-to-dusk song count of the red-eyed vireo, the aggressive displays of woodpeckers—are an amalgam of details from her private letters, her scholarly studies, and the popular pieces she published. As much as possible, I preserved her style and tone, but I urge readers to search out Louise in the original, especially in her books *The Lovely and the Wild, Another Winter, Another Spring*, and *To Whom the Wilderness Speaks*.

During this project I have been inspired by invisible women who moved ornithology forward—Miss Jessica A. Potter with her brilliant trap, a design that has not been improved on in a hundred years; Miss E.I. Turner, who gave the bird world one of its favourite words—jizz; Harriet Sheppard, who was parsing birdsong before Canada became itself; Elsie Cassels, whose husband destroyed her life's work of bird records after her death; and all the other women who moved mountains to tramp field and forest in their search to understand the natural world and their place in it. If it seems I overemphasize the contribution of women, I do. It gives me great pleasure, in *Woman, Watching*, to make these women visible again.

I have taken to heart Oliver Austin's advice to Louise and removed not only most of the Latin names of birds, but also the officially recognized way of spelling bird names. And so I removed capital letters from all bird names in the text—red-eyed vireo instead of Red-eyed Vireo—including within letters and studies, for the sake of smoother reading. I ask the forgiveness of ornithological scholars, and point out that I do retain scholarly style in the titles of published articles.

Acknowledgements

In 1989, the year my article on Louise was published in *Harrowsmith* magazine, I received a letter from Barry Penhale, Louise's publisher, telling me that Louise wished me to be her biographer. At the time I was a single mother of two teenage sons, desperately trying to earn a living as a freelance writer. I couldn't imagine taking the years I would need to gather the resources to write a life history. My circumstances changed and birds returned to my life, but it wasn't until 2018, when my house was destroyed in a flood and I came upon that dripping issue of *Harrowsmith*, that I thought, Yes. Now.

I am grateful to Barry for making that first suggestion, for opening his basement hoard and his memory to me, and for granting permission to quote from Louise's vast archive as I fulfilled that long-ago obligation. My apologies for taking so long.

My greatest debt of gratitude is to Louise for being such a fervent letter-writer, for her honesty and openness in those thousands of missives. She made my job both easier and harder.

Without savers and hoarders there would be no archives to consult, and so I thank Louise, Margaret Morse Nice, Percy A. Taverner, Roy Ivor, Alexander Skutch, W. Earl Godfrey, Doris Speirs, and dozens of others who kept the letters they received from Louise and copies of the letters they sent. More than published histories, these personal letters reveal the passion and the dogged quest to understand the place of birds and humans in the natural world. Thank you to their heirs for permission to quote from these letters: Anne Bishop, niece of Dorothy Bishop; Ken Boyer, grandson of Margaret Morse Nice; and John Sabean, literary executor for Doris Speirs.

Researching a biography during the Covid-19 pandemic presented particular challenges. Archives were closed, and staff struggled to continue their work from home, where they had deeper digital access than the general public, but no access to physical files. My thanks to all these hard-working keepers of the past, for researching what they could and sending copies when possible, and most of all for their enthusiasm and unfailing good humour. Special thanks to Heather Home at Queen's University; Chantal Dussault and Greg Rand at the Canadian Museum of Nature; Lynn Lafontaine, Karine Gélinas, Annabelle Schattmann, Masha Davidovic, and so many others at Library and Archives Canada, including Jacqueline Vincent and the digitizers at The Brechlin Group; Tad Bennicoff at the Smithsonian Institution; Peter Corina in the division of Rare and Manuscript Collections at Cornell University; Kim Stathers at the Northern BC Archives and Special Collections at the George R. Weller Library at the Prince George Campus of the University of Northern British Columbia; Rick Stapleton at McMaster University; Pearce Carefoot and John Shoesmith at the Thomas Fisher Rare Book Library at the University of Toronto; Jason Ramsay-Brown at the Toronto Field Naturalists; and Ann MacKenzie at the Ottawa Field-Naturalists' Club, the oldest nature organization in Canada. And my thanks to the Royal Ontario Museum for opening their vaults of skins and nests to me.

I am particularly grateful to Marianne (Marika) G. Ainley, a feminist historian of science who gathered notes on Louise, Doris Huestis Speirs, and Margaret Morse Nice toward a project she died before completing. I am grateful for her archival instincts in collecting material that proved vital in writing *Woman, Watching*. Marika wrote passionately about the history of women watchers and amateurs in the AOU. Twenty-seven years later, Amy Wallace, now of Carleton University in Ottawa, curated an exhibit of Louise's life and work at the Artlab Concourse Gallery at the University of Western Ontario in London, Ontario, and the WKP Kennedy Gallery in North Bay, Ontario; as part of the exhibition, she produced paintings inspired by Louise and the Loghouse Nest, as well as a booklet. Marika, Amy, me: a slender thread connects those of us who have not forgotten Louise and her inspiring work in expanding human understanding of breeding songbirds in the north.

Astrid Mohr was my invaluable research assistant through the writing of this book. She brought a passion for finding answers and young feminist eyes to the project, which made the book better than it might otherwise have been.

Bob Montgomerie, author, researcher, eminent ornithologist, and emeritus professor of biology at Queen's University, walked beside me from the beginning, even though he wasn't convinced there was a book in Louise's life. He introduced me to VertNet, SORA (Searchable Ornithological Research Archive at the University of New Mexico), and countless other resources, lent me books, and informed my work with his own writings on birds. Bob was a young graduate student when Louise was publishing her final works; he guided me through the history of ornithology in Canada and was a perceptive, critical first reader of the manuscript. For his commentary and especially for his support, I am deeply grateful.

Thank you also to Victoria Ryan who translated Louise's early letters and telegrams from Swedish into English, and to Wayne Grady who provided translations from the French; to Robert Wright of the Tamworth Bookshop who found me books I wasn't sure still existed; and to Craig Gagnon and Michelle Brisson for allowing me to spend a month in Louise's Loghouse Nest. And special thanks to Dan Strickland, aka Mr. Canada Jay, who helped put Louise's first nesting study in ornithological context.

A Marian Hebb Research Grant from the Access Copyright Foundation was instrumental in completing this work. Marian has been a dear friend and comrade through many copyright battles at the Writers' Union of Canada: I thought of her often as once again I trolled letters for a story that draws the past into the present.

I value my birder friends: the gang that gathers every May on Pelee Island, hosted for decades by Margaret Atwood and Graeme Gibson; Trevor Herriot out in Saskatchewan; Rodrigo Lopez, who introduced me to so many birds of Mexico; Sean Dooley in Australia and David Lindo in Spain; nearby Cathy and Richard Cooper who are endlessly welcoming in their avian paradise; Steve Pitt on Talon Lake who has kept the Louise light burning brightly in myriad ways; and all my other friends, especially the non-birders among them, who patiently listen to the ongoing saga that is the writing of a book, offering their encouragement and support.

A huge thank you to my editor, Susan Renouf, for her sensitivity and strength, her commitment to her writers, and her deep interest in women and their history. With the gentlest touch, she prods me where I need to go. And a sweet birdsong to the amazing flock at ECW Press, especially editorial coordinator Pia Singhal, art director Jessica Albert, designer of the stunning cover Michel Vrana, copy editor Rachel Ironstone, proofreader Crissy Calhoun, the marketing and promotion team led by Claire Pokorchak, and publishers David Caron and Jack David for their unwavering support of Canadian writers. And my gratitude to my agent, Martha Webb of CookeMcDermid, for her steadfast support and skill in negotiating the ups and downs of the publishing industry.

Writers always thank their partners, but I feel doubly grateful to share my life with a person who is not only equally engaged in wrestling with words but who is also a watcher. Together we are calmed and uplifted in the presence of birds.

Credits

Excerpts from the letters of Dorothy Bishop are used with permission of Ann Bishop.

Excerpts from the letters of Margaret Morse Nice are used with permission of Ken Boyer.

Excerpts from the letters of Doris Speirs are used with the permission of her literary executor, John Sabean.

Comments from a conversation with Jane Gibson are used with her permission.

Excerpts from the materials of Louise de Kiriline Lawrence, including the letters of her mother, Hillevid Neergaard, and her husbands, Gleb Nikolayevich and Len Lawrence, are used with the permission of her literary executor, Barry Penhale. Also used with his permission are brief excerpts from his Ontario Medical Association interview with Louise de Kiriline Lawrence and from his CBC-Radio documentary *She Is One of Us*.

Photo Credits

Photo Credits

PAGE 97: Merilyn Simonds

PAGE 103: The Canadian Field-Naturalist/ECW Press

PAGE 110: Doris Huestis Speirs/Thomas Fisher Rare Book Library

PAGE 113: Louise de Kiriline Lawrence/Library and Archives Canada/e011443250

PAGE 121: Royal Ontario Museum/Merilyn Simonds

PAGE 128: Louise de Kiriline Lawrence/Library and Archives Canada/e011443239

PAGE 139: Louise de Kiriline Lawrence/Library and Archives Canada/e011443246

PAGE 143: ECW Press

PAGE 148: *Farmer's Magazine*/Merilyn Simonds

PAGE 153: Louise de Kiriline Lawrence/Library and Archives Canada/e011443248

PAGE 168: *Audubon Magazine*/Thomas Fisher Rare Book Library

PAGE 180: Louise de Kiriline Lawrence/Library and Archives Canada/e011504692

PAGE 196: Associated Press/440401030

PAGE 208: Merilyn Simonds

PAGE 213: Louise de Kiriline Lawrence/Library and Archives Canada/e011443241

PAGE 218: Louise de Kiriline Lawrence/Library and Archives Canada/e011443256

PAGE 229: Louise de Kiriline Lawrence/Library and Archives Canada/e011504690

PAGE 236: Louise de Kiriline Lawrence/Library and Archives Canada/e010783326

PAGE 244: Louise de Kiriline Lawrence/Library and Archives Canada/e011443247

PAGE 249: ECW Press

PAGE 254: Merilyn Simonds

PAGE 258: Louise de Kiriline Lawrence/Library and Archives Canada/e011443238

PAGE 261: Louise de Kiriline Lawrence /Library and Archives Canada/e011504695

PAGE 269: ECW Press

PAGE 284: Barry Penhale Collection/ECW Press

PAGE 309: Louise de Kiriline Lawrence/Library and Archives Canada/e011443214

PAGE 313: Louise de Kiriline Lawrence/Library and Archives Canada/e011443252

PAGE 323: Merilyn Simonds

PAGE 334: Merilyn Simonds

PAGE 350: Merilyn Simonds

PAGE 368: Louise de Kiriline Lawrence/Library and Archives Canada/e010783334

Bibliography of Works by
Louise de Kiriline Lawrence

BOOKS

The Quintuplets' First Year: The Survival of the Five Famous Dionne Babies and Its Significance for All Mothers. Toronto: Macmillan Canada, 1936.

The Loghouse Nest. Toronto: S.J.R. Saunders Canada, 1945. Illustrated by Thoreau MacDonald.

——. Toronto: Natural Heritage Books, 1988.

A Comparative Life-History Study of Four Species of Woodpeckers. Monograph Series, #5. The American Ornithologists' Union, 1967.

The Lovely and the Wild. New York: McGraw-Hill, 1968. Illustrated by Glen Loates.

——. Toronto: McGraw-Hill Ryerson, 1968.

——. Toronto: Natural Heritage Books, 1987.

Mar: A Glimpse into the Natural Life of a Bird. Toronto: Clarke, Irwin Canada, 1976.

——. Toronto: Natural Heritage Books, 1986.

Another Winter, Another Spring: A Love Remembered. New York: McGraw-Hill, 1977.

——. Toronto: McGraw-Hill Ryerson, 1977.

——. Toronto: Natural Heritage Books, 1987.

To Whom the Wilderness Speaks. Toronto: McGraw-Hill Ryerson, 1980. Illustrated
by Aletha Karstad.

——. Toronto: Natural Heritage Books, 1989.

ANTHOLOGIES

"The White-Tailed Deer of Pimisi Bay," "Irrepressible Nuthatch," and "My
Conditioned Chickadees" in *The Audubon Book of True Nature Stories*, selected
and edited by John K. Terres, editor, *Audubon Magazine*. Published by Thomas
Y. Crowell Company. New York: 1958.

"Blackburnians of the Pines" in *This Is Nature*, edited by Richard Westwood.
Published by Thomas Crowell. New York: 1959.

"The Voluble Singer of the Treetops" in *A Treasury of Birdlore*, edited by Joseph
Wood Krutch and Paul S. Eriksson. Published by Doubleday & Company Inc.
New York: 1962.

"The Apartment" in *The Pleasure of Birds: An Audubon Treasury*, selected and edited
by Les Line. Published by J.B. Lippincott in cooperation with the National
Audubon Society. New York: 1975.

"The White-Tailed Deer of Pimisi Bay" in *Animals Can Be Almost Human*, by
the Reader's Digest Association, edited by Alma E. Guinness. Published by
Random House Inc. New York: 1980.

"The Lovely" in *Birdwatching with American Women: A Selection of Nature Writings*,
edited by Deborah Strom. Published by W.W. Norton. New York: 1986.

"An Exercise in Tolerance" in *Living in Harmony: Nature Writing by Women in*
Canada, edited with an introduction by Andrea Pinto Lebowitz. Published by
Orca Books. Victoria, BC: 1996.

"Voluble Singer of the Tree-Tops" in *Bright Stars, Dark Trees, Clear Water: Nature*
Writing from North of the Border, selected and edited by Wayne Grady. Published
by David R. Godine. Boston: 1999.

ARTICLES

1935   Five-part series on the Dionne quintuplets for the *New York World Telegram*.
1936–7   "The Quintuplets' First Year," *Chatelaine*, serialized in eight parts.
1937   "Why Did I Come to Canada?" *Chatelaine*, October.

1937   "Christmas in Another Land," *North Bay Nugget*, December.

1938   "With Chicks Among Rocks," *Chatelaine*.

1939   "3 Golden Keys," *Baby Talk Magazine*.

1939   "Lost Feathers," *Baby Talk Magazine*.

1940   "That Most Important Safeguard," *Baby Talk Magazine*.

1941   "Such Is Life with the Birds," *Farmer's Magazine* 41(4): 20–21, 25, 27. Illustrated by Louise de Kiriline Lawrence.

1942   "The Love Life of a Dove," *Farmer's Magazine* 39(12): 22–23, 33.

1943   "Much Depends on Dinner," *Farmer's Magazine* 40(2): 18–19.

1943   "The Birds Are My Friends," *Farmer's Magazine* 40(6): 24.

1944   "Mrs. Citizen Objects," *Canadian Forum*, April.

1945   "With Rose Underwing," *Farmer's Magazine* 41(3): 20, 23.

1945   "Winter Motif in Red," *Farmer's Magazine* 42(2): 18–19.

1945   "My Friend the Bachelor," *Farmer's Magazine* 42(4): 18, 21, 29.

1945   "The Grey Lady," *Farmer's Magazine* 42(6): 20, 27–28. Illustrated by Louise de Kiriline Lawrence.

1946   "A Bird in the Hand," *Audubon Magazine* 48(5): 284–93. Illustrated by Louise de Kiriline Lawrence.

1946   "The Nest in the Raspberry Bush," *Farmer's Magazine* 43(3): 20–21, 25. Illustrated by Louise de Kiriline Lawrence.

1946   "Satin Tails," *Farmer's Magazine* 43(5): 20–21. Illustrated by Louise de Kiriline Lawrence.

1947   "Five Days with a Pair of Nesting Canada Jays," *The Canadian Field-Naturalist* 61(1): 1–11. Illustrated by Louise de Kiriline Lawrence.

1948   "Comparative Study of the Nesting Behaviour of Chestnut-sided and Nashville Warblers," *The Auk* 65(2): 204–19.

1948   "Night Life at Peak Hill," *Audubon Magazine* 50(4): 232–37.

1948   "A White-throat Trio and a Warbler Incident," *Bird-Banding* 19(3): 122–23.

1948   "Least Flycatcher," *Audubon Magazine*, May-June.

1949   "January Singing in the Black-capped Chickadee and Other Species," *The Auk* 66(3): 289–90.

1949   "Thus They Shall Perish," *Audubon Magazine* 51(1), 42–48.

1949   "Notes on Nesting Pigeon Hawks at Pimisi Bay, Ontario," *The Wilson Bulletin* 61(1): 15–25.

1949   "Golden-crowned Kinglet Wintering Near the Mattawa River, Ontario,"
        The Canadian Field-Naturalist (63)3: 117–18.

1949   "The Red Crossbill at Pimisi Bay, Ontario," *The Canadian Field-Naturalist*
        63(4): 147–60. Illustrated by Louise de Kiriline Lawrence.

1949   Winter Birds at the Loghouse," *Audubon Magazine* 51(6), 356–60. Ill. By LKL.

1950   "A Strange Winter Visitor at Pimisi Bay," *The Wood Duck* (Hamilton
        Naturalists' Club) (6)3: 1–3.

1950   "Kicki," *Audubon Magazine* 52: 330–35.

1950   "Winter record of a Cape May Warbler, *Dendroica tigrina*, at Pimisi Bay,"
        The Auk 67(4): 520.

1950   "Among the Birds," Eastern Bird Banding Association newsletter.

1951   "Birds in Unusual Plumages at Pimisi Bay, Ontario," *The Canadian Field-
        Naturalist* 65(1): 45–46.

1951   "A Phoebe Builds a Nest," *The Wood Duck* (Hamilton Naturalists' Club)
        4: 1–3.

1951   "Trials of a Phoebe Family," *Audubon Magazine* 53(3): 150–55.

1951   "Flight South," *Audubon Magazine* 53(5): 290–95.

1951   "Autumn at Pimisi Bay," *The Wood Duck* (Hamilton Naturalists' Club) 5: 1–3.

1952   "Red-breast Makes a Home," *Audubon Magazine* 54(11): 16–21.

1952   "New Sight Records of Three Species at Pimisi Bay, Ontario," *The
        Canadian Field-Naturalist* 66(2): 67–68.

1952   "The Spraying of Roadsides," *Federation of Ontario Naturalists Bulletin* 58: 16.

1952   "The White-tailed Deer of Pimisi Bay," *Audubon Magazine* 54(6): 350.

1953   "Behaviour of a Female Eastern Kingbird," *The Wilson Bulletin* 65(1): 40.

1953   "Blackburnians of the Pines," *Nature Magazine* 46(5): 233.

1953   "Tent Caterpillar Outbreak at Pimisi Bay," *Federation of Ontario Naturalists
        Bulletin.*

1953   "Nesting Life and Behaviour of the Red-eyed Vireo," *The Canadian
        Field-Naturalist* 67(2): 47–77.

1953   "Notes on the Nesting Behaviour of the Blackburnian Warbler," *The
        Wilson Bulletin* 65 (3): 135–44.

1954   "Jays in My Woods," *The Wood Duck* (Hamilton Naturalists' Club) 7(5): 1.

1954   "We've Been Thinking About . . . Roadside Spraying," *Federation of
        Ontario Naturalists Bulletin* 68: 4–6.

1954   "Enchanted Singer of the Treetops," *Audubon Magazine* 56(3): 109–11.

1954   "Irrepressible Nuthatch," *Audubon Magazine* 56(6): 264–67.

1955   "Red-wing Roost," *Federation of Ontario Naturalists Bulletin* 69: 10–11.

1955   "Is the Sapsucker Destructive?" *Nature Magazine* 48(9): 487–88, 500.

1956   "Flight Home to Sweden," *Toronto Field Naturalists Newsletter* 141: 1.

1956   "Birding in Sweden," *Toronto Field Naturalists Newsletter* 142.

1956   "My Conditioned Chickadees," *Audubon Magazine* 58(6): 254–55, 300.

1956   "We've Been Thinking . . . of Harmonious Association," *Federation of Ontario Naturalists Bulletin* 73: 4–.

1956   "Birds on an Island," *Federation of Ontario Naturalists Bulletin* 73: 18.

1956   "An Interesting Displacement Movement in a Slate-colored Junco," *The Auk* 73(2): 267.

1956   "The Following Reaction in a Brood of Mute Swans," *The Auk* 73(2): 268.

1957   "Displacement Singing in a Canada Jay (*Perisoreus canadensis*)," *The Auk* 74(2): 260–61.

1958   "On Regional Movements and Body Weight of Black-capped Chickadees in Winter," *The Auk* 75(4): 415–43.

1958   "My Most Exciting First," *The South Peel Naturalist* 5(10): 7–8.

1958   "Slippers the Skunk," *Family Herald*.

1960   "Jays of a Northern Forest," *Audubon Magazine* 62(6): 266–7, 286–7.

1962   "Recent Additions to the Nipissing Region, Ontario, Birdlists," *The Canadian Field-Naturalist* 76(4): 225.

1962   "A Noteworthy Reverse Migration of Snow Geese in Central Ontario," *The Auk* 79(4): 718.

1968   "Note: On Hoarding Nesting Material, Display, and Flycatching in the Gray Jay, *Perisoreus canadensis*," *The Auk* 85(1): 139.

1970   "The Apartment," *Audubon* 72(2): 4–7.

1970   "Comments," *Canadian Author & Bookman*, Fall Issue, 46 (1).

1972   "Thus They Shall Survive," *Audubon* 74(1): 4–8.

1973   "The Great Disaster," *Nature Canada*.

1973   "Bird Feeders," *Hinterland Who's Who*, Canadian Wildlife Service, Ottawa.

1973   "Gray Jay," *Hinterland Who's Who*, Canadian Wildlife Service, Ottawa.

1973   "Black-capped Chickadee," *Hinterland Who's Who*, Canadian Wildlife Service, Ottawa. Reprinted 1988.

1973   "Downy Woodpecker," *Hinterland Who's Who*, Canadian Wildlife
        Service, Ottawa. Reprinted 1988.

1974   "Ruby-throated Hummingbird," *Hinterland Who's Who*, Canadian
        Wildlife Service, Ottawa. Reprinted 2007.

1974   "Whippoorwill," *Hinterland Who's Who*, Canadian Wildlife Service,
        Ottawa.

1975   Canadian Nature Federation Calendar. Various artists. Text by Louise de
        Kiriline Lawrence. Clark, Irwin & Company.

1975   "The Walk at Dawn," *Audubon* 77(4): 26–29.

1976   "Cold Spring," *Audubon* 78(3): 40–45.

1976   "A Wilderness Feeding Station," *Nature Canada* 5(4): 5–6.

1978   "The Eternal Alliance," *Audubon* 80(2): 4–7.

1980   "The Pairing and Displays of a Red-breasted Nuthatch," *Pickering
        Naturalist* 5(2): 67–68.

1982   "A Dash of Salt," *Nature Canada* 11(4): 28–32.

1982   "A Plea for Reassessment," *Park News*, Fall Issue.

1984   "From Hostility to Amity," *The Living Bird Quarterly* 3(2): 14–17.

1985   "A Springtime Affair," *Audubon* 87(2): 70–71.

From 1956 into the late 1980s, Louise published over five hundred reviews and abstracts of Swedish and French ornithological books and articles in *The Auk*, *The Wilson Bulletin*, *Bird-Banding*, and others.

Note: *The Auk*, *The Wilson Bulletin*, *The Canadian Field-Naturalist*, and *Bird-Banding* are peer-reviewed ornithological journals.

Index

LKL stands for Louise de Kiriline Lawrence, except for her early writings, where "LK" is used to match her signature. Bird topics related to LKL are found at the topic, for example "banding." Page numbers in italics refer to photos.

This book is also available as a Global Certified Accessible™ (GCA) ebook. ECW Press's ebooks are screen reader friendly and are built to meet the needs of those who are unable to read standard print due to blindness, low vision, dyslexia, or a physical disability.

At ECW Press, we want you to enjoy our books in whatever format you like. If you've bought a print copy just send an email to ebook@ecwpress.com and include:

- the book title
- the name of the store where you purchased it
- a screenshot or picture of your order/receipt number and your name
- your preference of file type: PDF (for desktop reading), ePub (for a phone/tablet, Kobo, or Nook), mobi (for Kindle)

A real person will respond to your email with your ebook attached. Please note this offer is only for copies bought for personal use and does not apply to school or library copies.

Thank you for supporting an independently owned Canadian publisher with your purchase!